Friendly Neighborhood SPIDER-MAN

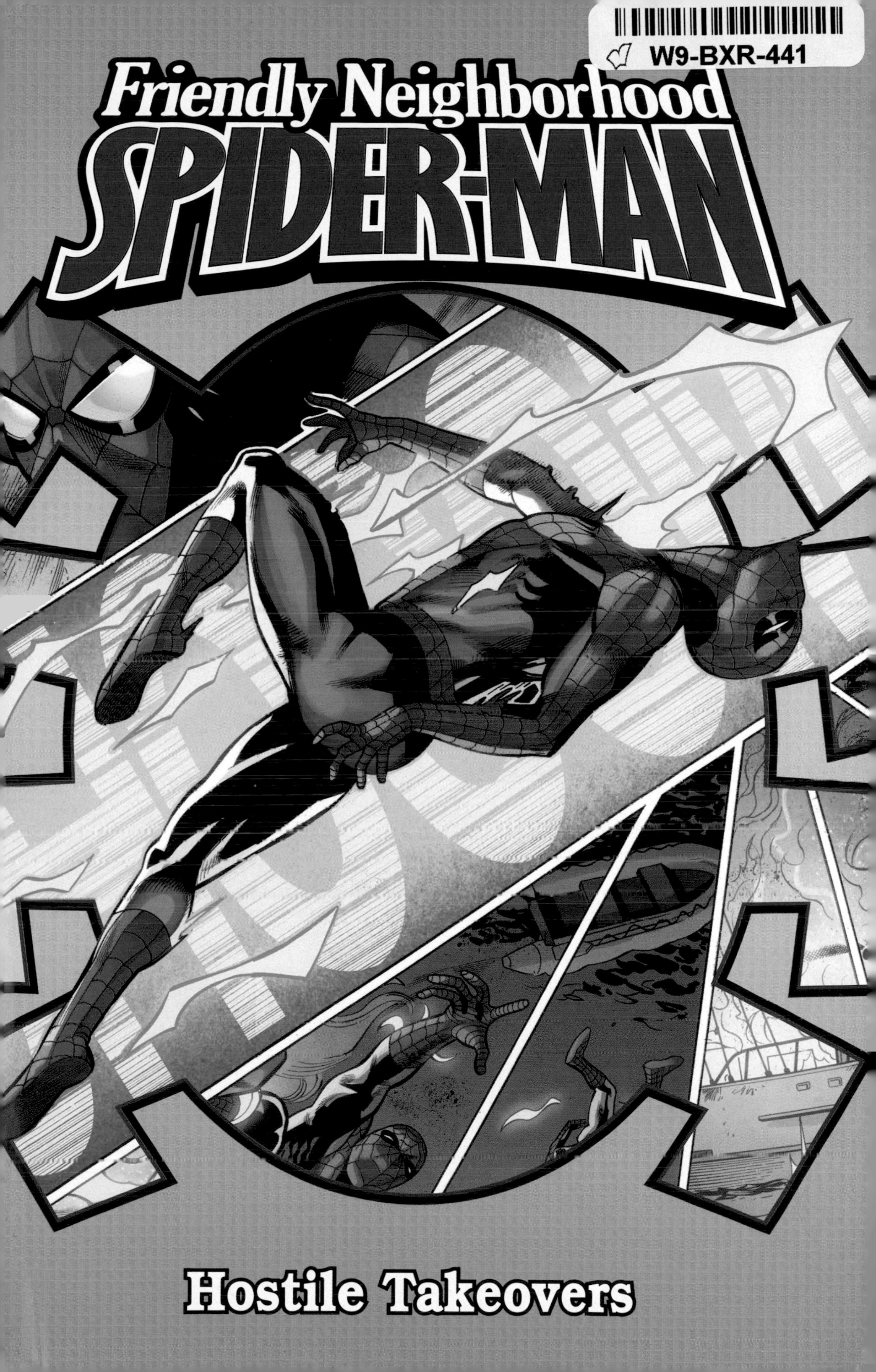

Hostile Takeovers

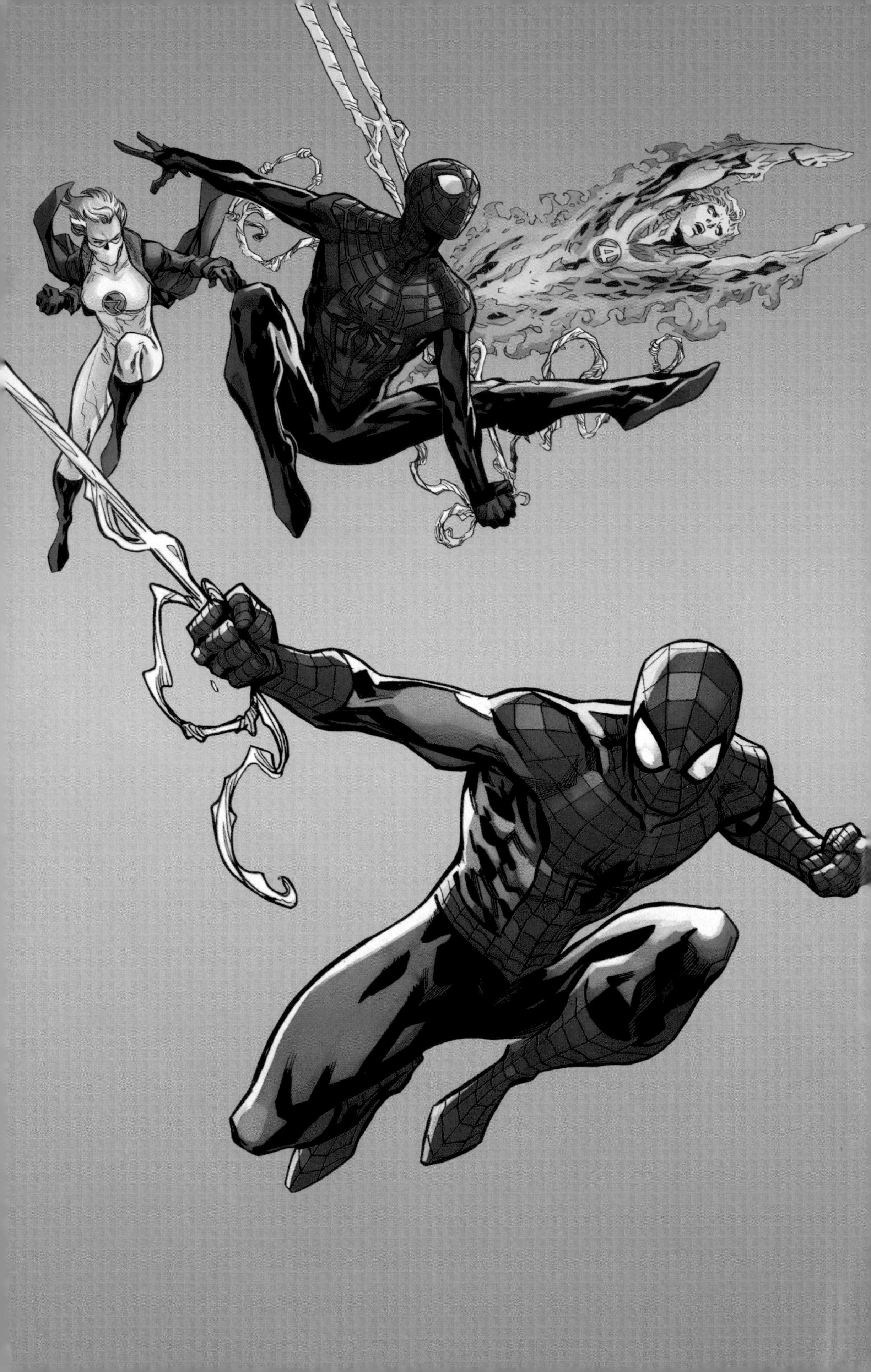

Friendly Neighborhood Spider-Man

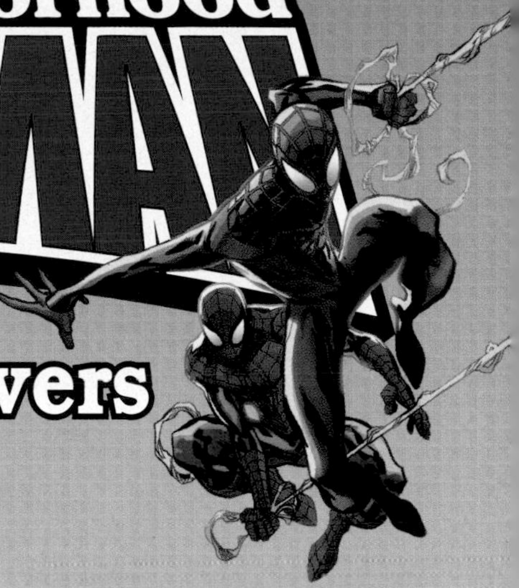

Hostile Takeovers

Tom Taylor
Writer

Ken Lashley (#7-10, 13-14), **Juann Cabal** (#9, 11), **Scott Hanna** (#10), **Luca Maresca** (#10, pages 18-20), **Pere Pérez** (#12), **Todd Nauck** (#13), **Ig Guara** (#13), **Dike Ruan** (#13) and **Marguerite Sauvage** (#14 flashback)
Artists

Scott Hanna (Finishes: #8, page 15) and **Jay Leisten** (#12)
Inkers

Nolan Woodard (#7-9), **Marcio Menyz** (#9), **Rachelle Rosenberg** (#11-14) and **Marguerite Sauvage** (#14 flashback)
Color Artists

VC's Travis Lanham
Letterer

Andrew C. Robinson
Cover Artist

Kathleen Wisneski
Assistant Editor

Nick Lowe
Editor

Spider-Man created by **Stan Lee** & **Steve Ditko**

Collection Editor **Mark D. Beazley**
Assistant Editor **Caitlin O'Connell**
Associate Managing Editor **Kateri Woody**
Senior Editor, Special Projects **Jennifer Grünwald**
VP Production & Special Projects **Jeff Youngquist**
Book Designer **Stacie Zucker** with **Adam Del Re**

SVP Print, Sales & Marketing **David Gabriel**
Director, Licensed Publishing **Sven Larsen**
Editor in Chief **C.B. Cebulski**
Chief Creative Officer **Joe Quesada**
President **Dan Buckley**
Executive Producer **Alan Fine**

FRIENDLY NEIGHBORHOOD SPIDER-MAN VOL. 2: HOSTILE TAKEOVERS. Contains material originally published in magazine form as FRIENDLY NEIGHBORHOOD SPIDER-MAN (2019) #7-14. First printing 2019. ISBN 978-1-302-91691-6. Published by MARVEL WORLDWIDE, INC., a subsidiary of MARVEL ENTERTAINMENT, LLC. OFFICE OF PUBLICATION: 135 West 50th Street, New York, NY 10020. **Printed in the U.S.A.** DAN BUCKLEY, President, Marvel Entertainment; JOHN NEE, Publisher; JOE QUESADA, Chief Creative Officer; TOM BREVOORT, SVP of Publishing; DAVID BOGART, Associate Publisher & SVP of Talent Affairs; DAVID GABRIEL, VP of Print & Digital Publishing; JEFF YOUNGQUIST, VP of Production & Special Projects; DAN CARR, Executive Director of Publishing Technology; ALEX MORALES, Director of Publishing Operations; DAN EDINGTON, Managing Editor; SUSAN CRESPI, Production Manager; STAN LEE, Chairman Emeritus. For information regarding advertising in Marvel Comics or on Marvel.com, please contact Vit DeBellis, Custom Solutions & Integrated Advertising Manager, at vdebellis@marvel.com. For Marvel subscription inquiries, please call 888-511-5480. **Manufactured between 10/25/2019 and 11/26/2019 by LSC COMMUNICATIONS INC., KENDALLVILLE, IN, USA.**

10 9 8 7 6 5 4 3 2 1

7

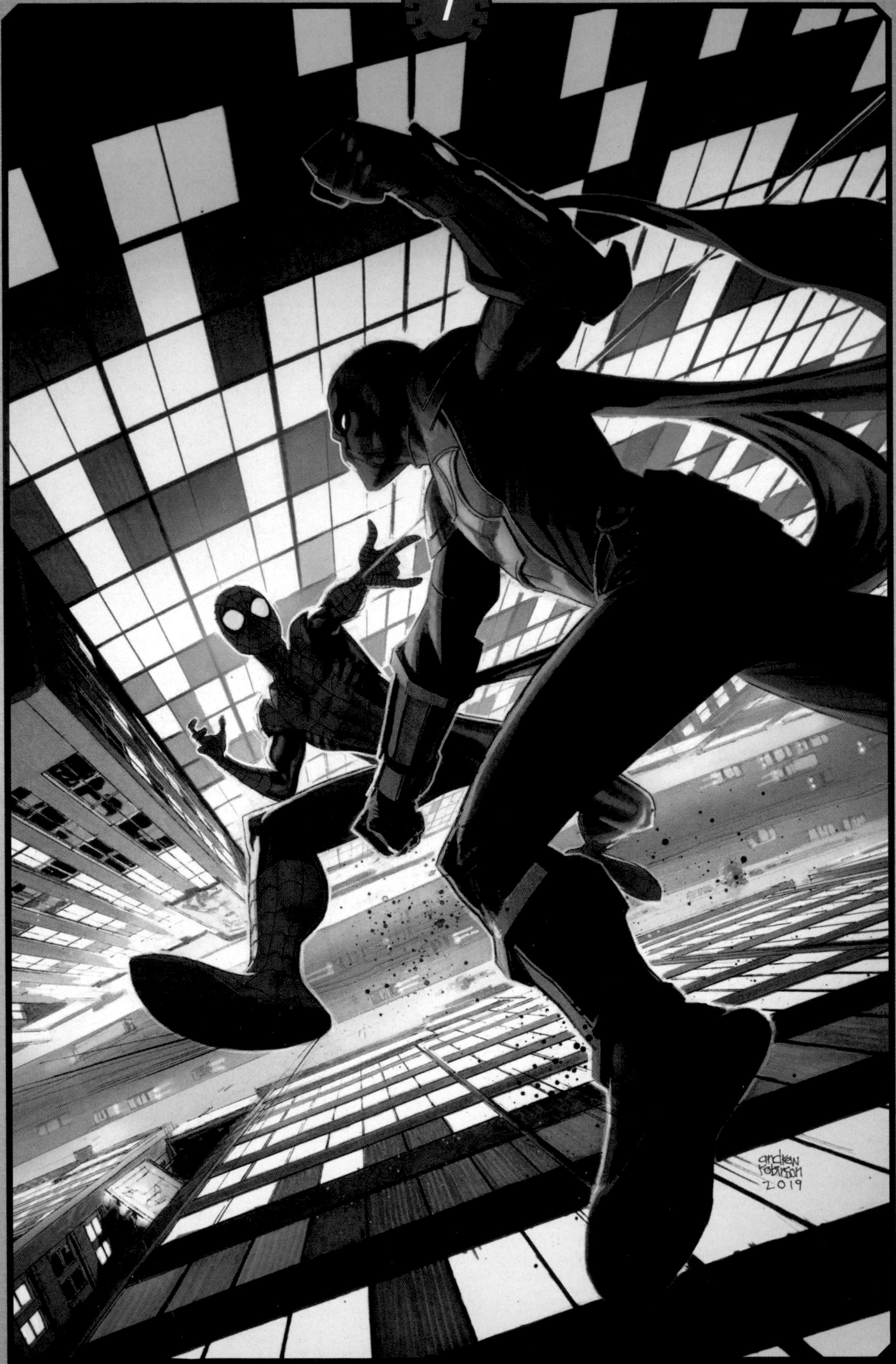
andrew robinson 2019

Feast or Famine: Part One

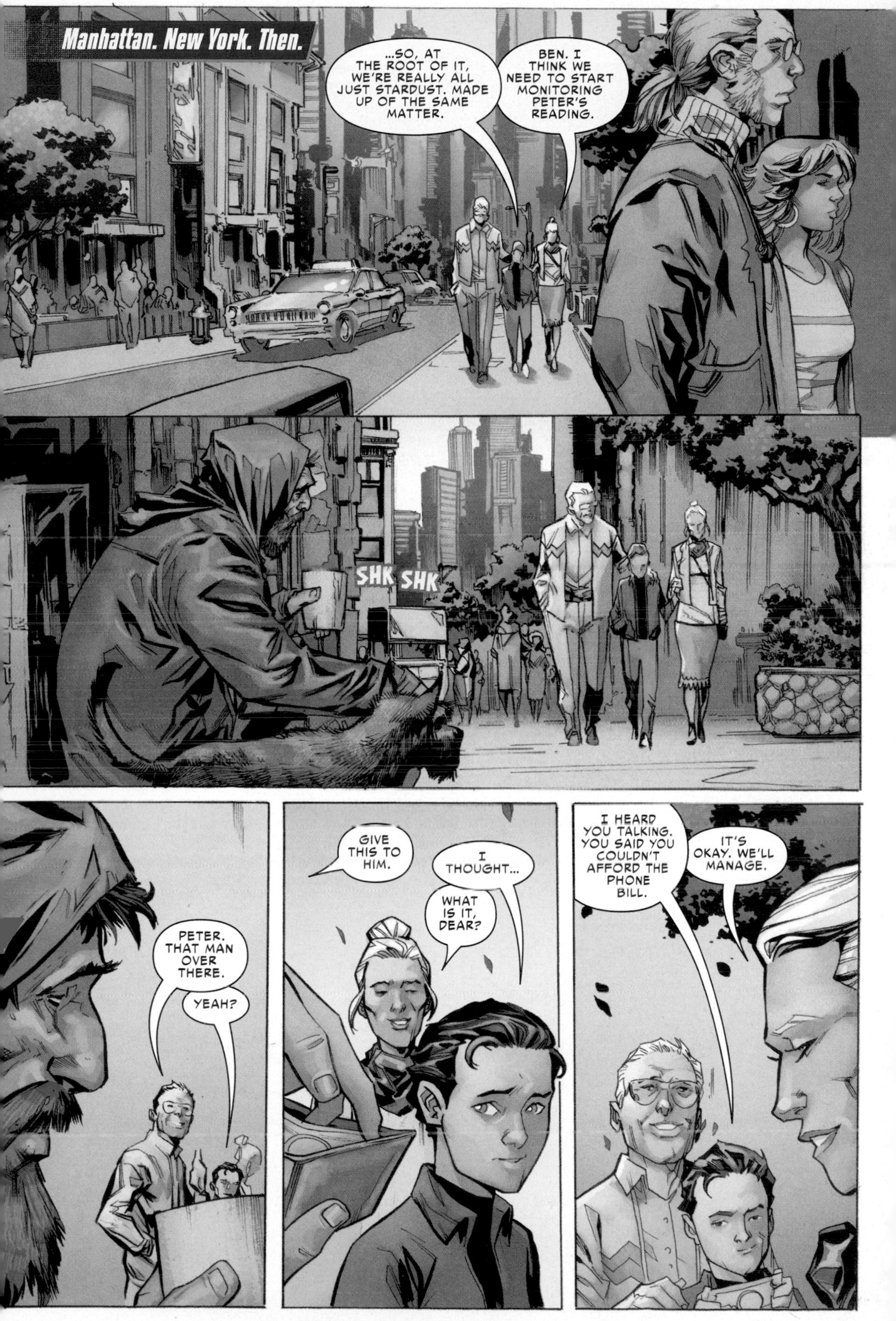
Manhattan. New York. Then.
...SO, AT THE ROOT OF IT, WE'RE REALLY ALL JUST STARDUST. MADE UP OF THE SAME MATTER.
BEN. I THINK WE NEED TO START MONITORING PETER'S READING.
SHK SHK
PETER. THAT MAN OVER THERE.
YEAH?
GIVE THIS TO HIM.
I THOUGHT...
WHAT IS IT, DEAR?
I HEARD YOU TALKING. YOU SAID YOU COULDN'T AFFORD THE PHONE BILL.
IT'S OKAY. WE'LL MANAGE.

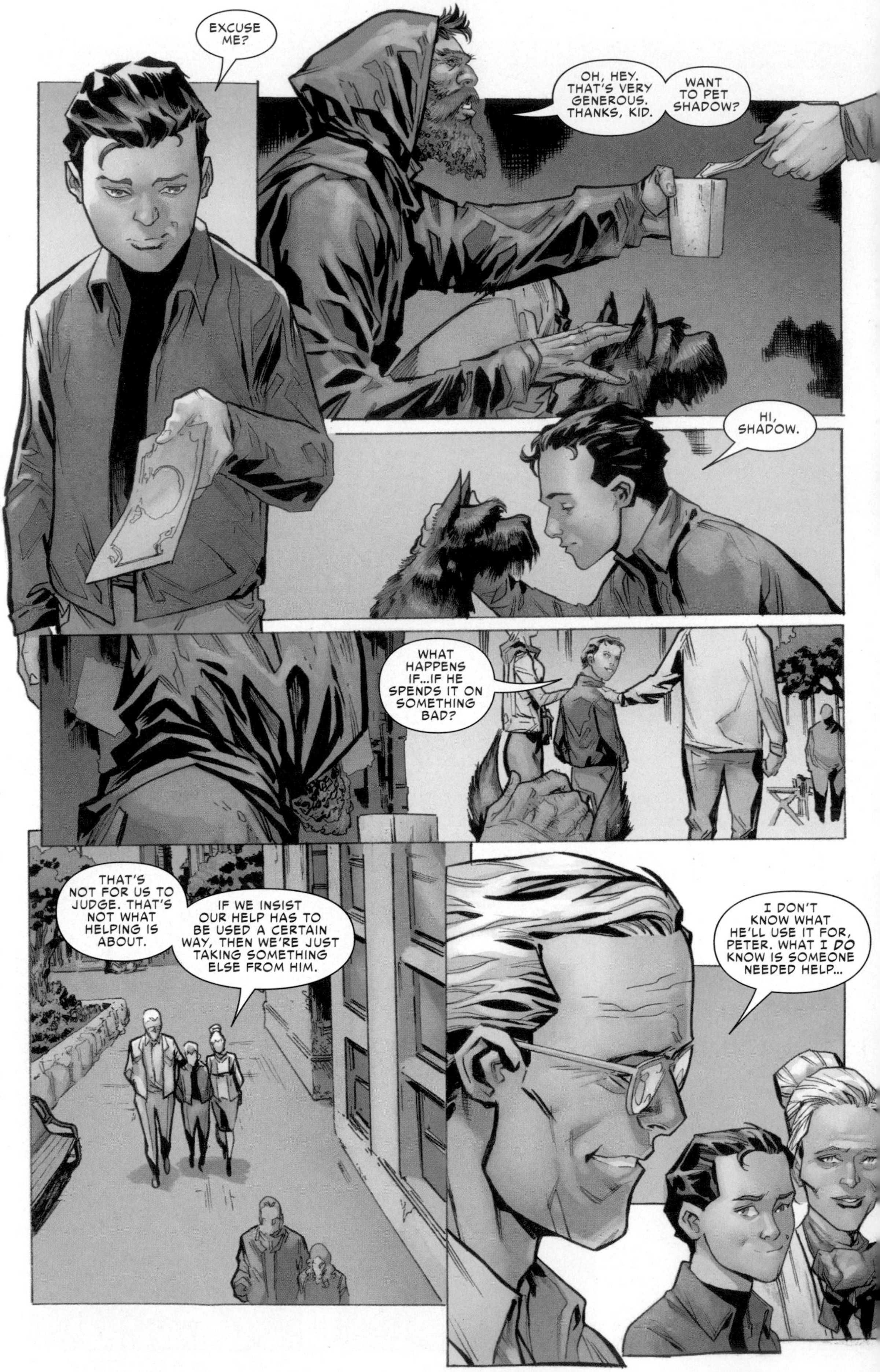
EXCUSE ME?
OH, HEY. THAT'S VERY GENEROUS. THANKS, KID.
WANT TO PET SHADOW?
HI, SHADOW.
WHAT HAPPENS IF...IF HE SPENDS IT ON SOMETHING BAD?
THAT'S NOT FOR US TO JUDGE. THAT'S NOT WHAT HELPING IS ABOUT.
IF WE INSIST OUR HELP HAS TO BE USED A CERTAIN WAY, THEN WE'RE JUST TAKING SOMETHING ELSE FROM HIM.
I DON'T KNOW WHAT HE'LL USE IT FOR, PETER. WHAT I *DO* KNOW IS SOMEONE NEEDED HELP...

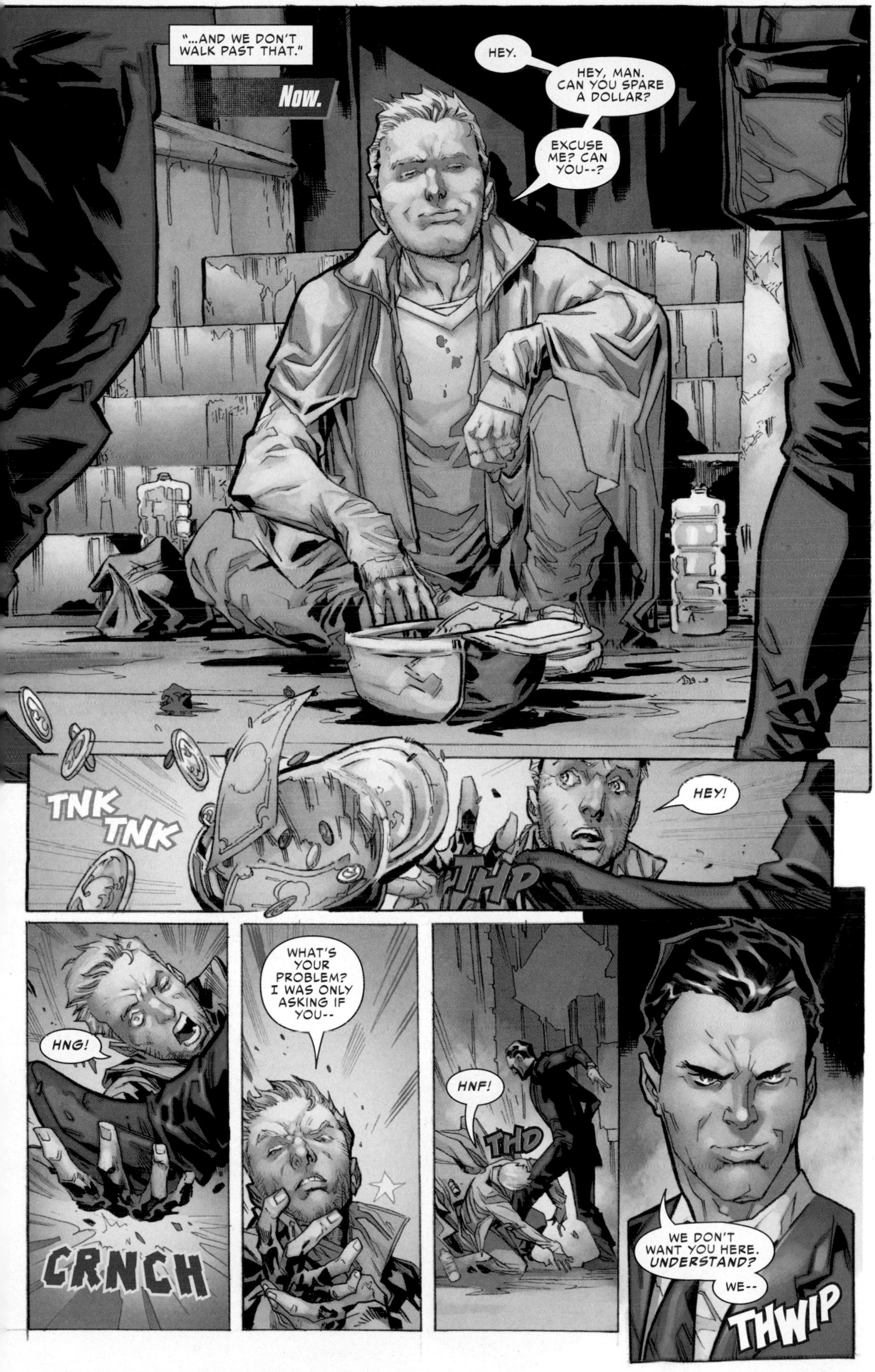
"...AND WE DON'T WALK PAST THAT."
Now.
HEY.
HEY, MAN. CAN YOU SPARE A DOLLAR?
EXCUSE ME? CAN YOU--?
TNK TNK
HEY!
THP
HNG!
CRNCH
WHAT'S YOUR PROBLEM? I WAS ONLY ASKING IF YOU--
HNF!
THD
WE DON'T WANT YOU HERE. UNDERSTAND?
WE--
THWIP

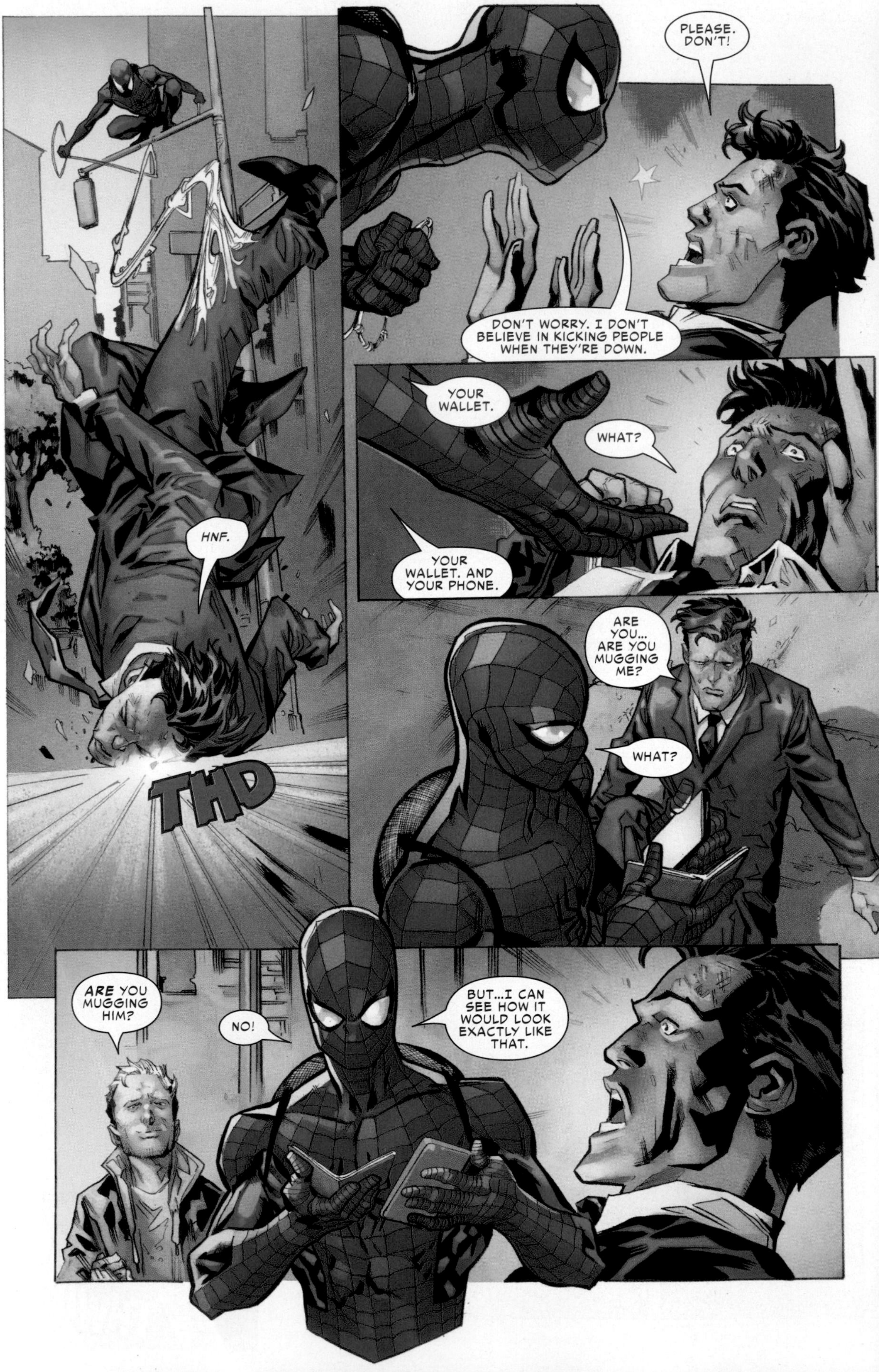
PLEASE. DON'T!
DON'T WORRY. I DON'T BELIEVE IN KICKING PEOPLE WHEN THEY'RE DOWN.
HNF.
THD
YOUR WALLET.
WHAT?
YOUR WALLET. AND YOUR PHONE.
ARE YOU... ARE YOU MUGGING ME?
WHAT?
ARE YOU MUGGING HIM?
NO!
BUT...I CAN SEE HOW IT WOULD LOOK EXACTLY LIKE THAT.

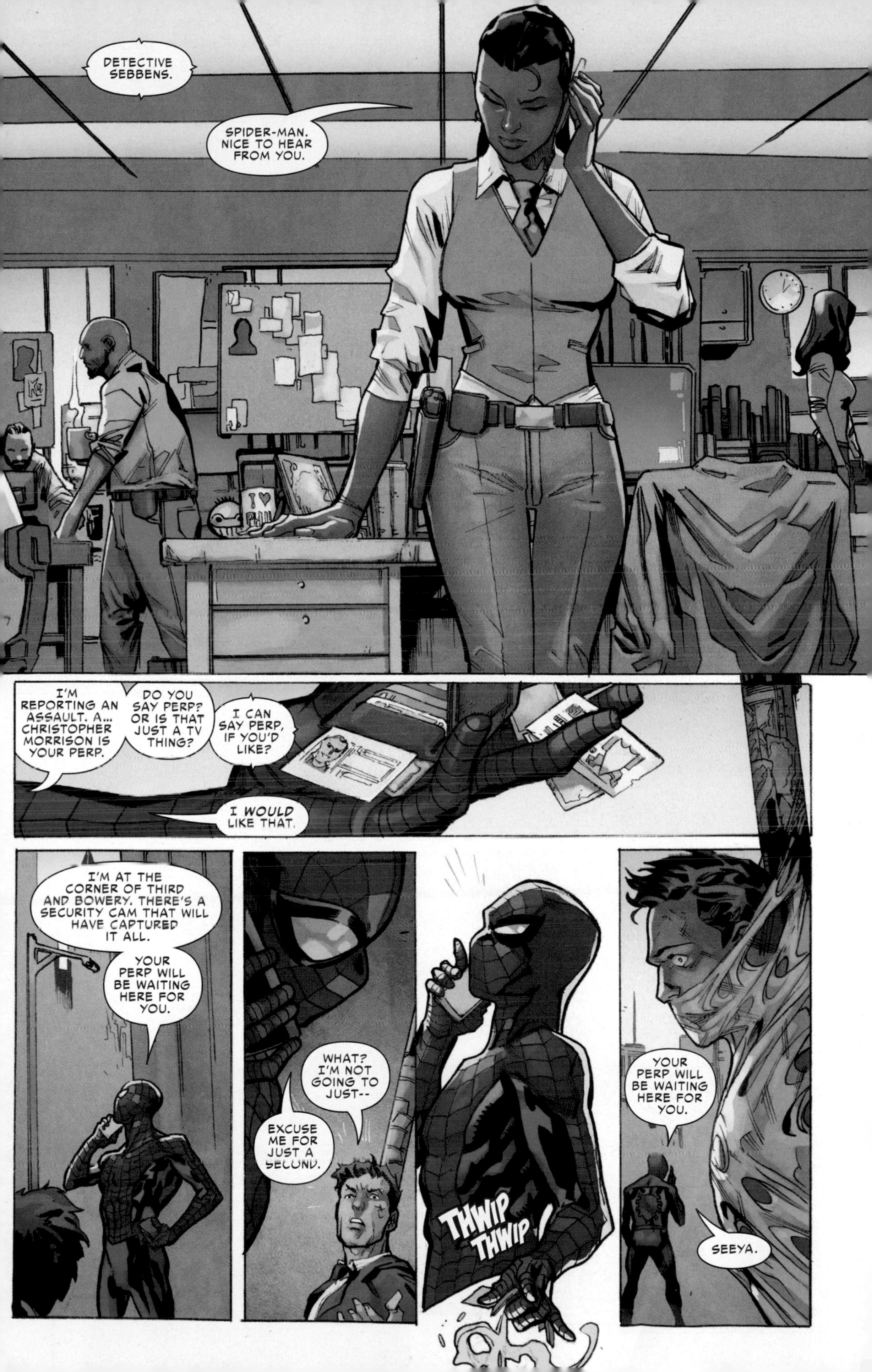
DETECTIVE SEBBENS.
SPIDER-MAN. NICE TO HEAR FROM YOU.
I'M REPORTING AN ASSAULT. A... CHRISTOPHER MORRISON IS YOUR PERP.
DO YOU SAY PERP? OR IS THAT JUST A TV THING?
I CAN SAY PERP, IF YOU'D LIKE?
I WOULD LIKE THAT.
I'M AT THE CORNER OF THIRD AND BOWERY. THERE'S A SECURITY CAM THAT WILL HAVE CAPTURED IT ALL.
YOUR PERP WILL BE WAITING HERE FOR YOU.
WHAT? I'M NOT GOING TO JUST--
EXCUSE ME FOR JUST A SECOND.
THWIP THWIP
YOUR PERP WILL BE WAITING HERE FOR YOU.
SEEYA.

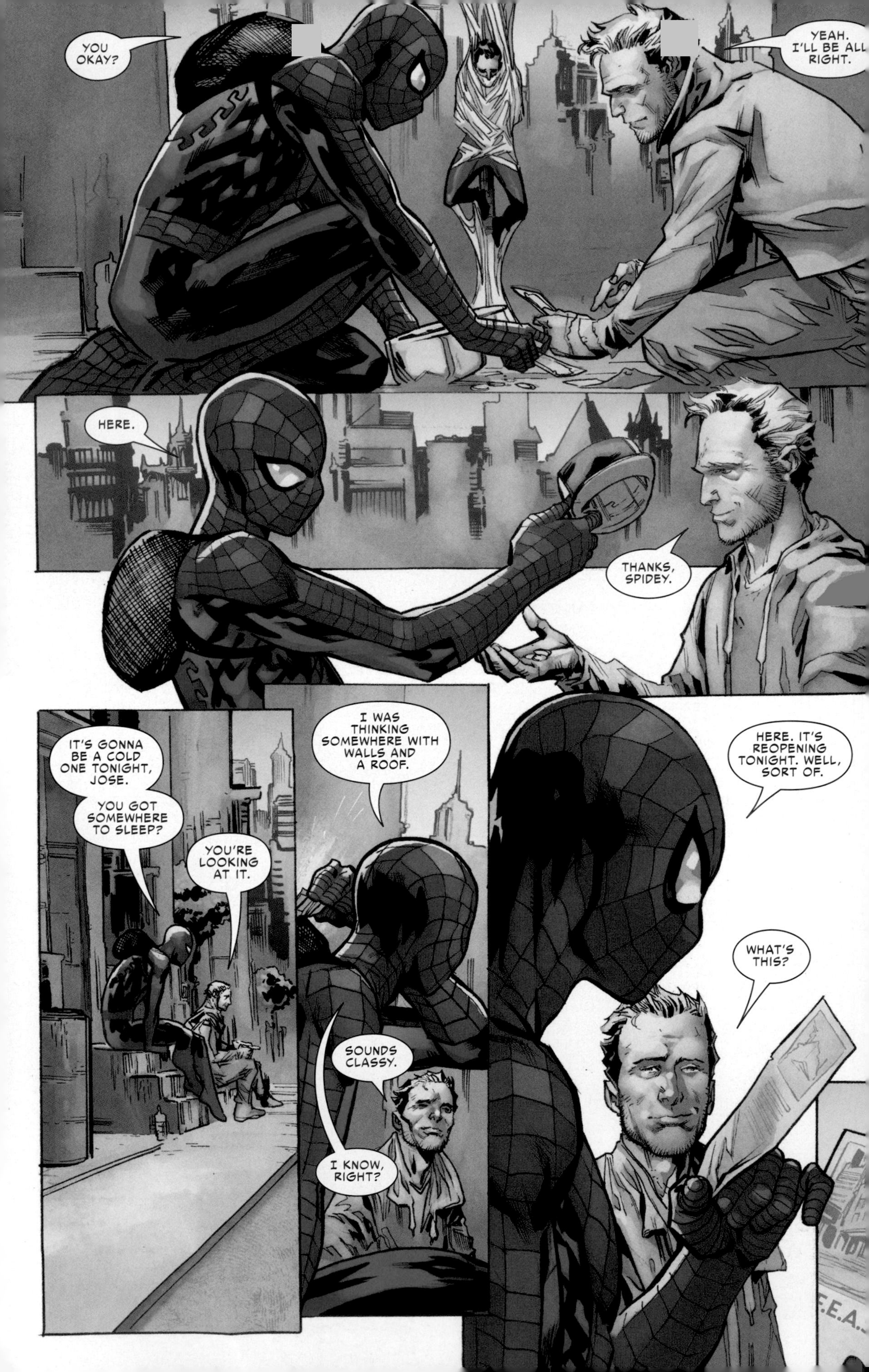
YOU OKAY?
YEAH. I'LL BE ALL RIGHT.
HERE.
THANKS, SPIDEY.
IT'S GONNA BE A COLD ONE TONIGHT, JOSE.
YOU GOT SOMEWHERE TO SLEEP?
YOU'RE LOOKING AT IT.
I WAS THINKING SOMEWHERE WITH WALLS AND A ROOF.
SOUNDS CLASSY.
I KNOW, RIGHT?
HERE. IT'S REOPENING TONIGHT. WELL, SORT OF.
WHAT'S THIS?

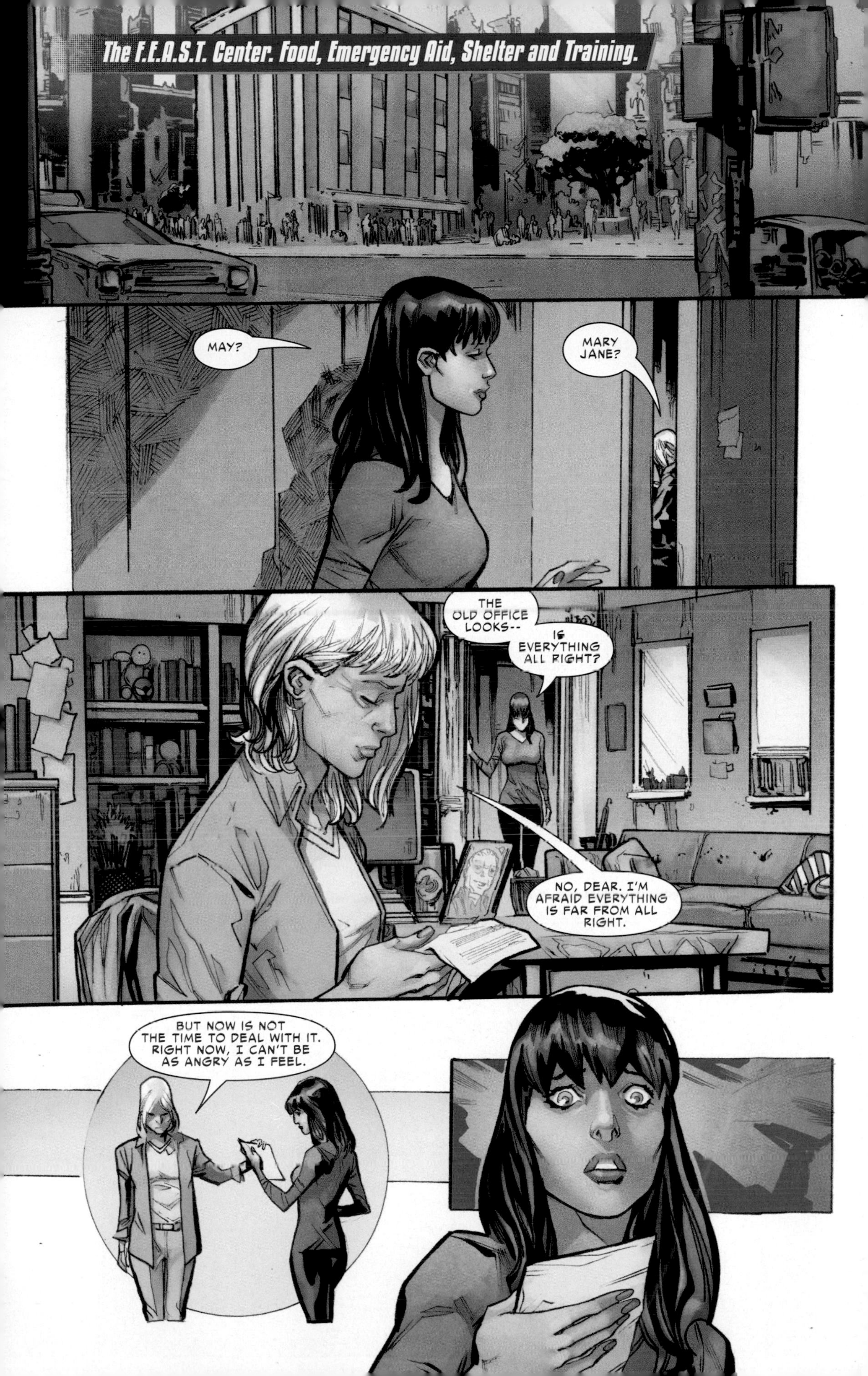
The F.E.A.S.T. Center. Food, Emergency Aid, Shelter and Training.
MAY?
MARY JANE?
THE OLD OFFICE LOOKS--
IS EVERYTHING ALL RIGHT?
NO, DEAR. I'M AFRAID EVERYTHING IS FAR FROM ALL RIGHT.
BUT NOW IS NOT THE TIME TO DEAL WITH IT. RIGHT NOW, I CAN'T BE AS ANGRY AS I FEEL.

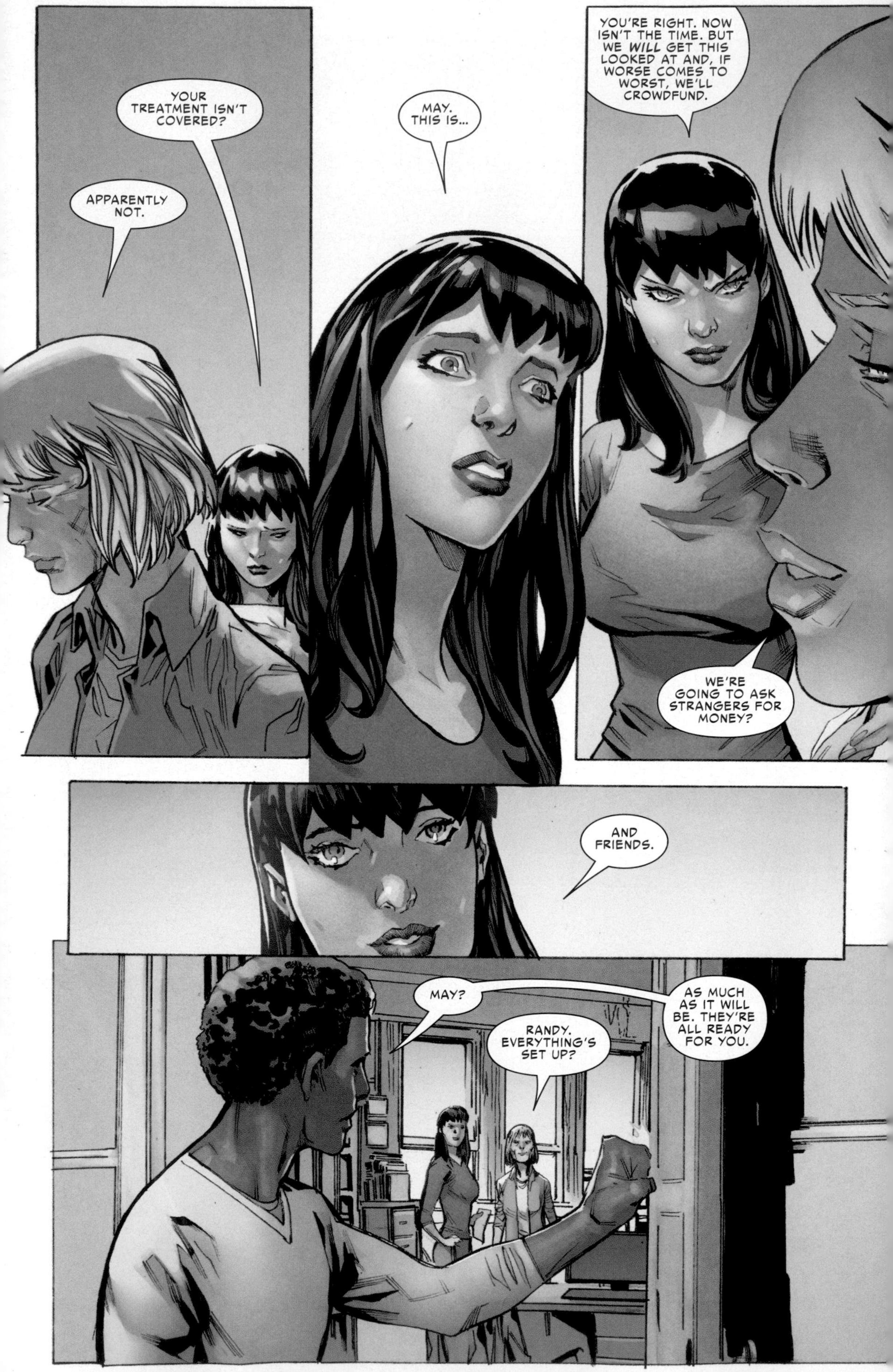
YOUR TREATMENT ISN'T COVERED?
APPARENTLY NOT.
MAY. THIS IS...
YOU'RE RIGHT. NOW ISN'T THE TIME. BUT WE WILL GET THIS LOOKED AT AND, IF WORSE COMES TO WORST, WE'LL CROWDFUND.
WE'RE GOING TO ASK STRANGERS FOR MONEY?
AND FRIENDS.
MAY?
RANDY. EVERYTHING'S SET UP?
AS MUCH AS IT WILL BE. THEY'RE ALL READY FOR YOU.

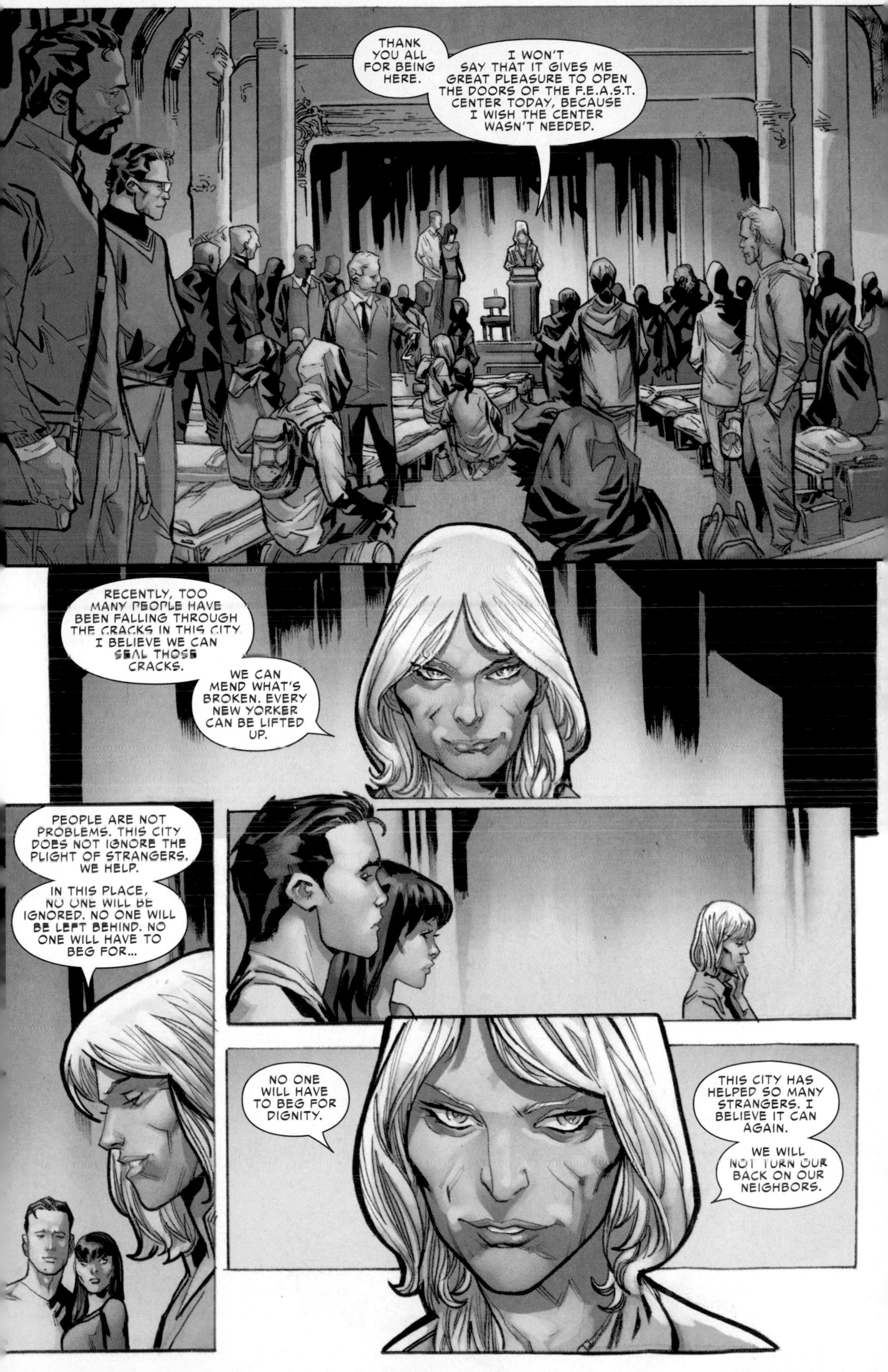
THANK YOU ALL FOR BEING HERE.
I WON'T SAY THAT IT GIVES ME GREAT PLEASURE TO OPEN THE DOORS OF THE F.E.A.S.T. CENTER TODAY, BECAUSE I WISH THE CENTER WASN'T NEEDED.
RECENTLY, TOO MANY PEOPLE HAVE BEEN FALLING THROUGH THE CRACKS IN THIS CITY. I BELIEVE WE CAN SEAL THOSE CRACKS.
WE CAN MEND WHAT'S BROKEN. EVERY NEW YORKER CAN BE LIFTED UP.
PEOPLE ARE NOT PROBLEMS. THIS CITY DOES NOT IGNORE THE PLIGHT OF STRANGERS. WE HELP.
IN THIS PLACE, NO ONE WILL BE IGNORED. NO ONE WILL BE LEFT BEHIND. NO ONE WILL HAVE TO BEG FOR...
NO ONE WILL HAVE TO BEG FOR DIGNITY.
THIS CITY HAS HELPED SO MANY STRANGERS. I BELIEVE IT CAN AGAIN.
WE WILL NOT TURN OUR BACK ON OUR NEIGHBORS.

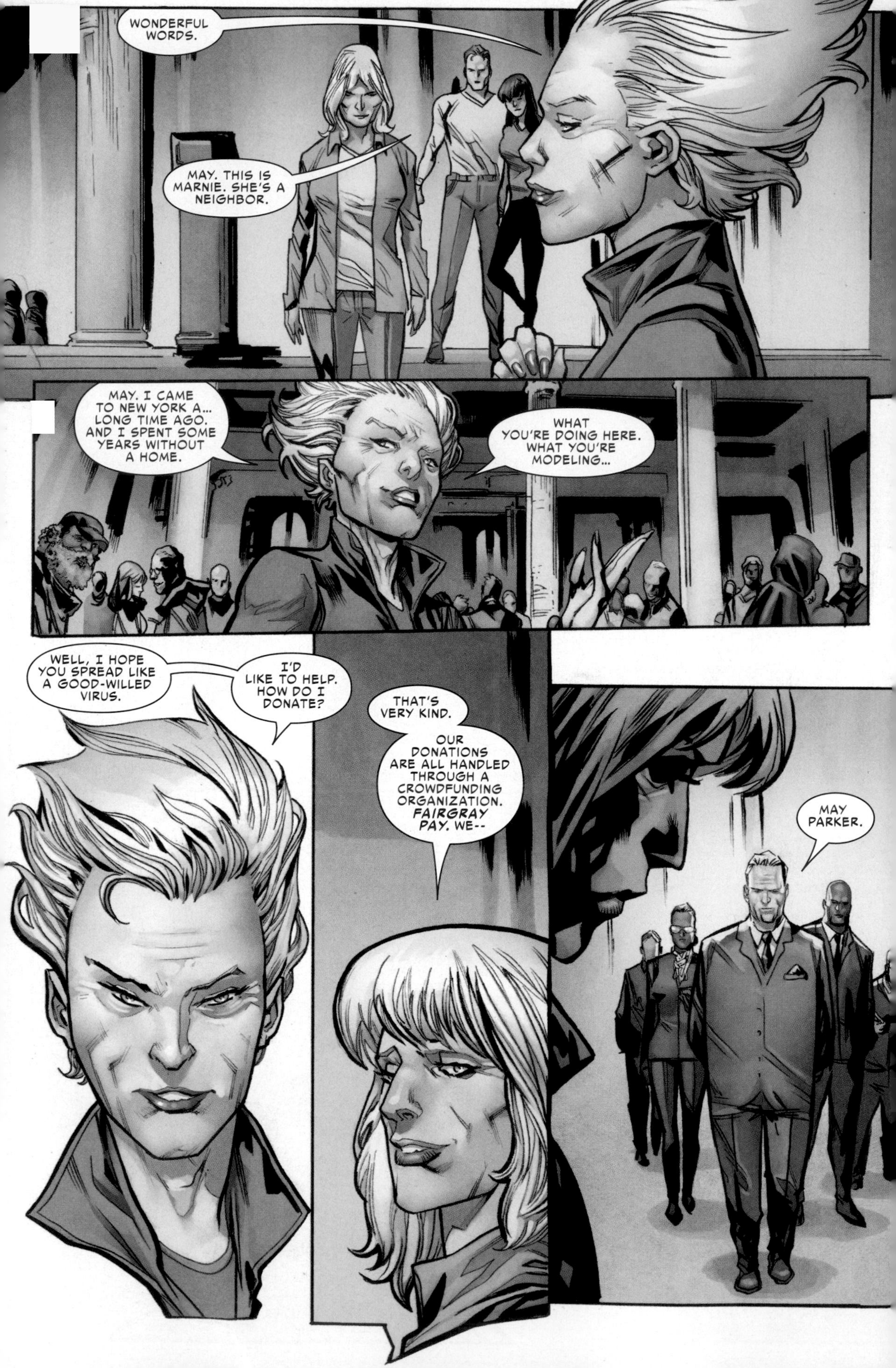
WONDERFUL WORDS.
MAY. THIS IS MARNIE. SHE'S A NEIGHBOR.
MAY. I CAME TO NEW YORK A... LONG TIME AGO. AND I SPENT SOME YEARS WITHOUT A HOME.
WHAT YOU'RE DOING HERE. WHAT YOU'RE MODELING...
WELL, I HOPE YOU SPREAD LIKE A GOOD-WILLED VIRUS.
I'D LIKE TO HELP. HOW DO I DONATE?
THAT'S VERY KIND.
OUR DONATIONS ARE ALL HANDLED THROUGH A CROWDFUNDING ORGANIZATION. FAIRGRAY PAY. WE--
MAY PARKER.

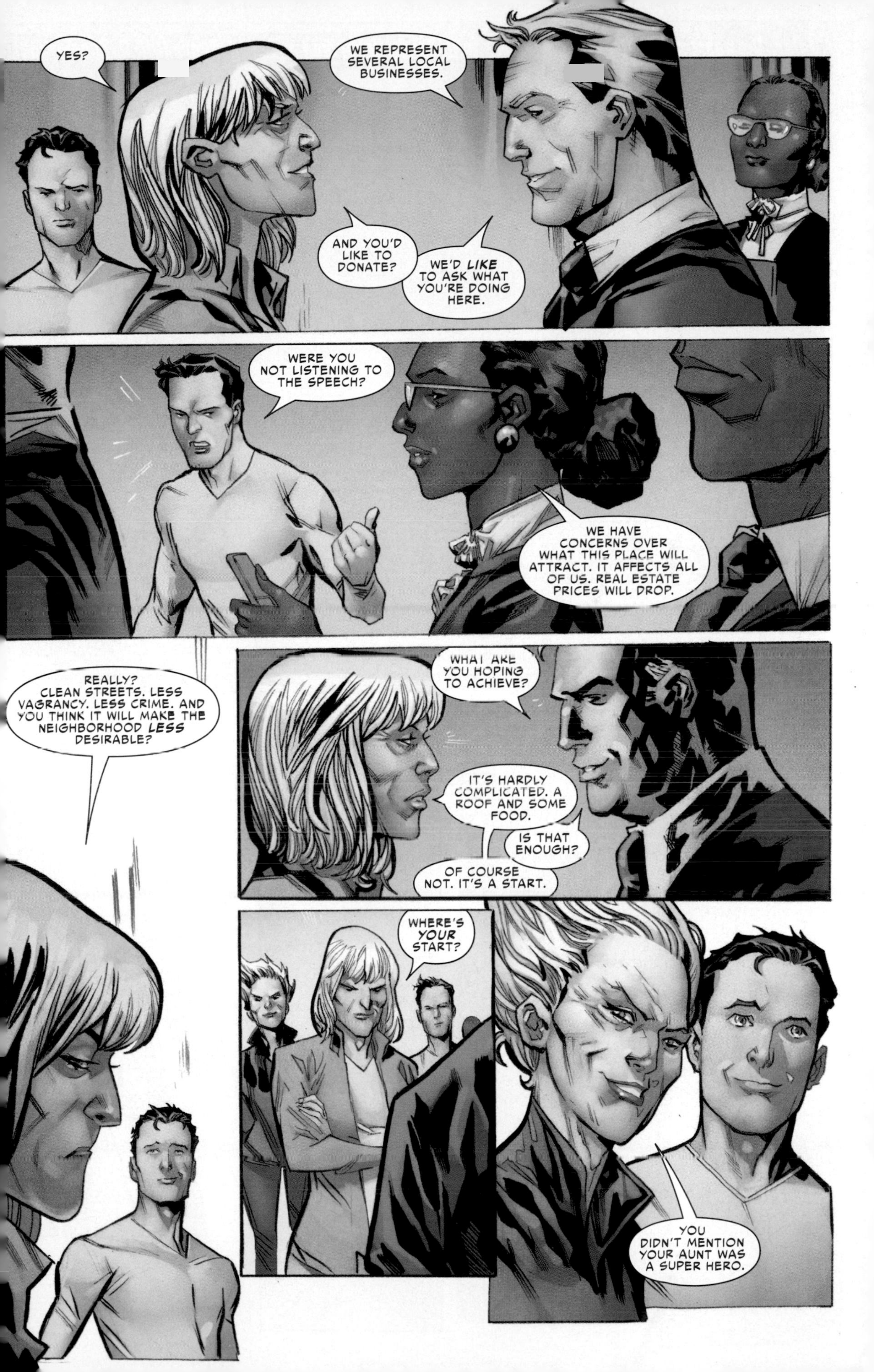
YES?
WE REPRESENT SEVERAL LOCAL BUSINESSES.
AND YOU'D LIKE TO DONATE?
WE'D *LIKE* TO ASK WHAT YOU'RE DOING HERE.
WERE YOU NOT LISTENING TO THE SPEECH?
WE HAVE CONCERNS OVER WHAT THIS PLACE WILL ATTRACT. IT AFFECTS ALL OF US. REAL ESTATE PRICES WILL DROP.
REALLY? CLEAN STREETS. LESS VAGRANCY. LESS CRIME. AND YOU THINK IT WILL MAKE THE NEIGHBORHOOD *LESS* DESIRABLE?
WHAT ARE YOU HOPING TO ACHIEVE?
IT'S HARDLY COMPLICATED. A ROOF AND SOME FOOD.
IS THAT ENOUGH?
OF COURSE NOT. IT'S A START.
WHERE'S *YOUR* START?
YOU DIDN'T MENTION YOUR AUNT WAS A SUPER HERO.

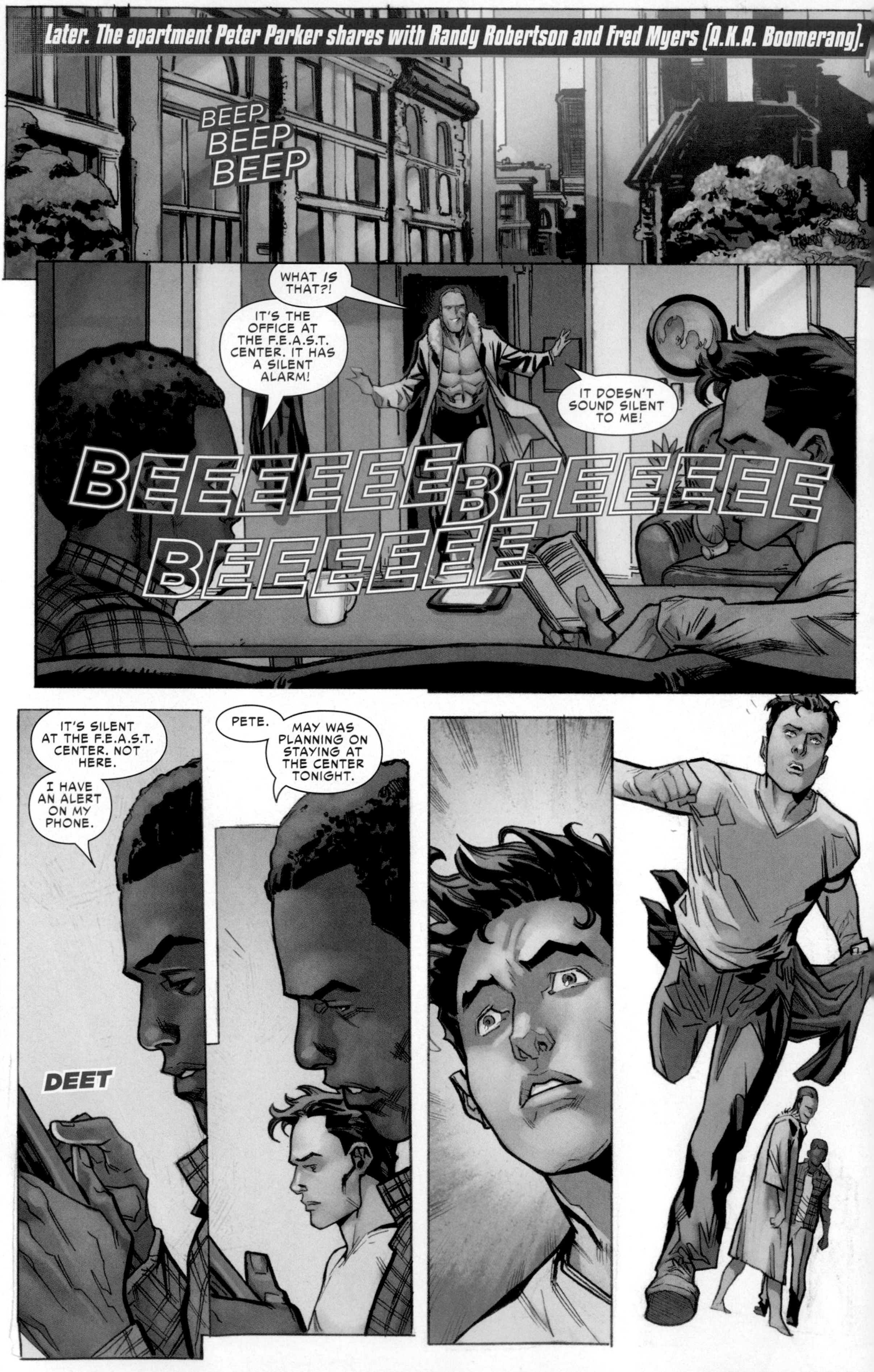
Later. The apartment Peter Parker shares with Randy Robertson and Fred Myers (A.K.A. Boomerang).
BEEP BEEP BEEP
WHAT IS THAT?!
IT'S THE OFFICE AT THE F.E.A.S.T. CENTER. IT HAS A SILENT ALARM!
IT DOESN'T SOUND SILENT TO ME!
BEEEEEE BEEEEEEE BEEEEEE
IT'S SILENT AT THE F.E.A.S.T. CENTER. NOT HERE.
I HAVE AN ALERT ON MY PHONE.
DEET
PETE.
MAY WAS PLANNING ON STAYING AT THE CENTER TONIGHT.

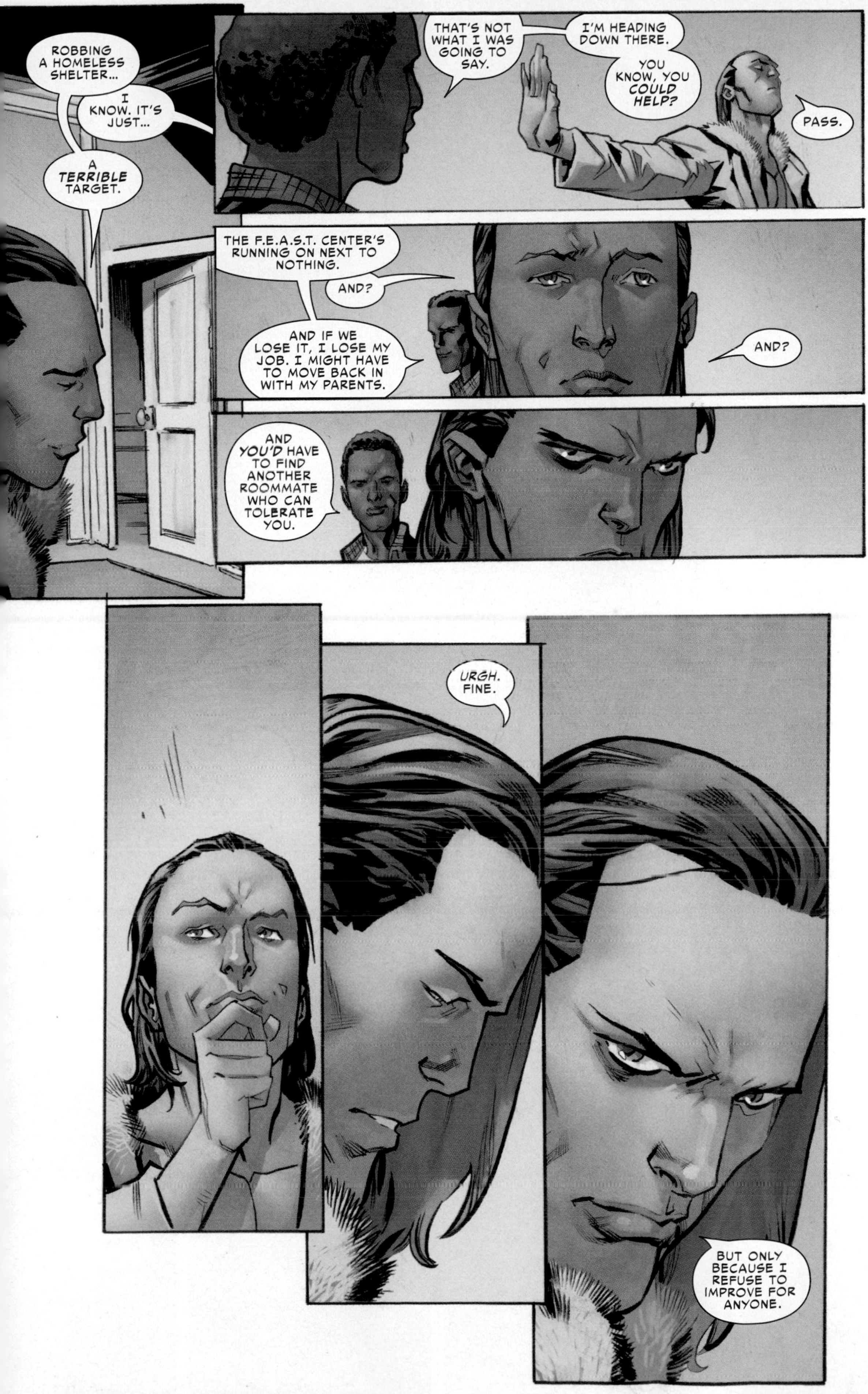

ROBBING A HOMELESS SHELTER...
I KNOW. IT'S JUST...
A TERRIBLE TARGET.
THAT'S NOT WHAT I WAS GOING TO SAY.
I'M HEADING DOWN THERE.
YOU KNOW, YOU COULD HELP?
PASS.
THE F.E.A.S.T. CENTER'S RUNNING ON NEXT TO NOTHING.
AND?
AND IF WE LOSE IT, I LOSE MY JOB. I MIGHT HAVE TO MOVE BACK IN WITH MY PARENTS.
AND?
AND YOU'D HAVE TO FIND ANOTHER ROOMMATE WHO CAN TOLERATE YOU.
URGH. FINE.
BUT ONLY BECAUSE I REFUSE TO IMPROVE FOR ANYONE.

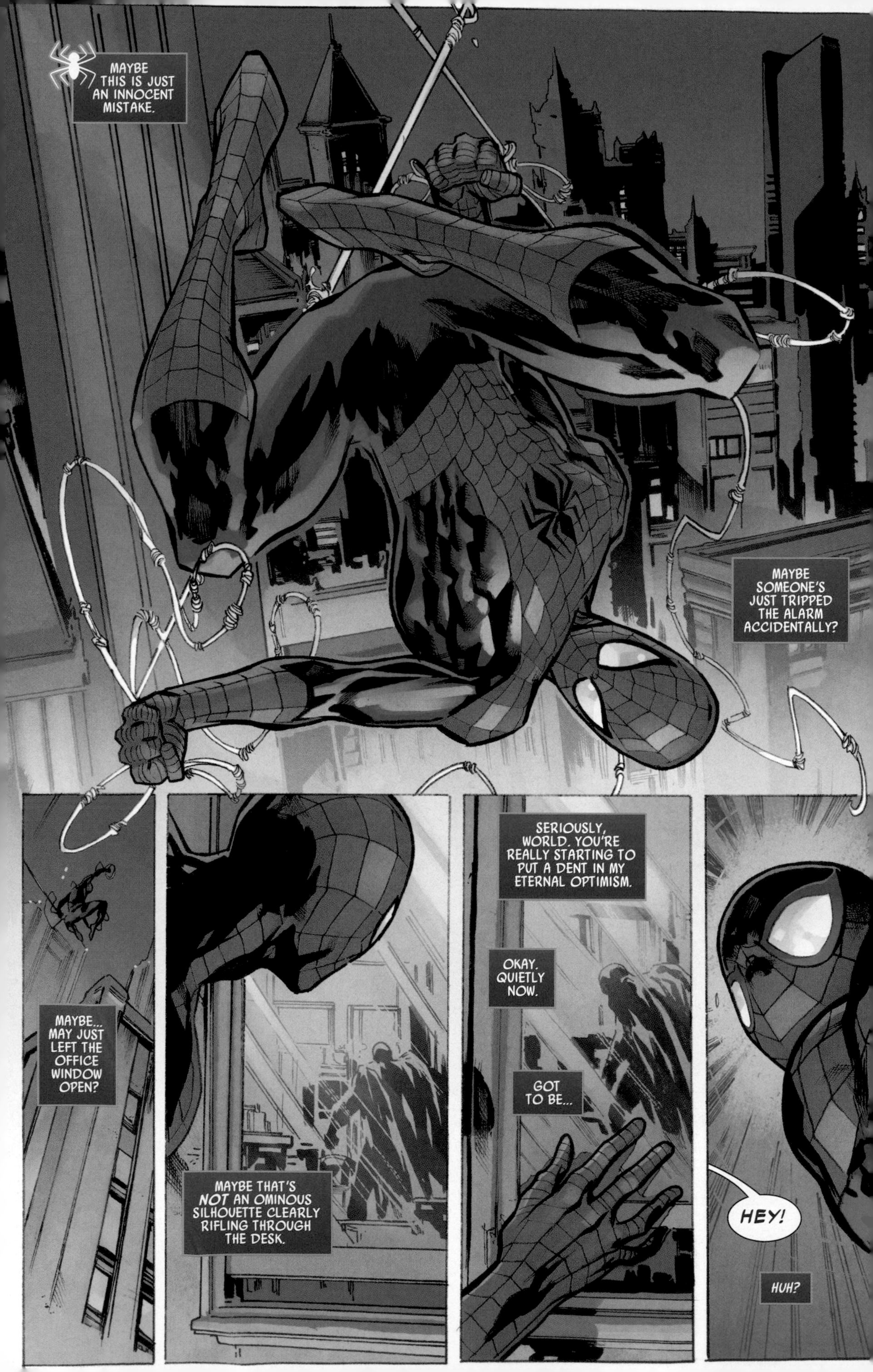
MAYBE THIS IS JUST AN INNOCENT MISTAKE.
MAYBE SOMEONE'S JUST TRIPPED THE ALARM ACCIDENTALLY?
MAYBE... MAY JUST LEFT THE OFFICE WINDOW OPEN?
MAYBE THAT'S NOT AN OMINOUS SILHOUETTE CLEARLY RIFLING THROUGH THE DESK.
SERIOUSLY, WORLD. YOU'RE REALLY STARTING TO PUT A DENT IN MY ETERNAL OPTIMISM.
OKAY. QUIETLY NOW.
GOT TO BE...
HEY!
HUH?

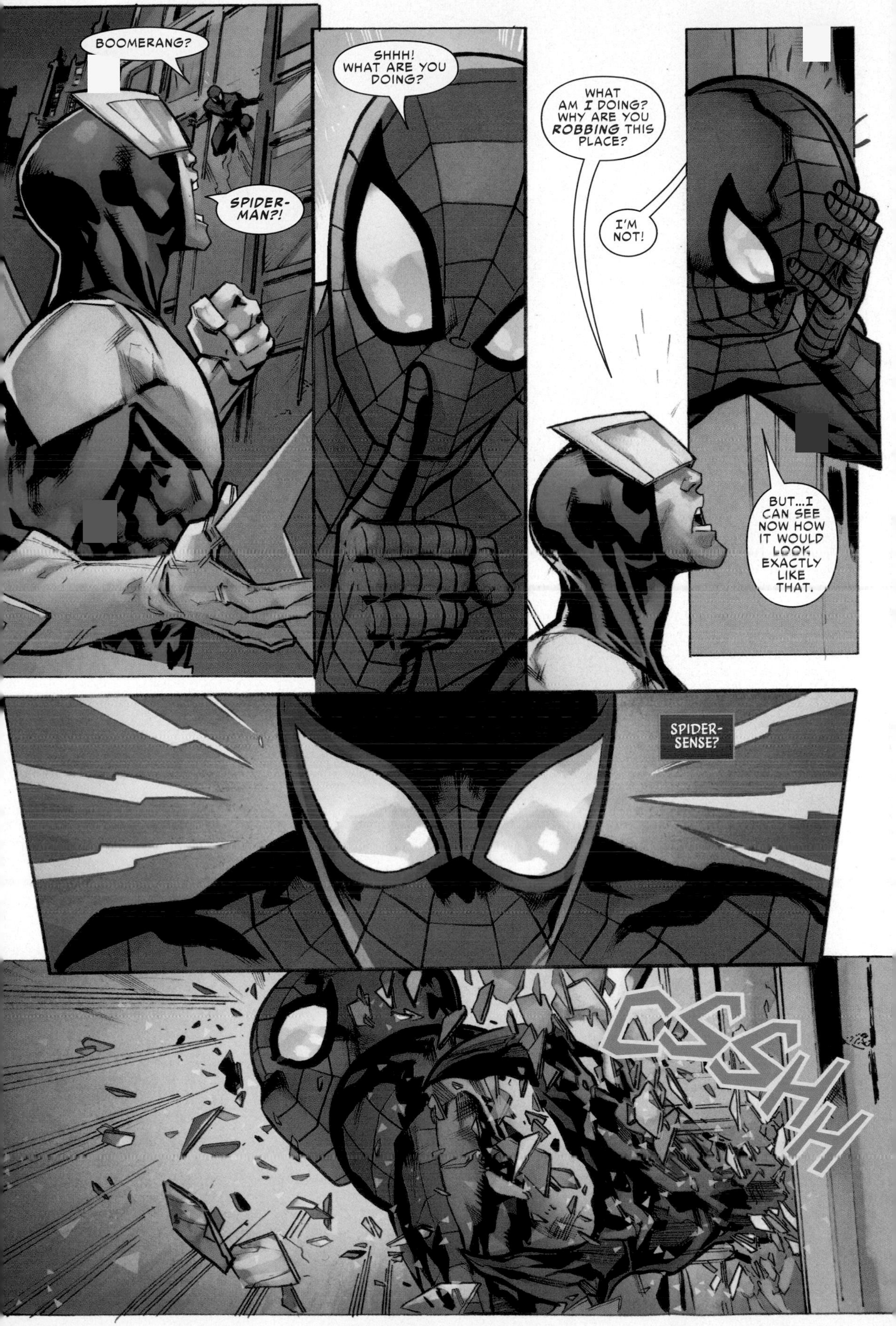
BOOMERANG?
SPIDER-MAN?!
SHHH! WHAT ARE YOU DOING?
WHAT AM I DOING? WHY ARE YOU ROBBING THIS PLACE?
I'M NOT!
BUT...I CAN SEE NOW HOW IT WOULD LOOK EXACTLY LIKE THAT.
SPIDER-SENSE?
CSSHH

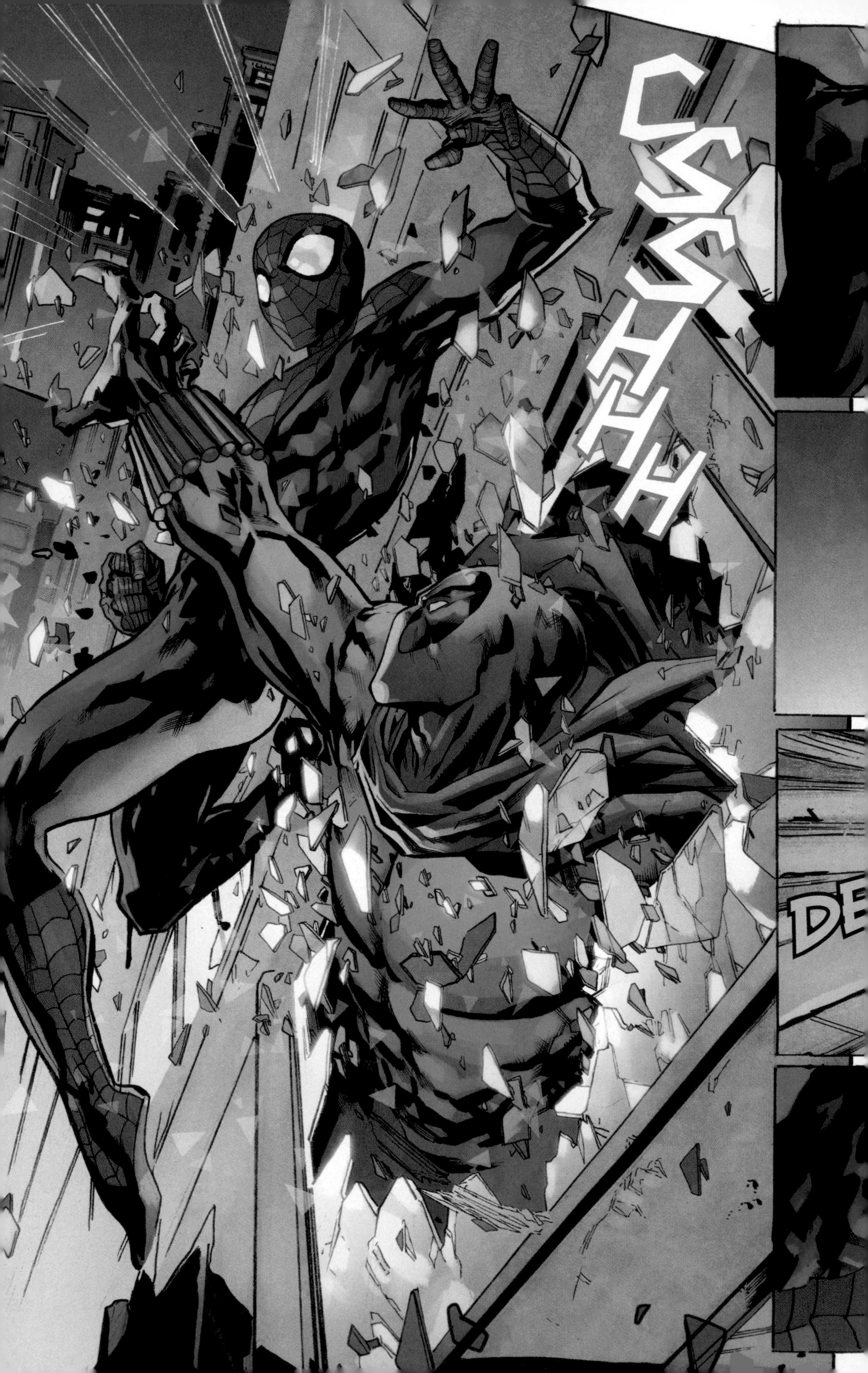
CSSHHH
DE

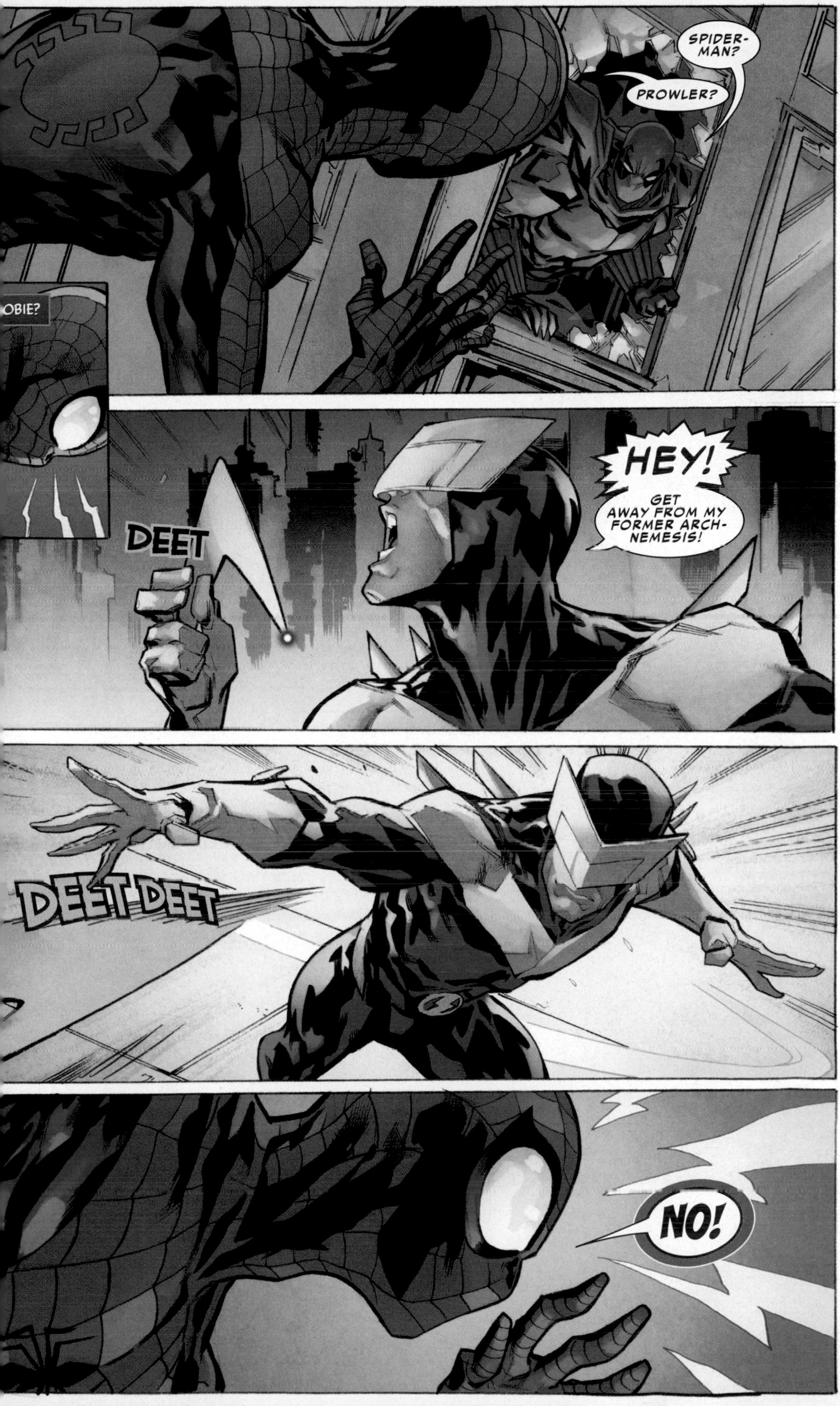
SPIDER-MAN?
PROWLER?
OBIE?
HEY!
GET AWAY FROM MY FORMER ARCH-NEMESIS!
DEET
DEET DEET
NO!

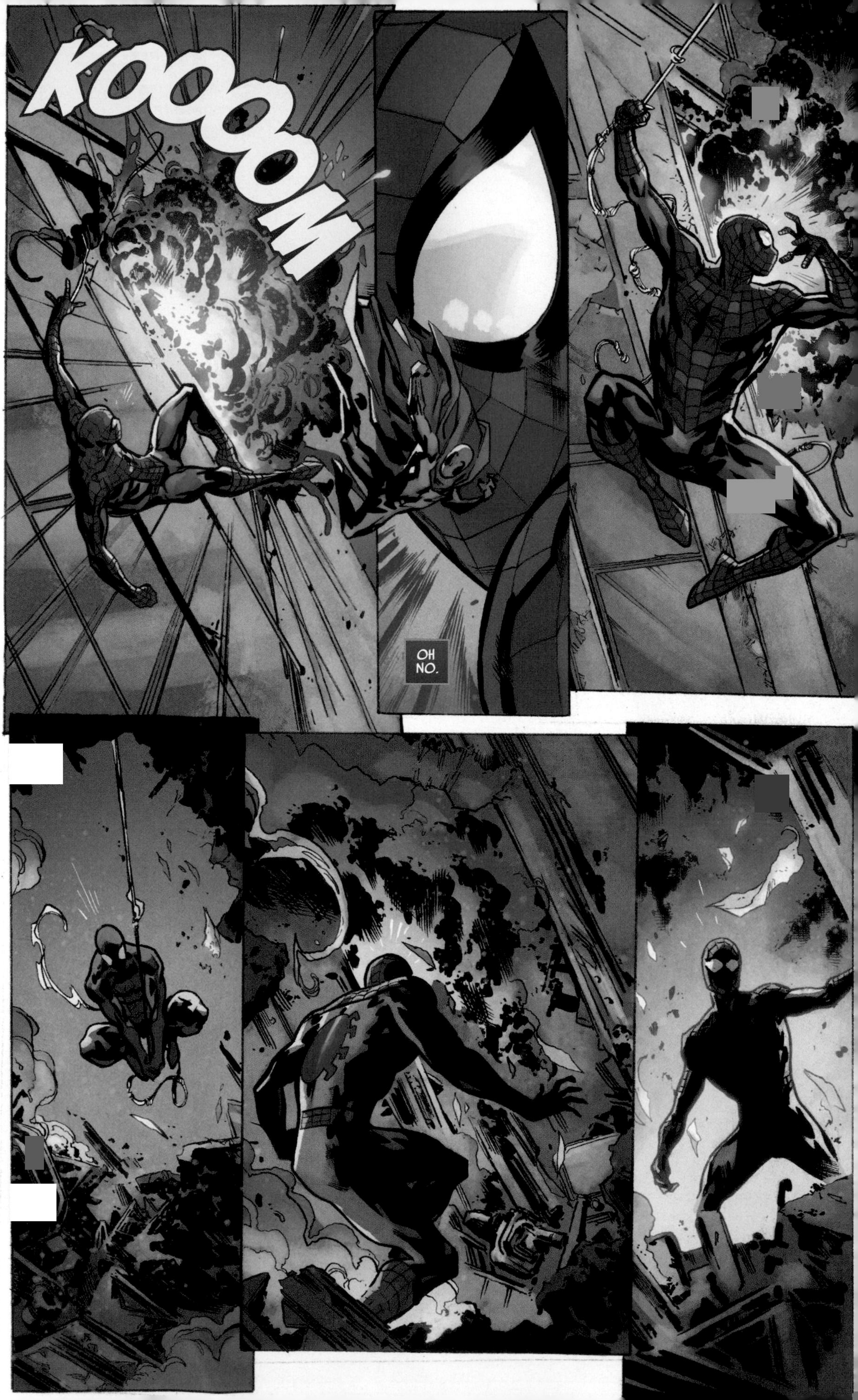
KOOOOM
OH NO.

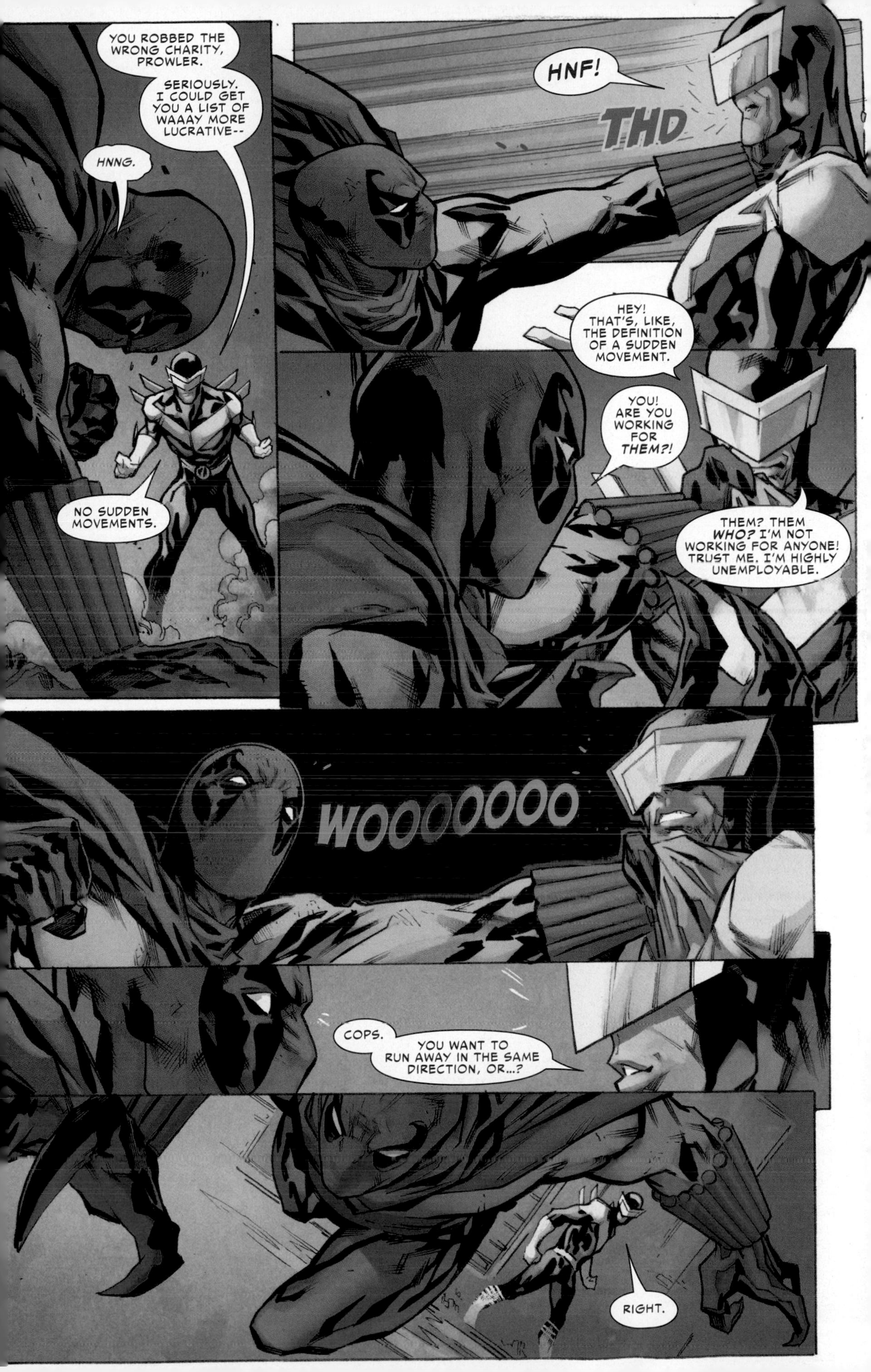
YOU ROBBED THE WRONG CHARITY, PROWLER.
SERIOUSLY. I COULD GET YOU A LIST OF WAAAY MORE LUCRATIVE--
HNNG.
NO SUDDEN MOVEMENTS.
HNF!
THD
HEY! THAT'S, LIKE, THE DEFINITION OF A SUDDEN MOVEMENT.
YOU! ARE YOU WORKING FOR THEM?!
THEM? THEM WHO? I'M NOT WORKING FOR ANYONE! TRUST ME. I'M HIGHLY UNEMPLOYABLE.
WOOOOOOO
COPS.
YOU WANT TO RUN AWAY IN THE SAME DIRECTION, OR...?
RIGHT.

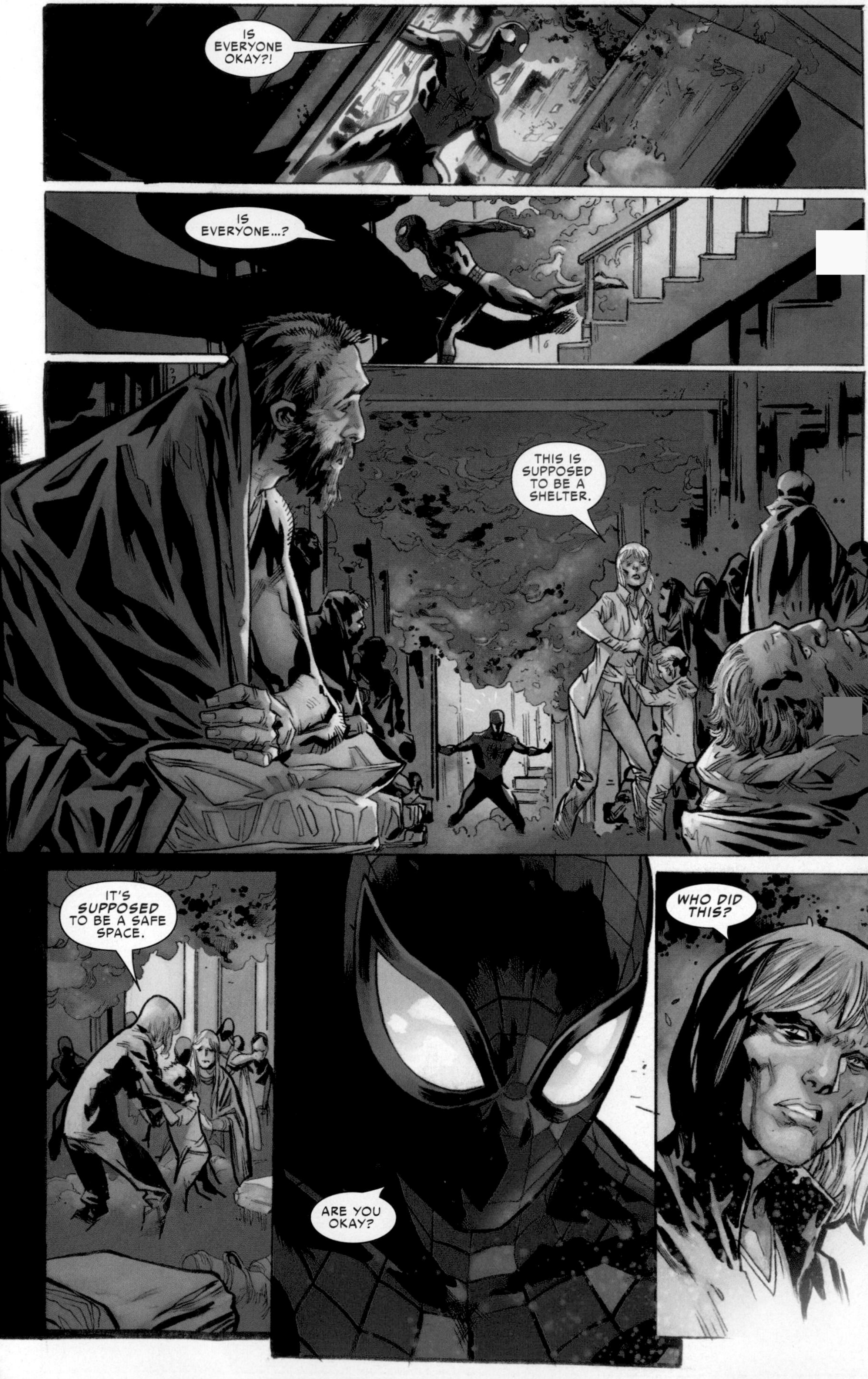
IS EVERYONE OKAY?!
IS EVERYONE...?
THIS IS SUPPOSED TO BE A SHELTER.
IT'S SUPPOSED TO BE A SAFE SPACE.
ARE YOU OKAY?
WHO DID THIS?

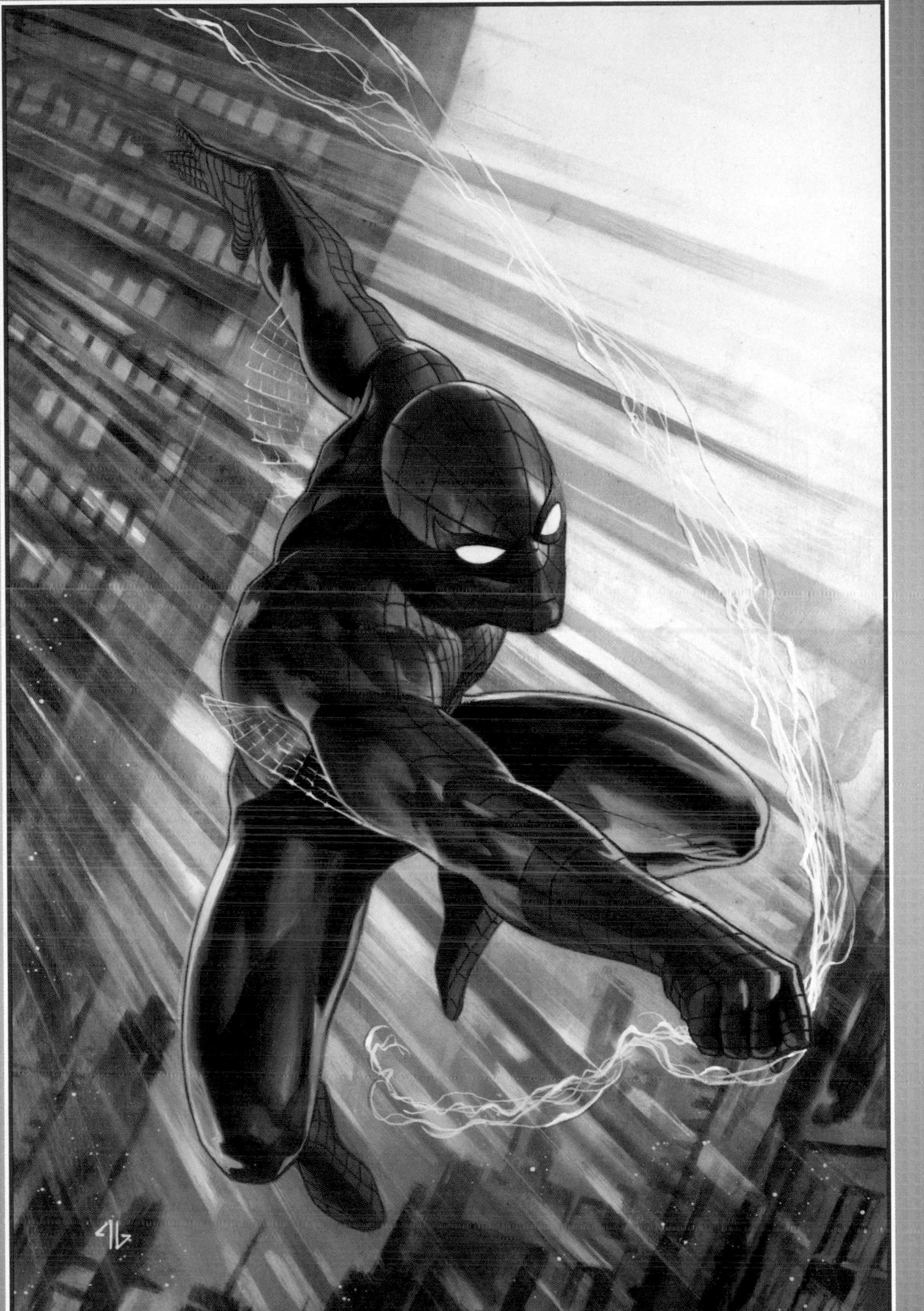

Adi Granov
#8 Variant

8

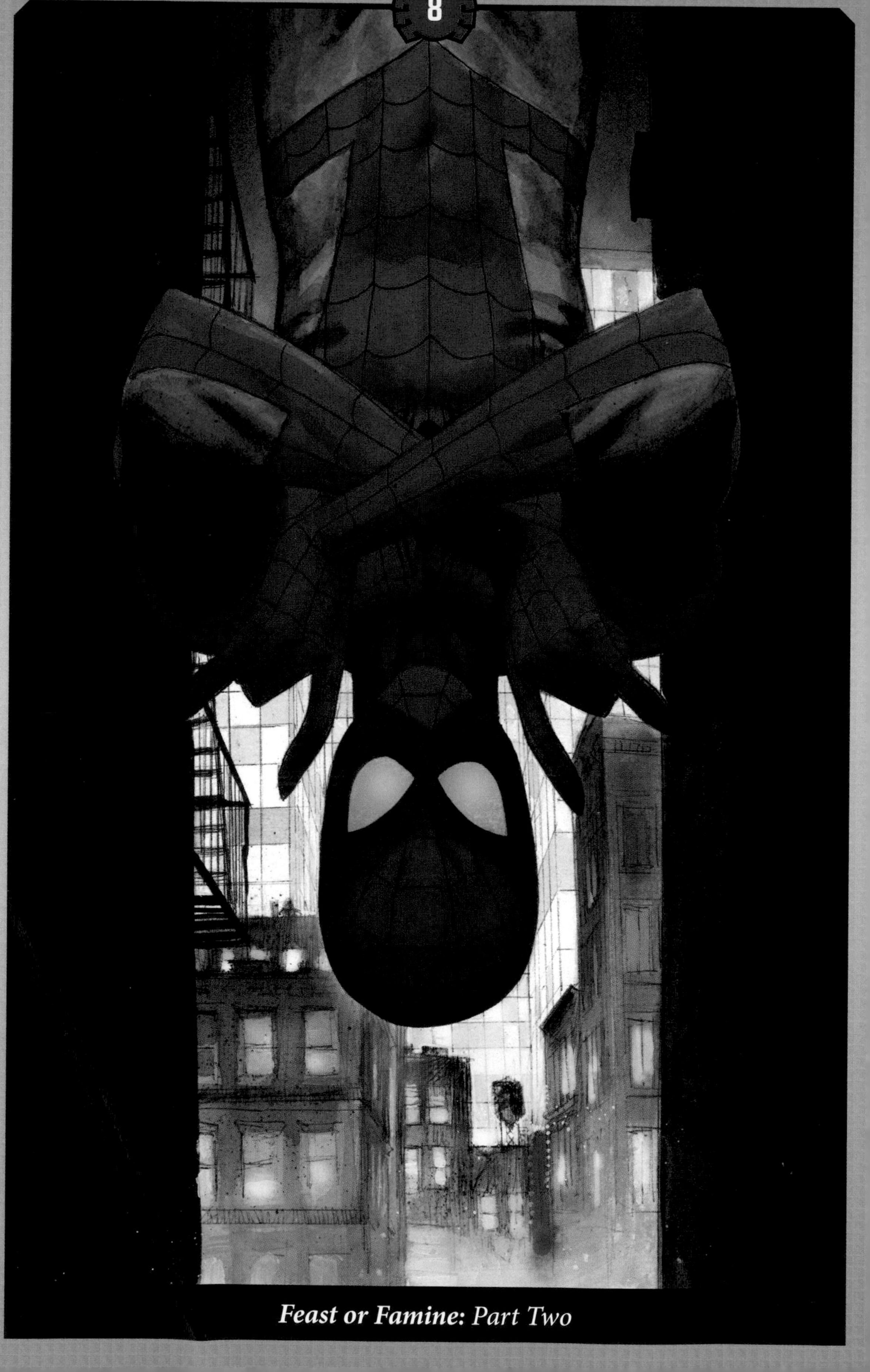

Feast or Famine: Part Two

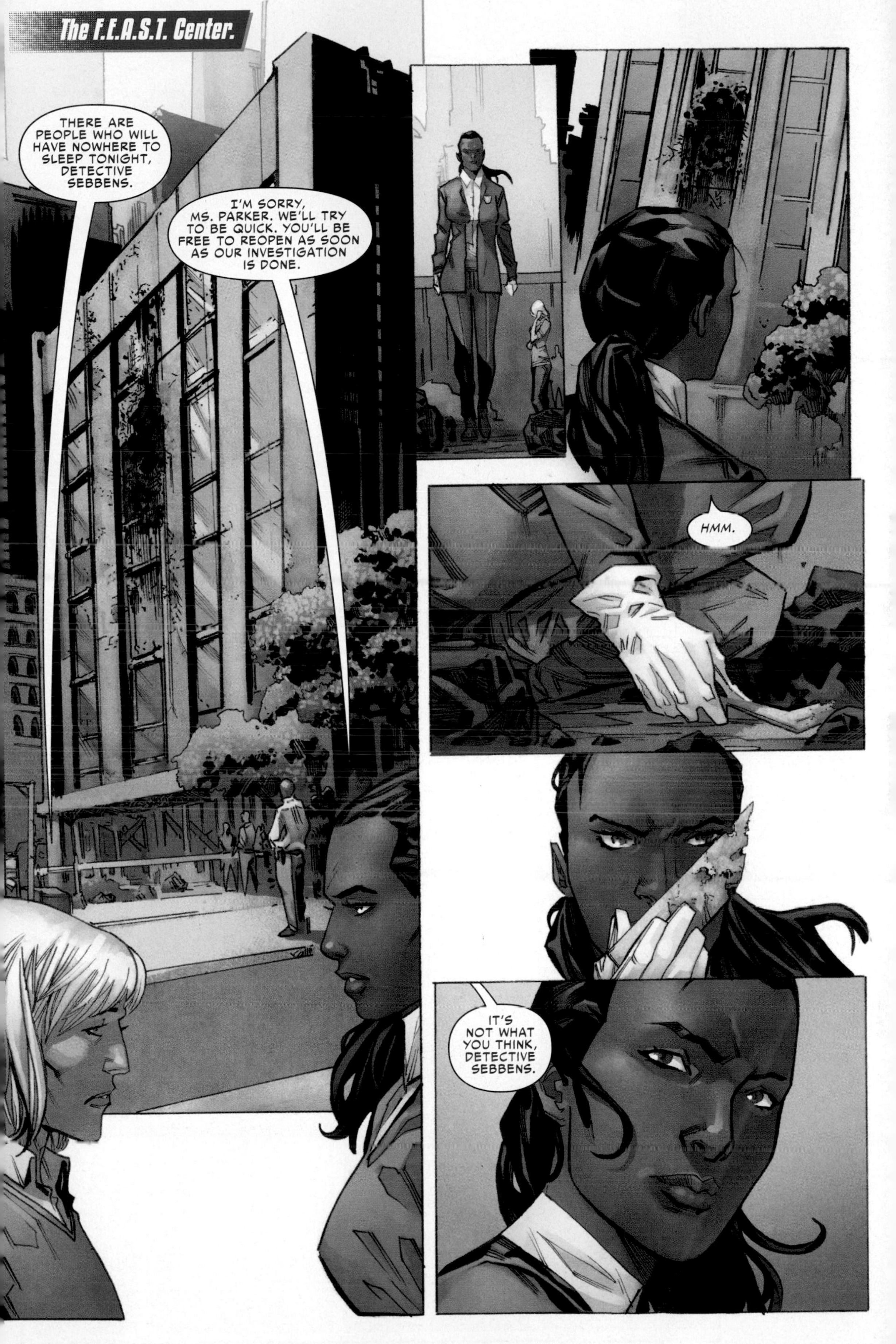
The F.E.A.S.T. Center.
THERE ARE PEOPLE WHO WILL HAVE NOWHERE TO SLEEP TONIGHT, DETECTIVE SEBBENS.
I'M SORRY, MS. PARKER. WE'LL TRY TO BE QUICK. YOU'LL BE FREE TO REOPEN AS SOON AS OUR INVESTIGATION IS DONE.
HMM.
IT'S NOT WHAT YOU THINK, DETECTIVE SEBBENS.

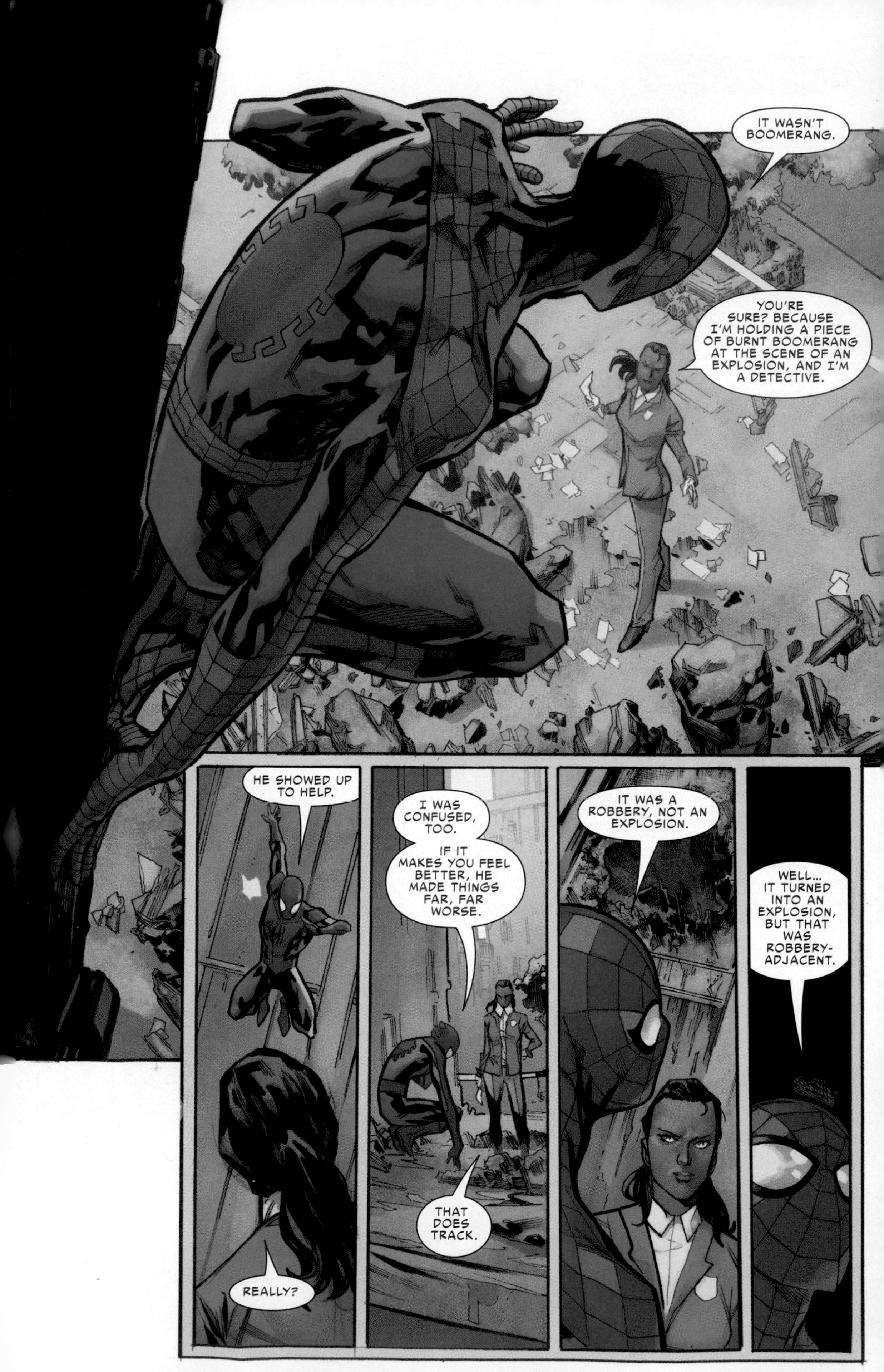
IT WASN'T BOOMERANG.
YOU'RE SURE? BECAUSE I'M HOLDING A PIECE OF BURNT BOOMERANG AT THE SCENE OF AN EXPLOSION, AND I'M A DETECTIVE.
HE SHOWED UP TO HELP.
REALLY?
I WAS CONFUSED, TOO.
IF IT MAKES YOU FEEL BETTER, HE MADE THINGS FAR, FAR WORSE.
THAT DOES TRACK.
IT WAS A ROBBERY, NOT AN EXPLOSION.
WELL... IT TURNED INTO AN EXPLOSION, BUT THAT WAS ROBBERY-ADJACENT.

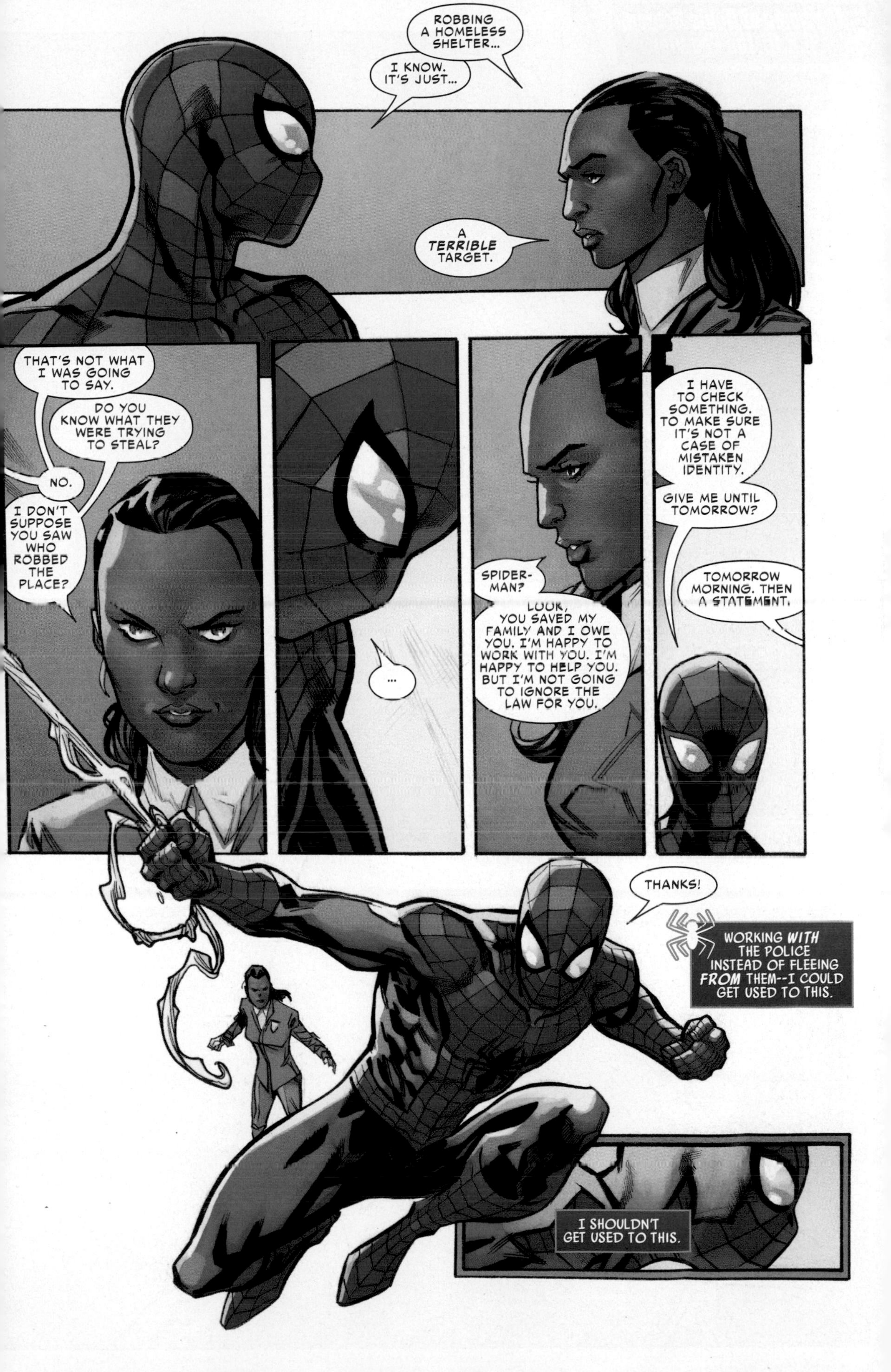
ROBBING A HOMELESS SHELTER...
I KNOW. IT'S JUST...
A *TERRIBLE* TARGET.
THAT'S NOT WHAT I WAS GOING TO SAY.
DO YOU KNOW WHAT THEY WERE TRYING TO STEAL?
NO.
I DON'T SUPPOSE YOU SAW WHO ROBBED THE PLACE?
...
SPIDER-MAN?
LOOK, YOU SAVED MY FAMILY AND I OWE YOU. I'M HAPPY TO WORK WITH YOU. I'M HAPPY TO HELP YOU. BUT I'M NOT GOING TO IGNORE THE LAW FOR YOU.
I HAVE TO CHECK SOMETHING. TO MAKE SURE IT'S NOT A CASE OF MISTAKEN IDENTITY.
GIVE ME UNTIL TOMORROW?
TOMORROW MORNING. THEN A STATEMENT.
THANKS!
WORKING *WITH* THE POLICE INSTEAD OF FLEEING *FROM* THEM--I COULD GET USED TO THIS.
I SHOULDN'T GET USED TO THIS.

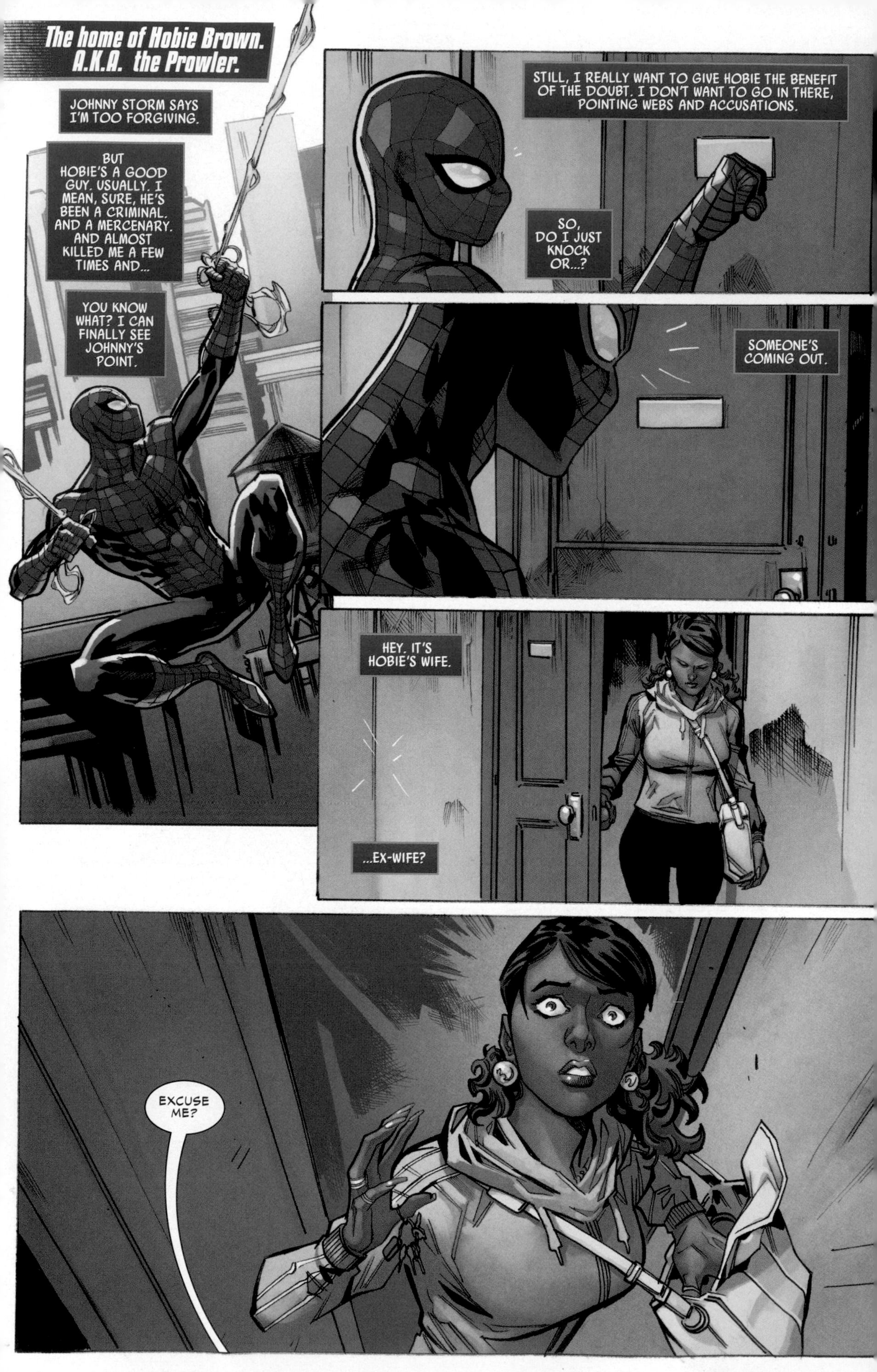
The home of Hobie Brown. A.K.A. the Prowler.
JOHNNY STORM SAYS I'M TOO FORGIVING.
BUT HOBIE'S A GOOD GUY. USUALLY. I MEAN, SURE, HE'S BEEN A CRIMINAL. AND A MERCENARY. AND ALMOST KILLED ME A FEW TIMES AND...
YOU KNOW WHAT? I CAN FINALLY SEE JOHNNY'S POINT.
STILL, I REALLY WANT TO GIVE HOBIE THE BENEFIT OF THE DOUBT. I DON'T WANT TO GO IN THERE, POINTING WEBS AND ACCUSATIONS.
SO, DO I JUST KNOCK OR...?
SOMEONE'S COMING OUT.
HEY. IT'S HOBIE'S WIFE.
...EX-WIFE?
EXCUSE ME?

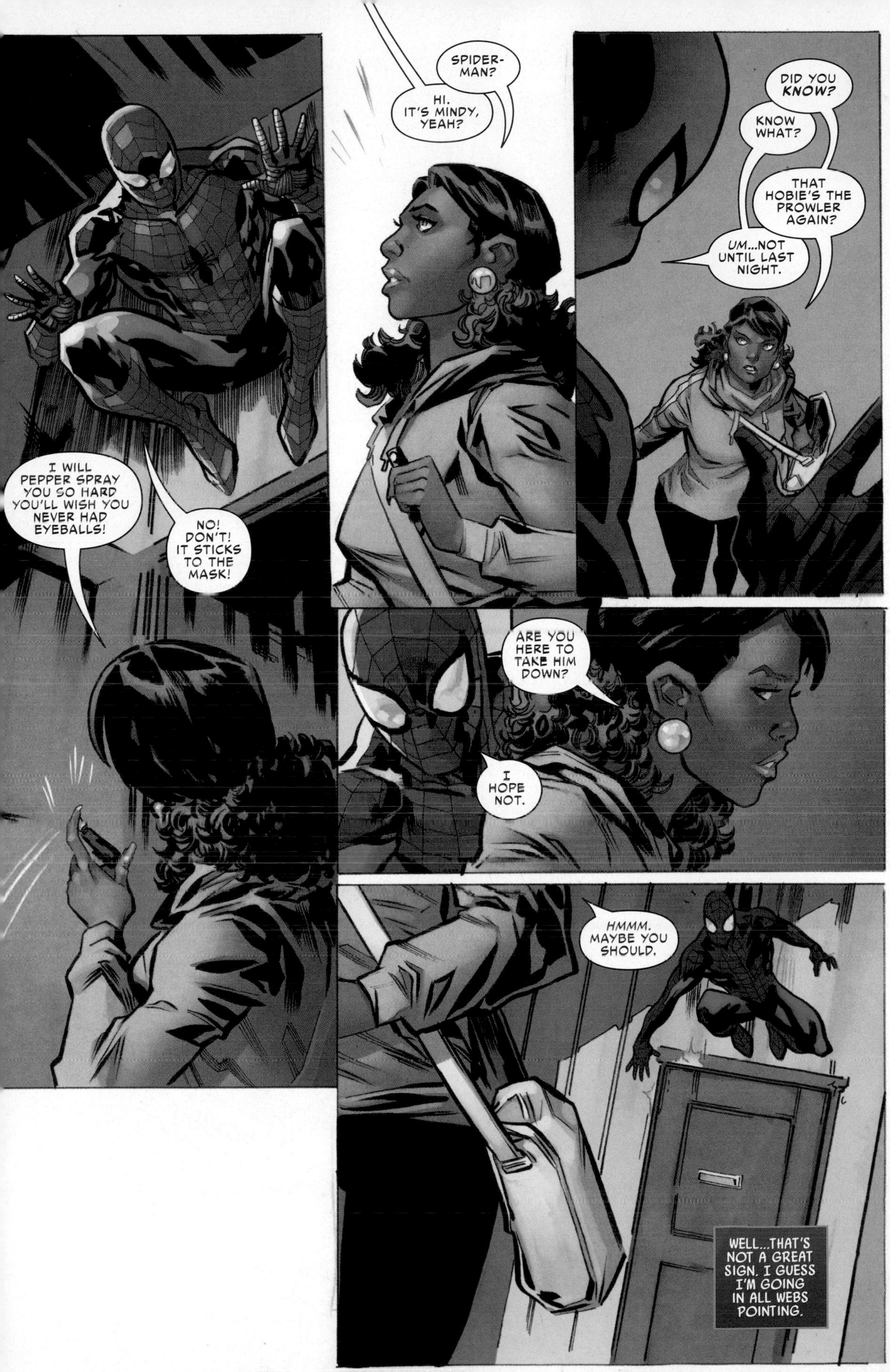
I WILL PEPPER SPRAY YOU SO HARD YOU'LL WISH YOU NEVER HAD EYEBALLS!
NO! DON'T! IT STICKS TO THE MASK!
SPIDER-MAN?
HI. IT'S MINDY, YEAH?
DID YOU KNOW?
KNOW WHAT?
THAT HOBIE'S THE PROWLER AGAIN?
UM...NOT UNTIL LAST NIGHT.
ARE YOU HERE TO TAKE HIM DOWN?
I HOPE NOT.
HMMM. MAYBE YOU SHOULD.
WELL...THAT'S NOT A GREAT SIGN. I GUESS I'M GOING IN ALL WEBS POINTING.

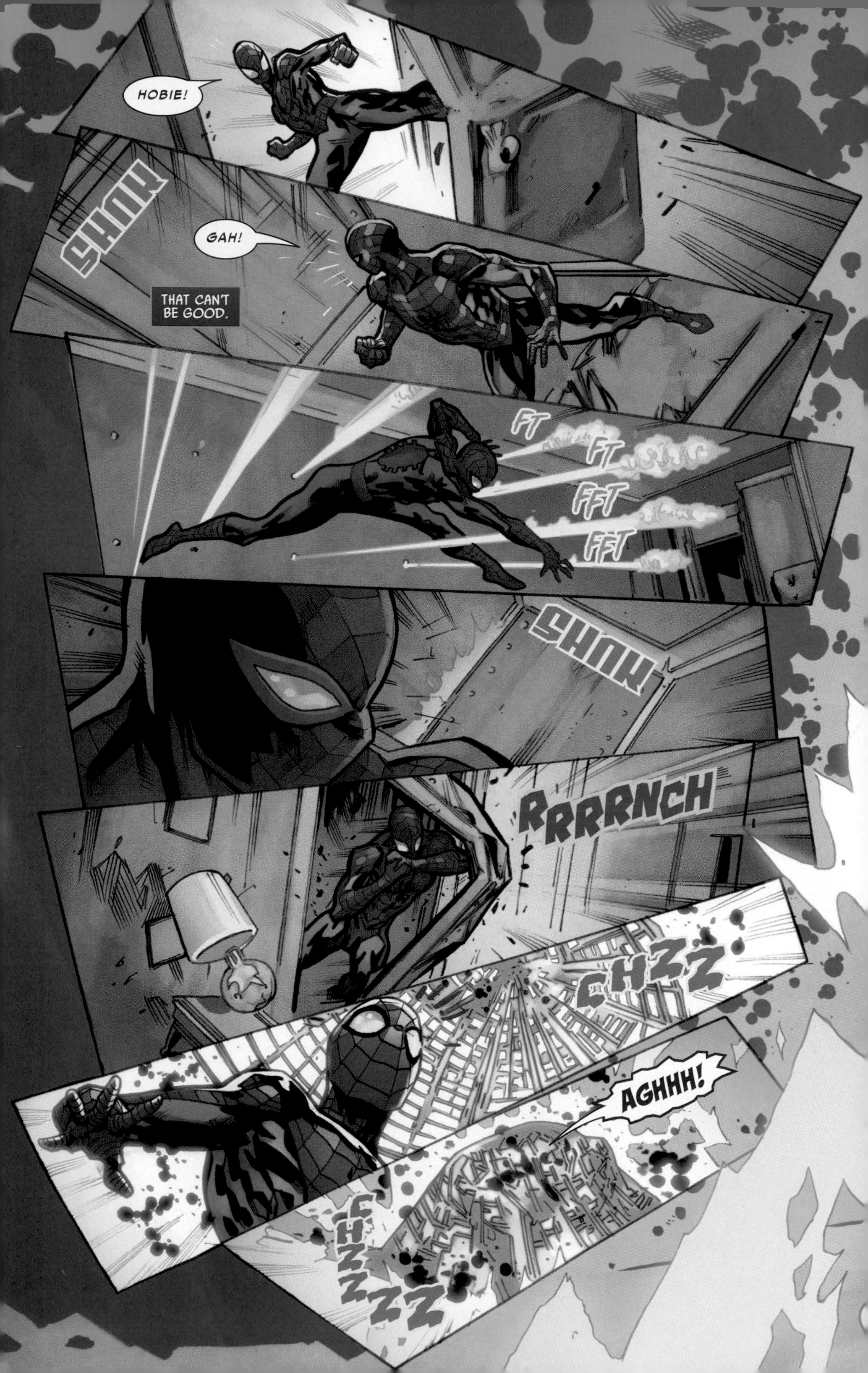
HOBIE!
SHUNK
GAH!
THAT CAN'T BE GOOD.
FT
FT
FFT
FFT
SHUNK
RRRRNCH
CHZZ
AGHHH!
CHZZZZZ

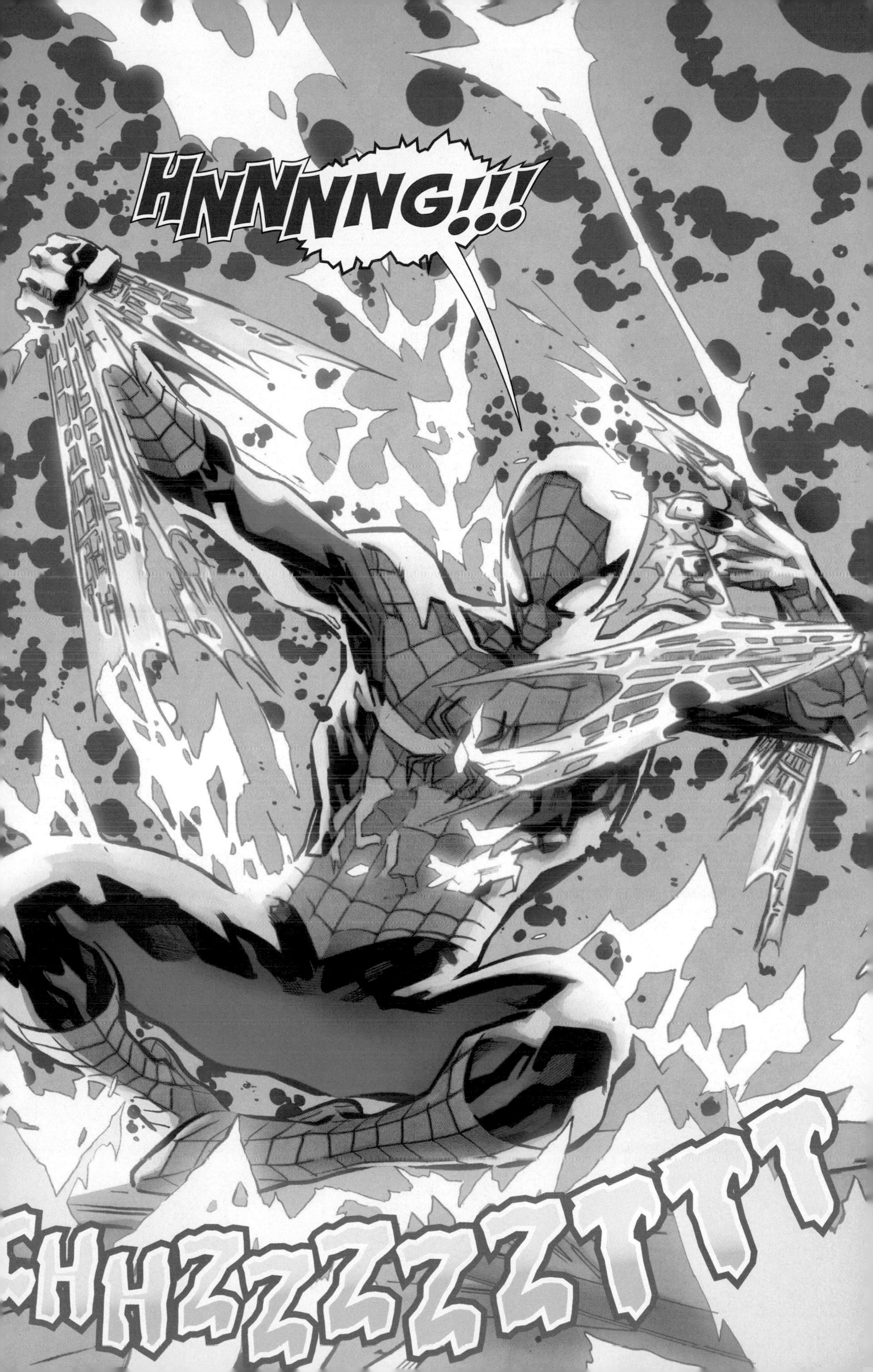
HNNNNG!!!
CHHZZZZZTTTT

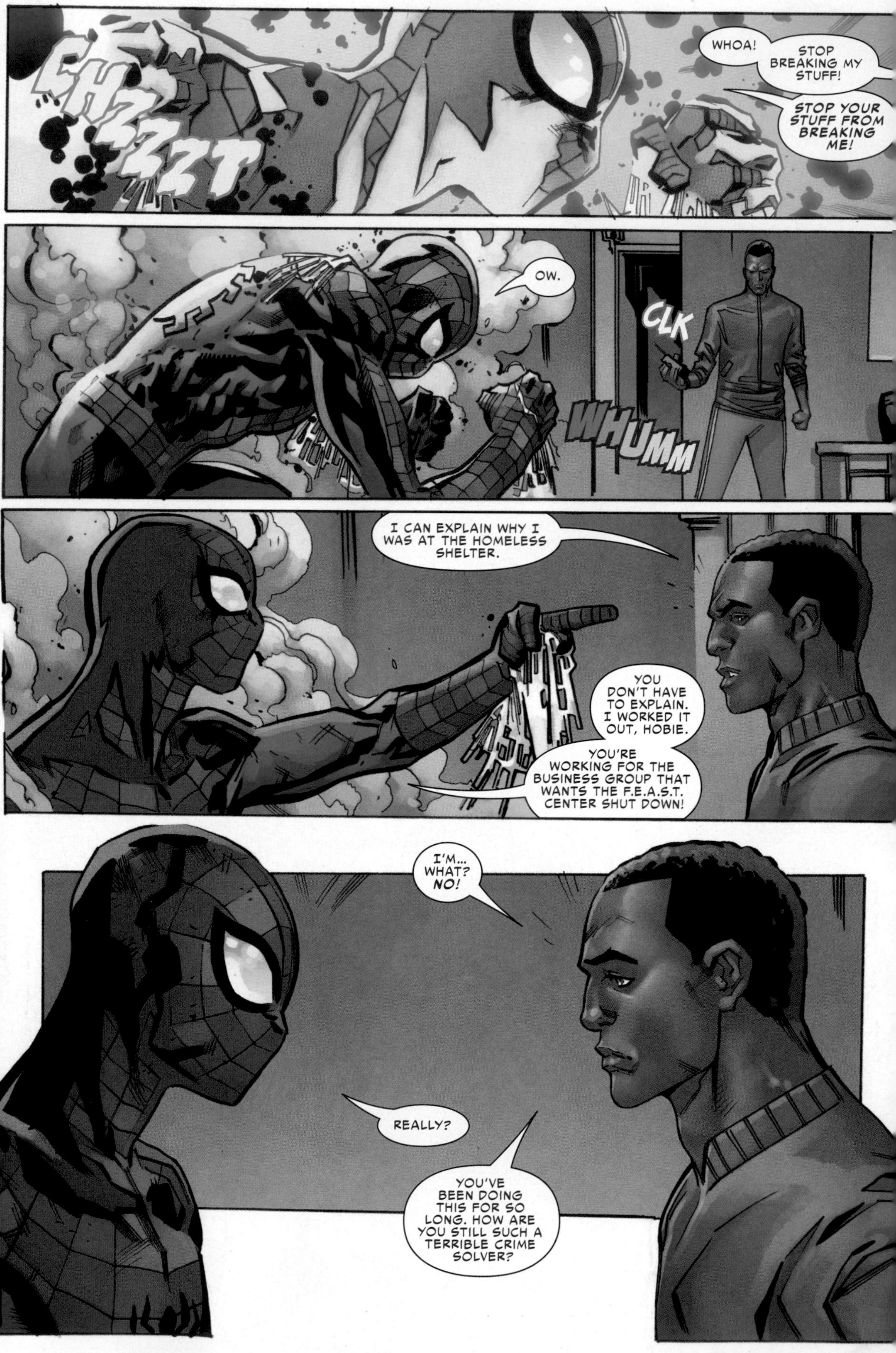
CHZZZZT
WHOA!
STOP BREAKING MY STUFF!
STOP YOUR STUFF FROM BREAKING ME!
OW.
CLK
WHUMM
I CAN EXPLAIN WHY I WAS AT THE HOMELESS SHELTER.
YOU DON'T HAVE TO EXPLAIN. I WORKED IT OUT, HOBIE.
YOU'RE WORKING FOR THE BUSINESS GROUP THAT WANTS THE F.E.A.S.T. CENTER SHUT DOWN!
I'M... WHAT? NO!
REALLY?
YOU'VE BEEN DOING THIS FOR SO LONG. HOW ARE YOU STILL SUCH A TERRIBLE CRIME SOLVER?

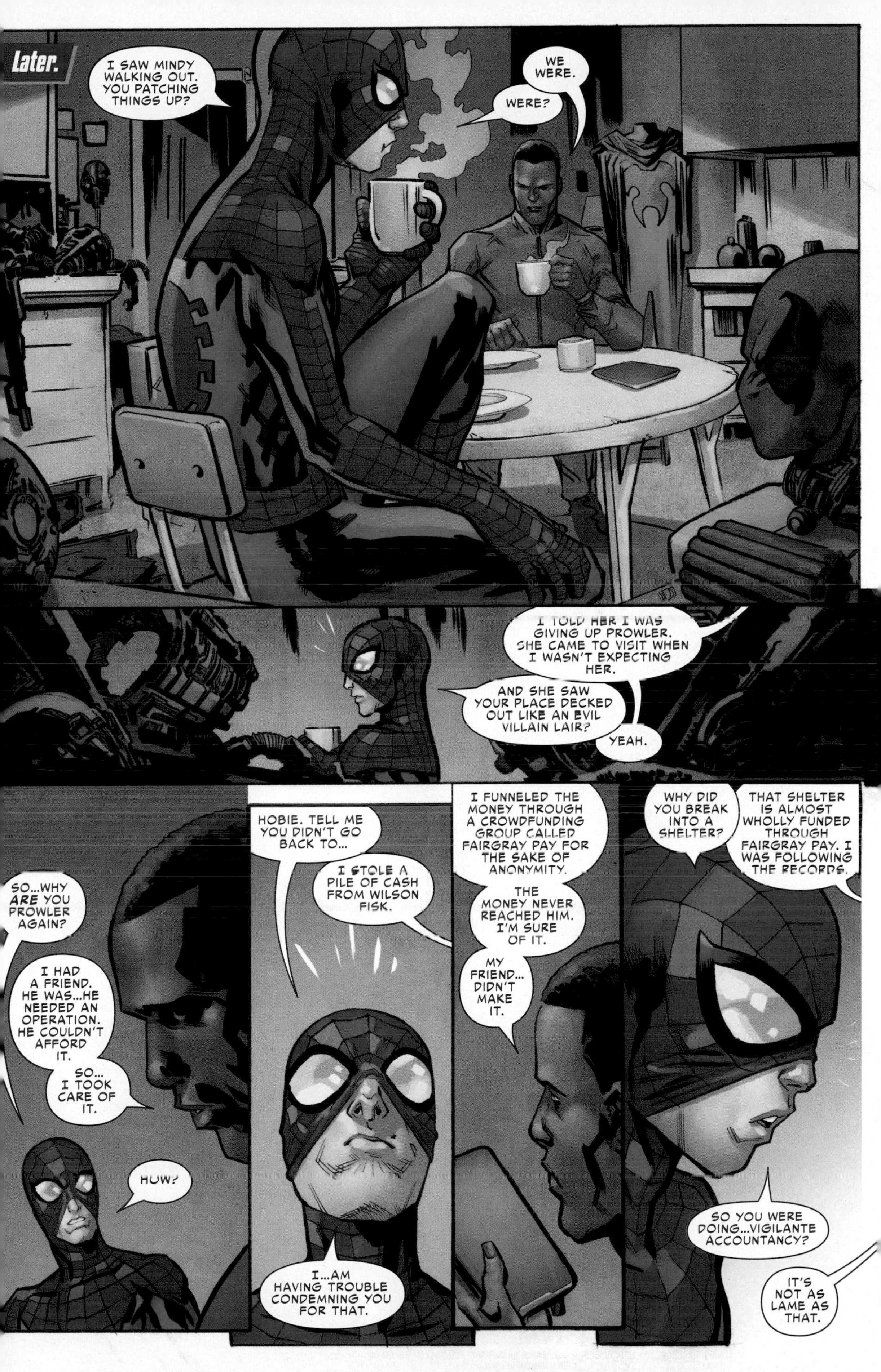
Later.
I SAW MINDY WALKING OUT. YOU PATCHING THINGS UP?
WE WERE.
WERE?
I TOLD HER I WAS GIVING UP PROWLER. SHE CAME TO VISIT WHEN I WASN'T EXPECTING HER.
AND SHE SAW YOUR PLACE DECKED OUT LIKE AN EVIL VILLAIN LAIR?
YEAH.
SO...WHY *ARE* YOU PROWLER AGAIN?
I HAD A FRIEND. HE WAS...HE NEEDED AN OPERATION. HE COULDN'T AFFORD IT.
SO... I TOOK CARE OF IT.
HOW?
HOBIE. TELL ME YOU DIDN'T GO BACK TO...
I STOLE A PILE OF CASH FROM WILSON FISK.
I...AM HAVING TROUBLE CONDEMNING YOU FOR THAT.
I FUNNELED THE MONEY THROUGH A CROWDFUNDING GROUP CALLED FAIRGRAY PAY FOR THE SAKE OF ANONYMITY.
THE MONEY NEVER REACHED HIM. I'M SURE OF IT.
MY FRIEND... DIDN'T MAKE IT.
WHY DID YOU BREAK INTO A SHELTER?
THAT SHELTER IS ALMOST WHOLLY FUNDED THROUGH FAIRGRAY PAY. I WAS FOLLOWING THE RECORDS.
SO YOU WERE DOING...VIGILANTE ACCOUNTANCY?
IT'S NOT AS LAME AS THAT.

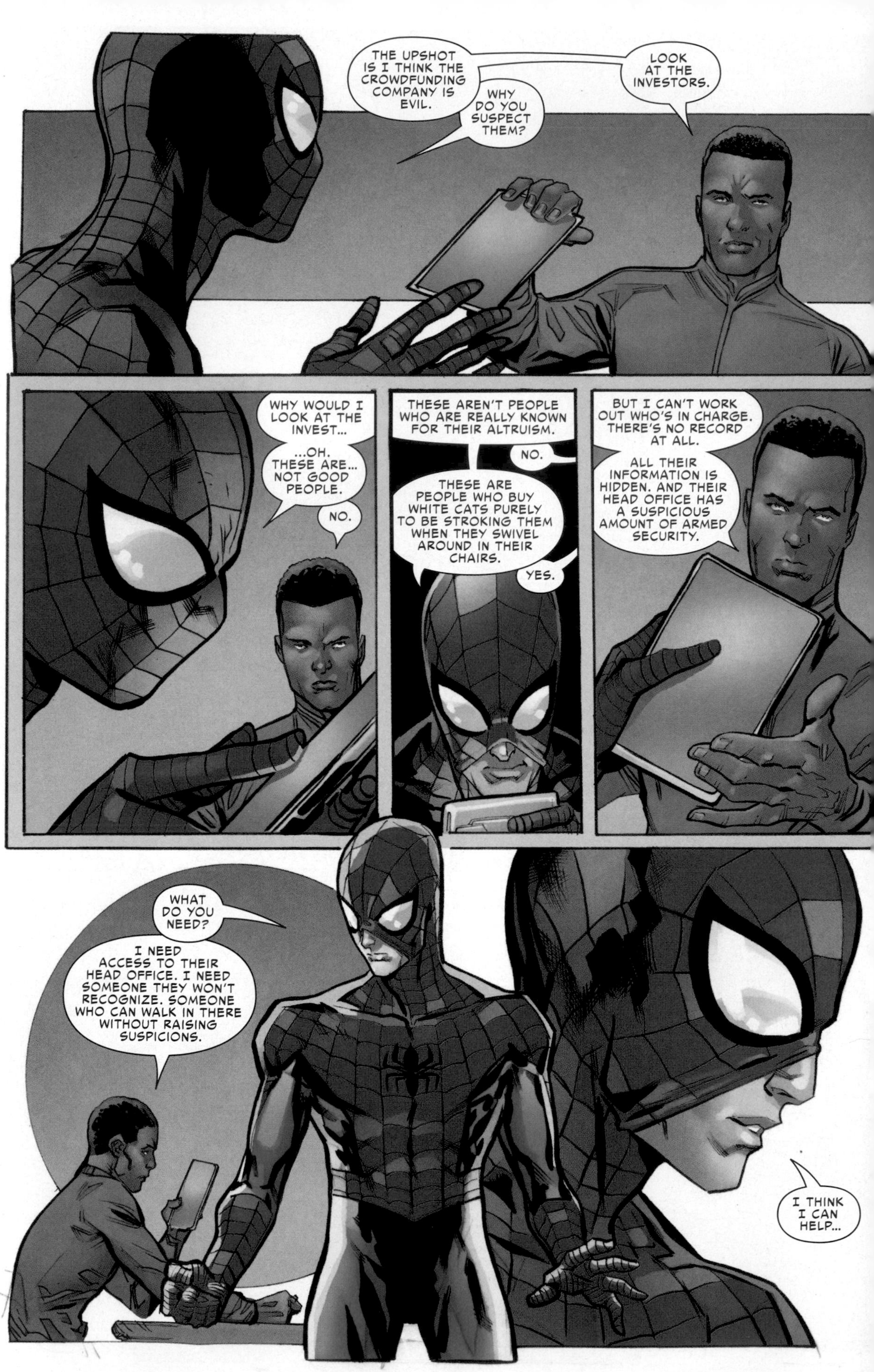
THE UPSHOT IS I THINK THE CROWDFUNDING COMPANY IS EVIL.
WHY DO YOU SUSPECT THEM?
LOOK AT THE INVESTORS.
WHY WOULD I LOOK AT THE INVEST...
...OH. THESE ARE... NOT GOOD PEOPLE.
NO.
THESE AREN'T PEOPLE WHO ARE REALLY KNOWN FOR THEIR ALTRUISM.
NO.
THESE ARE PEOPLE WHO BUY WHITE CATS PURELY TO BE STROKING THEM WHEN THEY SWIVEL AROUND IN THEIR CHAIRS.
YES.
BUT I CAN'T WORK OUT WHO'S IN CHARGE. THERE'S NO RECORD AT ALL.
ALL THEIR INFORMATION IS HIDDEN. AND THEIR HEAD OFFICE HAS A SUSPICIOUS AMOUNT OF ARMED SECURITY.
WHAT DO YOU NEED?
I NEED ACCESS TO THEIR HEAD OFFICE. I NEED SOMEONE THEY WON'T RECOGNIZE. SOMEONE WHO CAN WALK IN THERE WITHOUT RAISING SUSPICIONS.
I THINK I CAN HELP...

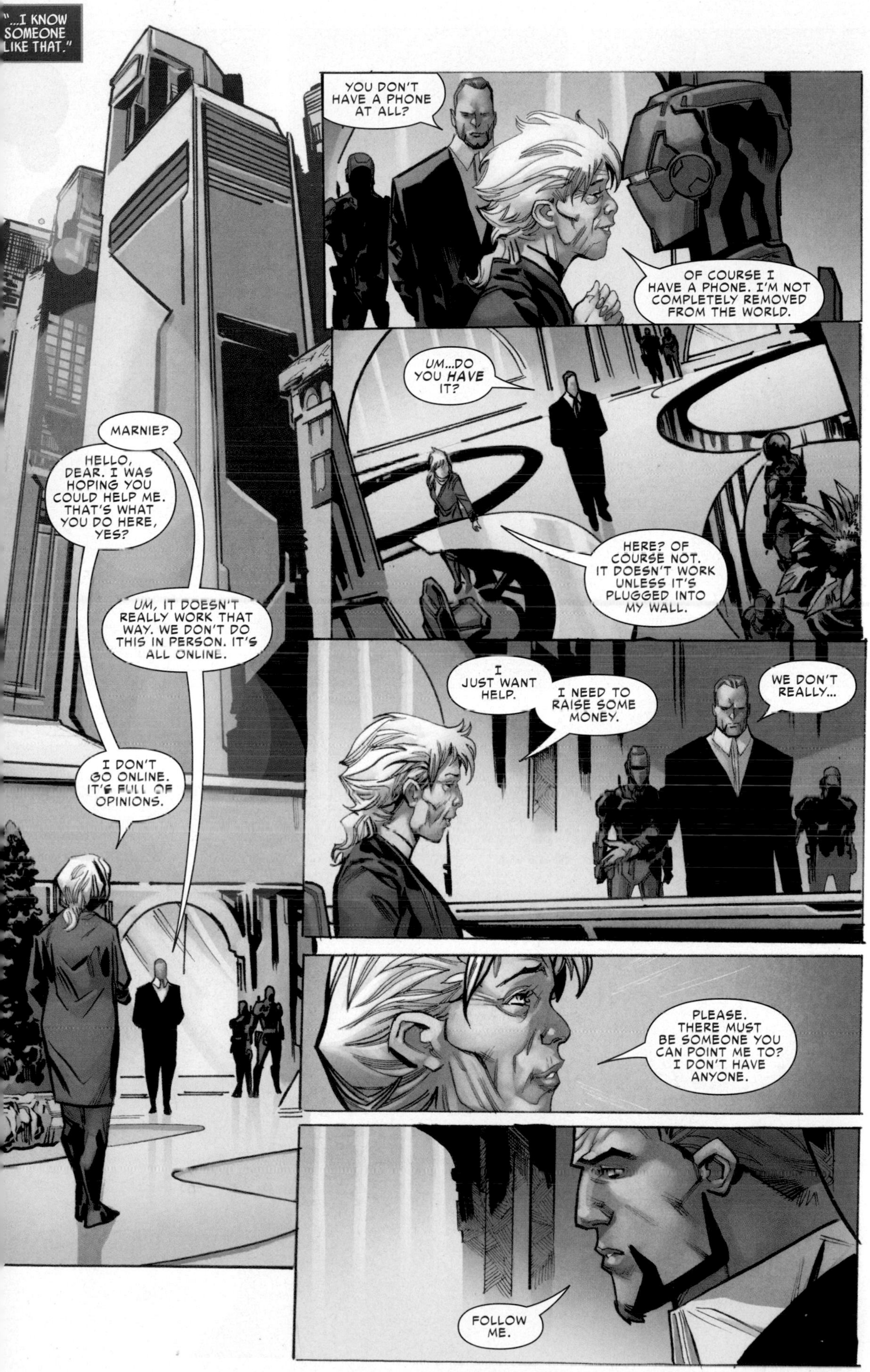
"...I KNOW SOMEONE LIKE THAT."
MARNIE?
HELLO, DEAR. I WAS HOPING YOU COULD HELP ME. THAT'S WHAT YOU DO HERE, YES?
UM, IT DOESN'T REALLY WORK THAT WAY. WE DON'T DO THIS IN PERSON. IT'S ALL ONLINE.
I DON'T GO ONLINE. IT'S FULL OF OPINIONS.
YOU DON'T HAVE A PHONE AT ALL?
OF COURSE I HAVE A PHONE. I'M NOT COMPLETELY REMOVED FROM THE WORLD.
UM...DO YOU HAVE IT?
HERE? OF COURSE NOT. IT DOESN'T WORK UNLESS IT'S PLUGGED INTO MY WALL.
I JUST WANT HELP.
I NEED TO RAISE SOME MONEY.
WE DON'T REALLY...
PLEASE. THERE MUST BE SOMEONE YOU CAN POINT ME TO? I DON'T HAVE ANYONE.
FOLLOW ME.

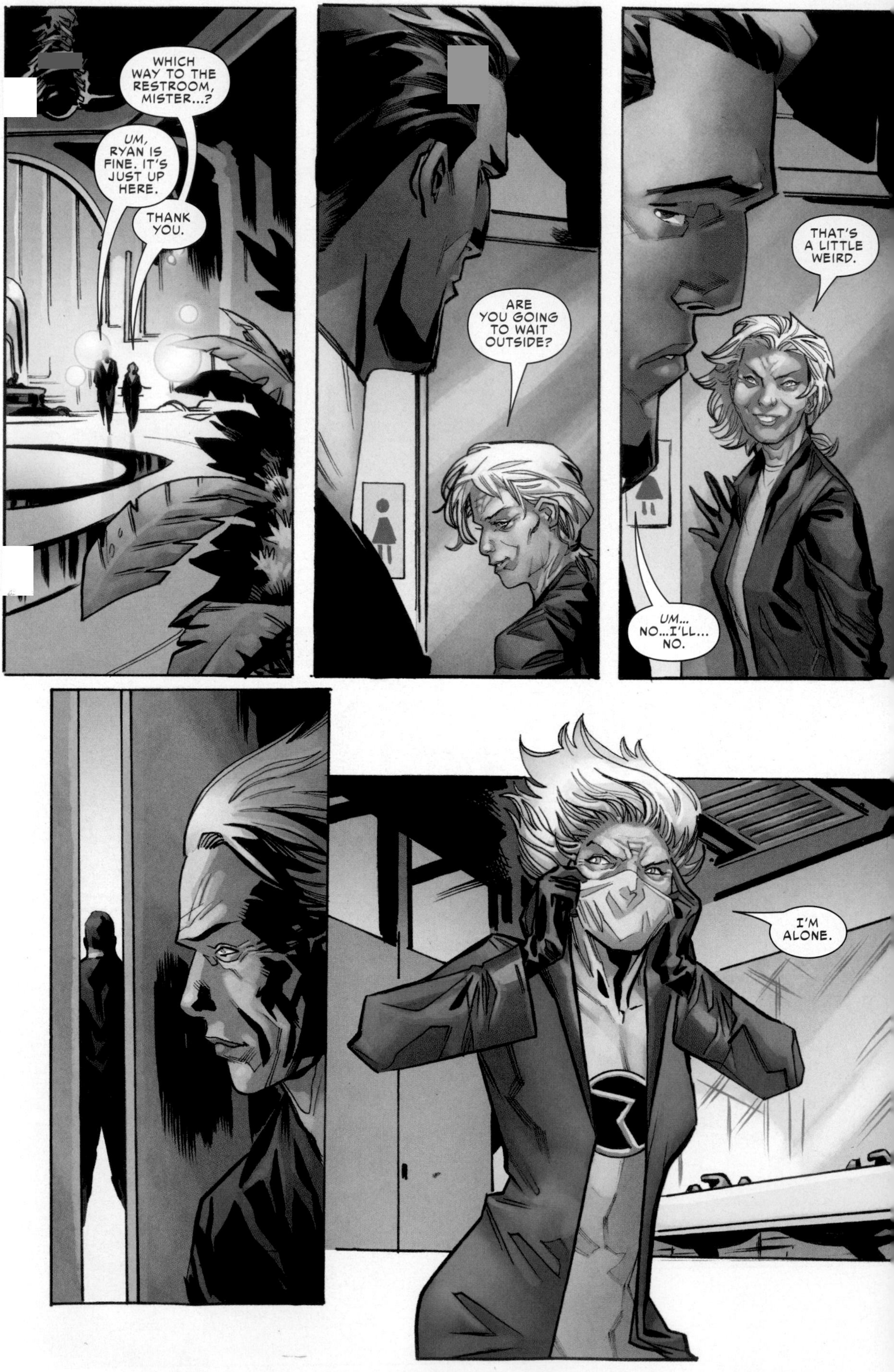
WHICH WAY TO THE RESTROOM, MISTER...?
UM, RYAN IS FINE. IT'S JUST UP HERE.
THANK YOU.
ARE YOU GOING TO WAIT OUTSIDE?
THAT'S A LITTLE WEIRD.
UM... NO...I'LL... NO.
I'M ALONE.

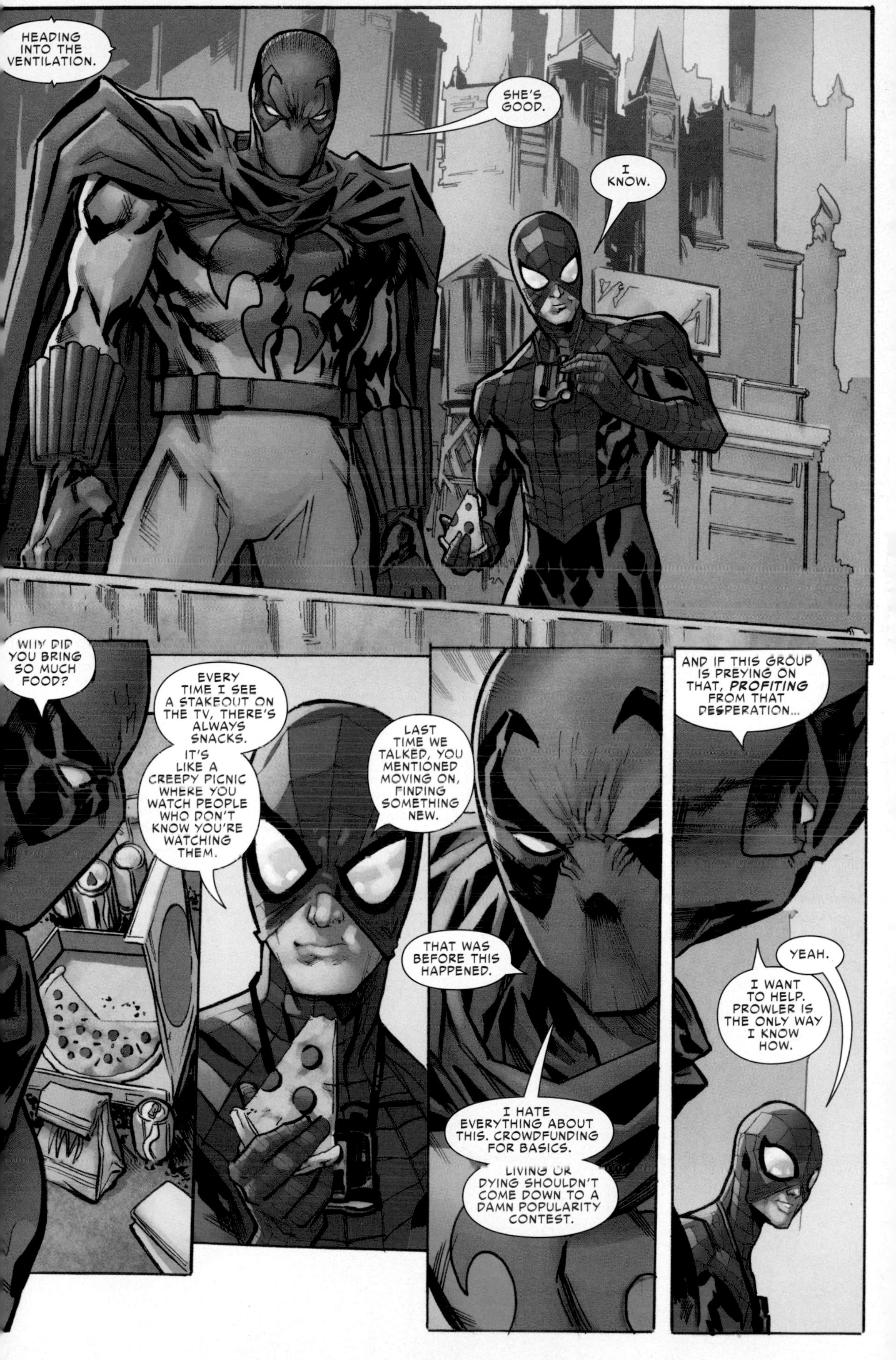
HEADING INTO THE VENTILATION.
SHE'S GOOD.
I KNOW.
WHY DID YOU BRING SO MUCH FOOD?
EVERY TIME I SEE A STAKEOUT ON THE TV, THERE'S ALWAYS SNACKS.
IT'S LIKE A CREEPY PICNIC WHERE YOU WATCH PEOPLE WHO DON'T KNOW YOU'RE WATCHING THEM.
LAST TIME WE TALKED, YOU MENTIONED MOVING ON, FINDING SOMETHING NEW.
THAT WAS BEFORE THIS HAPPENED.
I HATE EVERYTHING ABOUT THIS. CROWDFUNDING FOR BASICS.
LIVING OR DYING SHOULDN'T COME DOWN TO A DAMN POPULARITY CONTEST.
AND IF THIS GROUP IS PREYING ON THAT, PROFITING FROM THAT DESPERATION...
YEAH.
I WANT TO HELP. PROWLER IS THE ONLY WAY I KNOW HOW.

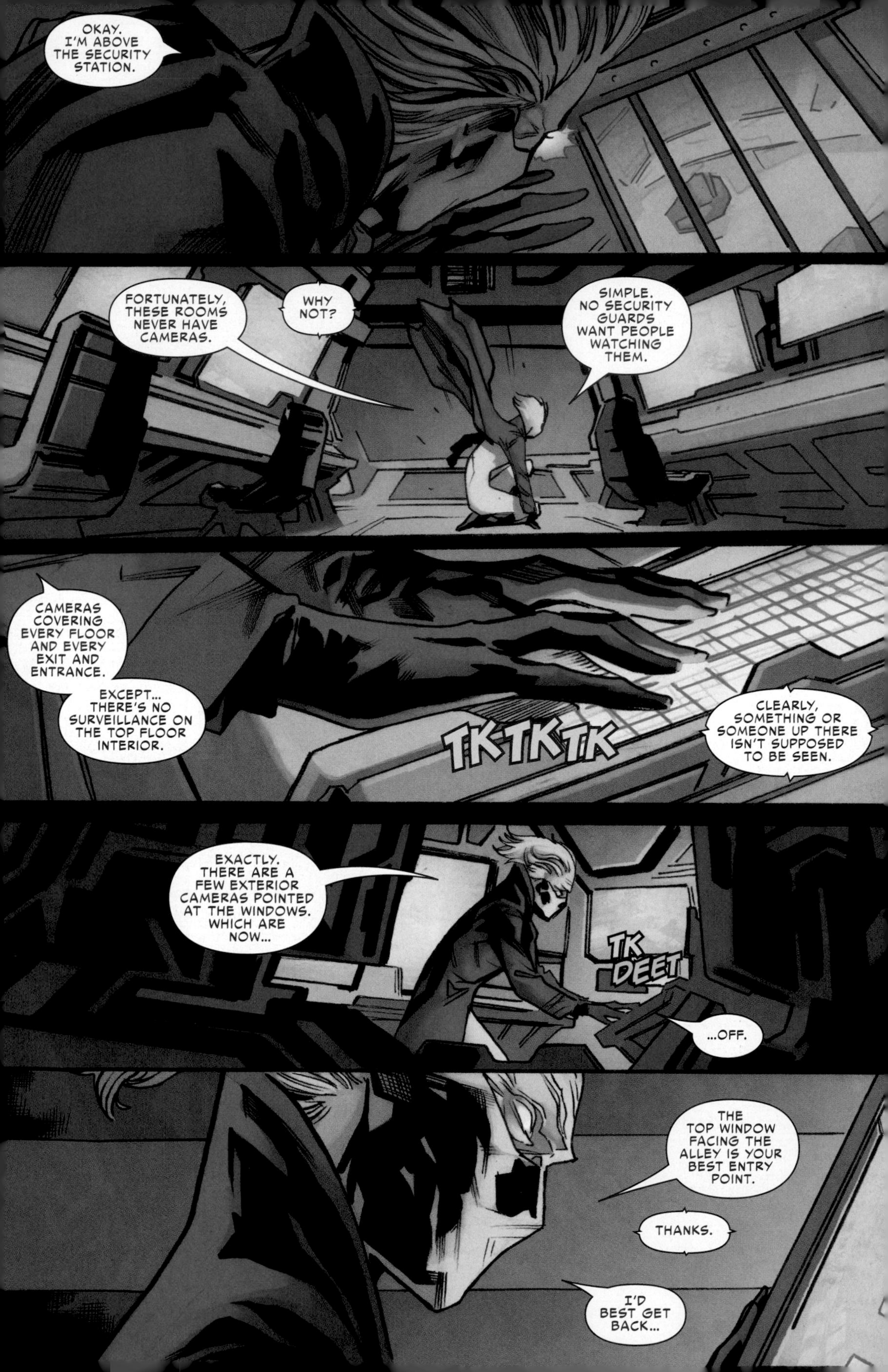
OKAY. I'M ABOVE THE SECURITY STATION.
FORTUNATELY, THESE ROOMS NEVER HAVE CAMERAS.
WHY NOT?
SIMPLE. NO SECURITY GUARDS WANT PEOPLE WATCHING THEM.
CAMERAS COVERING EVERY FLOOR AND EVERY EXIT AND ENTRANCE.
EXCEPT... THERE'S NO SURVEILLANCE ON THE TOP FLOOR INTERIOR.
TKTKTK
CLEARLY, SOMETHING OR SOMEONE UP THERE ISN'T SUPPOSED TO BE SEEN.
EXACTLY. THERE ARE A FEW EXTERIOR CAMERAS POINTED AT THE WINDOWS. WHICH ARE NOW...
TK DEET
...OFF.
THE TOP WINDOW FACING THE ALLEY IS YOUR BEST ENTRY POINT.
THANKS.
I'D BEST GET BACK...

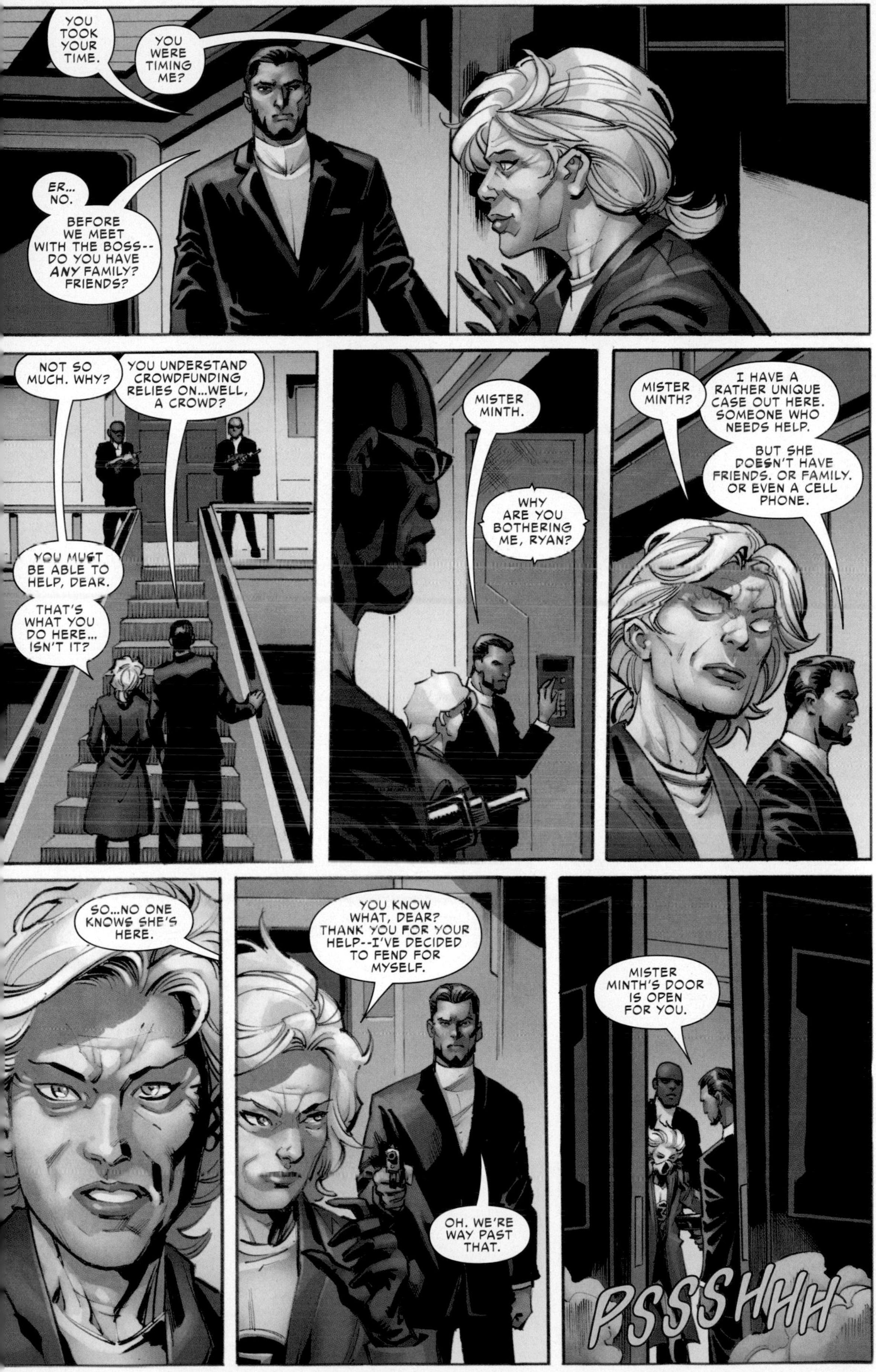
YOU TOOK YOUR TIME.
YOU WERE TIMING ME?
ER... NO.
BEFORE WE MEET WITH THE BOSS-- DO YOU HAVE ANY FAMILY? FRIENDS?
NOT SO MUCH. WHY?
YOU UNDERSTAND CROWDFUNDING RELIES ON...WELL, A CROWD?
YOU MUST BE ABLE TO HELP, DEAR.
THAT'S WHAT YOU DO HERE... ISN'T IT?
MISTER MINTH.
WHY ARE YOU BOTHERING ME, RYAN?
MISTER MINTH?
I HAVE A RATHER UNIQUE CASE OUT HERE. SOMEONE WHO NEEDS HELP.
BUT SHE DOESN'T HAVE FRIENDS. OR FAMILY. OR EVEN A CELL PHONE.
SO...NO ONE KNOWS SHE'S HERE.
YOU KNOW WHAT, DEAR? THANK YOU FOR YOUR HELP--I'VE DECIDED TO FEND FOR MYSELF.
OH. WE'RE WAY PAST THAT.
MISTER MINTH'S DOOR IS OPEN FOR YOU.
PSSSHHH

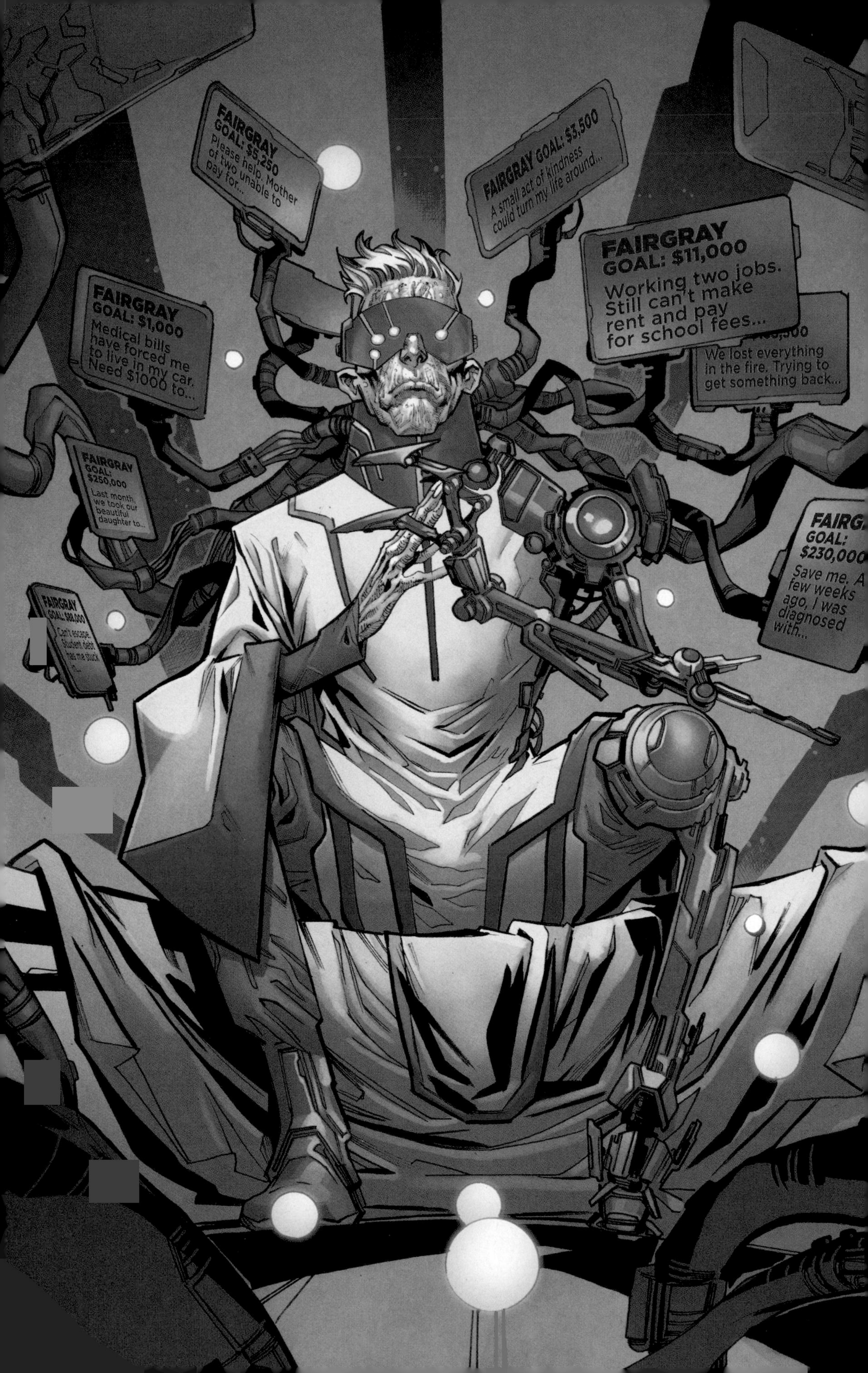
FAIRGRAY GOAL: $5,250
Please help. Mother of two unable to pay for...
FAIRGRAY GOAL: $3,500
A small act of kindness could turn my life around...
FAIRGRAY GOAL: $11,000
Working two jobs. Still can't make rent and pay for school fees...
We lost everything in the fire. Trying to get something back...
FAIRGRAY GOAL: $1,000
Medical bills have forced me to live in my car. Need $1000 to...
FAIRGRAY GOAL: $250,000
Last month, we took our beautiful daughter to...
FAIRGRAY GOAL: $98,000
Can't escape. Student debt has me stuck in...
FAIRG GOAL: $230,000
Save me. A few weeks ago, I was diagnosed with...

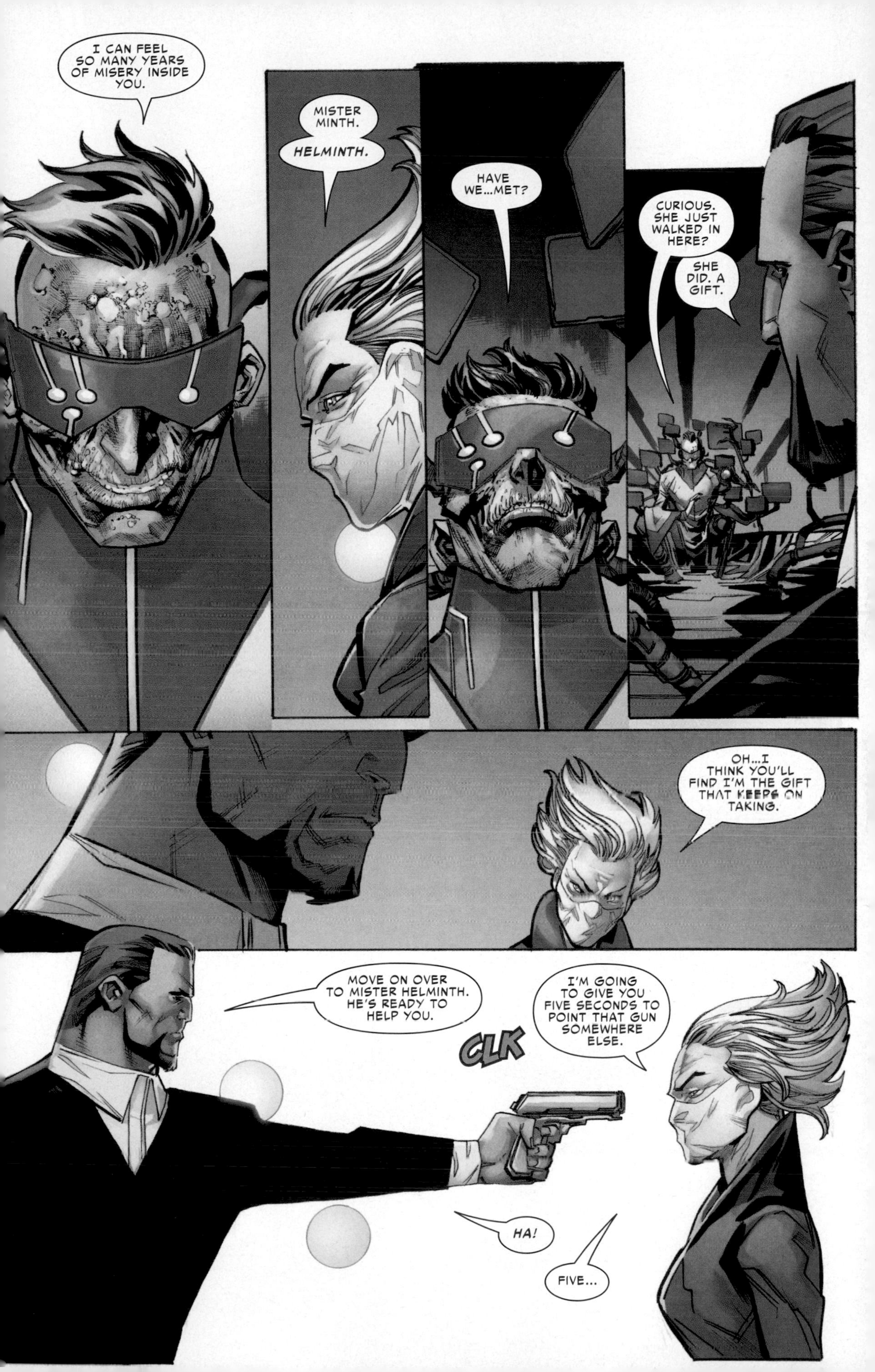
I CAN FEEL SO MANY YEARS OF MISERY INSIDE YOU.
MISTER MINTH.
HELMINTH.
HAVE WE...MET?
CURIOUS. SHE JUST WALKED IN HERE?
SHE DID. A GIFT.
OH...I THINK YOU'LL FIND I'M THE GIFT THAT KEEPS ON TAKING.
MOVE ON OVER TO MISTER HELMINTH. HE'S READY TO HELP YOU.
CLK
I'M GOING TO GIVE YOU FIVE SECONDS TO POINT THAT GUN SOMEWHERE ELSE.
HA!
FIVE...

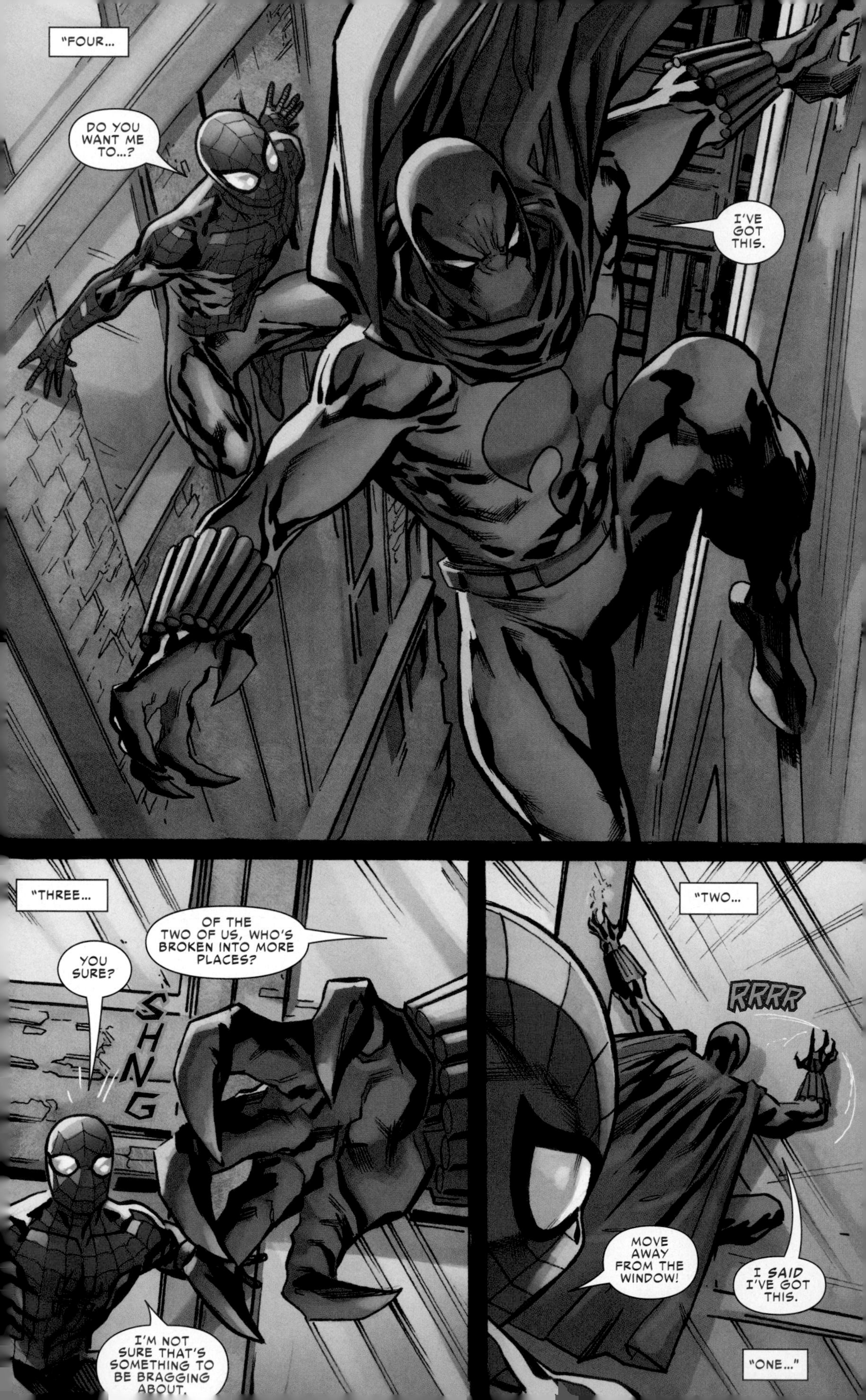
"FOUR...
DO YOU WANT ME TO...?
I'VE GOT THIS.
"THREE...
YOU SURE?
OF THE TWO OF US, WHO'S BROKEN INTO MORE PLACES?
SHNG
I'M NOT SURE THAT'S SOMETHING TO BE BRAGGING ABOUT.
"TWO...
RRRR
MOVE AWAY FROM THE WINDOW!
I SAID I'VE GOT THIS.
"ONE..."

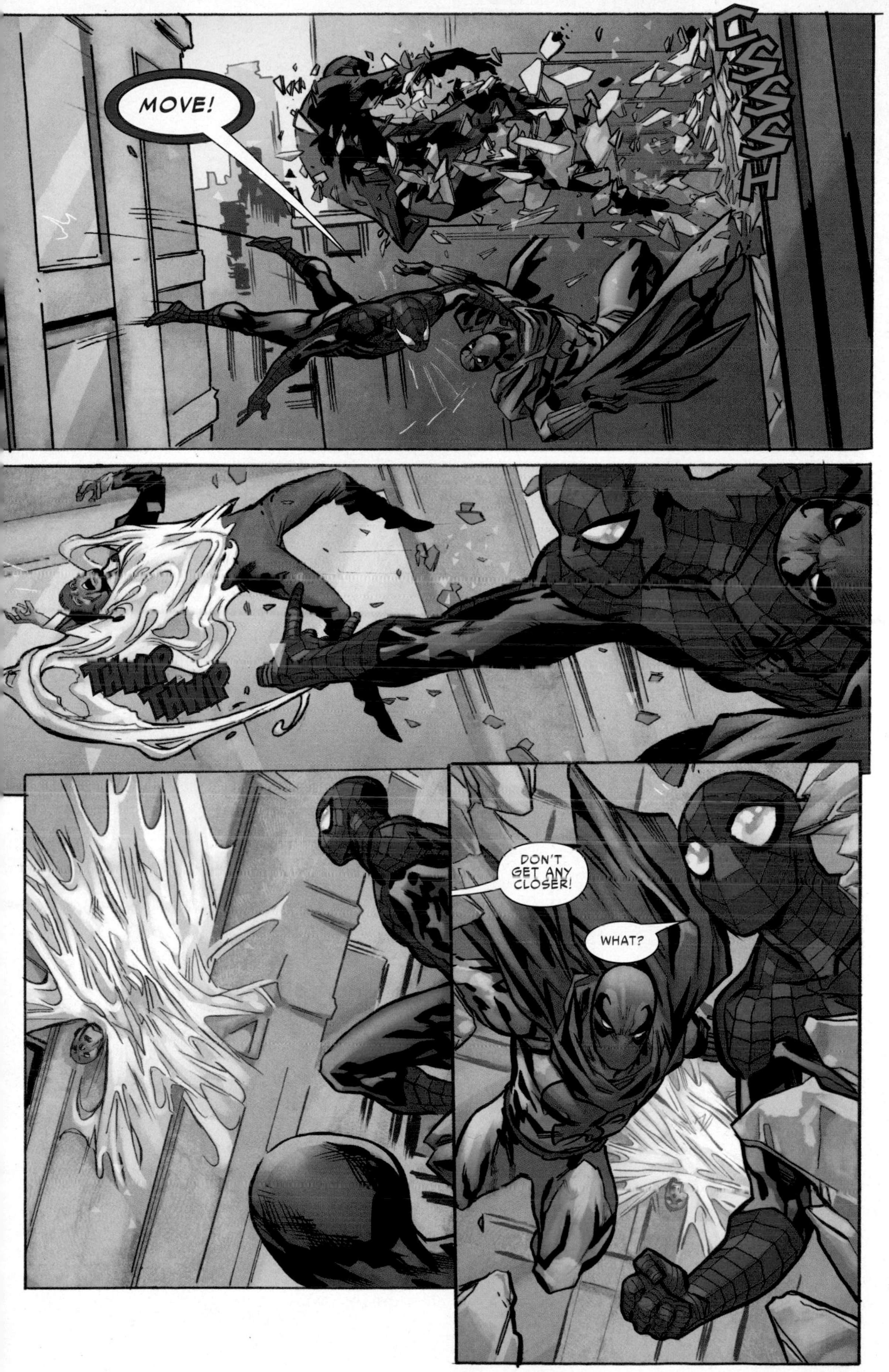
MOVE!
CSSSSH
THWIP THWIP
DON'T GET ANY CLOSER!
WHAT?

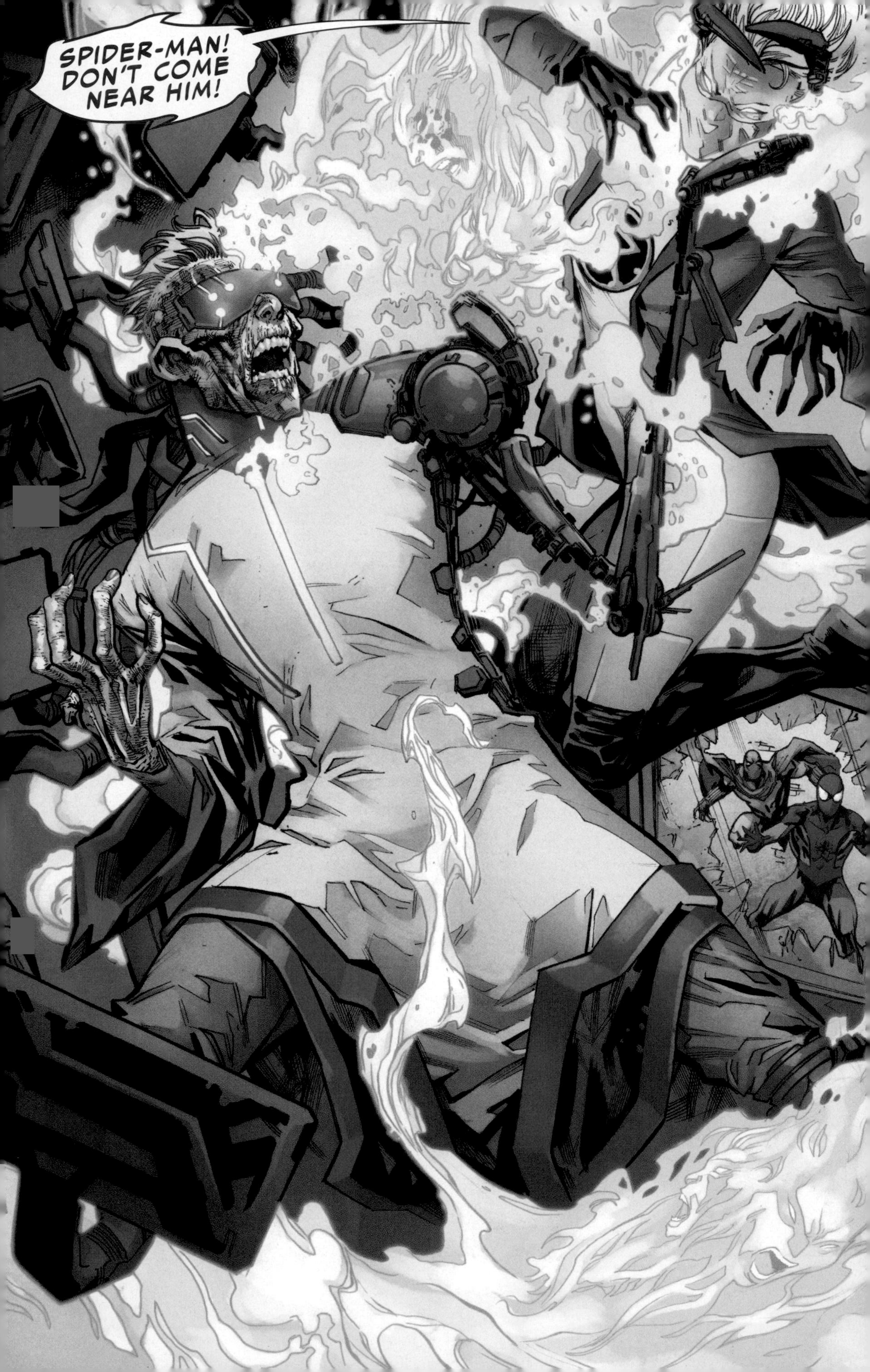
SPIDER-MAN! DON'T COME NEAR HIM!

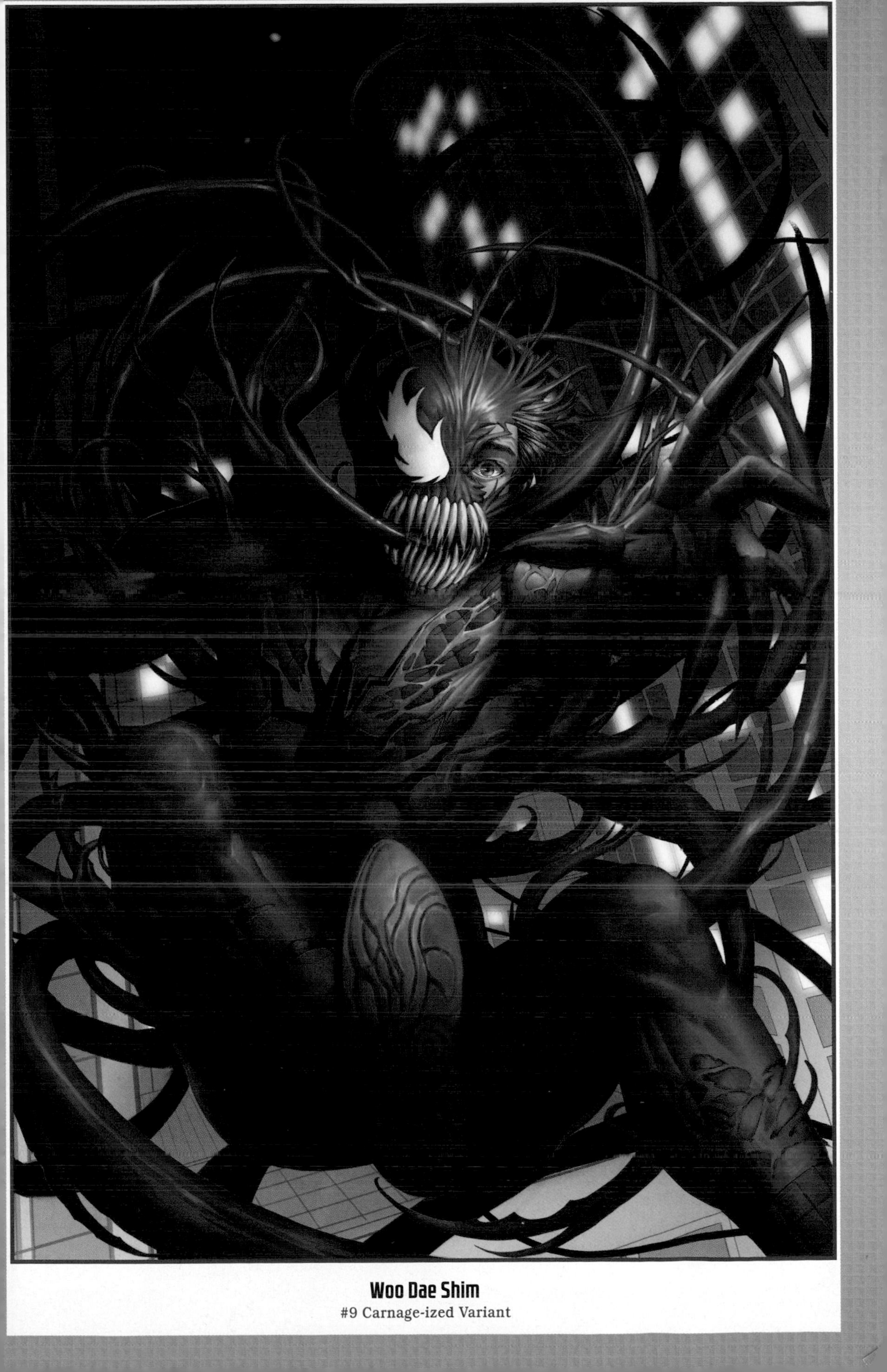

Woo Dae Shim
#9 Carnage-ized Variant

9

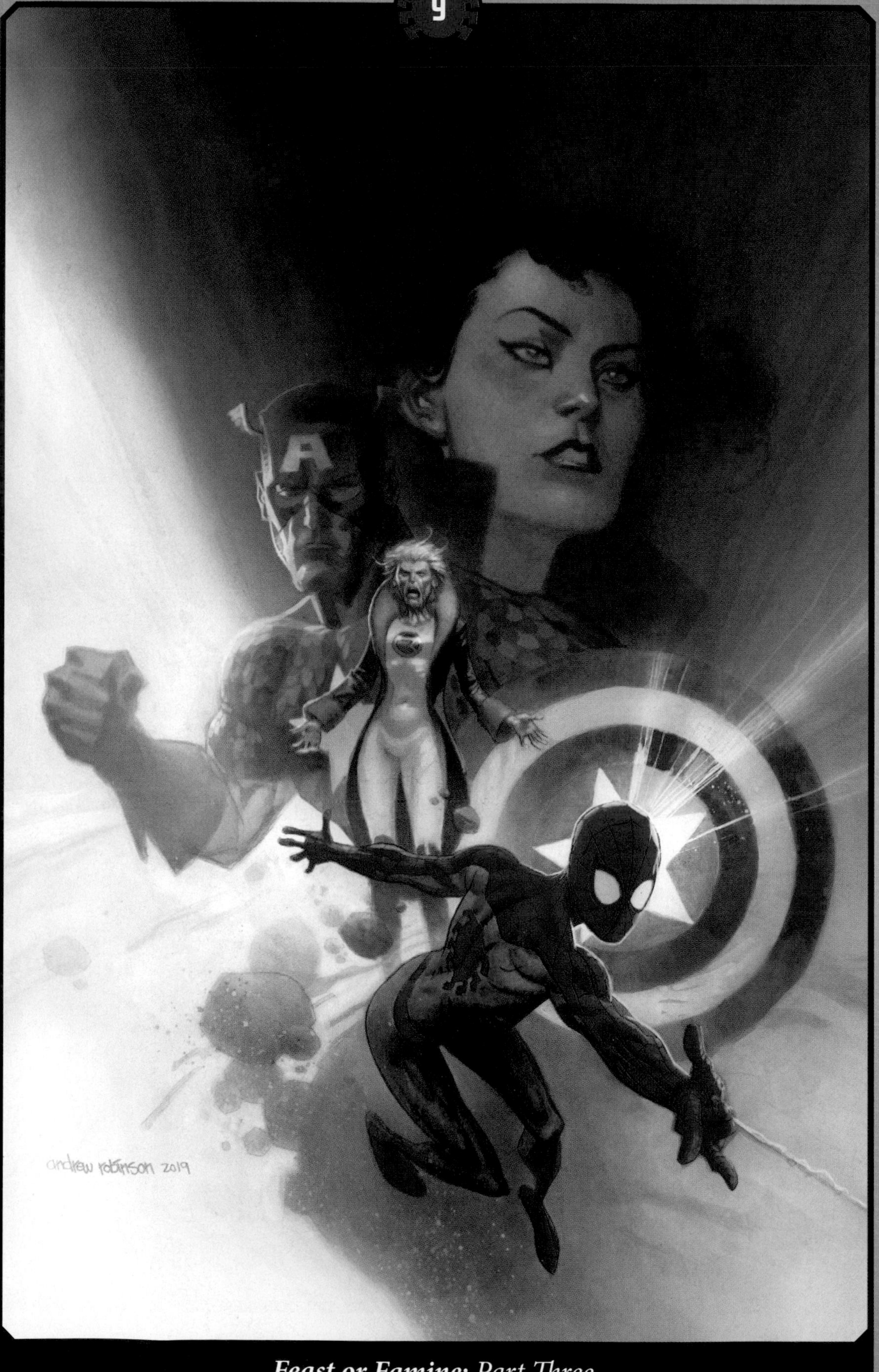
andrew robinson 2019

Feast or Famine: Part Three

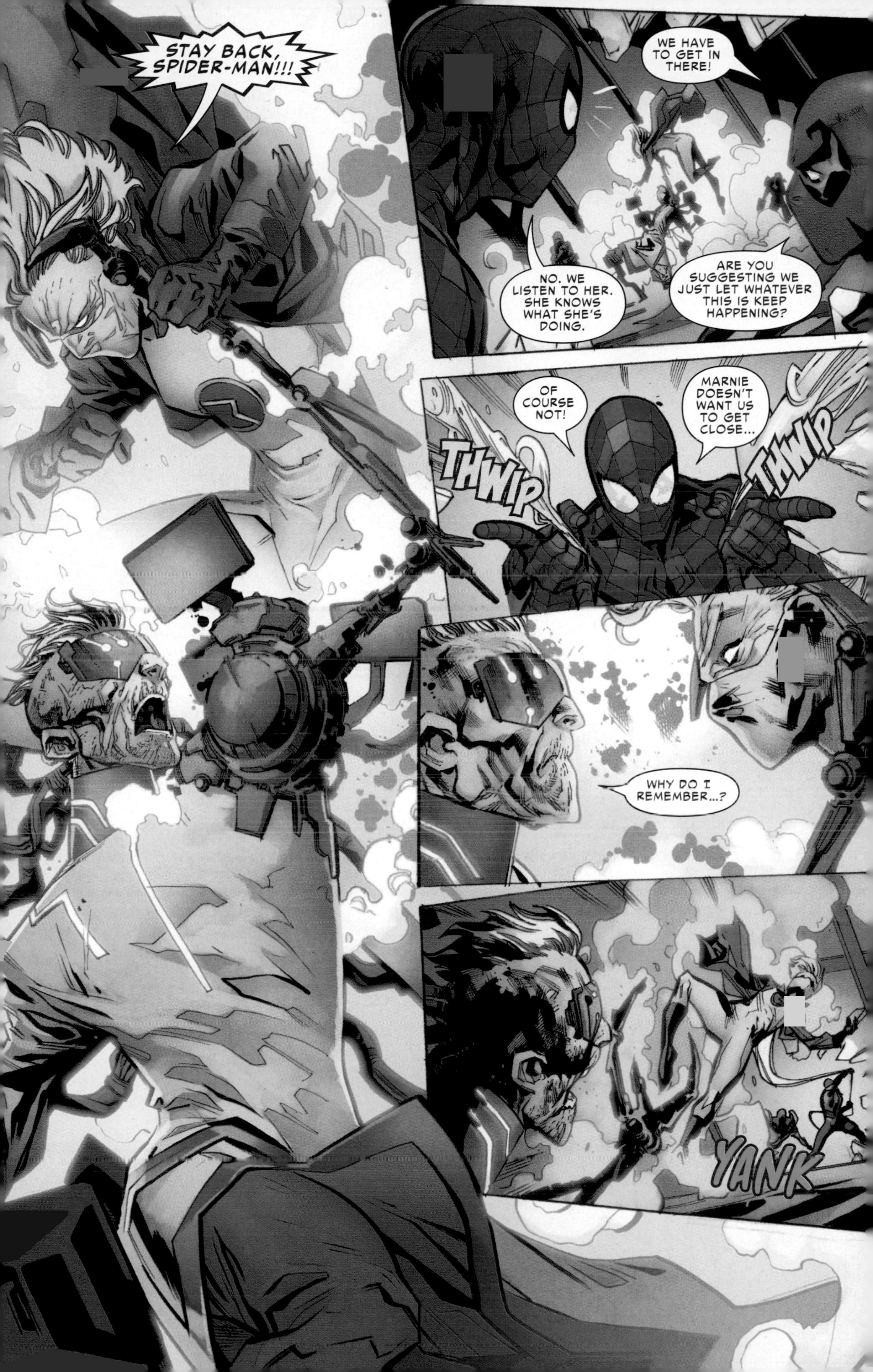
STAY BACK, SPIDER-MAN!!!
WE HAVE TO GET IN THERE!
NO. WE LISTEN TO HER. SHE KNOWS WHAT SHE'S DOING.
ARE YOU SUGGESTING WE JUST LET WHATEVER THIS IS KEEP HAPPENING?
OF COURSE NOT!
MARNIE DOESN'T WANT US TO GET CLOSE...
THWIP
THWIP
WHY DO I REMEMBER...?
YANK

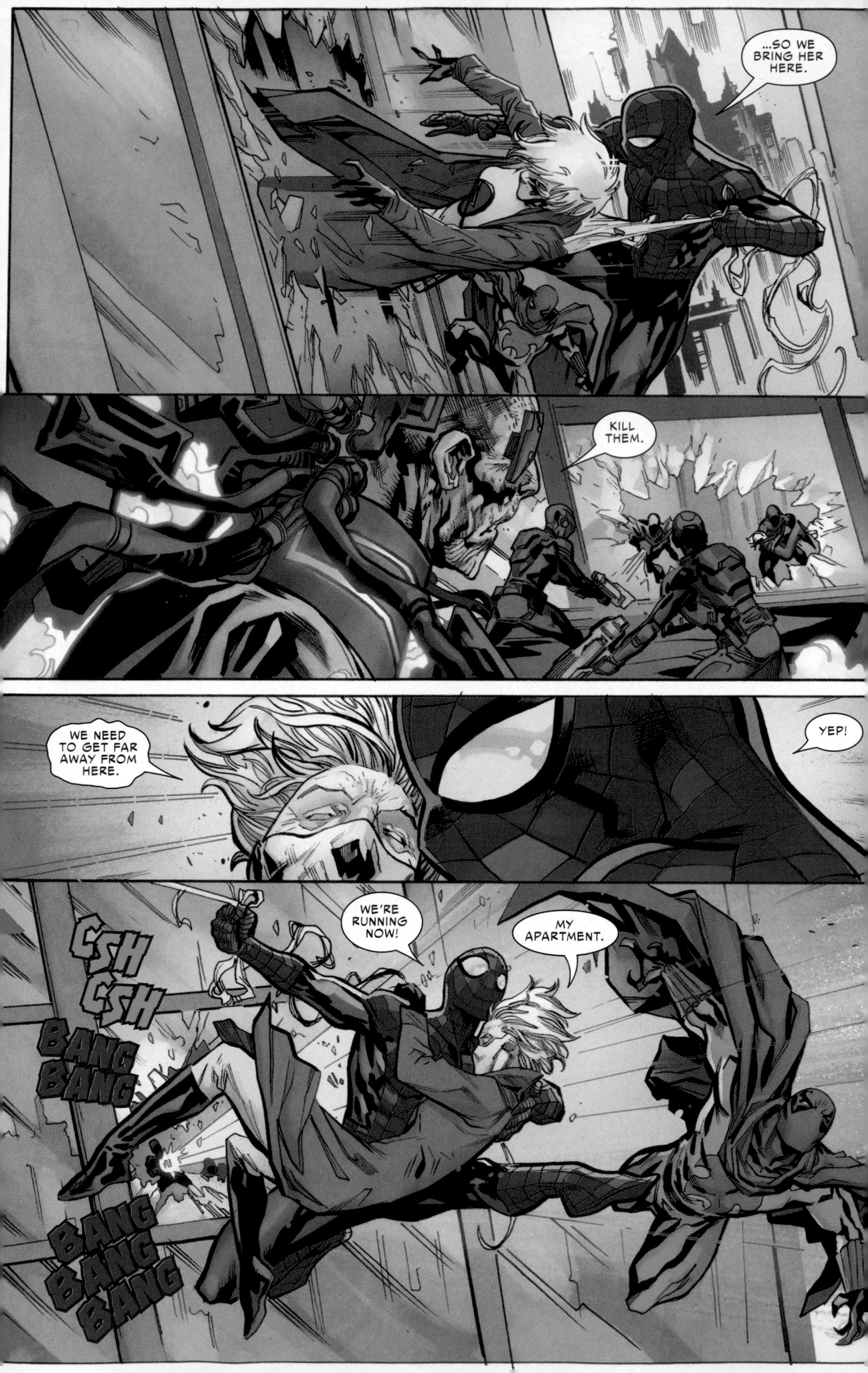
...SO WE BRING HER HERE.
KILL THEM.
WE NEED TO GET FAR AWAY FROM HERE.
YEP!
CSH CSH
BANG BANG
WE'RE RUNNING NOW!
MY APARTMENT.
BANG BANG BANG

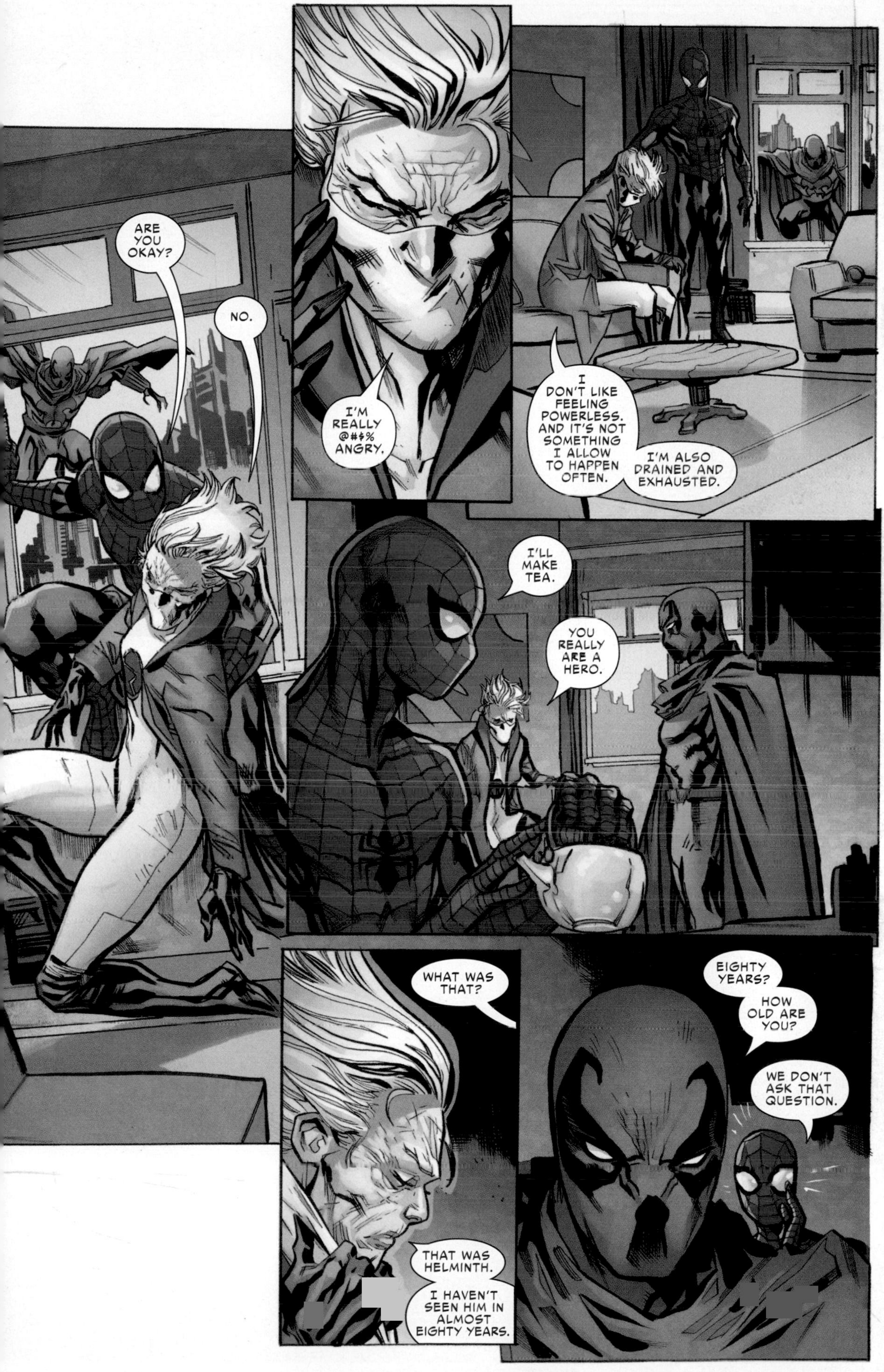
ARE YOU OKAY?
NO.
I'M REALLY @#$% ANGRY.
I DON'T LIKE FEELING POWERLESS. AND IT'S NOT SOMETHING I ALLOW TO HAPPEN OFTEN.
I'M ALSO DRAINED AND EXHAUSTED.
I'LL MAKE TEA.
YOU REALLY ARE A HERO.
WHAT WAS THAT?
THAT WAS HELMINTH.
I HAVEN'T SEEN HIM IN ALMOST EIGHTY YEARS.
EIGHTY YEARS?
HOW OLD ARE YOU?
WE DON'T ASK THAT QUESTION.

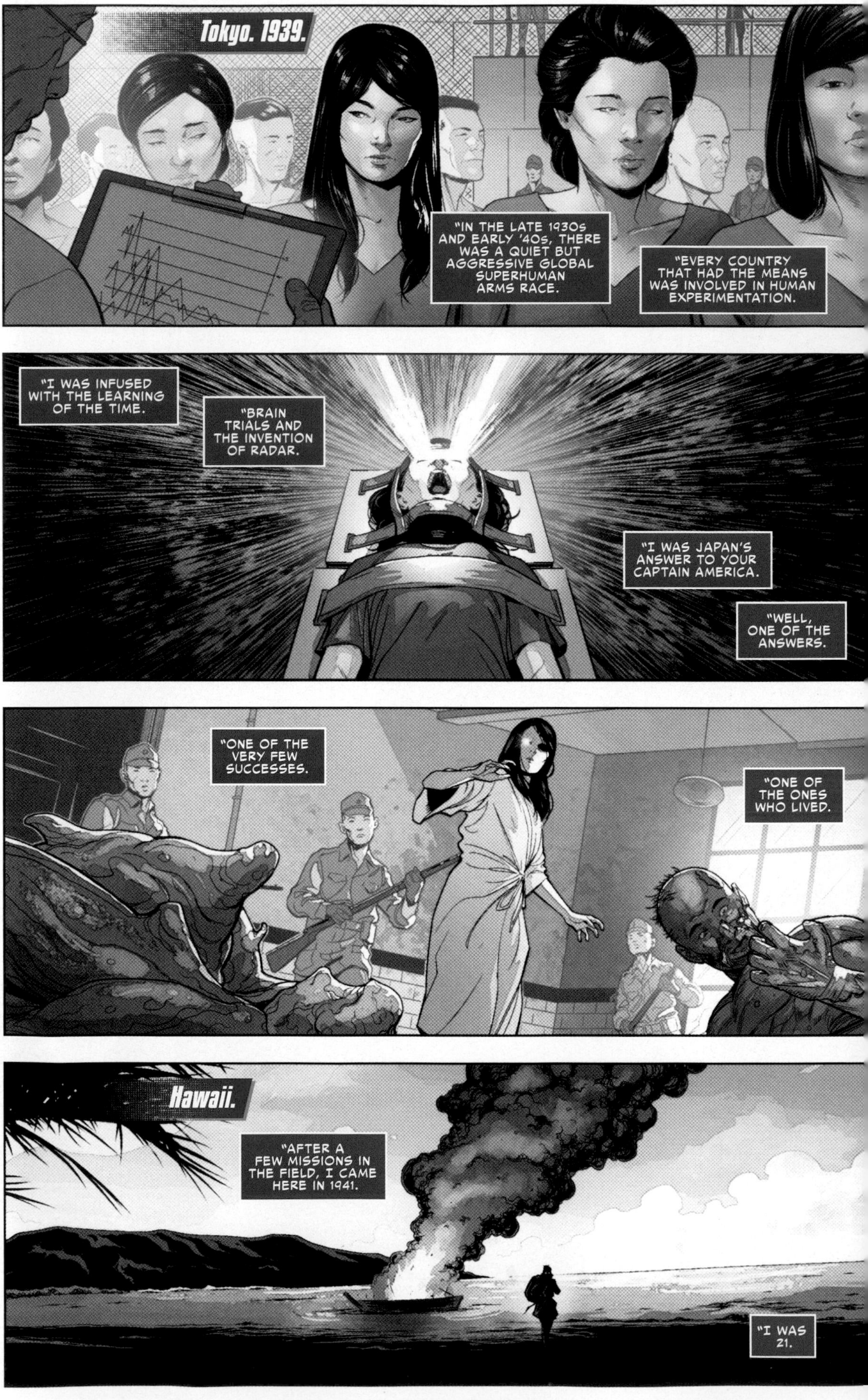
Tokyo. 1939.
"IN THE LATE 1930s AND EARLY '40s, THERE WAS A QUIET BUT AGGRESSIVE GLOBAL SUPERHUMAN ARMS RACE.
"EVERY COUNTRY THAT HAD THE MEANS WAS INVOLVED IN HUMAN EXPERIMENTATION.
"I WAS INFUSED WITH THE LEARNING OF THE TIME.
"BRAIN TRIALS AND THE INVENTION OF RADAR.
"I WAS JAPAN'S ANSWER TO YOUR CAPTAIN AMERICA.
"WELL, ONE OF THE ANSWERS.
"ONE OF THE VERY FEW SUCCESSES.
"ONE OF THE ONES WHO LIVED.
Hawaii.
"AFTER A FEW MISSIONS IN THE FIELD, I CAME HERE IN 1941.
"I WAS 21.

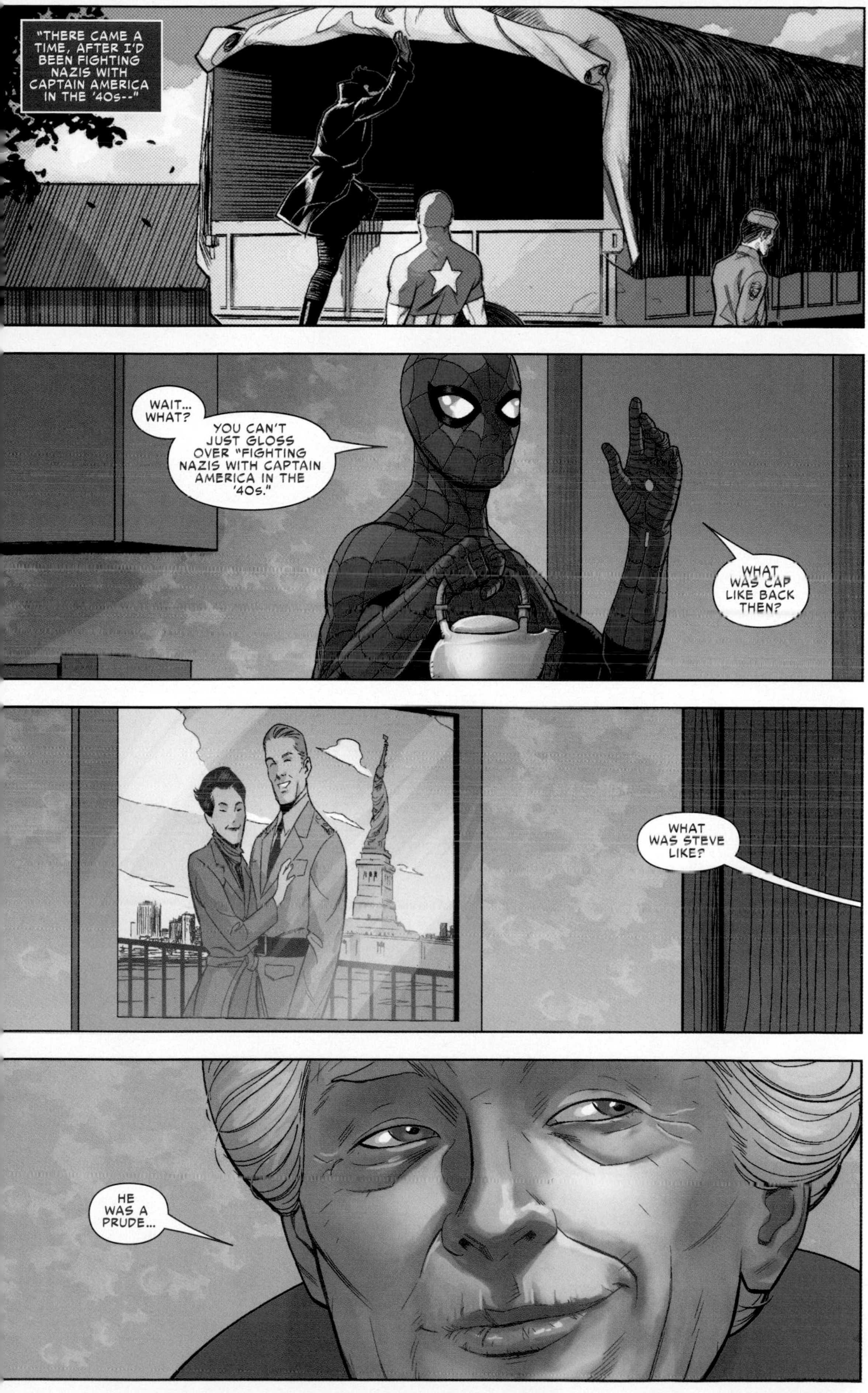
"THERE CAME A TIME, AFTER I'D BEEN FIGHTING NAZIS WITH CAPTAIN AMERICA IN THE '40s--"
WAIT... WHAT?
YOU CAN'T JUST GLOSS OVER "FIGHTING NAZIS WITH CAPTAIN AMERICA IN THE '40s."
WHAT WAS CAP LIKE BACK THEN?
WHAT WAS STEVE LIKE?
HE WAS A PRUDE...

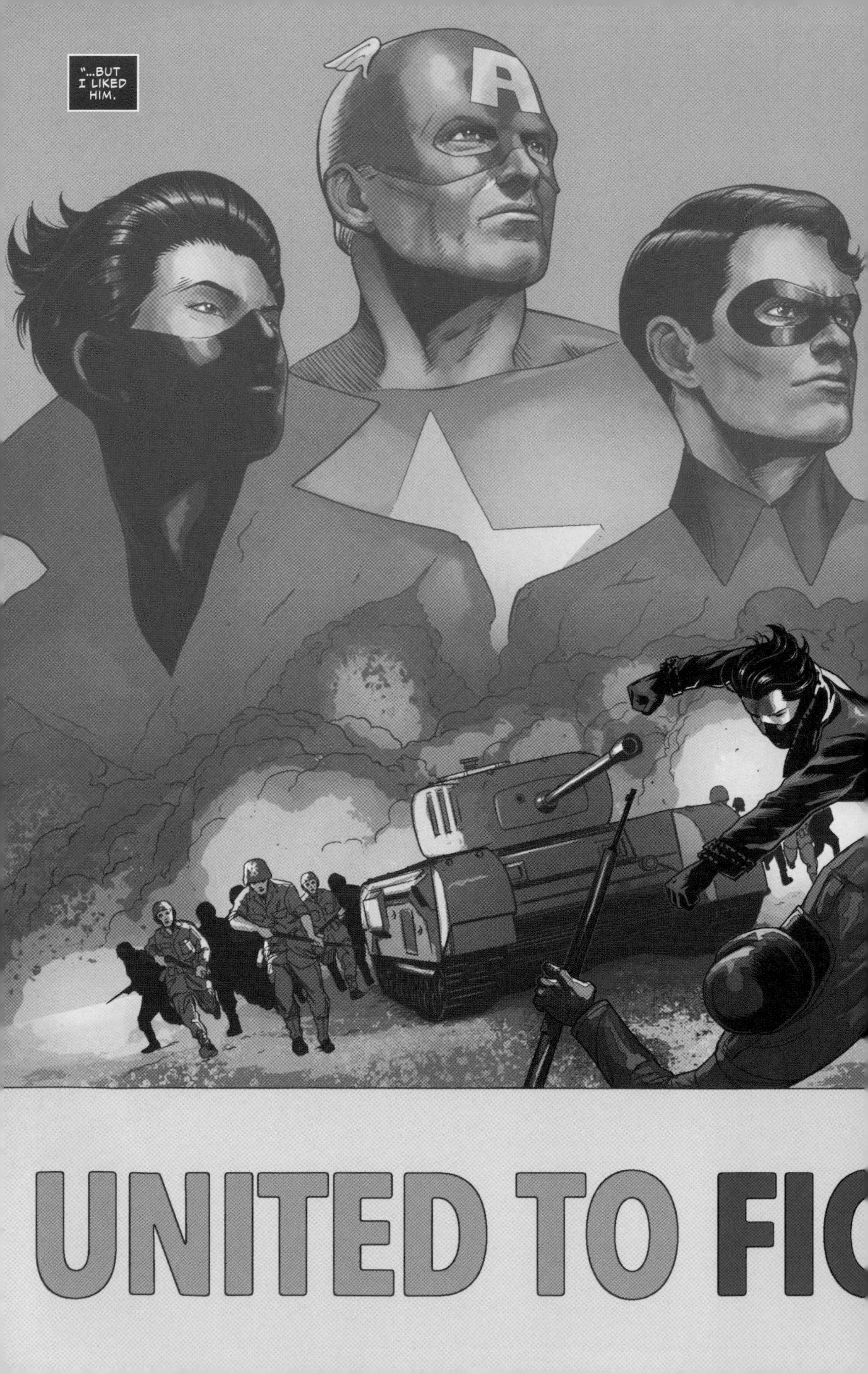
"...BUT I LIKED HIM.
UNITED TO FIG

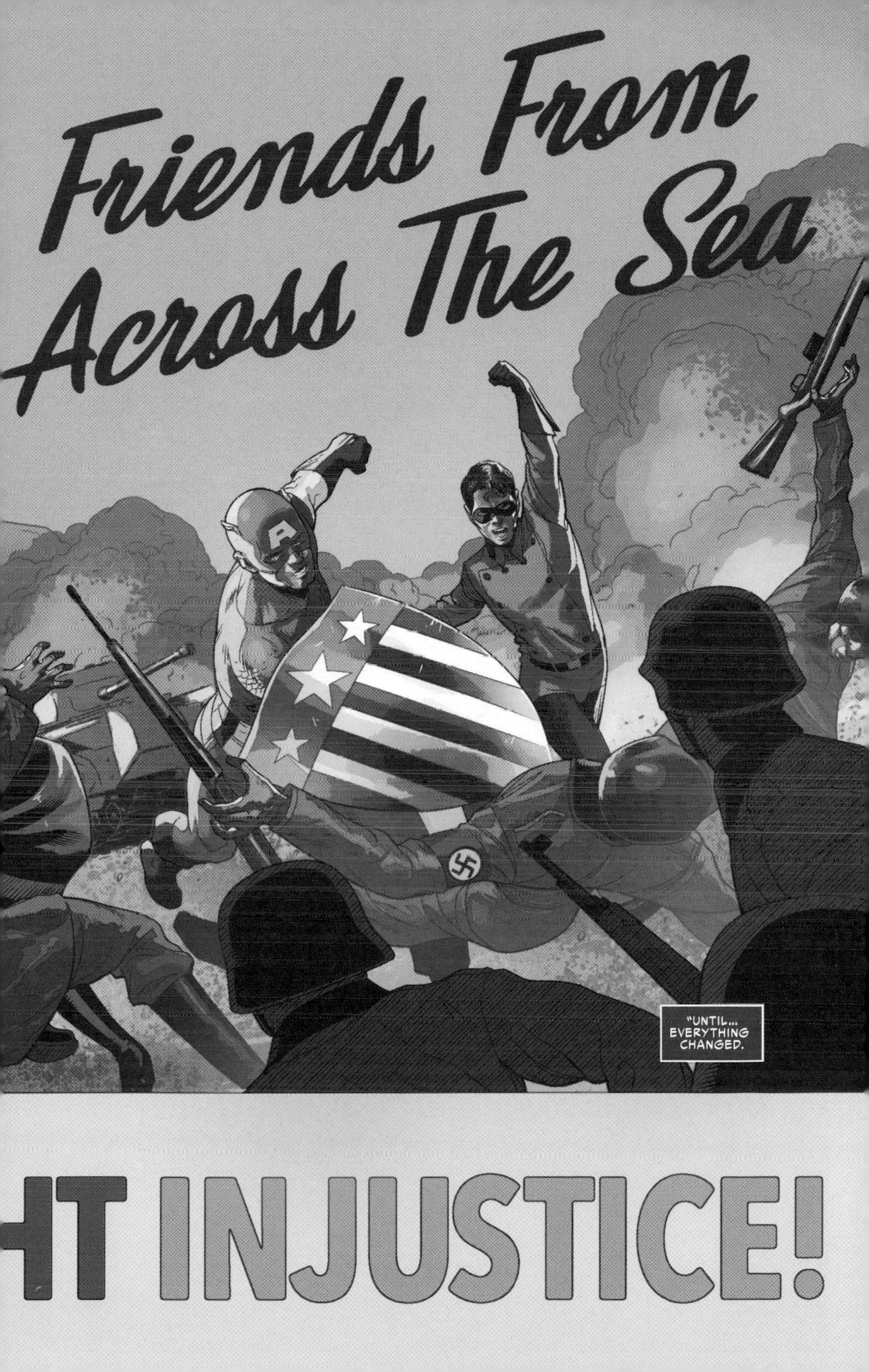

Friends From Across The Sea
"UNTIL... EVERYTHING CHANGED.
HT INJUSTICE!

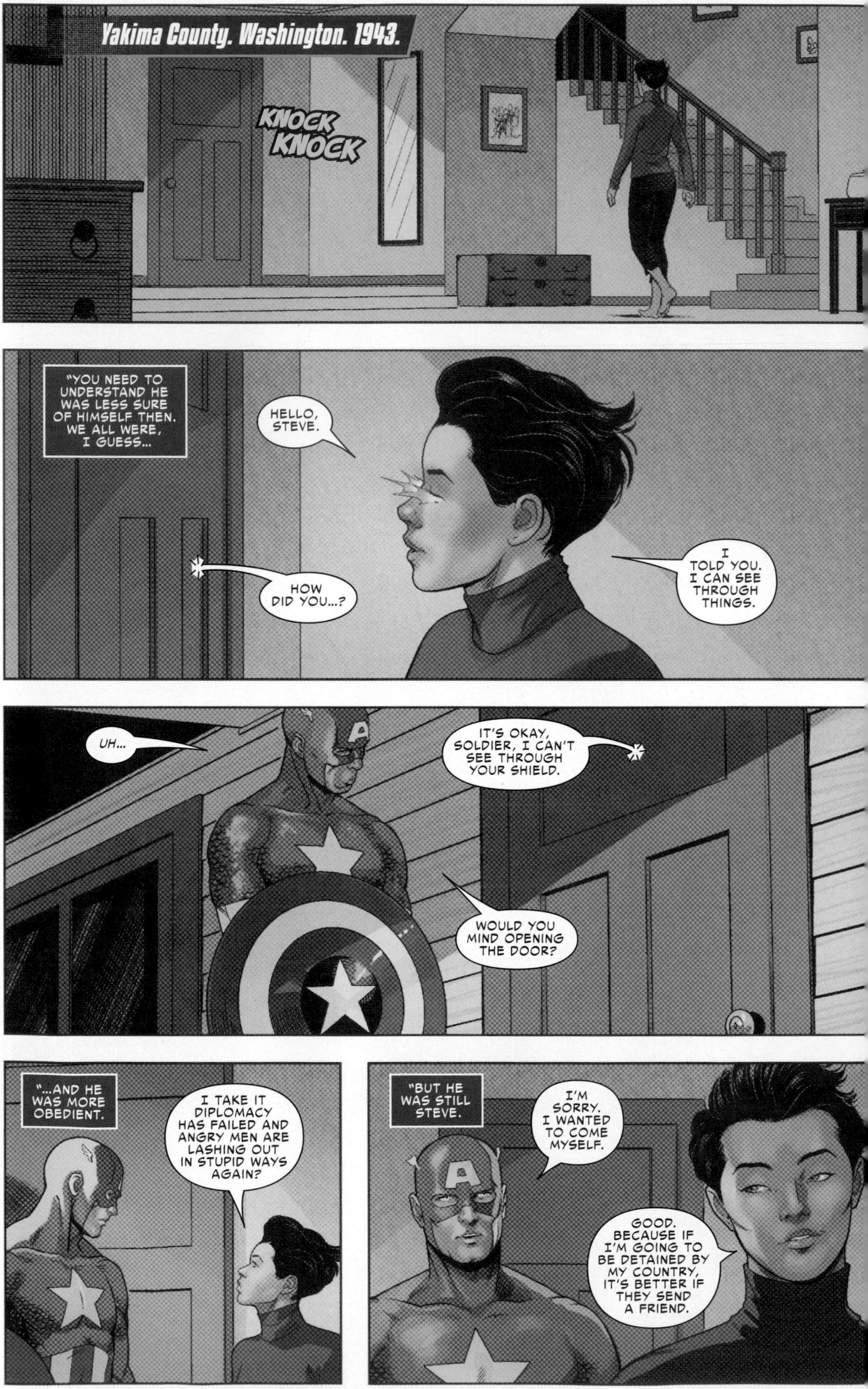
Yakima County. Washington. 1943.
KNOCK KNOCK
"YOU NEED TO UNDERSTAND HE WAS LESS SURE OF HIMSELF THEN. WE ALL WERE, I GUESS...
HELLO, STEVE.
HOW DID YOU...?
I TOLD YOU. I CAN SEE THROUGH THINGS.
UH...
IT'S OKAY, SOLDIER, I CAN'T SEE THROUGH YOUR SHIELD.
WOULD YOU MIND OPENING THE DOOR?
"...AND HE WAS MORE OBEDIENT.
I TAKE IT DIPLOMACY HAS FAILED AND ANGRY MEN ARE LASHING OUT IN STUPID WAYS AGAIN?
"BUT HE WAS STILL STEVE.
I'M SORRY. I WANTED TO COME MYSELF.
GOOD. BECAUSE IF I'M GOING TO BE DETAINED BY MY COUNTRY, IT'S BETTER IF THEY SEND A FRIEND.

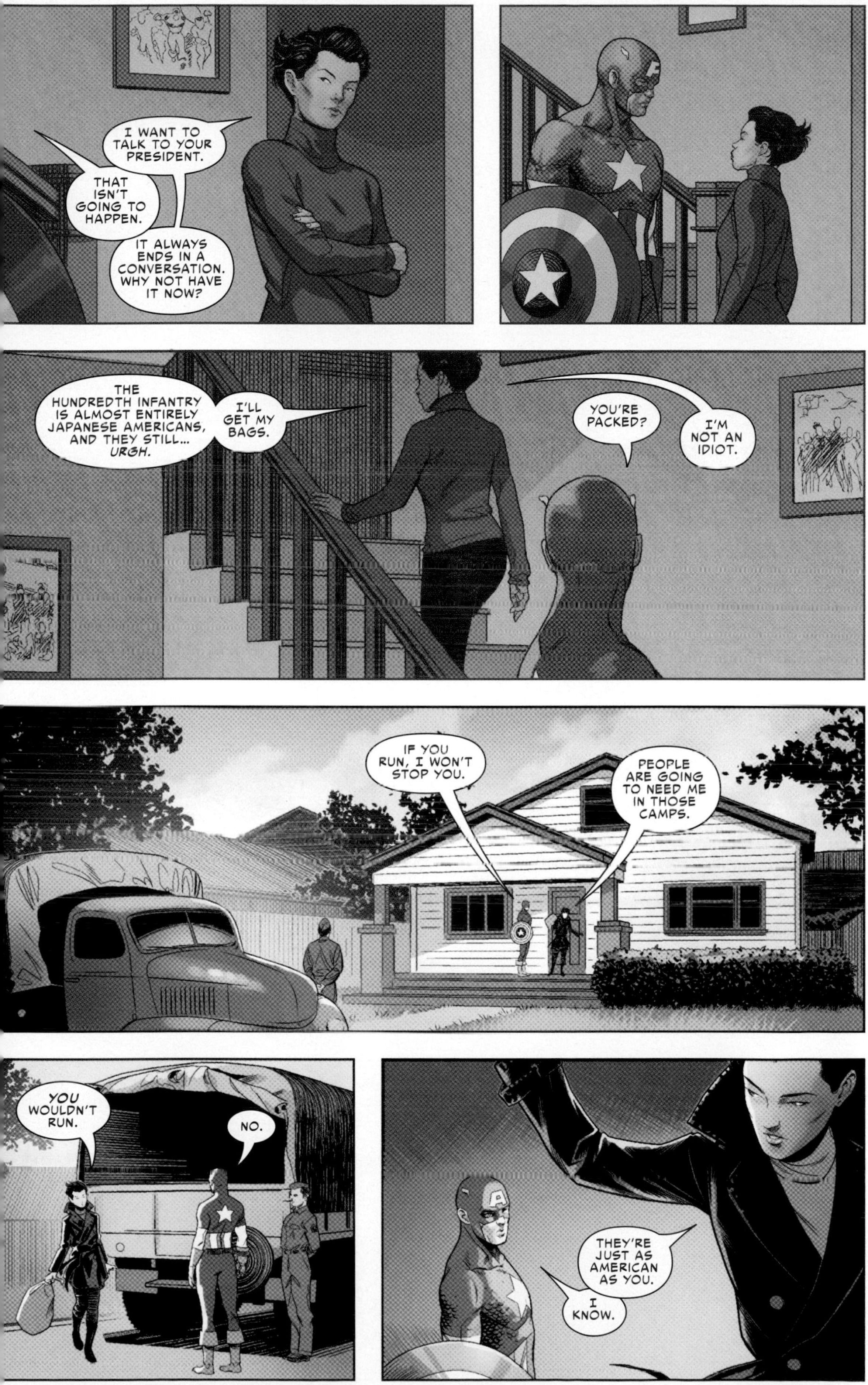
I WANT TO TALK TO YOUR PRESIDENT.
THAT ISN'T GOING TO HAPPEN.
IT ALWAYS ENDS IN A CONVERSATION. WHY NOT HAVE IT NOW?
THE HUNDREDTH INFANTRY IS ALMOST ENTIRELY JAPANESE AMERICANS, AND THEY STILL... *URGH.*
I'LL GET MY BAGS.
YOU'RE PACKED?
I'M NOT AN IDIOT.
IF YOU RUN, I WON'T STOP YOU.
PEOPLE ARE GOING TO NEED ME IN THOSE CAMPS.
YOU WOULDN'T RUN.
NO.
THEY'RE JUST AS AMERICAN AS YOU.
I KNOW.

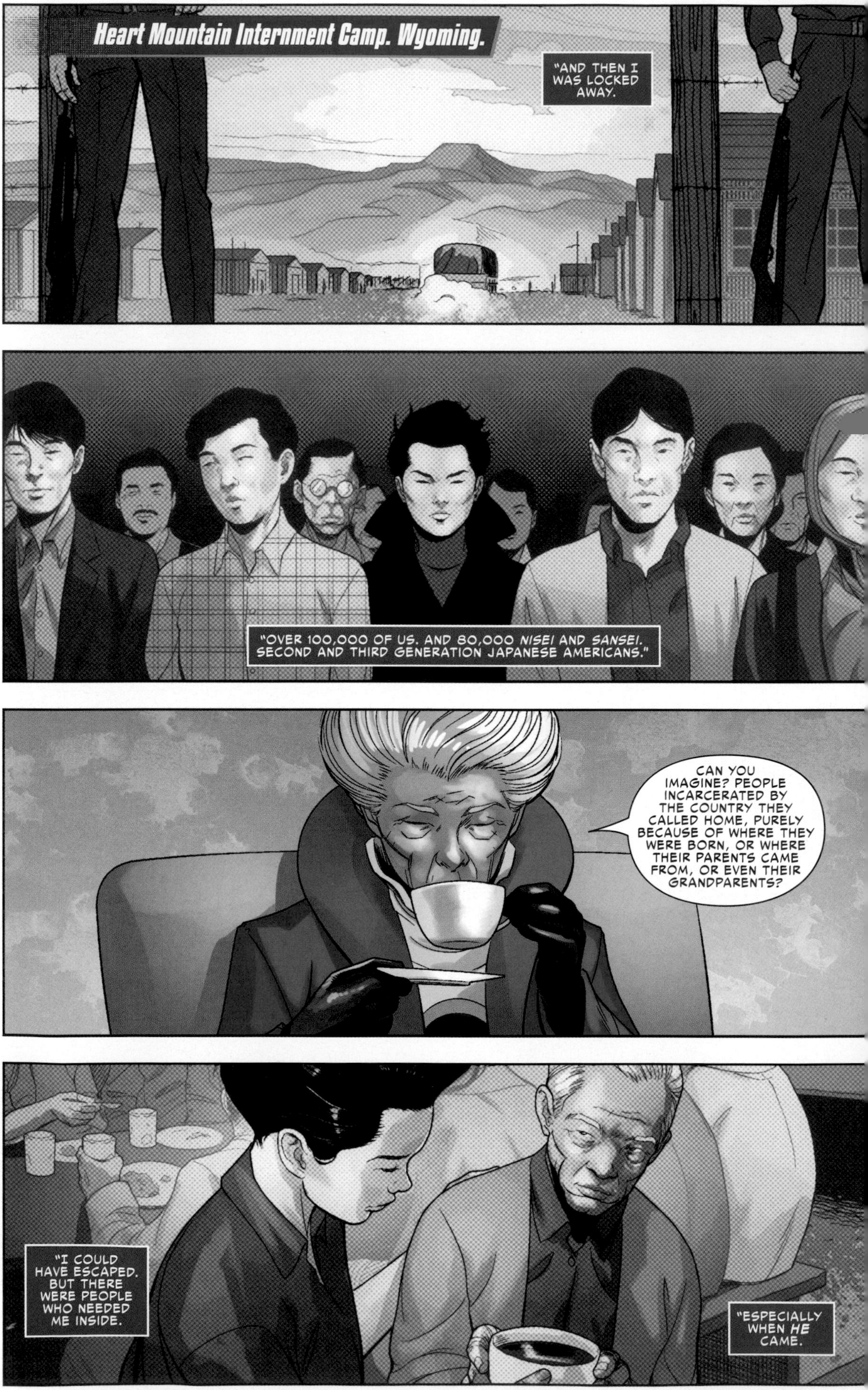
Heart Mountain Internment Camp. Wyoming.
"AND THEN I WAS LOCKED AWAY.
"OVER 100,000 OF US. AND 80,000 NISEI AND SANSEI. SECOND AND THIRD GENERATION JAPANESE AMERICANS."
CAN YOU IMAGINE? PEOPLE INCARCERATED BY THE COUNTRY THEY CALLED HOME, PURELY BECAUSE OF WHERE THEY WERE BORN, OR WHERE THEIR PARENTS CAME FROM, OR EVEN THEIR GRANDPARENTS?
"I COULD HAVE ESCAPED. BUT THERE WERE PEOPLE WHO NEEDED ME INSIDE.
"ESPECIALLY WHEN HE CAME.

"HELMINTH."

HIS FIRST NAME IS KENNETH.

THAT DOESN'T QUITE HAVE THE SAME MENACING RING.

NO.

"HE WAS ANOTHER ONE LIKE ME. SOMEONE MADE HIM. ANOTHER FAILURE.

"OR MAYBE HE WAS DEEMED A SUCCESS.

"HE PREYED ON MISERY. FED ON IT.

THD

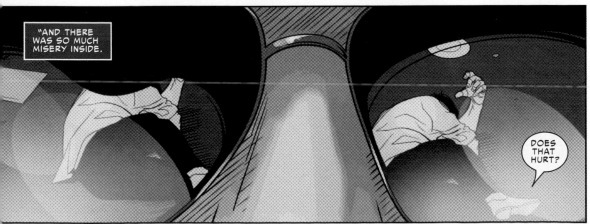

"AND THERE WAS SO MUCH MISERY INSIDE.

DOES THAT HURT?

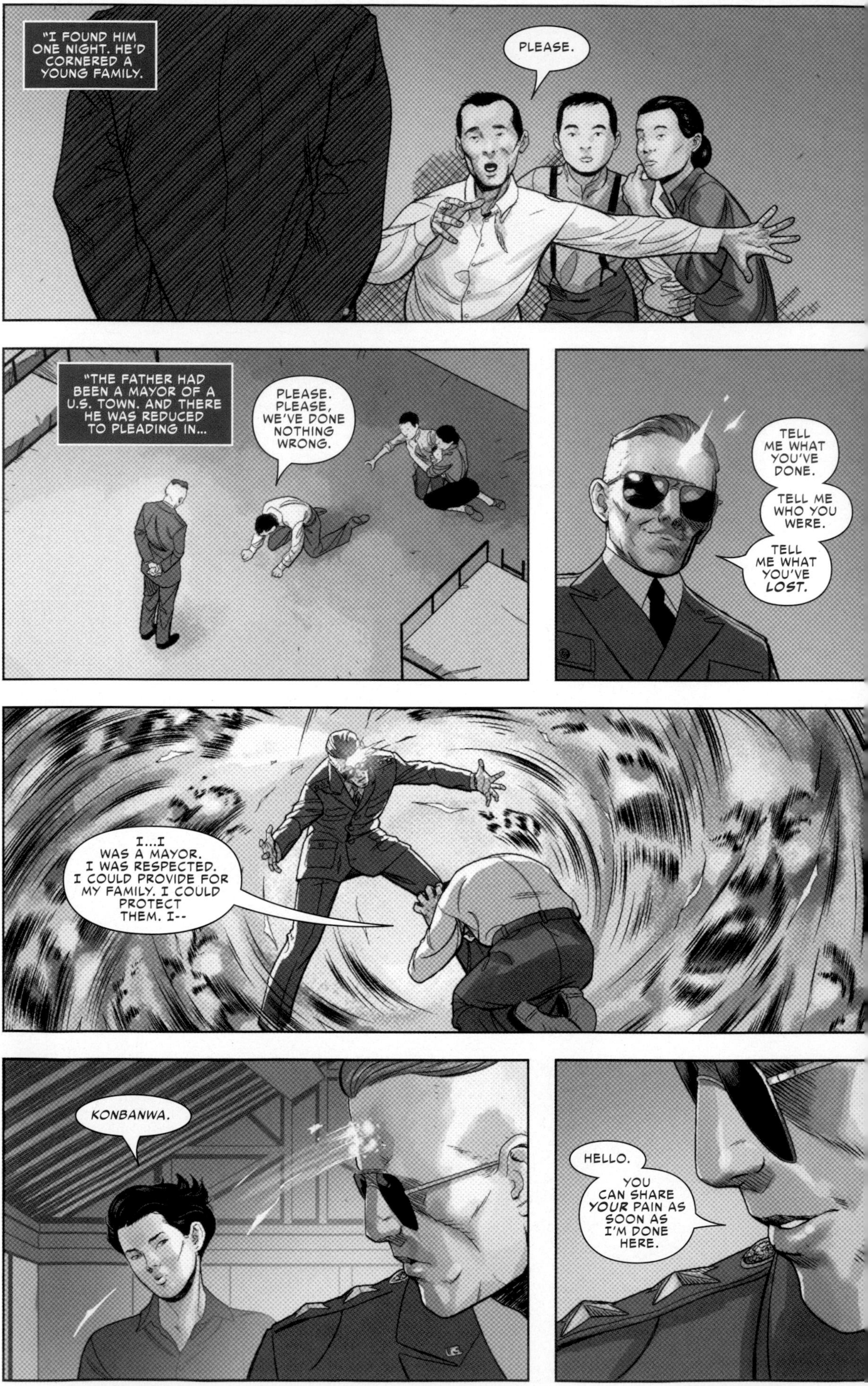
"I FOUND HIM ONE NIGHT. HE'D CORNERED A YOUNG FAMILY.
PLEASE.
"THE FATHER HAD BEEN A MAYOR OF A U.S. TOWN. AND THERE HE WAS REDUCED TO PLEADING IN...
PLEASE. PLEASE, WE'VE DONE NOTHING WRONG.
TELL ME WHAT YOU'VE DONE.
TELL ME WHO YOU WERE.
TELL ME WHAT YOU'VE *LOST.*
I...I WAS A MAYOR. I WAS RESPECTED. I COULD PROVIDE FOR MY FAMILY. I COULD PROTECT THEM. I--
KONBANWA.
HELLO.
YOU CAN SHARE *YOUR* PAIN AS SOON AS I'M DONE HERE.

"HE WASN'T EXPECTING ME.

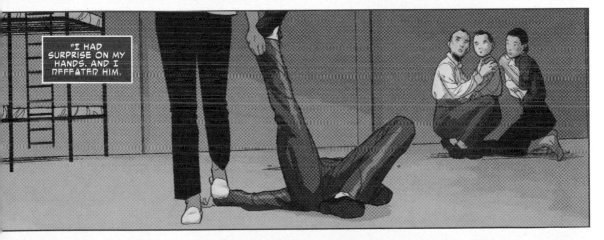

"OR WHAT I WAS CAPABLE OF.

"I HAD SURPRISE ON MY HANDS. AND I DEFEATED HIM.

"OR SO I THOUGHT."

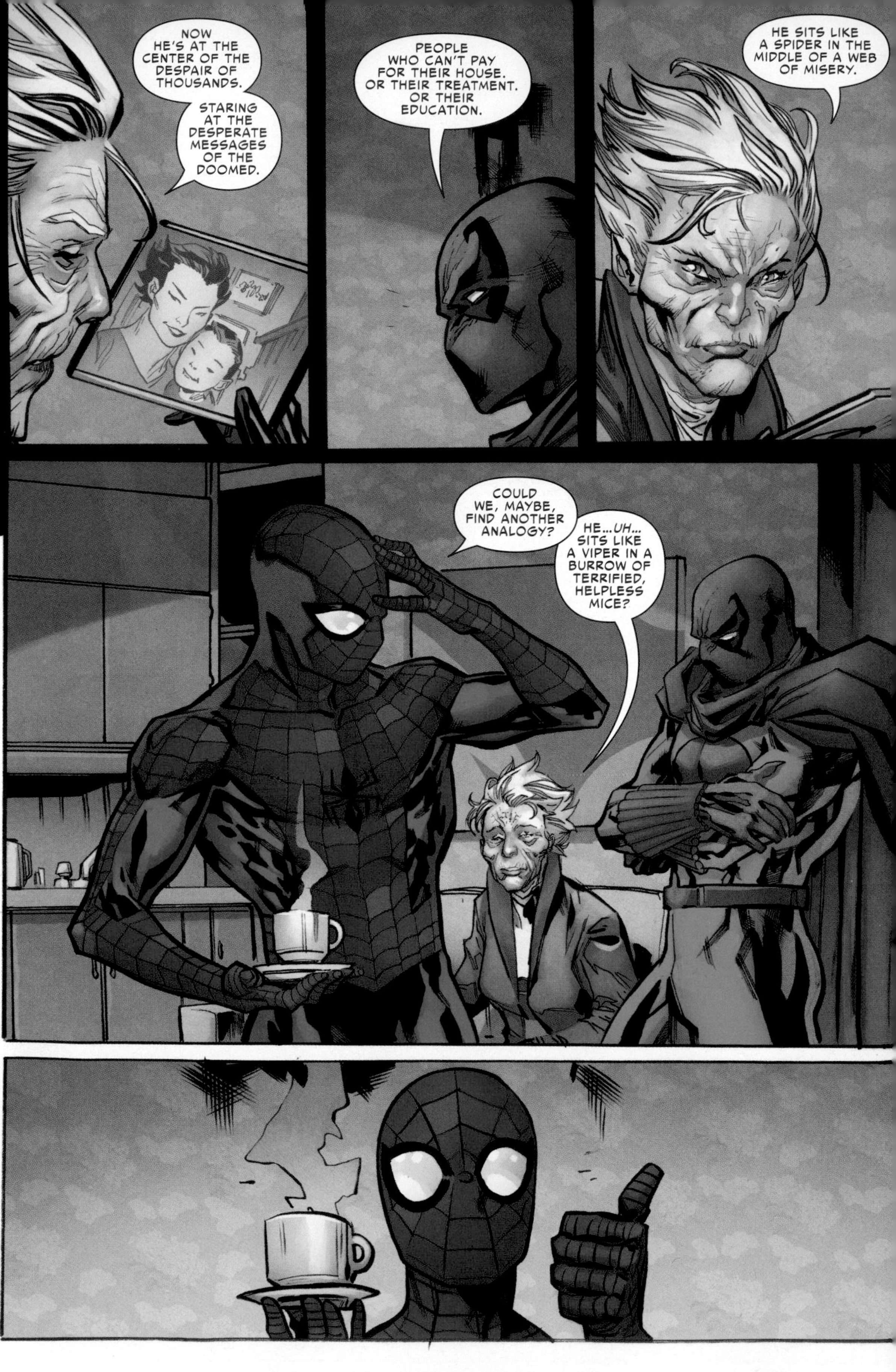
NOW HE'S AT THE CENTER OF THE DESPAIR OF THOUSANDS.
STARING AT THE DESPERATE MESSAGES OF THE DOOMED.
PEOPLE WHO CAN'T PAY FOR THEIR HOUSE. OR THEIR TREATMENT. OR THEIR EDUCATION.
HE SITS LIKE A SPIDER IN THE MIDDLE OF A WEB OF MISERY.
COULD WE, MAYBE, FIND ANOTHER ANALOGY?
HE...*UH*... SITS LIKE A VIPER IN A BURROW OF TERRIFIED, HELPLESS MICE?

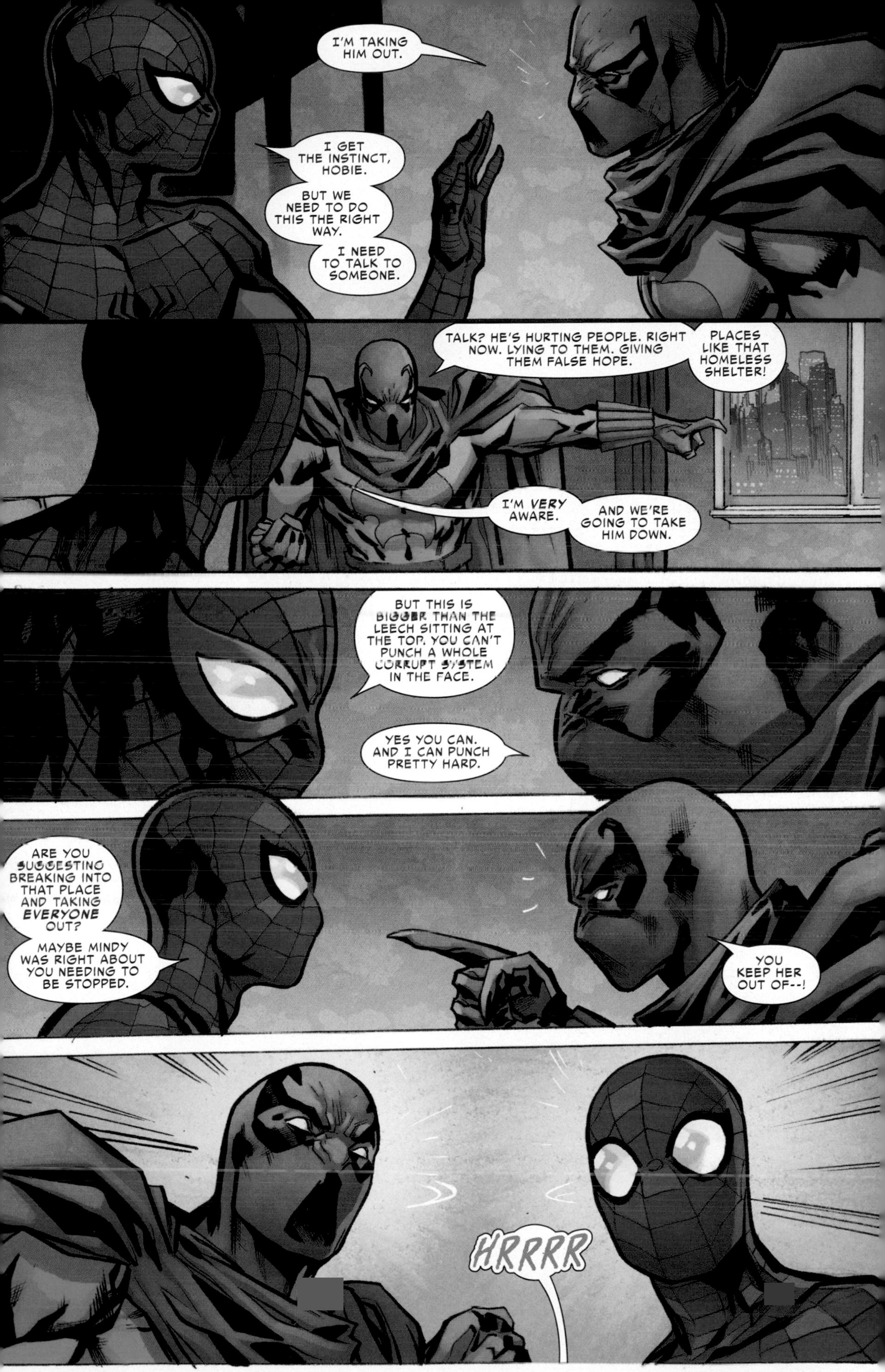
I'M TAKING HIM OUT.
I GET THE INSTINCT, HOBIE.
BUT WE NEED TO DO THIS THE RIGHT WAY.
I NEED TO TALK TO SOMEONE.
TALK? HE'S HURTING PEOPLE. RIGHT NOW. LYING TO THEM. GIVING THEM FALSE HOPE.
PLACES LIKE THAT HOMELESS SHELTER!
I'M *VERY* AWARE.
AND WE'RE GOING TO TAKE HIM DOWN.
BUT THIS IS BIGGER THAN THE LEECH SITTING AT THE TOP. YOU CAN'T PUNCH A WHOLE CORRUPT SYSTEM IN THE FACE.
YES YOU CAN. AND I CAN PUNCH PRETTY HARD.
ARE YOU SUGGESTING BREAKING INTO THAT PLACE AND TAKING ***EVERYONE*** OUT?
MAYBE MINDY WAS RIGHT ABOUT YOU NEEDING TO BE STOPPED.
YOU KEEP HER OUT OF--!
HRRRR

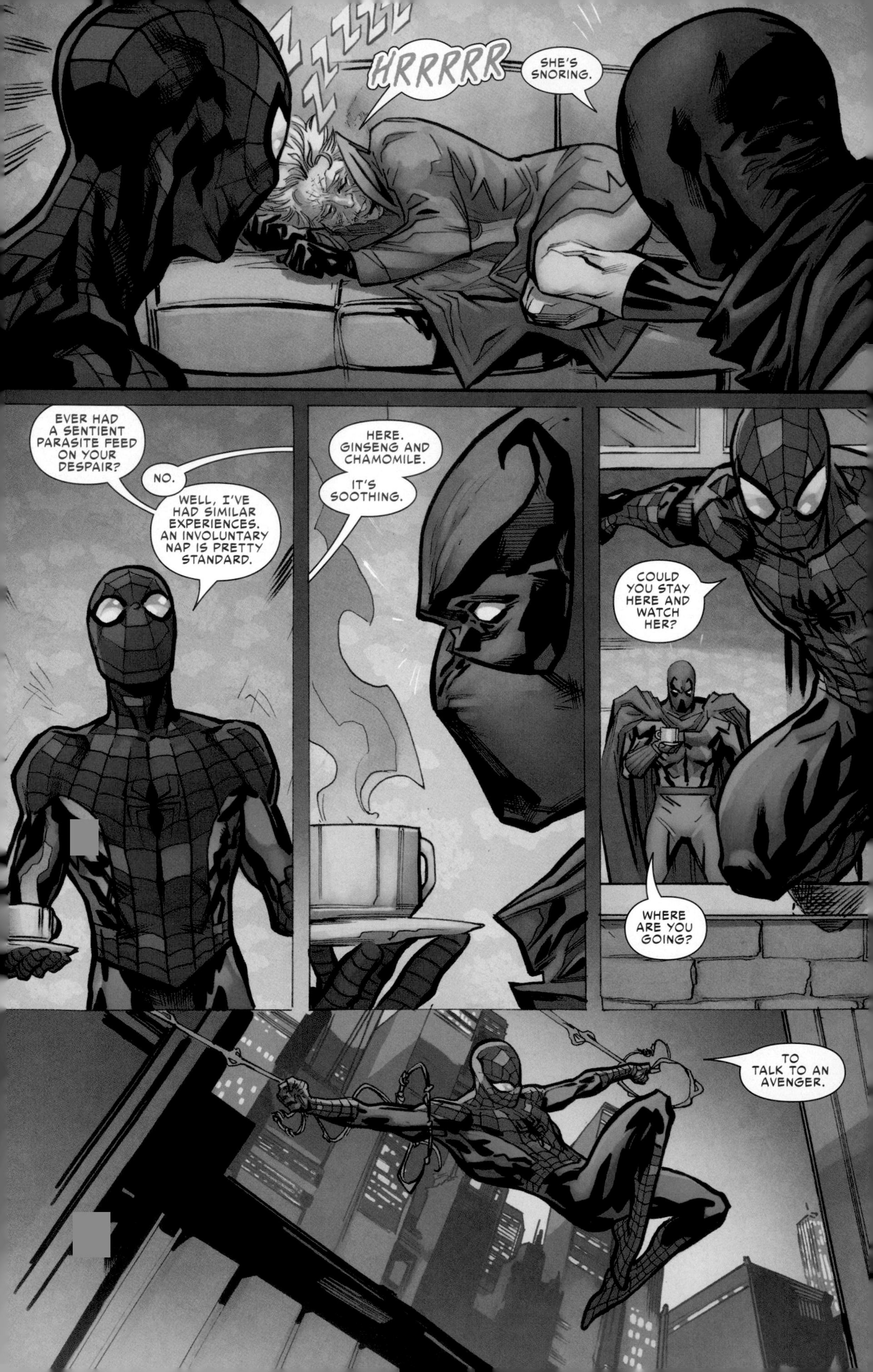
ZZZZZZ
HRRRRR
SHE'S SNORING.
EVER HAD A SENTIENT PARASITE FEED ON YOUR DESPAIR?
NO.
WELL, I'VE HAD SIMILAR EXPERIENCES. AN INVOLUNTARY NAP IS PRETTY STANDARD.
HERE. GINSENG AND CHAMOMILE.
IT'S SOOTHING.
COULD YOU STAY HERE AND WATCH HER?
WHERE ARE YOU GOING?
TO TALK TO AN AVENGER.

"I HAVE A DOOR. I HAVE A PHONE. YOU COULD TRY EITHER BEFORE THIS."

Stark Unlimited.

THIS GETS YOUR ATTENTION QUICKER, TONY.

I JUST HAD THOSE WINDOWS CLEANED.

AND?

YOU LEAVE A RESIDUE.

I DON'T LEAVE A RESIDUE.

...DO I?

WHY DON'T YOU COME INSIDE?

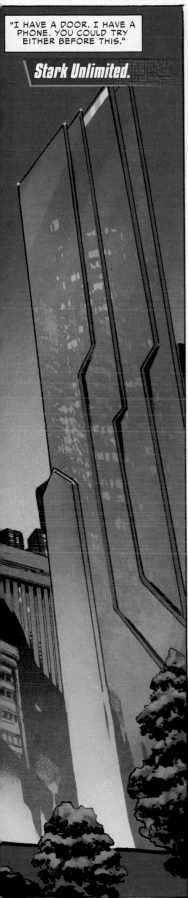

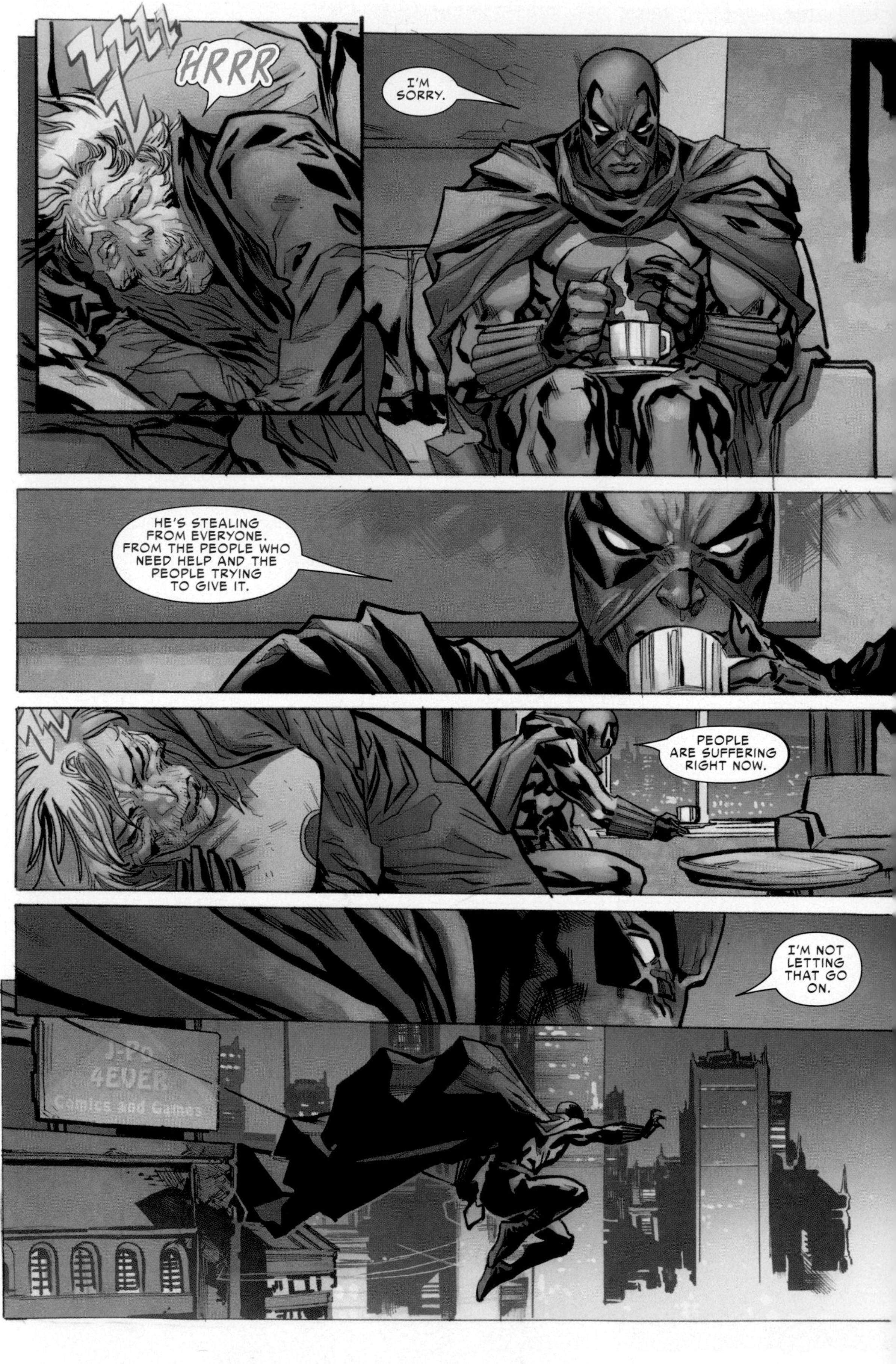
ZZSSL
HRRR
I'M SORRY.
HE'S STEALING FROM EVERYONE. FROM THE PEOPLE WHO NEED HELP AND THE PEOPLE TRYING TO GIVE IT.
PEOPLE ARE SUFFERING RIGHT NOW.
I'M NOT LETTING THAT GO ON.
J-Po 4EVER Comics and Games

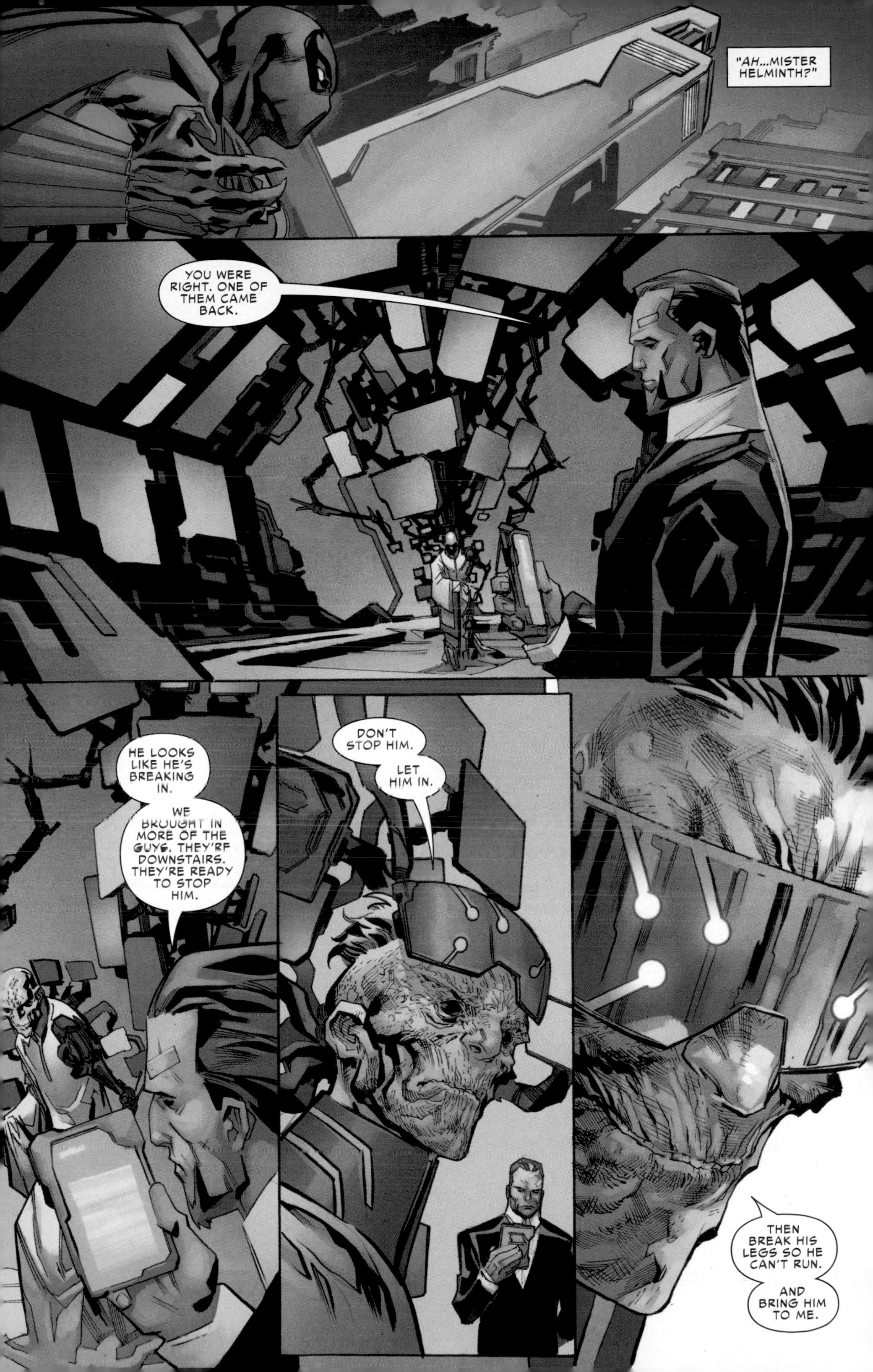
"AH...MISTER HELMINTH?"
YOU WERE RIGHT. ONE OF THEM CAME BACK.
HE LOOKS LIKE HE'S BREAKING IN.
WE BROUGHT IN MORE OF THE GUYS. THEY'RE DOWNSTAIRS. THEY'RE READY TO STOP HIM.
DON'T STOP HIM.
LET HIM IN.
THEN BREAK HIS LEGS SO HE CAN'T RUN.
AND BRING HIM TO ME.

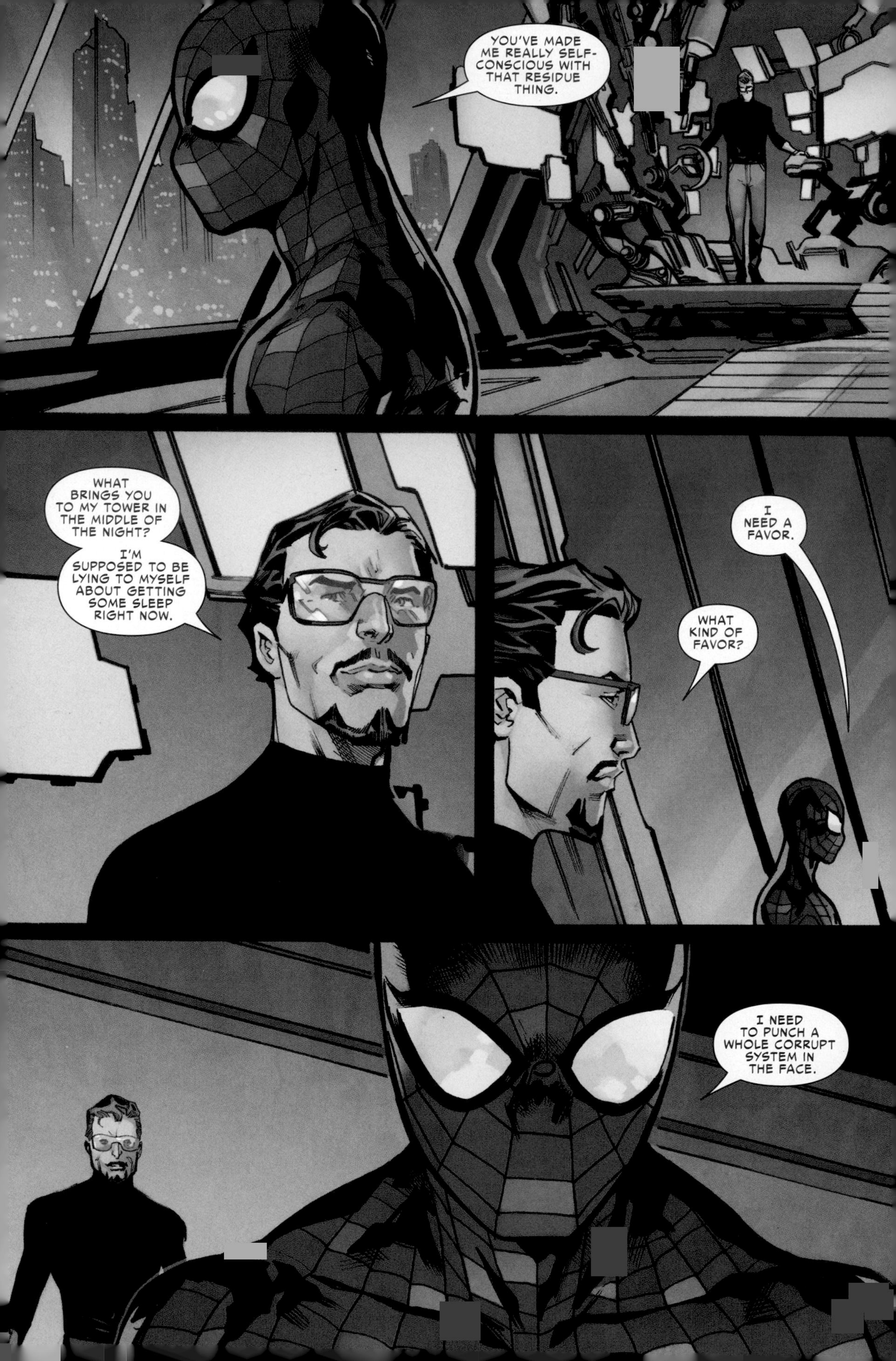
YOU'VE MADE ME REALLY SELF-CONSCIOUS WITH THAT RESIDUE THING.
WHAT BRINGS YOU TO MY TOWER IN THE MIDDLE OF THE NIGHT?
I'M SUPPOSED TO BE LYING TO MYSELF ABOUT GETTING SOME SLEEP RIGHT NOW.
I NEED A FAVOR.
WHAT KIND OF FAVOR?
I NEED TO PUNCH A WHOLE CORRUPT SYSTEM IN THE FACE.

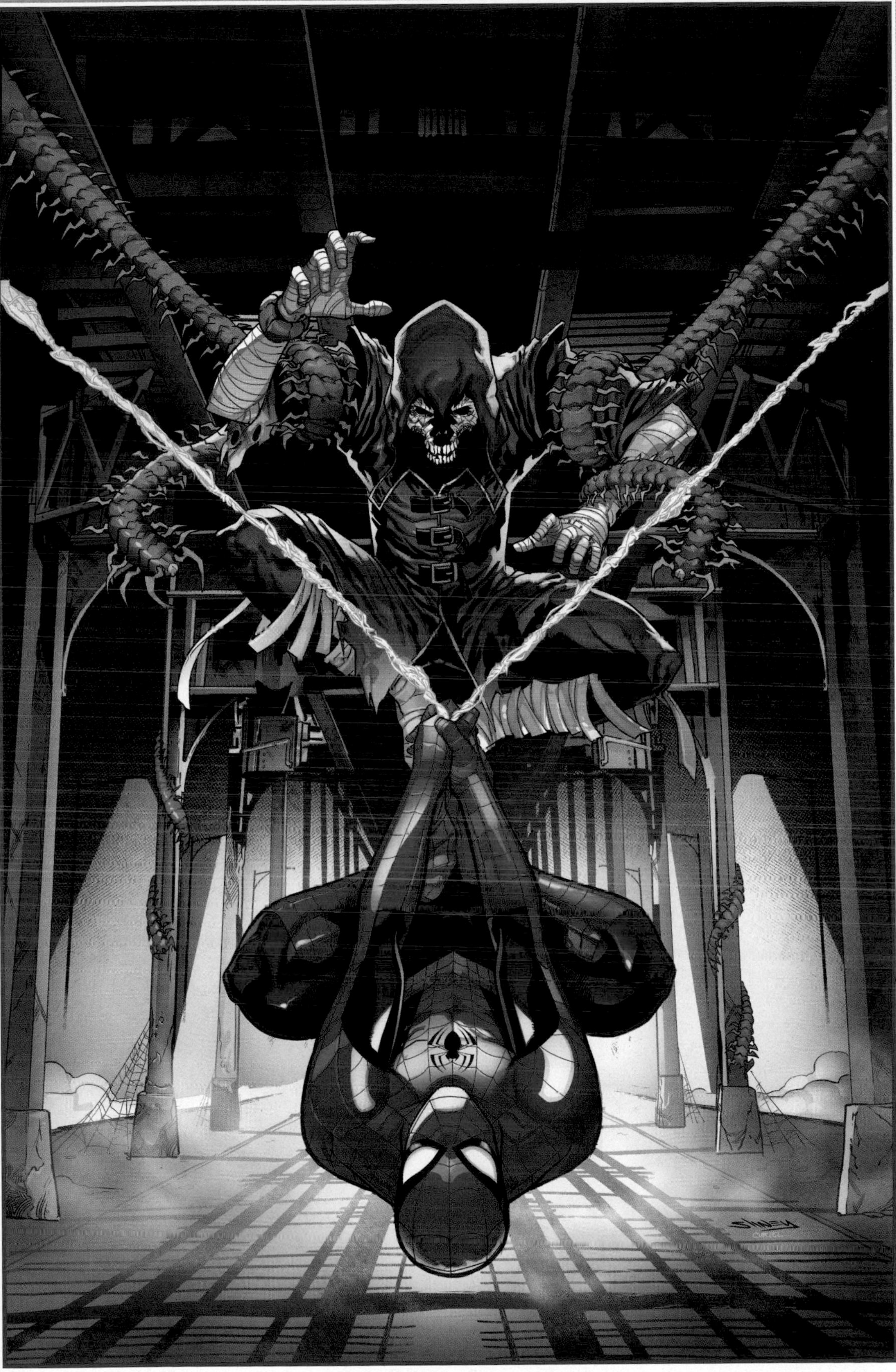

Will Sliney & David Curiel
#10 Bring on the Bad Guys Variant

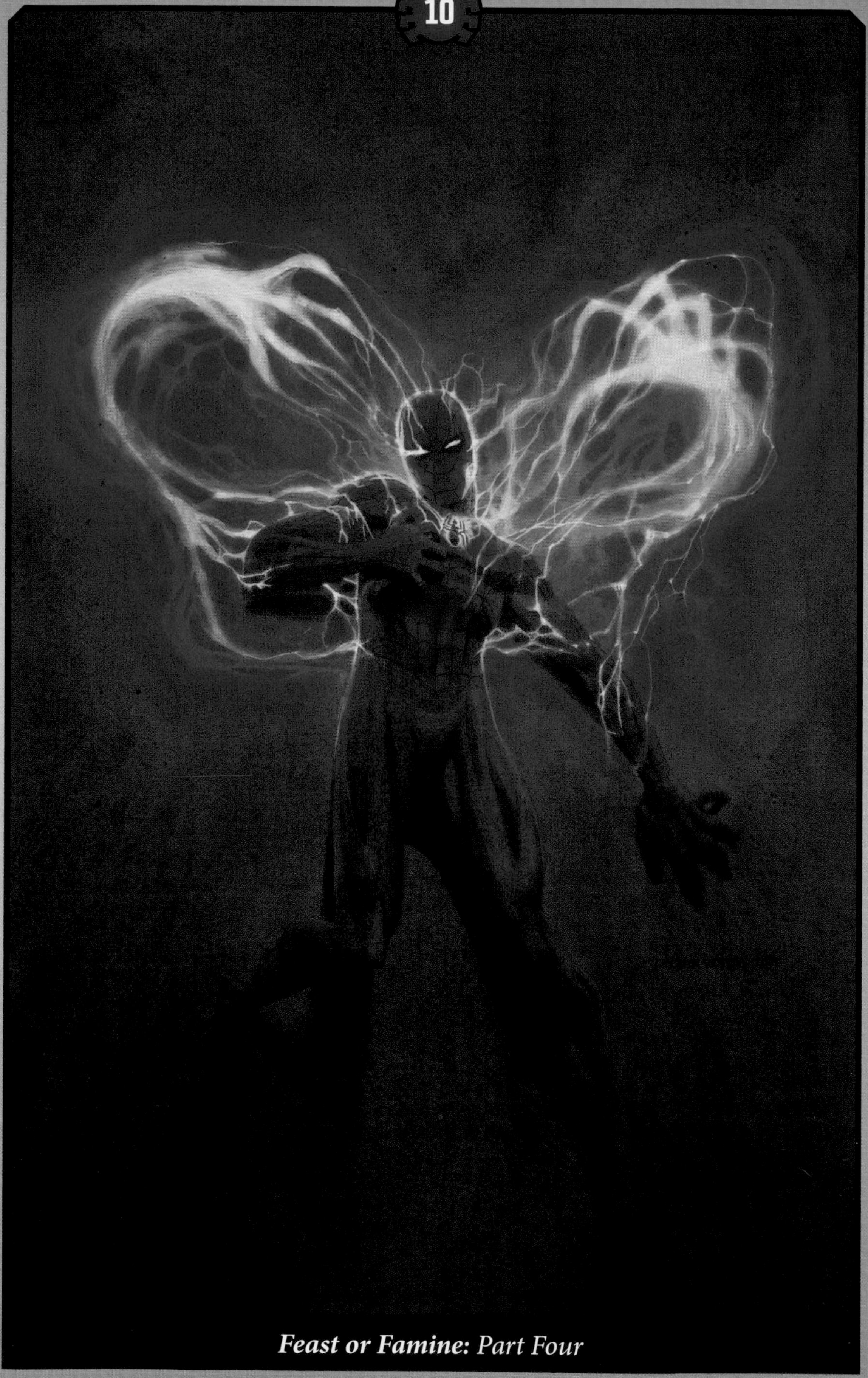

Feast or Famine: Part Four

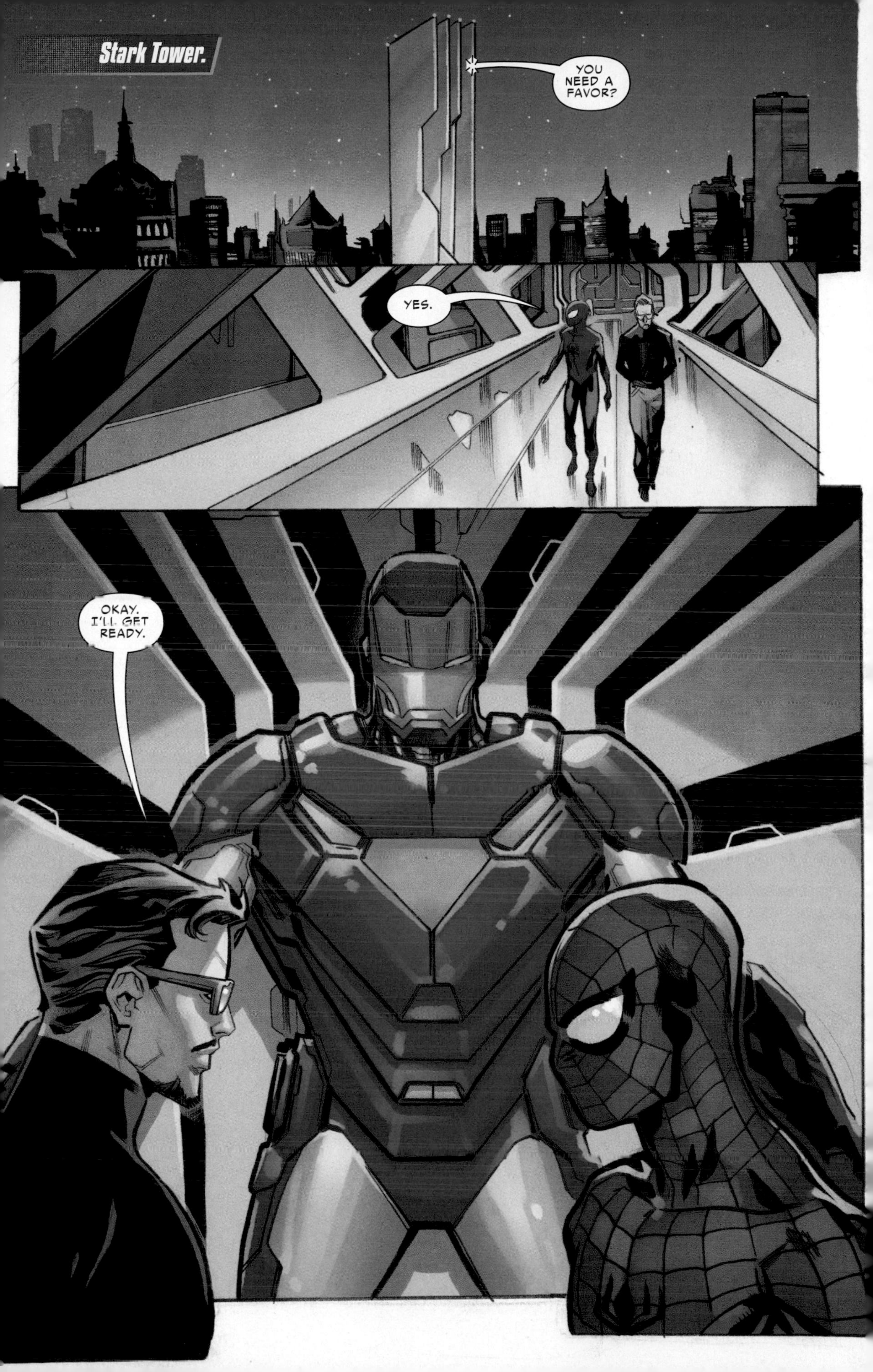
Stark Tower.
YOU NEED A FAVOR?
YES.
OKAY. I'LL GET READY.

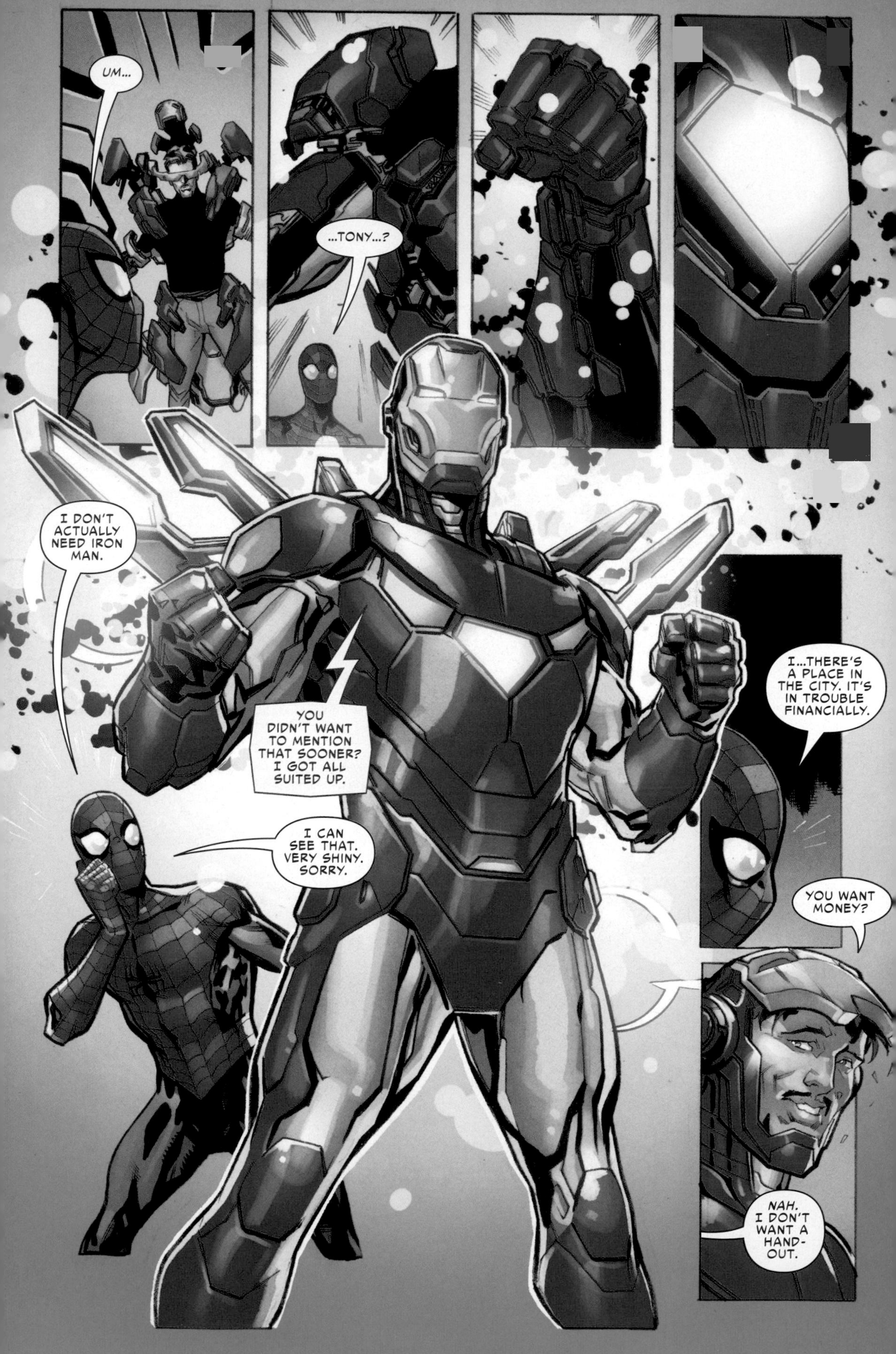
UM...
...TONY...?
I DON'T ACTUALLY NEED IRON MAN.
YOU DIDN'T WANT TO MENTION THAT SOONER? I GOT ALL SUITED UP.
I CAN SEE THAT. VERY SHINY. SORRY.
I...THERE'S A PLACE IN THE CITY. IT'S IN TROUBLE FINANCIALLY.
YOU WANT MONEY?
NAH. I DON'T WANT A HAND-OUT.

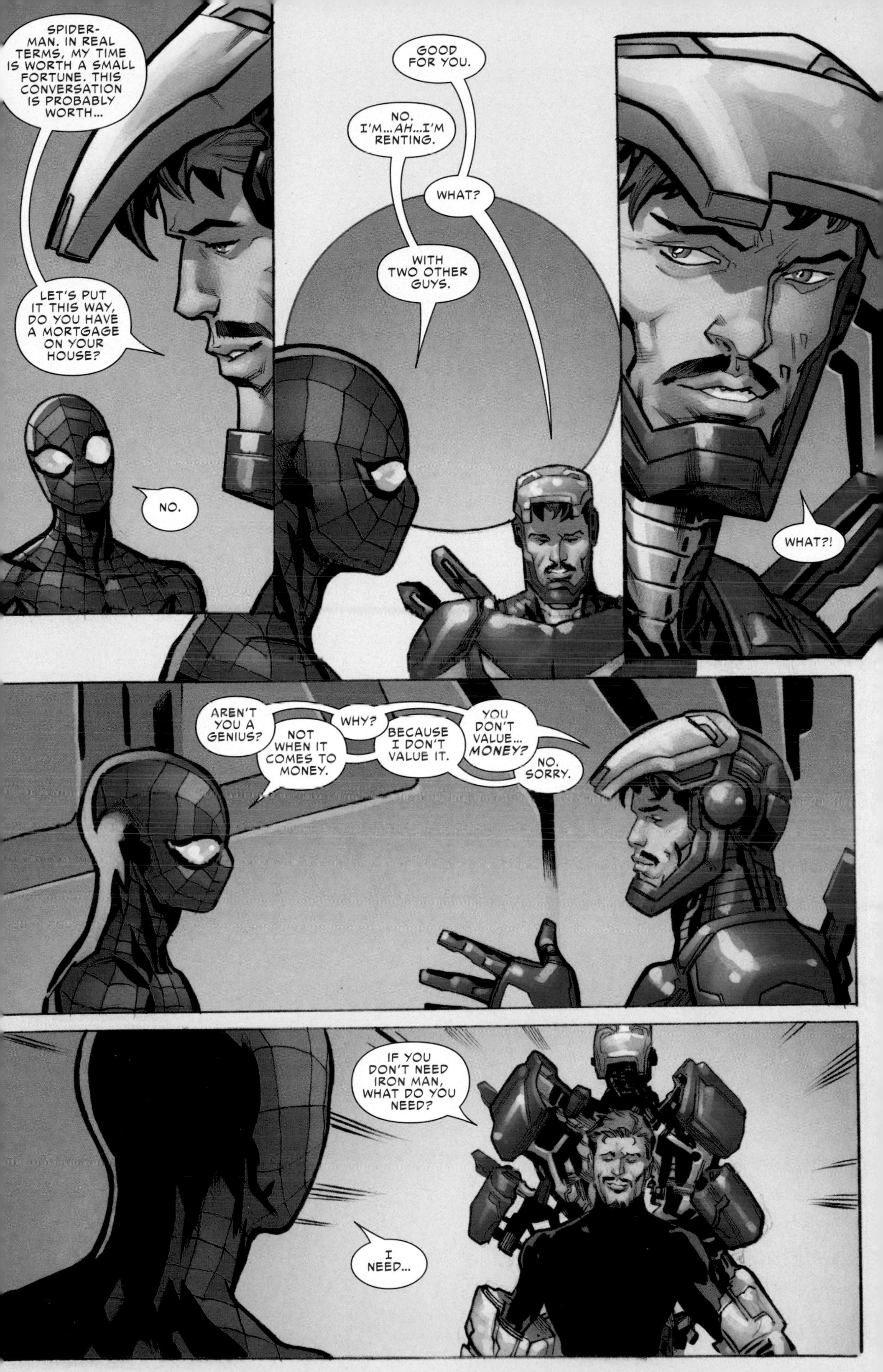

SPIDER-MAN. IN REAL TERMS, MY TIME IS WORTH A SMALL FORTUNE. THIS CONVERSATION IS PROBABLY WORTH...
LET'S PUT IT THIS WAY, DO YOU HAVE A MORTGAGE ON YOUR HOUSE?
NO.
GOOD FOR YOU.
NO. I'M...*AH*...I'M RENTING.
WHAT?
WITH TWO OTHER GUYS.
WHAT?!
AREN'T YOU A GENIUS?
NOT WHEN IT COMES TO MONEY.
WHY?
BECAUSE I DON'T VALUE IT.
YOU DON'T VALUE... *MONEY?*
NO. SORRY.
IF YOU DON'T NEED IRON MAN, WHAT DO YOU NEED?
I NEED...

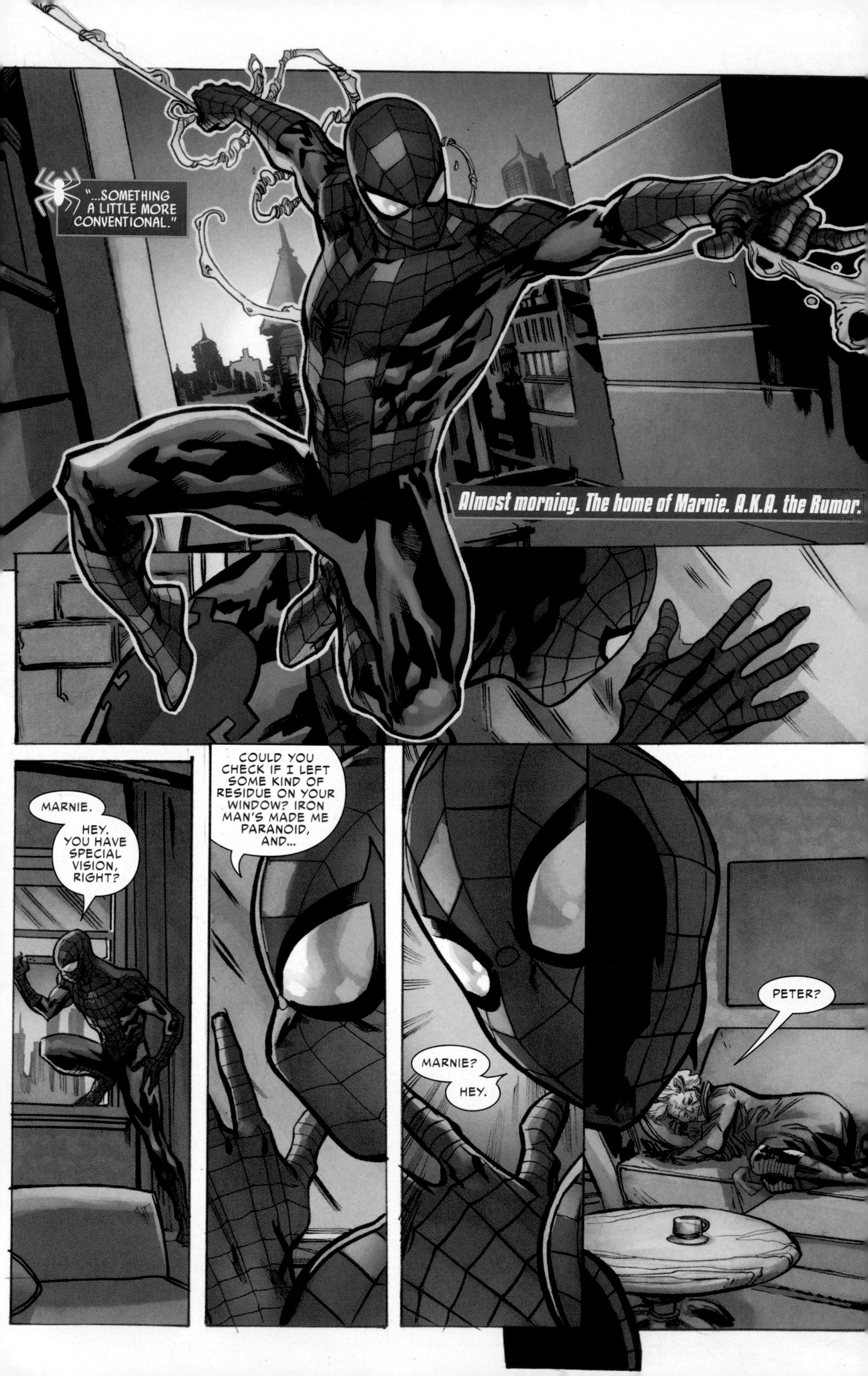
"...SOMETHING A LITTLE MORE CONVENTIONAL."
Almost morning. The home of Marnie. A.K.A. the Rumor.
MARNIE.
HEY. YOU HAVE SPECIAL VISION, RIGHT?
COULD YOU CHECK IF I LEFT SOME KIND OF RESIDUE ON YOUR WINDOW? IRON MAN'S MADE ME PARANOID, AND...
MARNIE?
HEY.
PETER?

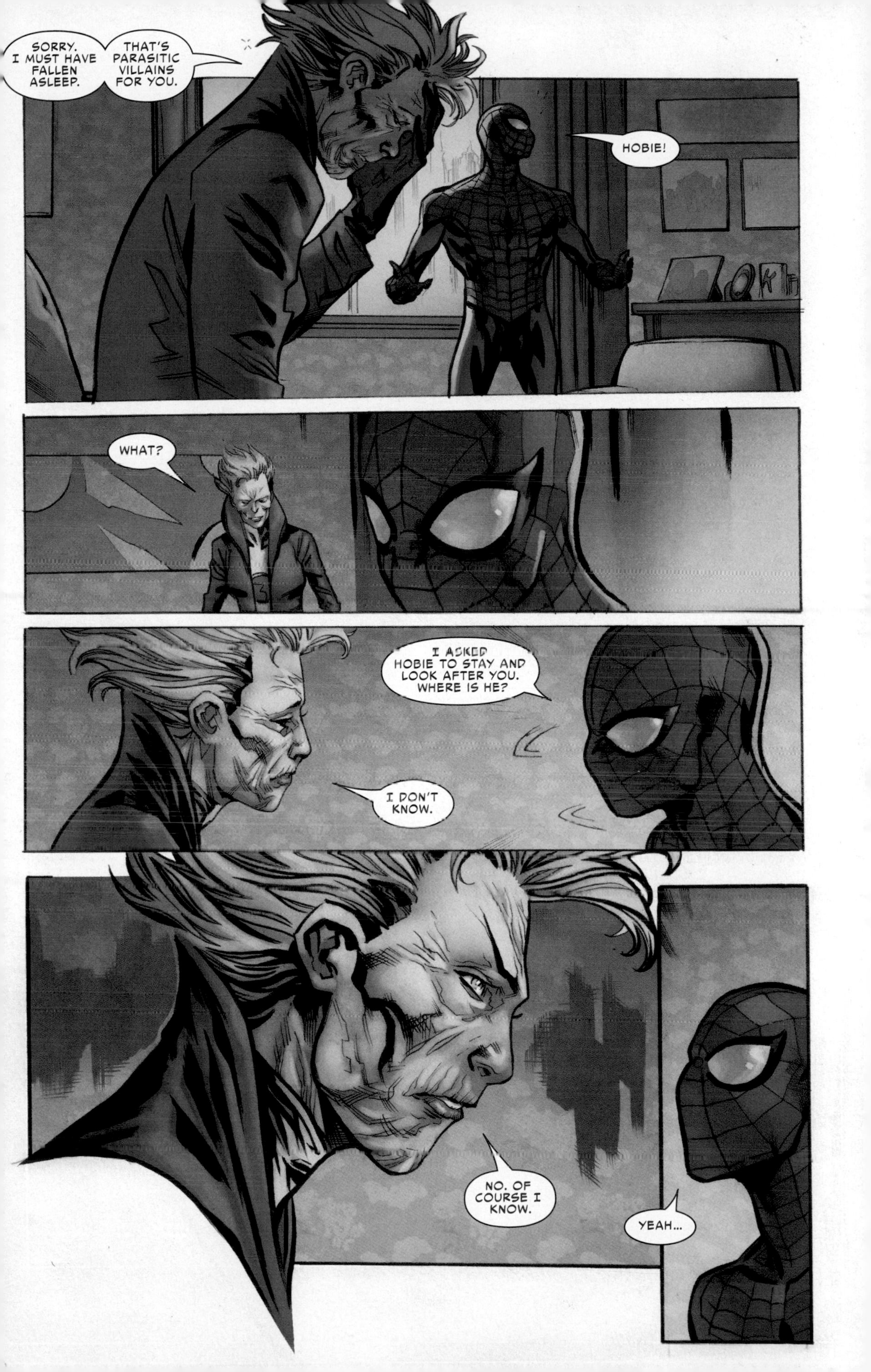
SORRY. I MUST HAVE FALLEN ASLEEP.
THAT'S PARASITIC VILLAINS FOR YOU.
HOBIE!
WHAT?
I ASKED HOBIE TO STAY AND LOOK AFTER YOU. WHERE IS HE?
I DON'T KNOW.
NO. OF COURSE I KNOW.
YEAH...

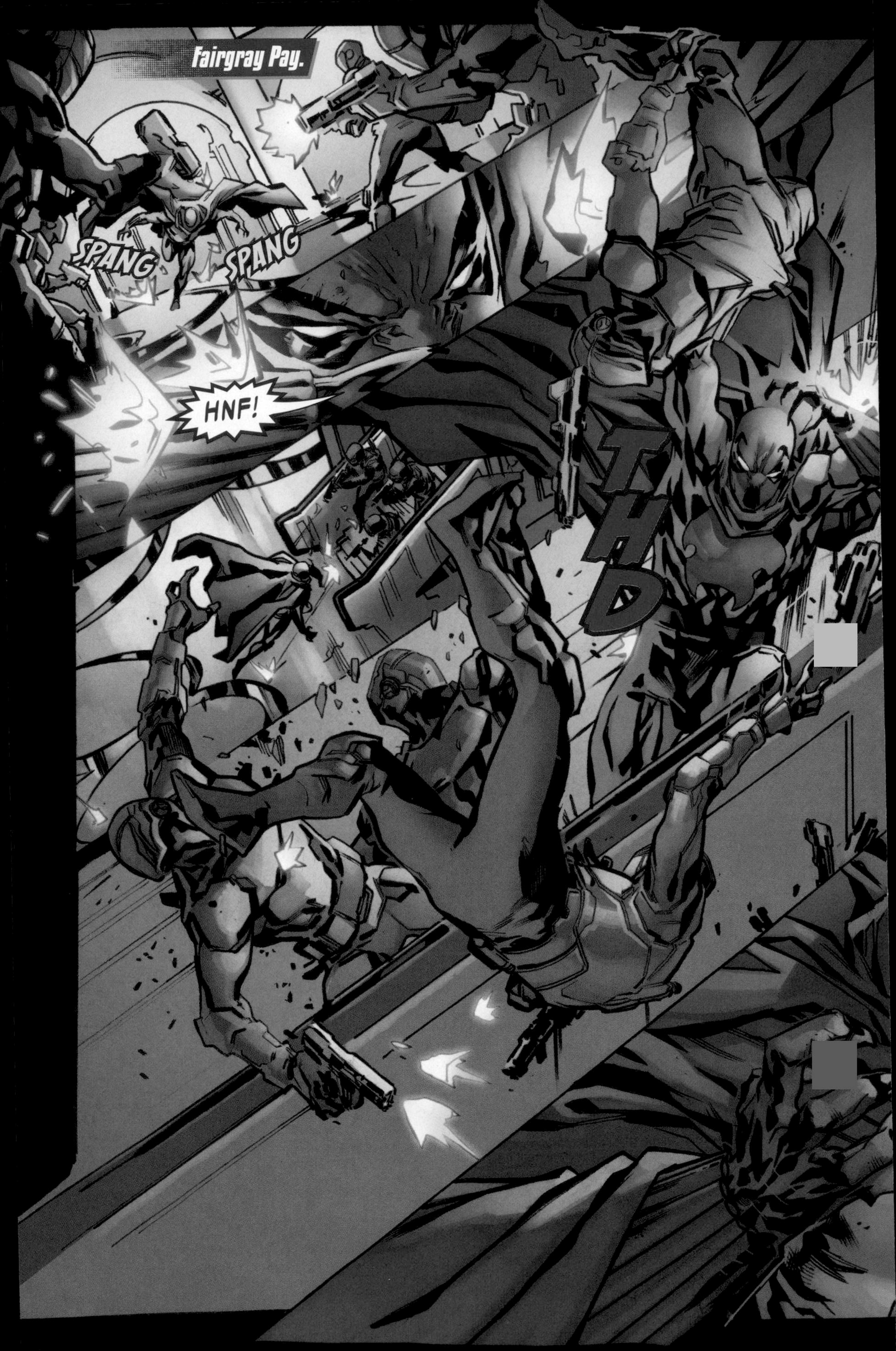
fairgray Pay.
SPANG
SPANG
HNF!
THD

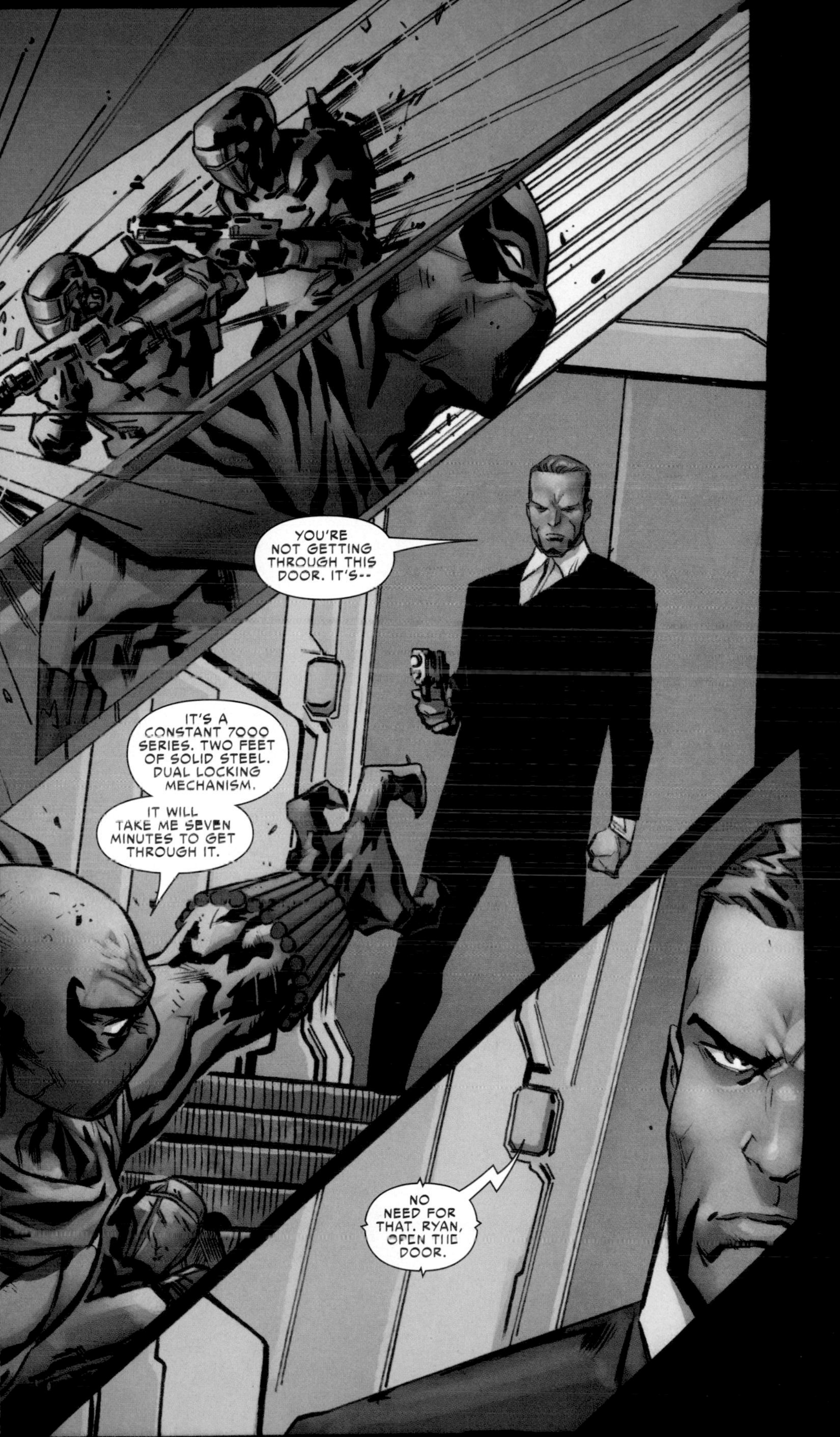
YOU'RE NOT GETTING THROUGH THIS DOOR. IT'S--
IT'S A CONSTANT 7000 SERIES. TWO FEET OF SOLID STEEL. DUAL LOCKING MECHANISM.
IT WILL TAKE ME SEVEN MINUTES TO GET THROUGH IT.
NO NEED FOR THAT. RYAN, OPEN THE DOOR.

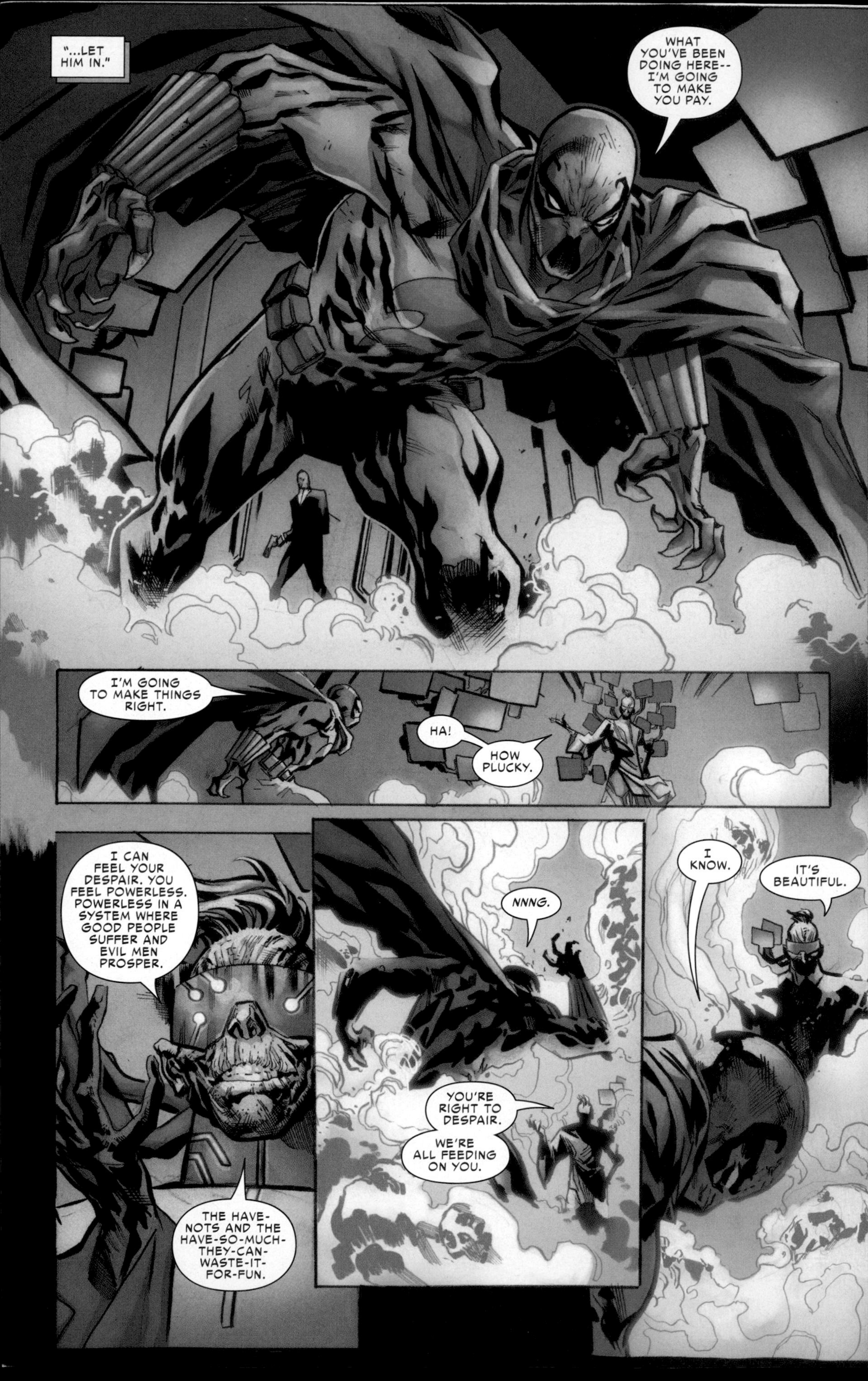
"...LET HIM IN."
WHAT YOU'VE BEEN DOING HERE-- I'M GOING TO MAKE YOU PAY.
I'M GOING TO MAKE THINGS RIGHT.
HA!
HOW PLUCKY.
I CAN FEEL YOUR DESPAIR. YOU FEEL POWERLESS. POWERLESS IN A SYSTEM WHERE GOOD PEOPLE SUFFER AND EVIL MEN PROSPER.
THE HAVE-NOTS AND THE HAVE-SO-MUCH-THEY-CAN-WASTE-IT-FOR-FUN.
NNNG.
YOU'RE RIGHT TO DESPAIR.
WE'RE ALL FEEDING ON YOU.
I KNOW.
IT'S BEAUTIFUL.

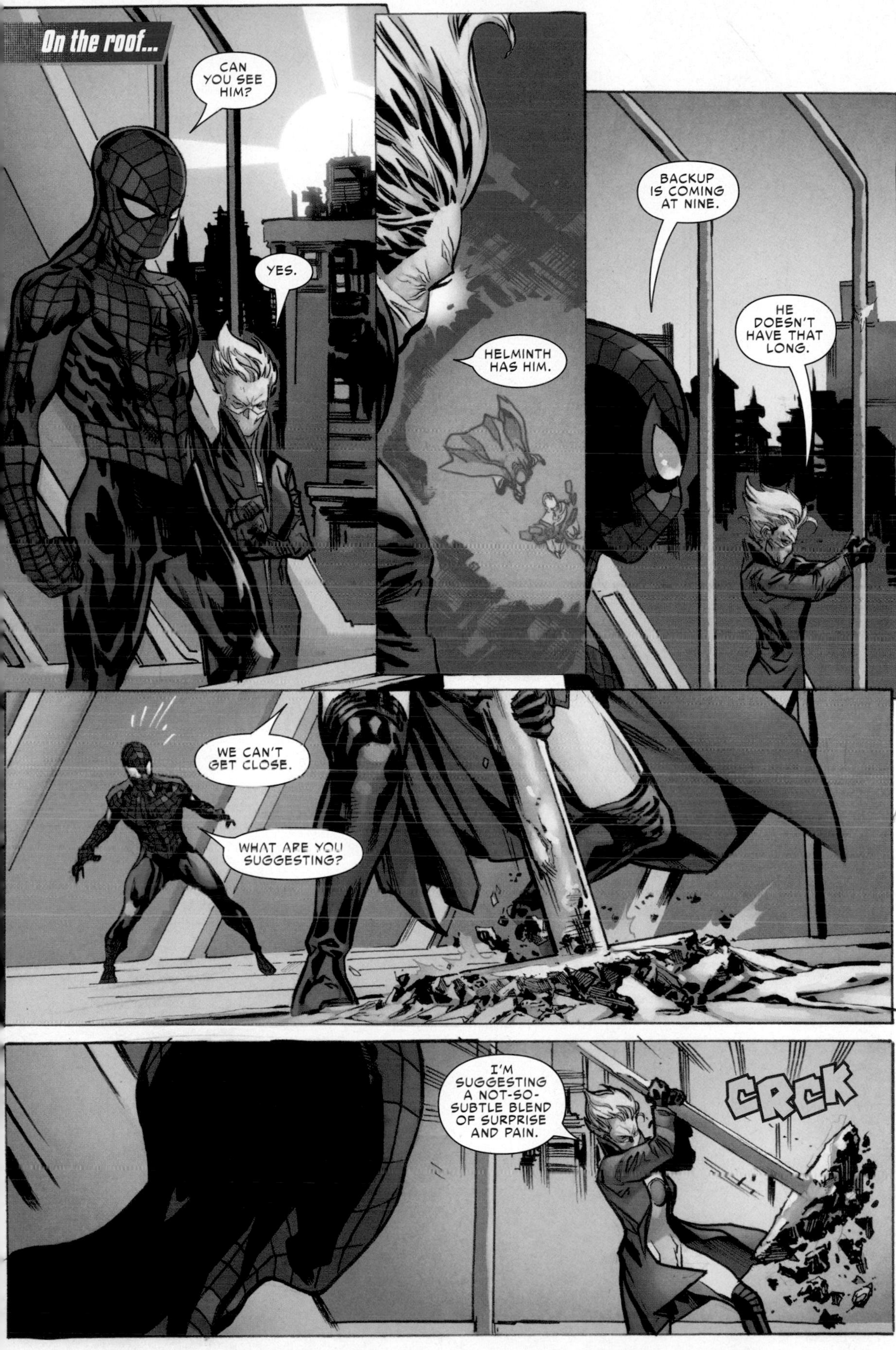
On the roof...
CAN YOU SEE HIM?
YES.
HELMINTH HAS HIM.
BACKUP IS COMING AT NINE.
HE DOESN'T HAVE THAT LONG.
WE CAN'T GET CLOSE.
WHAT ARE YOU SUGGESTING?
I'M SUGGESTING A NOT-SO-SUBTLE BLEND OF SURPRISE AND PAIN.
CRCK

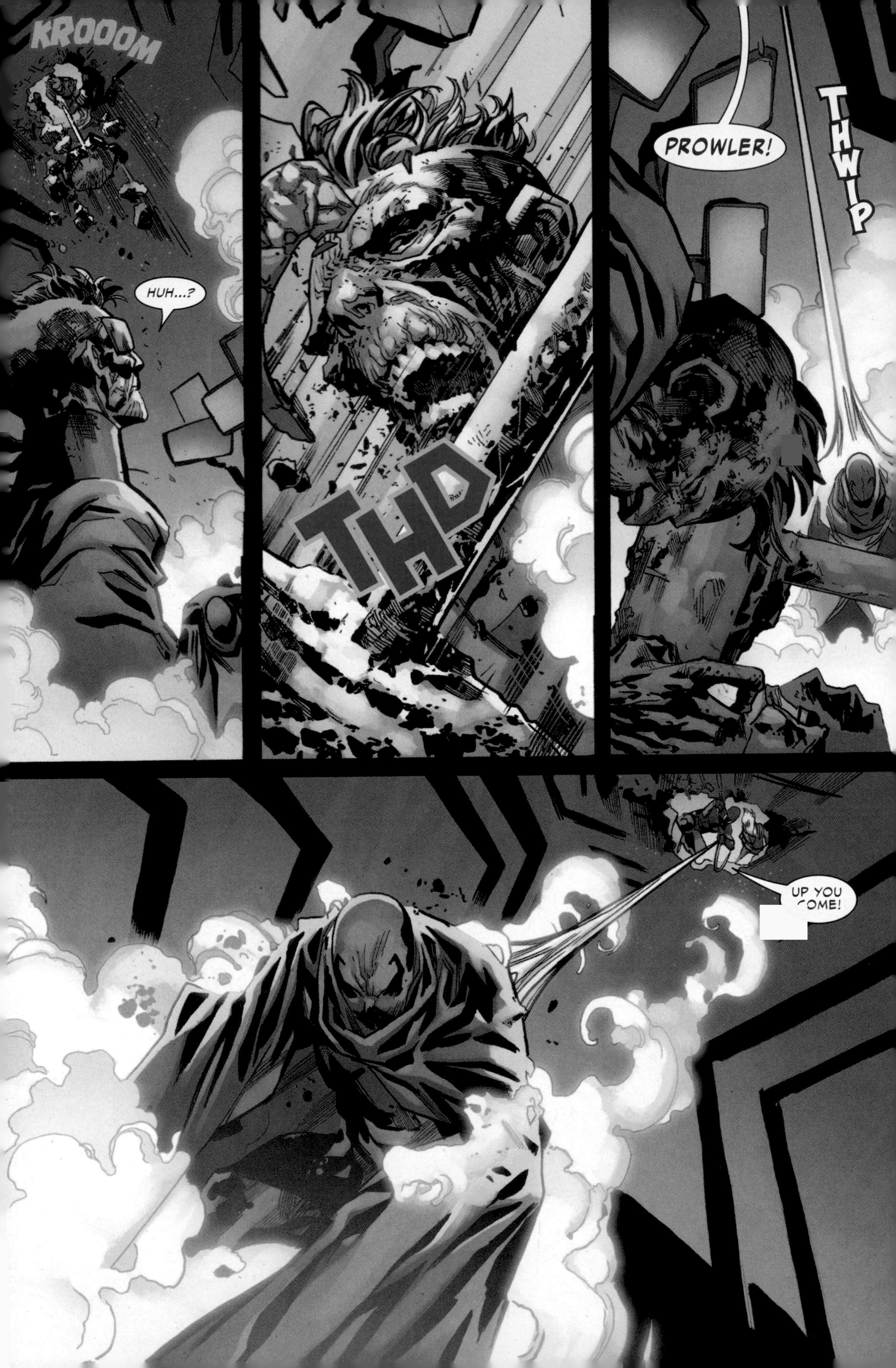
KROOOM
HUH...?
THD
PROWLER!
THWIP
UP YOU

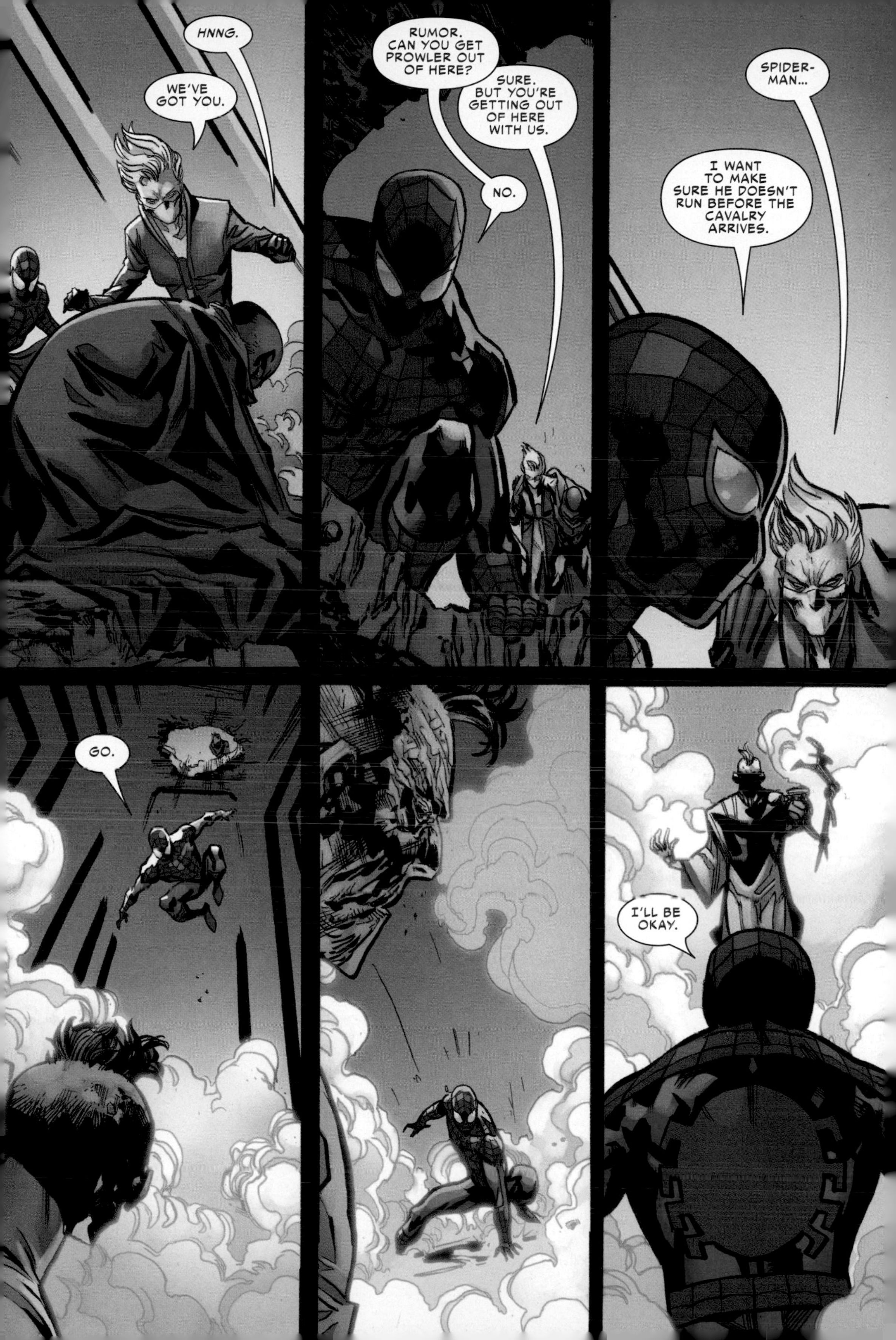
HNNG.
WE'VE GOT YOU.
RUMOR. CAN YOU GET PROWLER OUT OF HERE?
NO.
SURE. BUT YOU'RE GETTING OUT OF HERE WITH US.
SPIDER-MAN...
I WANT TO MAKE SURE HE DOESN'T RUN BEFORE THE CAVALRY ARRIVES.
GO.
I'LL BE OKAY.

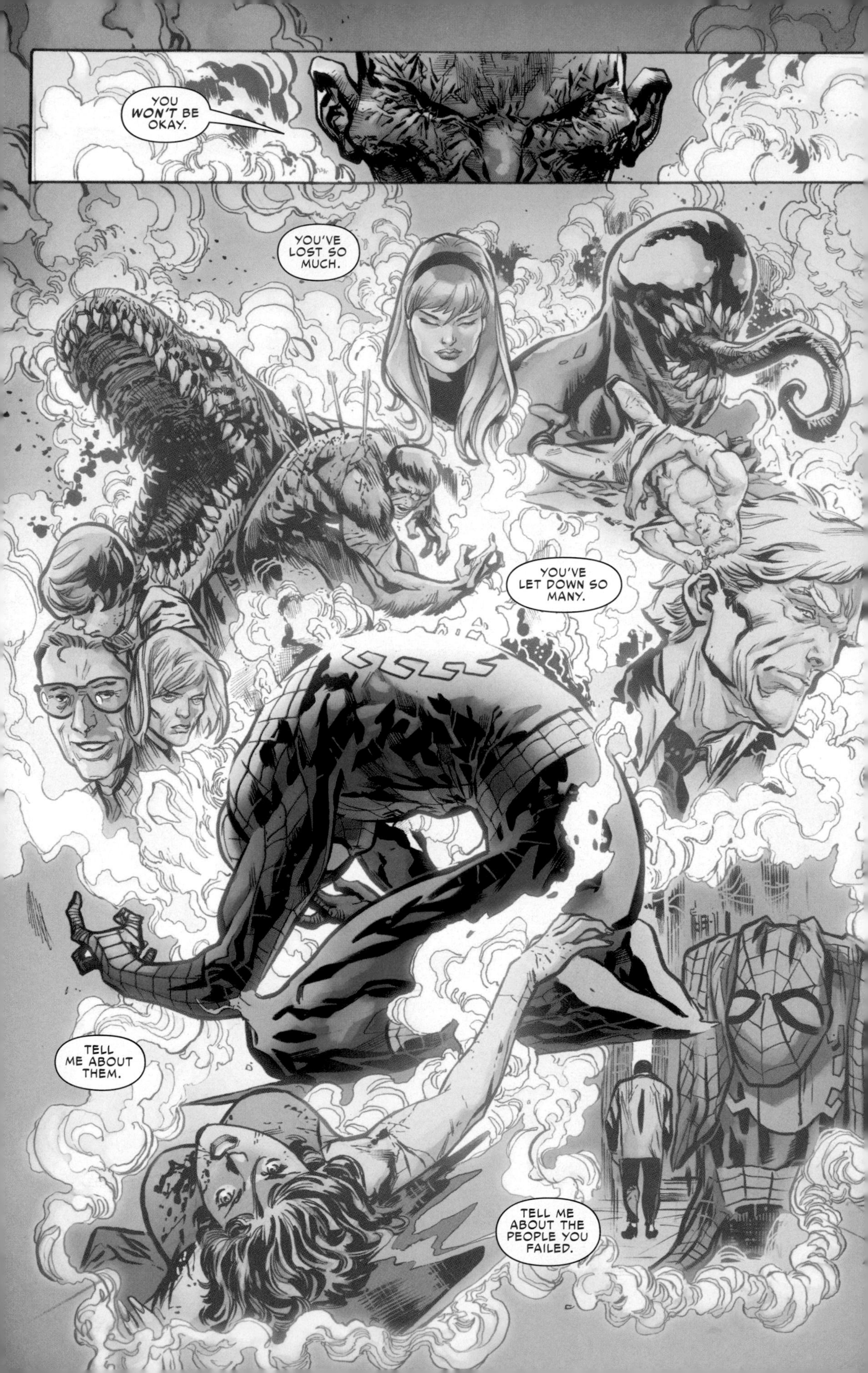
YOU WON'T BE OKAY.
YOU'VE LOST SO MUCH.
YOU'VE LET DOWN SO MANY.
TELL ME ABOUT THEM.
TELL ME ABOUT THE PEOPLE YOU FAILED.

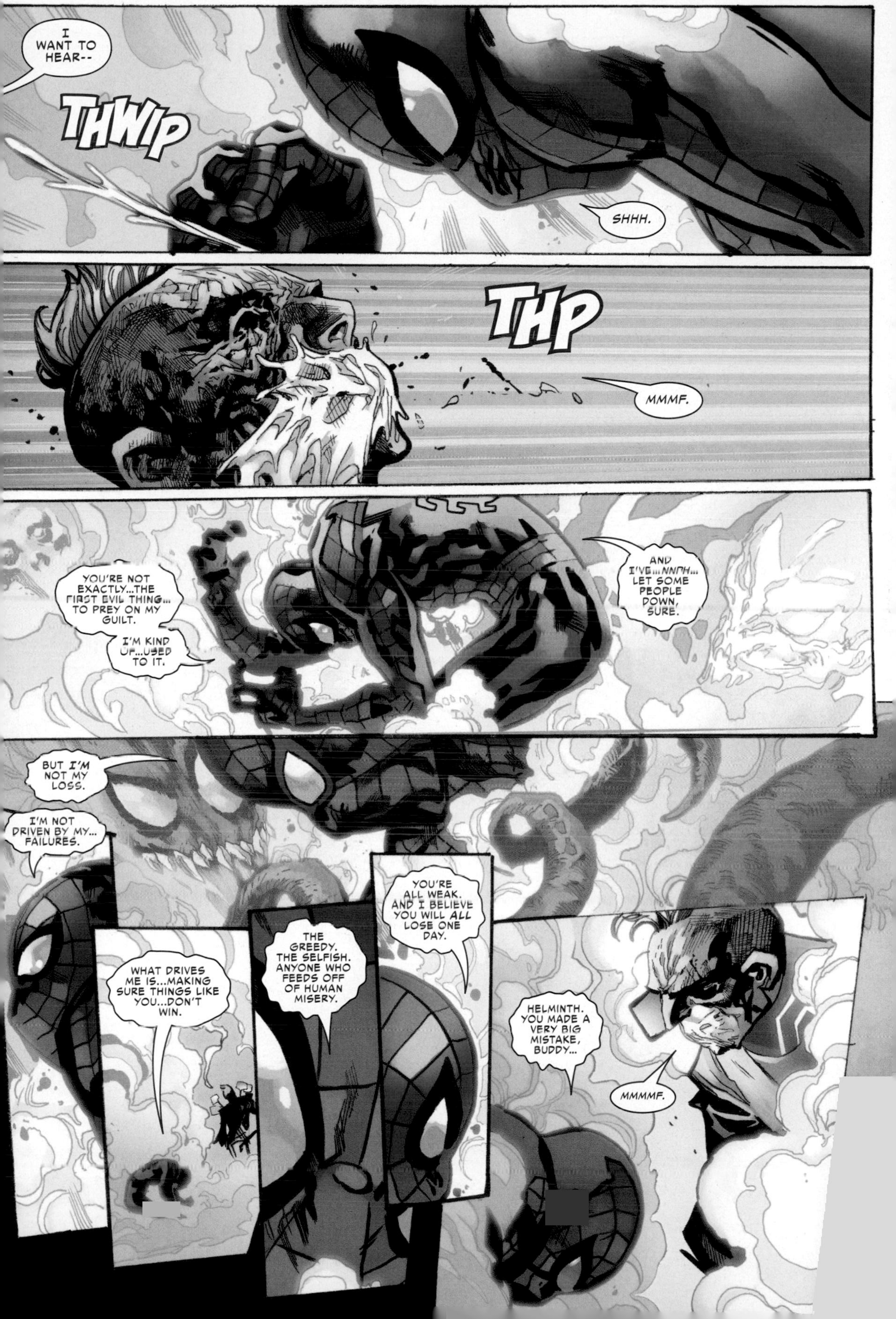
I WANT TO HEAR--
THWIP
SHHH.
THP
MMMF.
YOU'RE NOT EXACTLY...THE FIRST EVIL THING... TO PREY ON MY GUILT.
I'M KIND OF...USED TO IT.
AND I'VE...NNGH... LET SOME PEOPLE DOWN, SURE.
BUT I'M NOT MY LOSS.
I'M NOT DRIVEN BY MY... FAILURES.
WHAT DRIVES ME IS...MAKING SURE THINGS LIKE YOU...DON'T WIN.
THE GREEDY. THE SELFISH. ANYONE WHO FEEDS OFF OF HUMAN MISERY.
YOU'RE ALL WEAK. AND I BELIEVE YOU WILL ALL LOSE ONE DAY.
HELMINTH. YOU MADE A VERY BIG MISTAKE, BUDDY...
MMMMF.

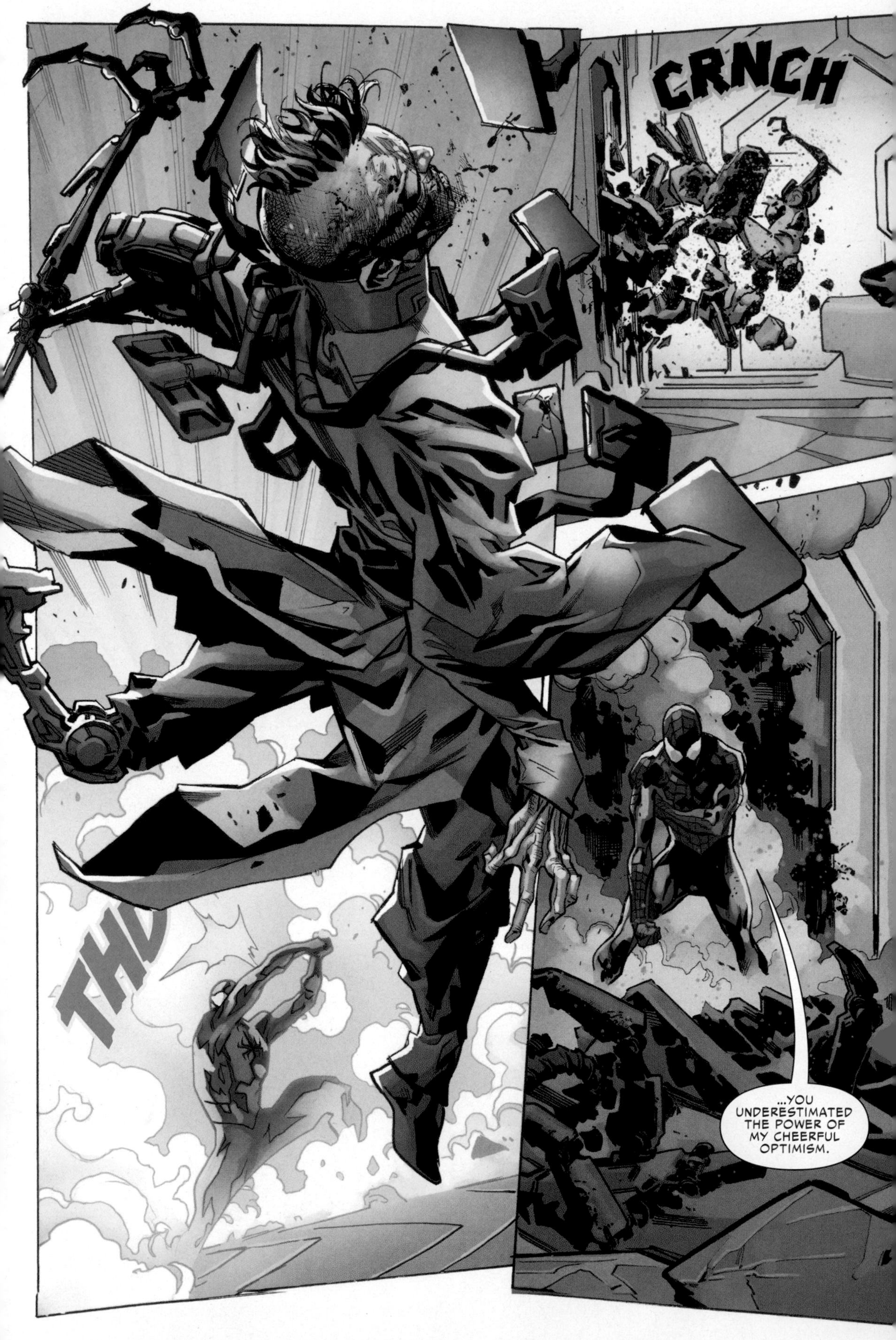
CRNCH
THD
...YOU UNDERESTIMATED THE POWER OF MY CHEERFUL OPTIMISM.

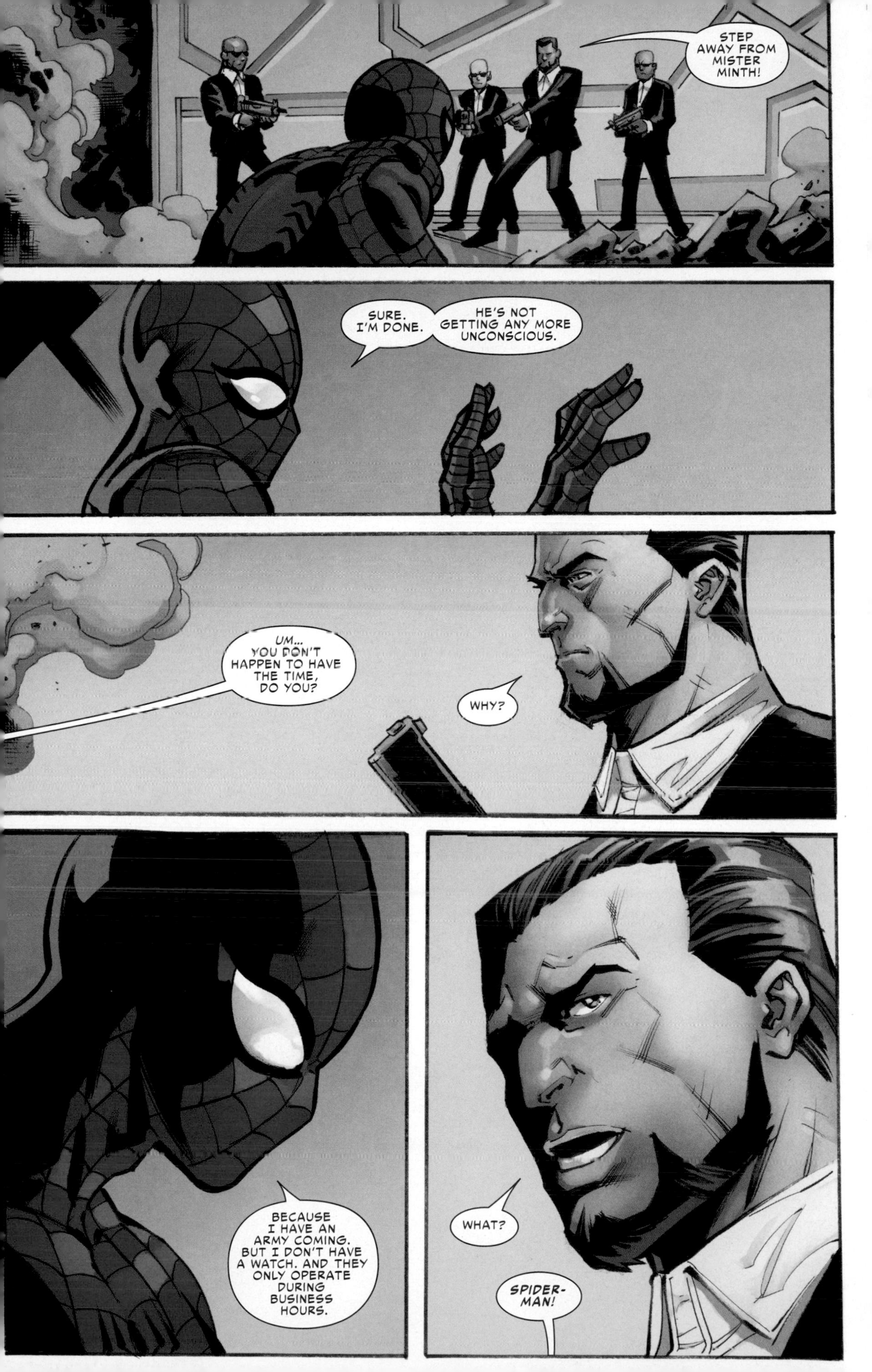
STEP AWAY FROM MISTER MINTH!
SURE. I'M DONE.
HE'S NOT GETTING ANY MORE UNCONSCIOUS.
UM... YOU DON'T HAPPEN TO HAVE THE TIME, DO YOU?
WHY?
BECAUSE I HAVE AN ARMY COMING. BUT I DON'T HAVE A WATCH. AND THEY ONLY OPERATE DURING BUSINESS HOURS.
WHAT?
SPIDER-MAN!

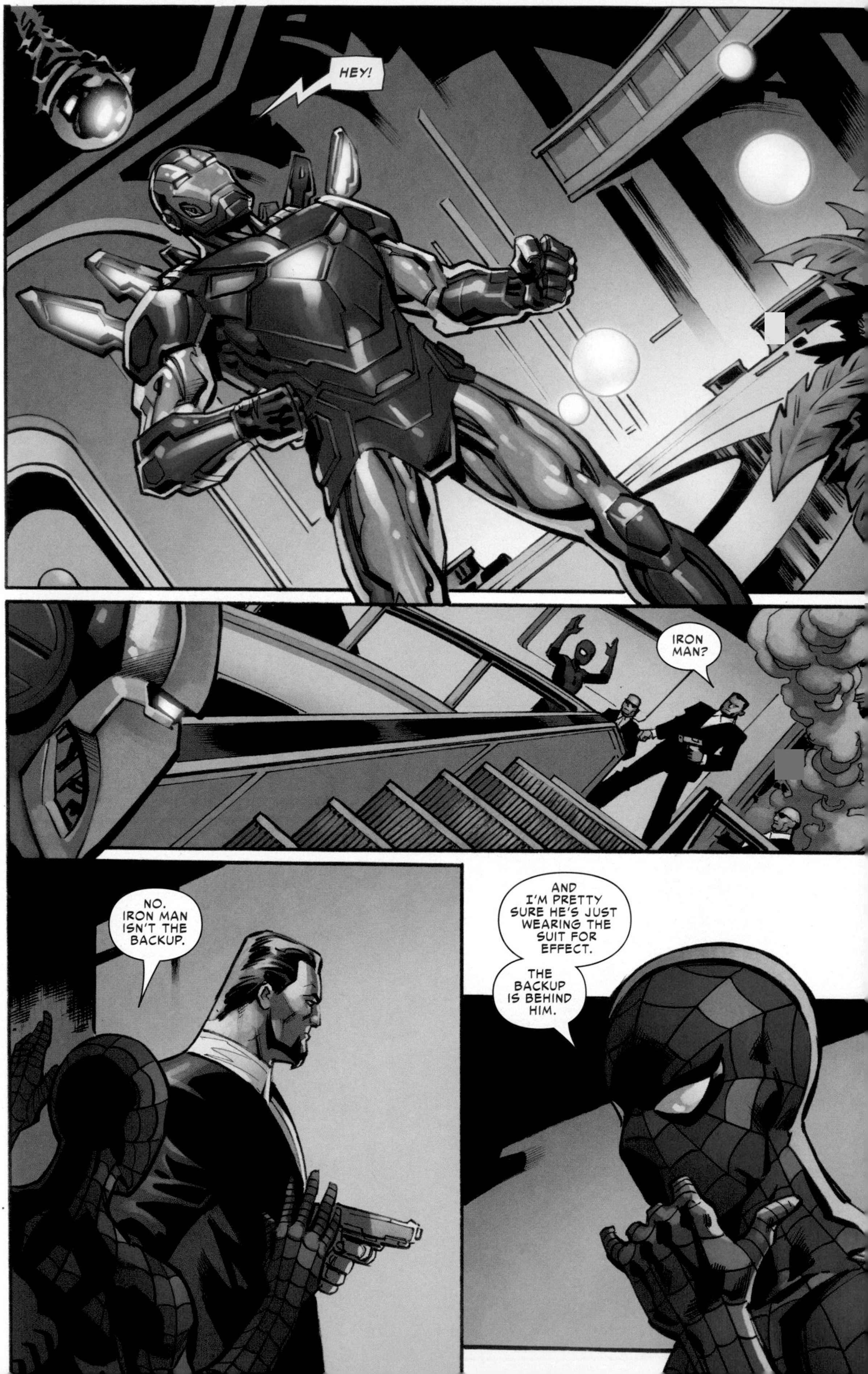
HEY!
IRON MAN?
NO. IRON MAN ISN'T THE BACKUP.
AND I'M PRETTY SURE HE'S JUST WEARING THE SUIT FOR EFFECT.
THE BACKUP IS BEHIND HIM.

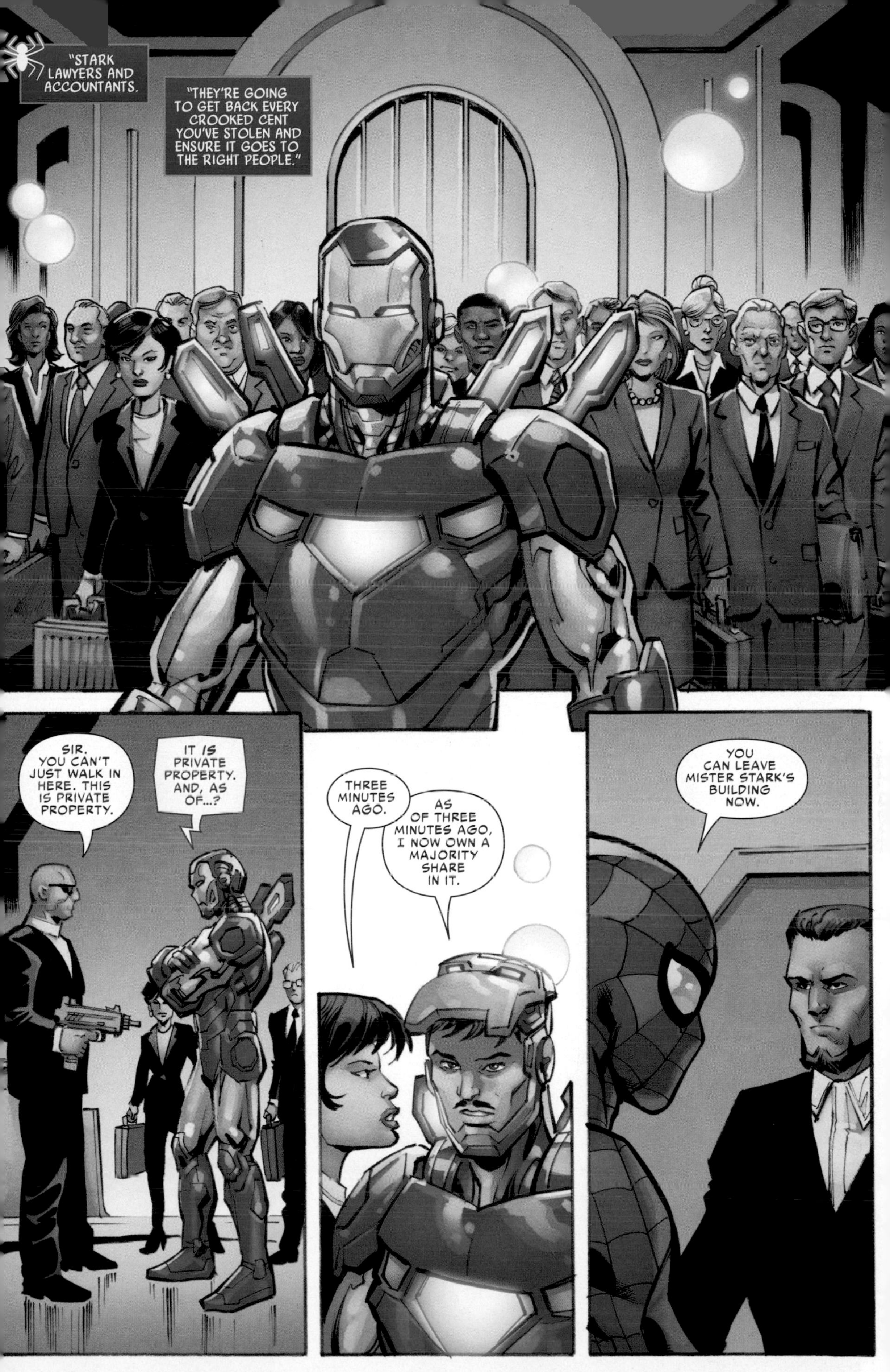
"STARK LAWYERS AND ACCOUNTANTS.
"THEY'RE GOING TO GET BACK EVERY CROOKED CENT YOU'VE STOLEN AND ENSURE IT GOES TO THE RIGHT PEOPLE."
SIR. YOU CAN'T JUST WALK IN HERE. THIS IS PRIVATE PROPERTY.
IT IS PRIVATE PROPERTY. AND, AS OF...?
THREE MINUTES AGO.
AS OF THREE MINUTES AGO, I NOW OWN A MAJORITY SHARE IN IT.
YOU CAN LEAVE MISTER STARK'S BUILDING NOW.

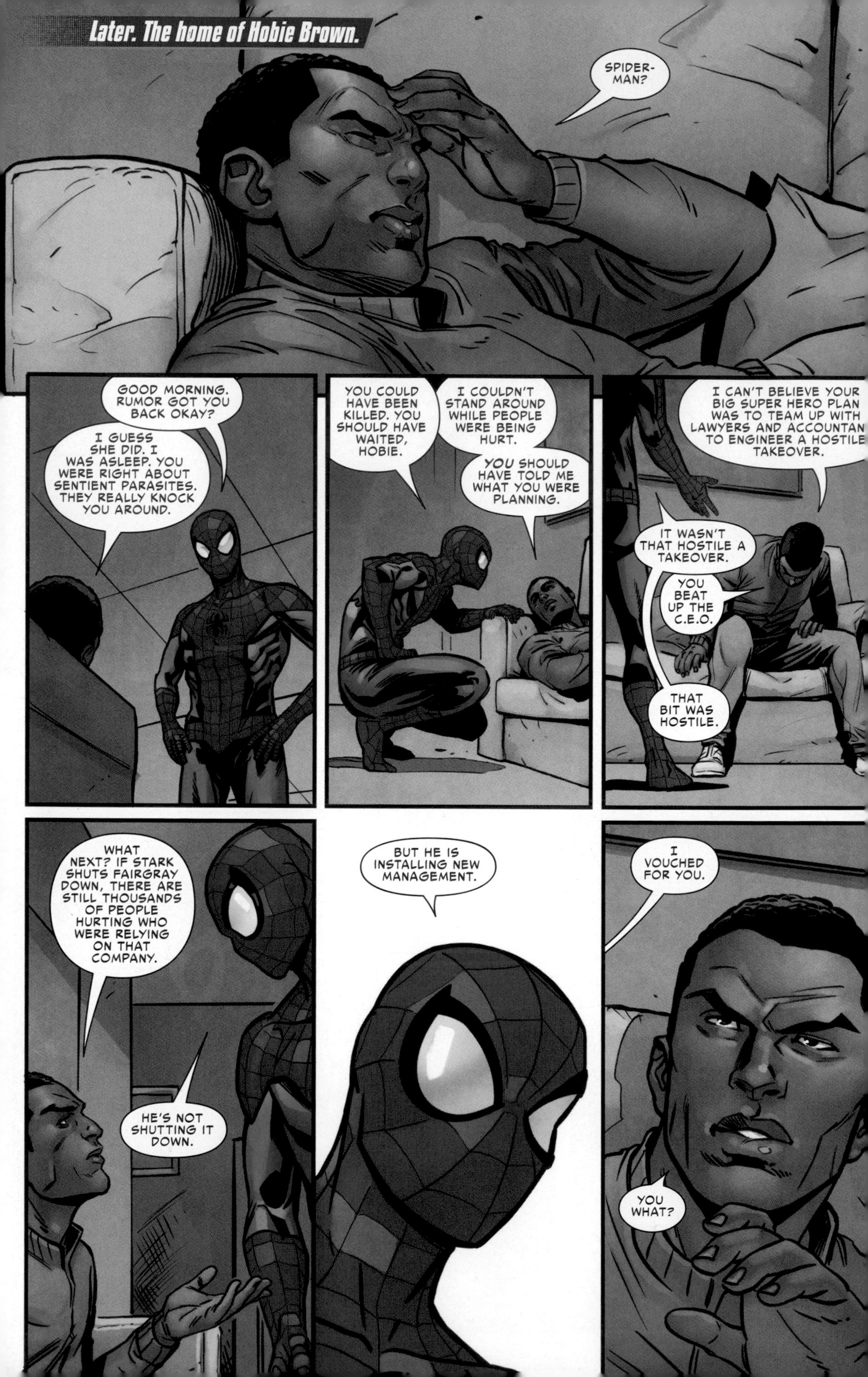
Later. The home of Hobie Brown.
SPIDER-MAN?
GOOD MORNING. RUMOR GOT YOU BACK OKAY?
I GUESS SHE DID. I WAS ASLEEP. YOU WERE RIGHT ABOUT SENTIENT PARASITES. THEY REALLY KNOCK YOU AROUND.
YOU COULD HAVE BEEN KILLED. YOU SHOULD HAVE WAITED, HOBIE.
I COULDN'T STAND AROUND WHILE PEOPLE WERE BEING HURT.
YOU SHOULD HAVE TOLD ME WHAT YOU WERE PLANNING.
I CAN'T BELIEVE YOUR BIG SUPER HERO PLAN WAS TO TEAM UP WITH LAWYERS AND ACCOUNTAN TO ENGINEER A HOSTILE TAKEOVER.
IT WASN'T THAT HOSTILE A TAKEOVER.
YOU BEAT UP THE C.E.O.
THAT BIT WAS HOSTILE.
WHAT NEXT? IF STARK SHUTS FAIRGRAY DOWN, THERE ARE STILL THOUSANDS OF PEOPLE HURTING WHO WERE RELYING ON THAT COMPANY.
HE'S NOT SHUTTING IT DOWN.
BUT HE IS INSTALLING NEW MANAGEMENT.
I VOUCHED FOR YOU.
YOU WHAT?

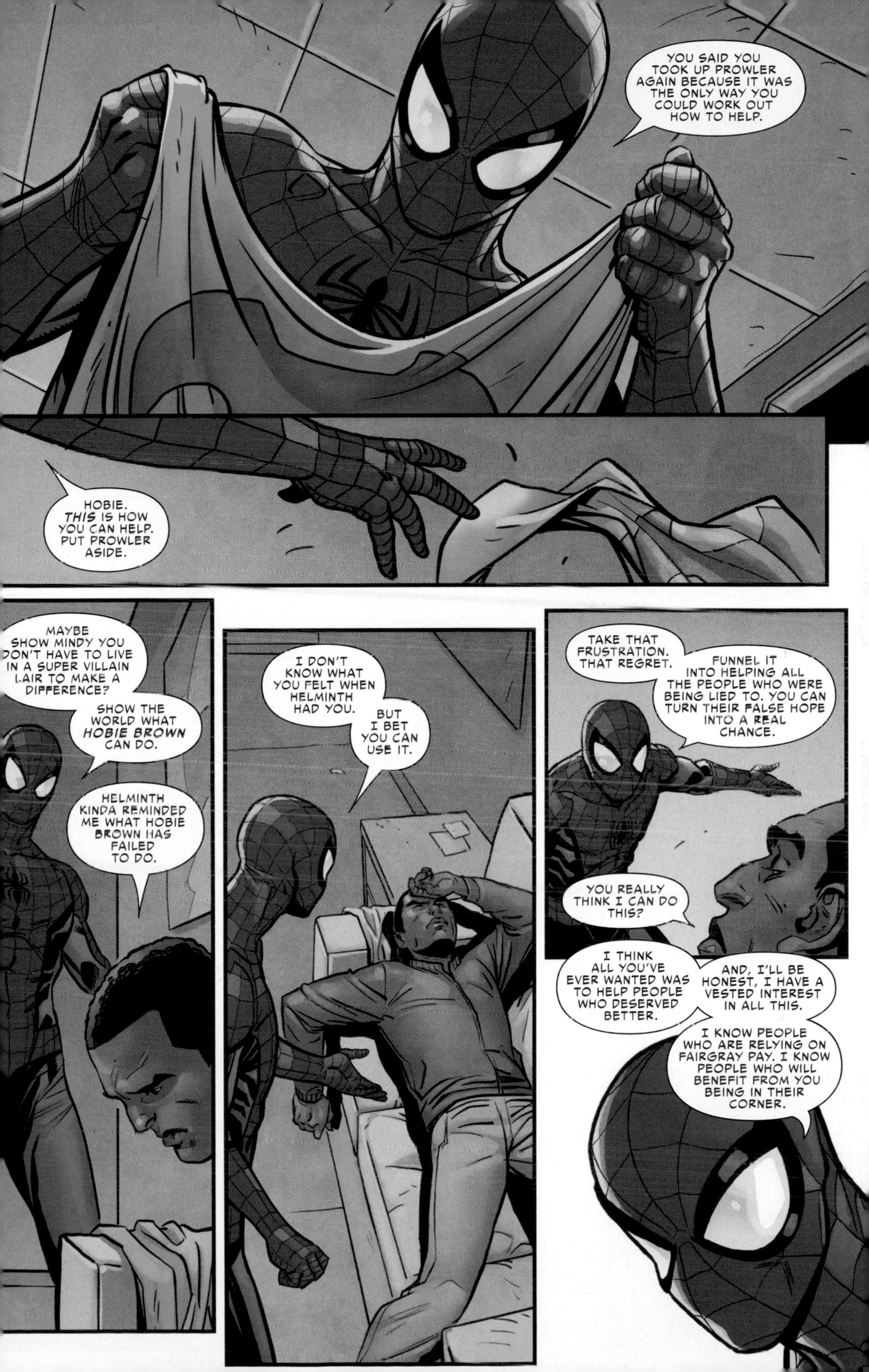
YOU SAID YOU TOOK UP PROWLER AGAIN BECAUSE IT WAS THE ONLY WAY YOU COULD WORK OUT HOW TO HELP.
HOBIE. THIS IS HOW YOU CAN HELP. PUT PROWLER ASIDE.
MAYBE SHOW MINDY YOU DON'T HAVE TO LIVE IN A SUPER VILLAIN LAIR TO MAKE A DIFFERENCE?
SHOW THE WORLD WHAT HOBIE BROWN CAN DO.
HELMINTH KINDA REMINDED ME WHAT HOBIE BROWN HAS FAILED TO DO.
I DON'T KNOW WHAT YOU FELT WHEN HELMINTH HAD YOU.
BUT I BET YOU CAN USE IT.
TAKE THAT FRUSTRATION. THAT REGRET.
FUNNEL IT INTO HELPING ALL THE PEOPLE WHO WERE BEING LIED TO. YOU CAN TURN THEIR FALSE HOPE INTO A REAL CHANCE.
YOU REALLY THINK I CAN DO THIS?
I THINK ALL YOU'VE EVER WANTED WAS TO HELP PEOPLE WHO DESERVED BETTER.
AND, I'LL BE HONEST, I HAVE A VESTED INTEREST IN ALL THIS.
I KNOW PEOPLE WHO ARE RELYING ON FAIRGRAY PAY. I KNOW PEOPLE WHO WILL BENEFIT FROM YOU BEING IN THEIR CORNER.

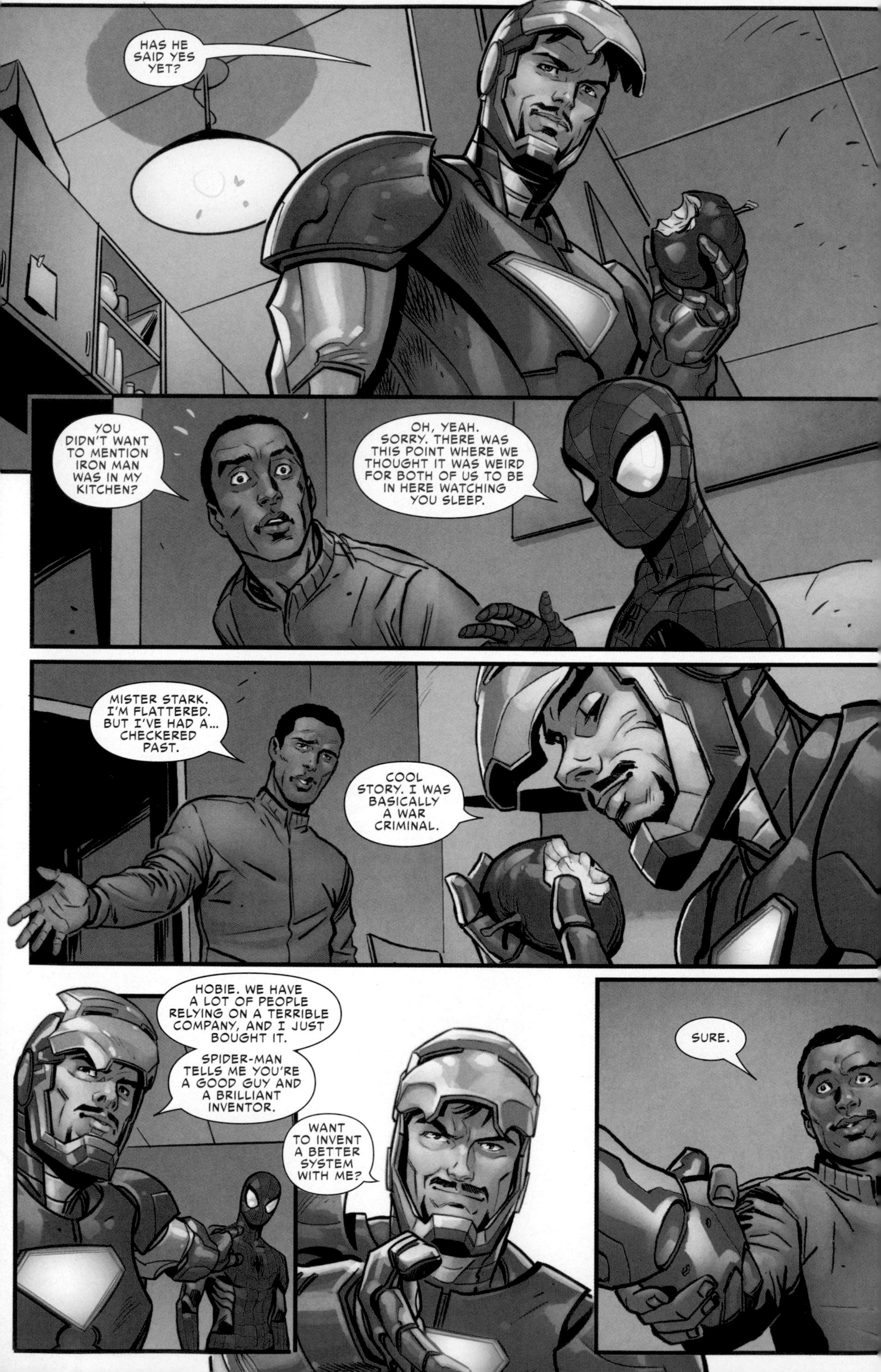
HAS HE SAID YES YET?
YOU DIDN'T WANT TO MENTION IRON MAN WAS IN MY KITCHEN?
OH, YEAH. SORRY. THERE WAS THIS POINT WHERE WE THOUGHT IT WAS WEIRD FOR BOTH OF US TO BE IN HERE WATCHING YOU SLEEP.
MISTER STARK. I'M FLATTERED. BUT I'VE HAD A... CHECKERED PAST.
COOL STORY. I WAS BASICALLY A WAR CRIMINAL.
HOBIE. WE HAVE A LOT OF PEOPLE RELYING ON A TERRIBLE COMPANY, AND I JUST BOUGHT IT.
SPIDER-MAN TELLS ME YOU'RE A GOOD GUY AND A BRILLIANT INVENTOR.
WANT TO INVENT A BETTER SYSTEM WITH ME?
SURE.

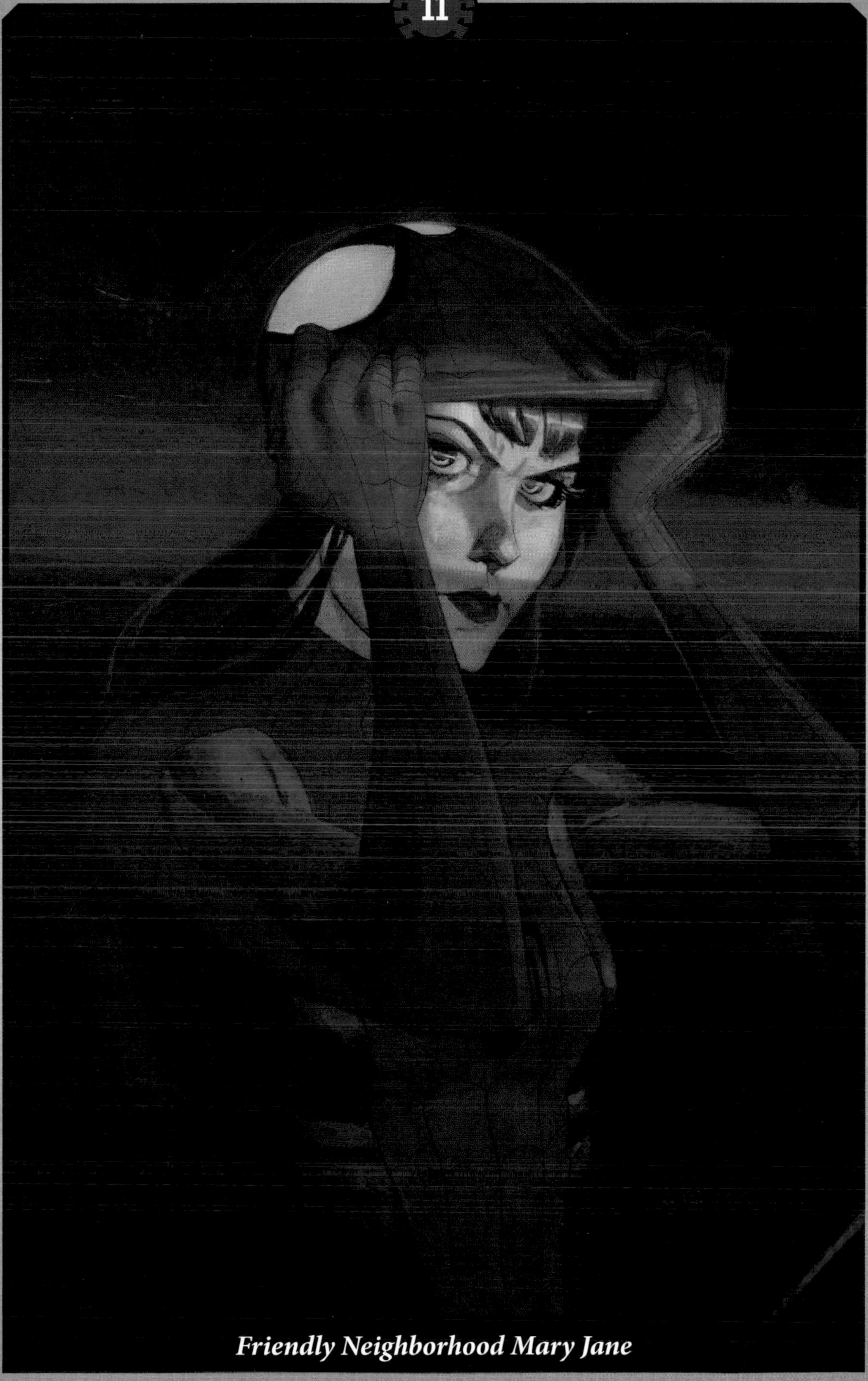

Friendly Neighborhood Mary Jane

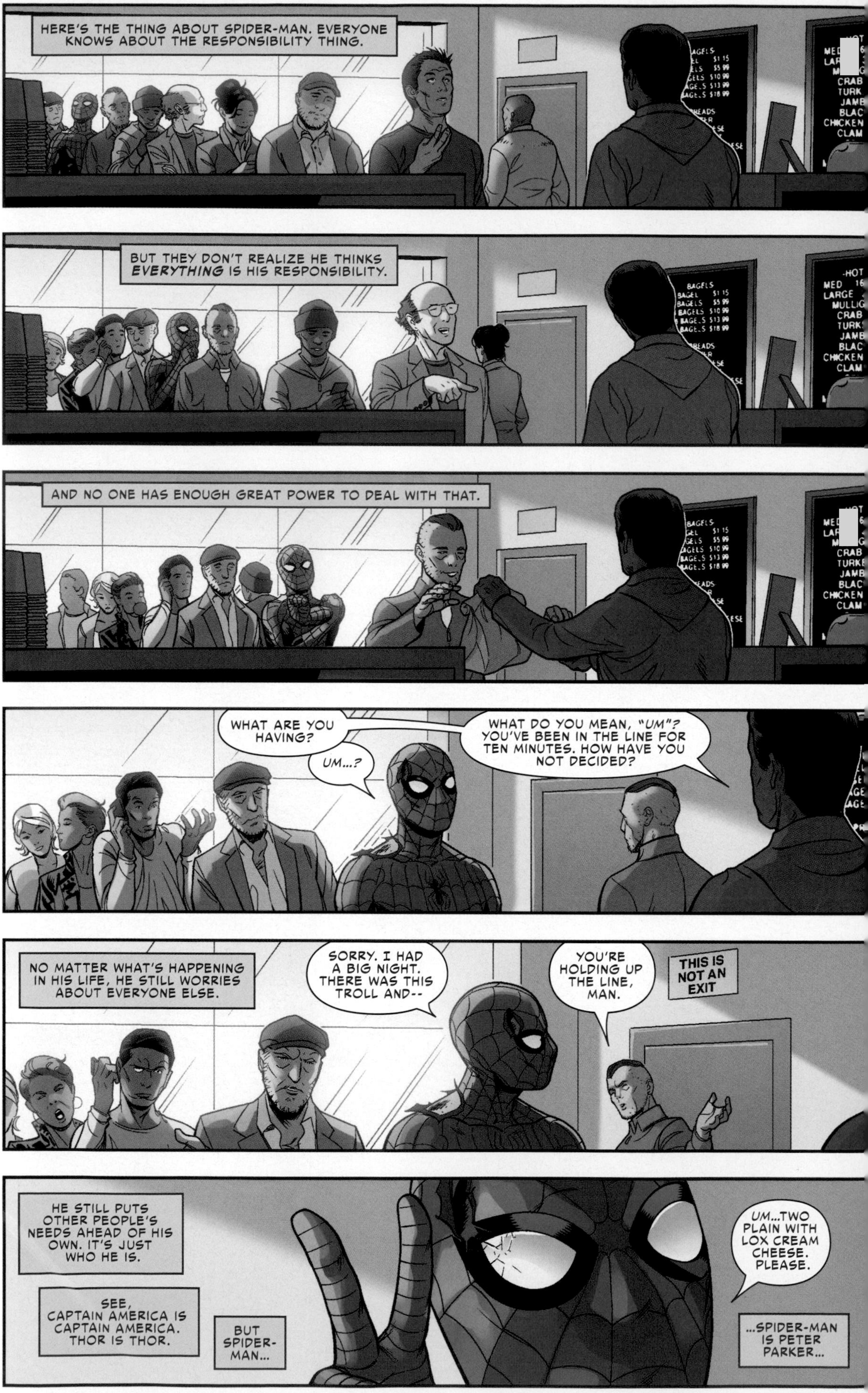

HERE'S THE THING ABOUT SPIDER-MAN. EVERYONE KNOWS ABOUT THE RESPONSIBILITY THING.
BUT THEY DON'T REALIZE HE THINKS *EVERYTHING* IS HIS RESPONSIBILITY.
AND NO ONE HAS ENOUGH GREAT POWER TO DEAL WITH THAT.
WHAT ARE YOU HAVING?
UM...?
WHAT DO YOU MEAN, *"UM"*? YOU'VE BEEN IN THE LINE FOR TEN MINUTES. HOW HAVE YOU NOT DECIDED?
NO MATTER WHAT'S HAPPENING IN HIS LIFE, HE STILL WORRIES ABOUT EVERYONE ELSE.
SORRY. I HAD A BIG NIGHT. THERE WAS THIS TROLL AND--
YOU'RE HOLDING UP THE LINE, MAN.
THIS IS NOT AN EXIT
HE STILL PUTS OTHER PEOPLE'S NEEDS AHEAD OF HIS OWN. IT'S JUST WHO HE IS.
SEE, CAPTAIN AMERICA IS CAPTAIN AMERICA. THOR IS THOR.
BUT SPIDER-MAN...
UM...TWO PLAIN WITH LOX CREAM CHEESE. PLEASE.
...SPIDER-MAN IS PETER PARKER...

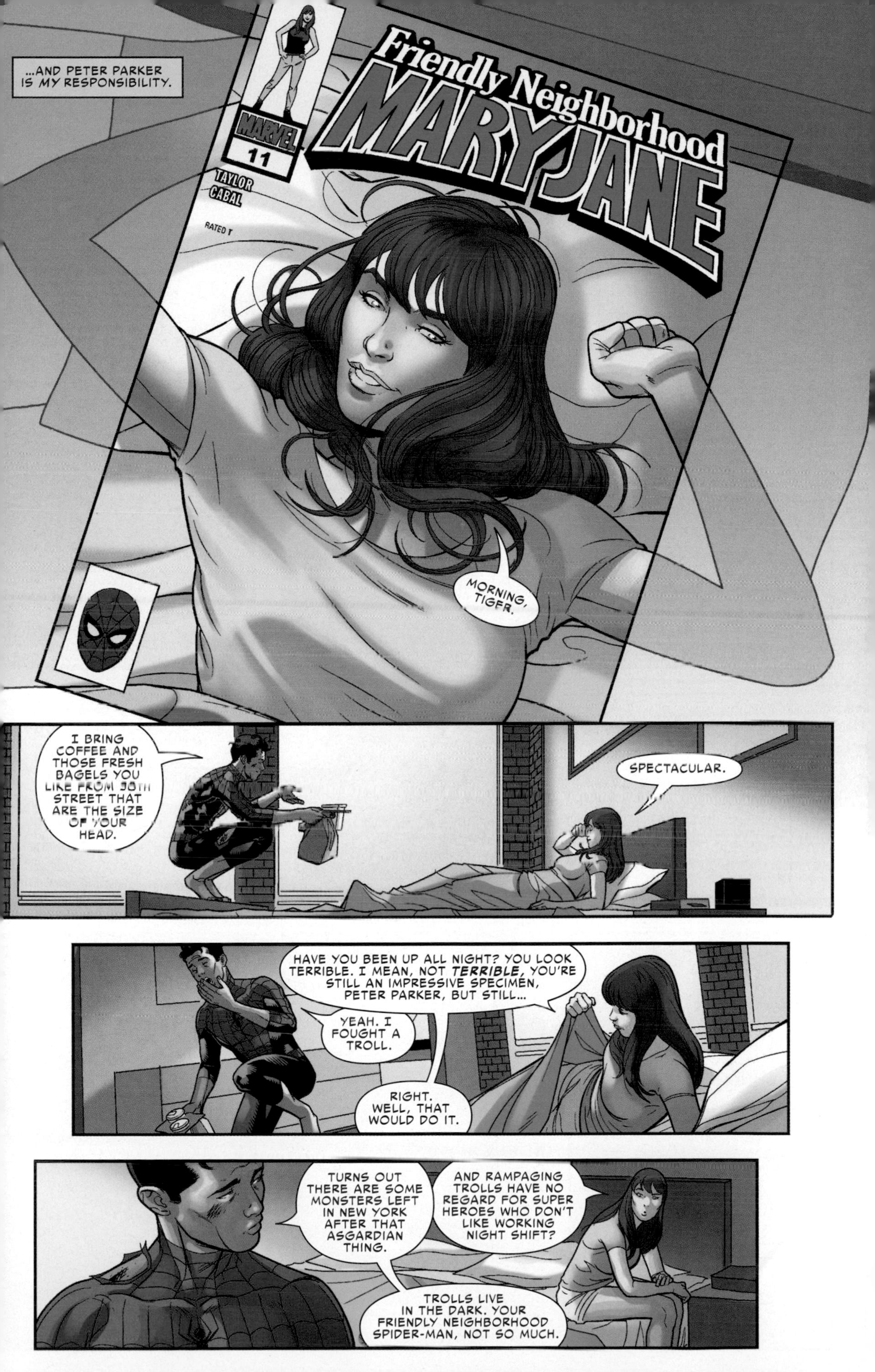
...AND PETER PARKER IS MY RESPONSIBILITY.
Friendly Neighborhood MARY JANE
MARVEL
11
TAYLOR
CABAL
RATED T
MORNING, TIGER.
I BRING COFFEE AND THOSE FRESH BAGELS YOU LIKE FROM 30TH STREET THAT ARE THE SIZE OF YOUR HEAD.
SPECTACULAR.
HAVE YOU BEEN UP ALL NIGHT? YOU LOOK TERRIBLE. I MEAN, NOT TERRIBLE, YOU'RE STILL AN IMPRESSIVE SPECIMEN, PETER PARKER, BUT STILL...
YEAH. I FOUGHT A TROLL.
RIGHT. WELL, THAT WOULD DO IT.
TURNS OUT THERE ARE SOME MONSTERS LEFT IN NEW YORK AFTER THAT ASGARDIAN THING.
AND RAMPAGING TROLLS HAVE NO REGARD FOR SUPER HEROES WHO DON'T LIKE WORKING NIGHT SHIFT?
TROLLS LIVE IN THE DARK. YOUR FRIENDLY NEIGHBORHOOD SPIDER-MAN, NOT SO MUCH.

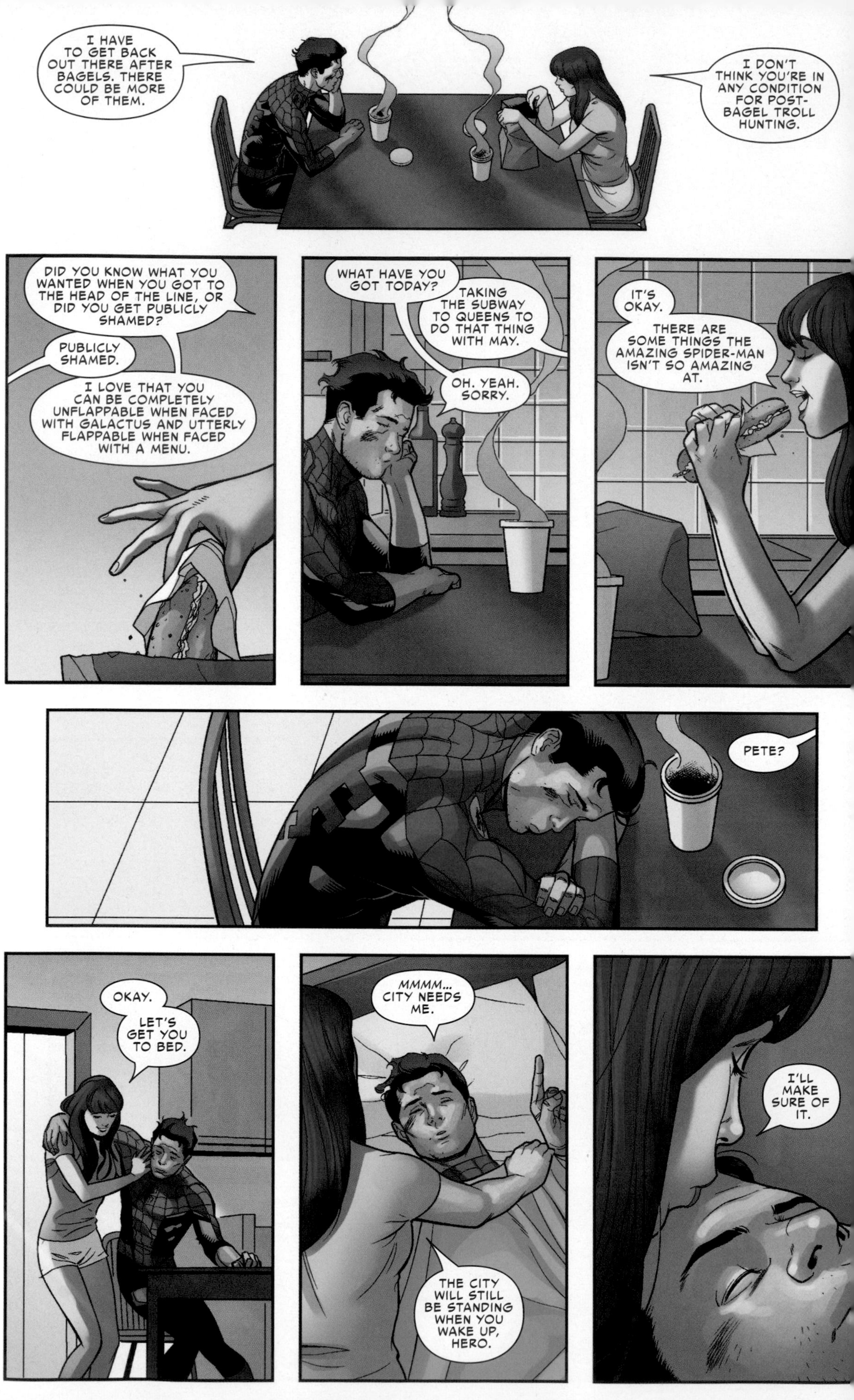
I HAVE TO GET BACK OUT THERE AFTER BAGELS. THERE COULD BE MORE OF THEM.
I DON'T THINK YOU'RE IN ANY CONDITION FOR POST-BAGEL TROLL HUNTING.
DID YOU KNOW WHAT YOU WANTED WHEN YOU GOT TO THE HEAD OF THE LINE, OR DID YOU GET PUBLICLY SHAMED?
PUBLICLY SHAMED.
I LOVE THAT YOU CAN BE COMPLETELY UNFLAPPABLE WHEN FACED WITH GALACTUS AND UTTERLY FLAPPABLE WHEN FACED WITH A MENU.
WHAT HAVE YOU GOT TODAY?
TAKING THE SUBWAY TO QUEENS TO DO THAT THING WITH MAY.
OH. YEAH. SORRY.
IT'S OKAY.
THERE ARE SOME THINGS THE AMAZING SPIDER-MAN ISN'T SO AMAZING AT.
PETE?
OKAY.
LET'S GET YOU TO BED.
MMMM... CITY NEEDS ME.
THE CITY WILL STILL BE STANDING WHEN YOU WAKE UP, HERO.
I'LL MAKE SURE OF IT.

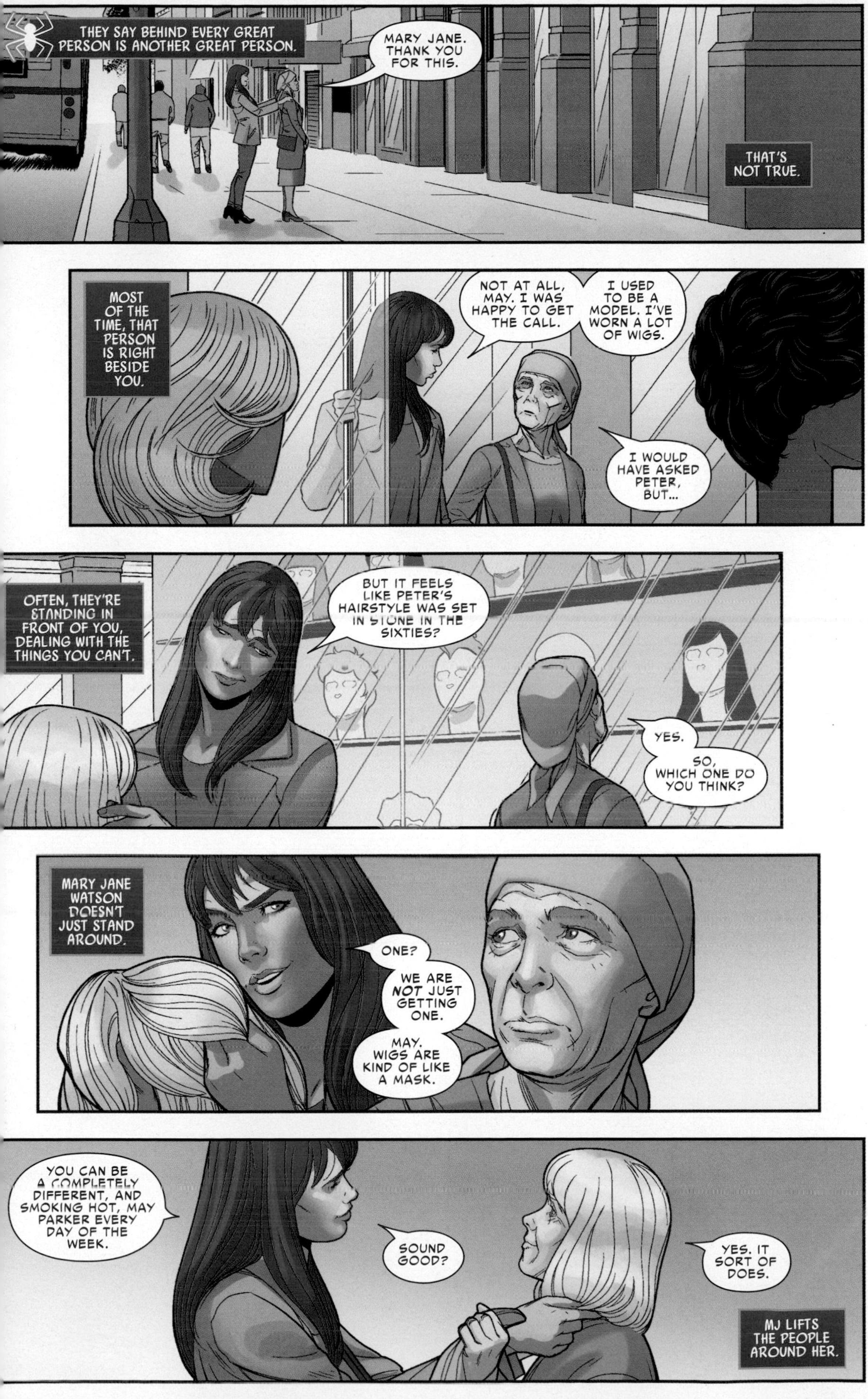
THEY SAY BEHIND EVERY GREAT PERSON IS ANOTHER GREAT PERSON.
MARY JANE. THANK YOU FOR THIS.
THAT'S NOT TRUE.
MOST OF THE TIME, THAT PERSON IS RIGHT BESIDE YOU.
NOT AT ALL, MAY. I WAS HAPPY TO GET THE CALL.
I USED TO BE A MODEL. I'VE WORN A LOT OF WIGS.
I WOULD HAVE ASKED PETER, BUT...
OFTEN, THEY'RE STANDING IN FRONT OF YOU, DEALING WITH THE THINGS YOU CAN'T.
BUT IT FEELS LIKE PETER'S HAIRSTYLE WAS SET IN STONE IN THE SIXTIES?
YES.
SO, WHICH ONE DO YOU THINK?
MARY JANE WATSON DOESN'T JUST STAND AROUND.
ONE?
WE ARE NOT JUST GETTING ONE.
MAY. WIGS ARE KIND OF LIKE A MASK.
YOU CAN BE A COMPLETELY DIFFERENT, AND SMOKING HOT, MAY PARKER EVERY DAY OF THE WEEK.
SOUND GOOD?
YES. IT SORT OF DOES.
MJ LIFTS THE PEOPLE AROUND HER.

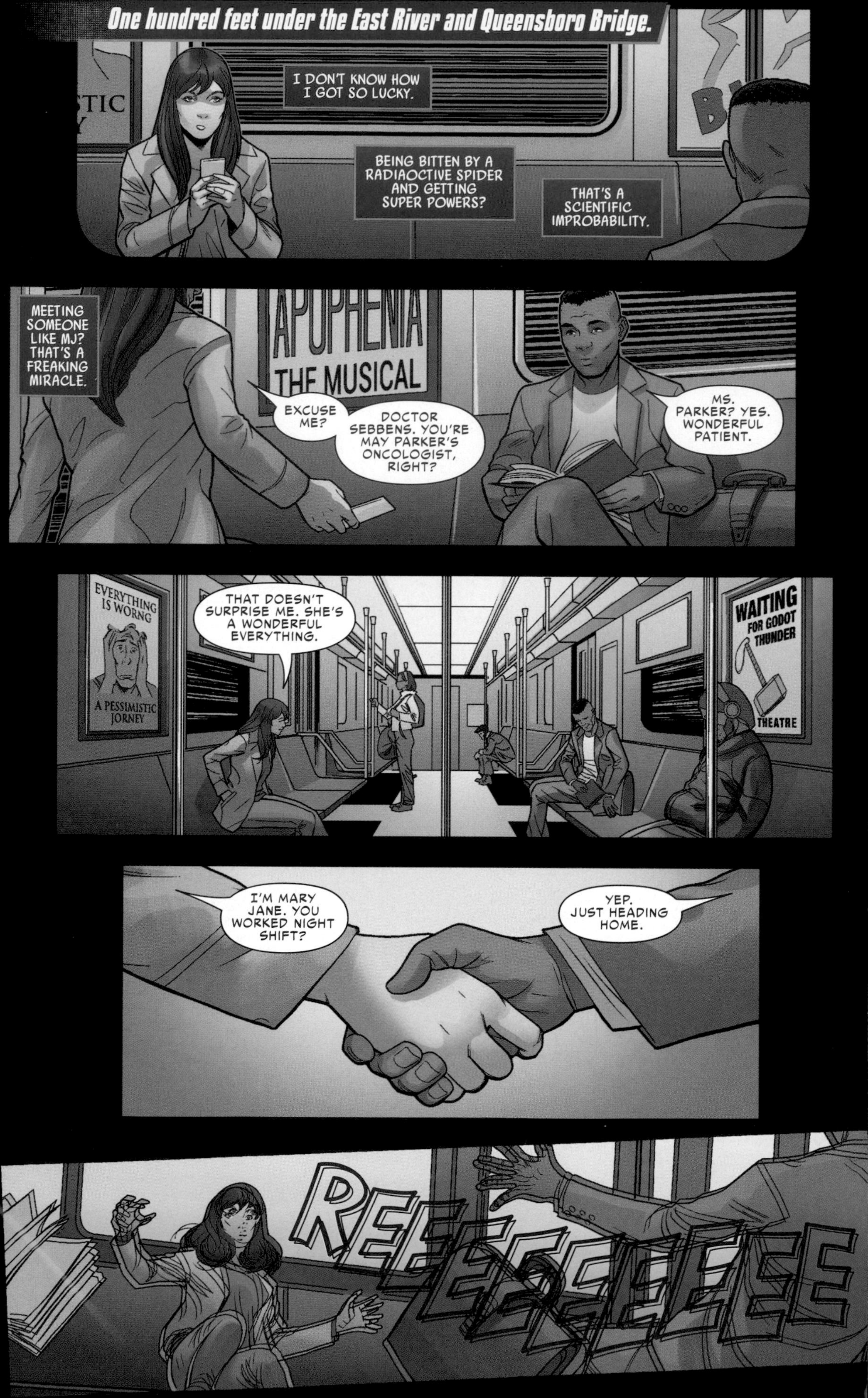
One hundred feet under the East River and Queensboro Bridge.
I DON'T KNOW HOW I GOT SO LUCKY.
BEING BITTEN BY A RADIAOCTIVE SPIDER AND GETTING SUPER POWERS?
THAT'S A SCIENTIFIC IMPROBABILITY.
MEETING SOMEONE LIKE MJ? THAT'S A FREAKING MIRACLE.
APOPHENIA THE MUSICAL
EXCUSE ME?
DOCTOR SEBBENS. YOU'RE MAY PARKER'S ONCOLOGIST, RIGHT?
MS. PARKER? YES. WONDERFUL PATIENT.
EVERYTHING IS WORNG
A PESSIMISTIC JORNEY
THAT DOESN'T SURPRISE ME. SHE'S A WONDERFUL EVERYTHING.
WAITING FOR GODOT THUNDER
THEATRE
I'M MARY JANE. YOU WORKED NIGHT SHIFT?
YEP. JUST HEADING HOME.
REEEEEEEEEEE

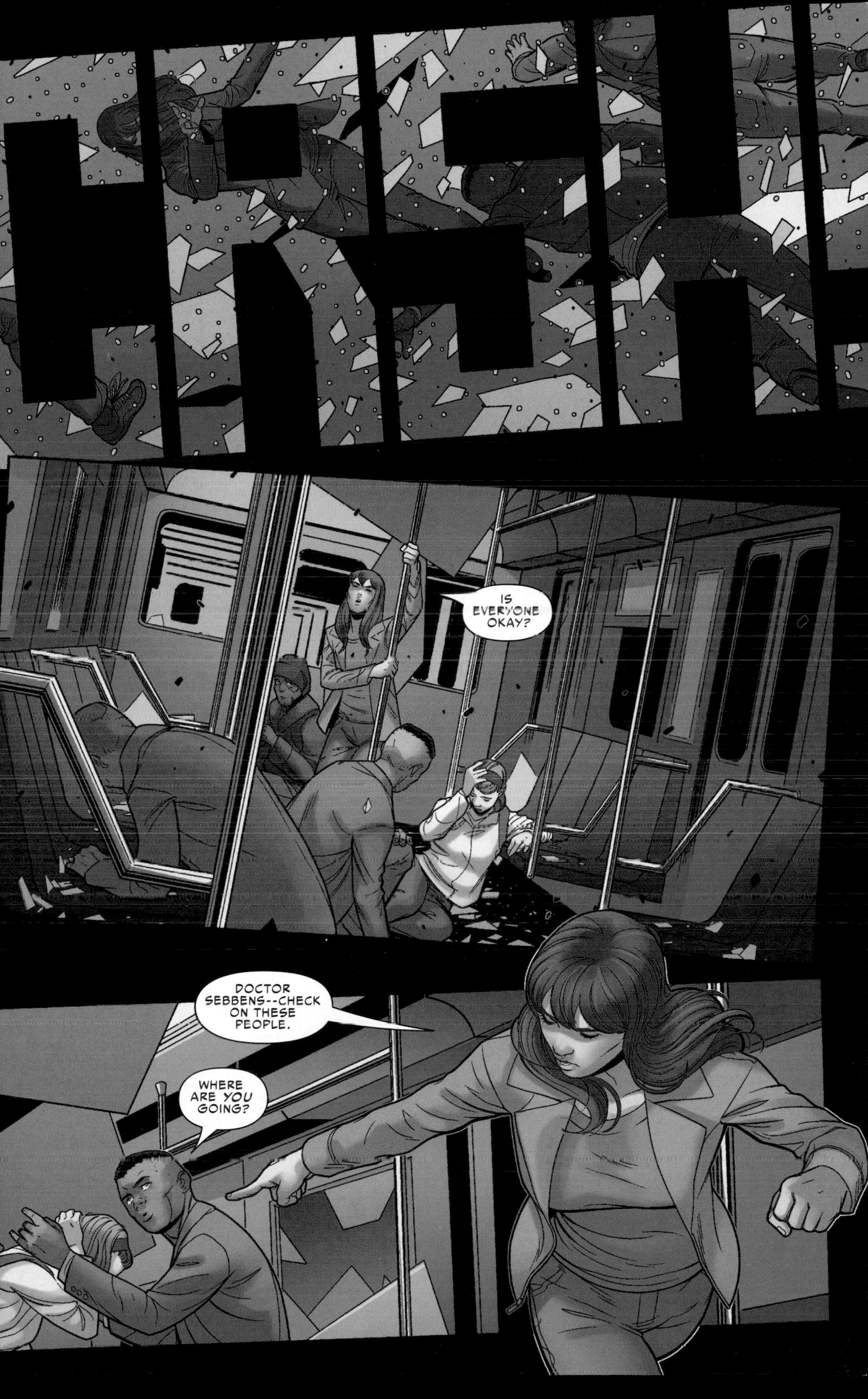
IS EVERYONE OKAY?
DOCTOR SEBBENS--CHECK ON THESE PEOPLE.
WHERE ARE YOU GOING?

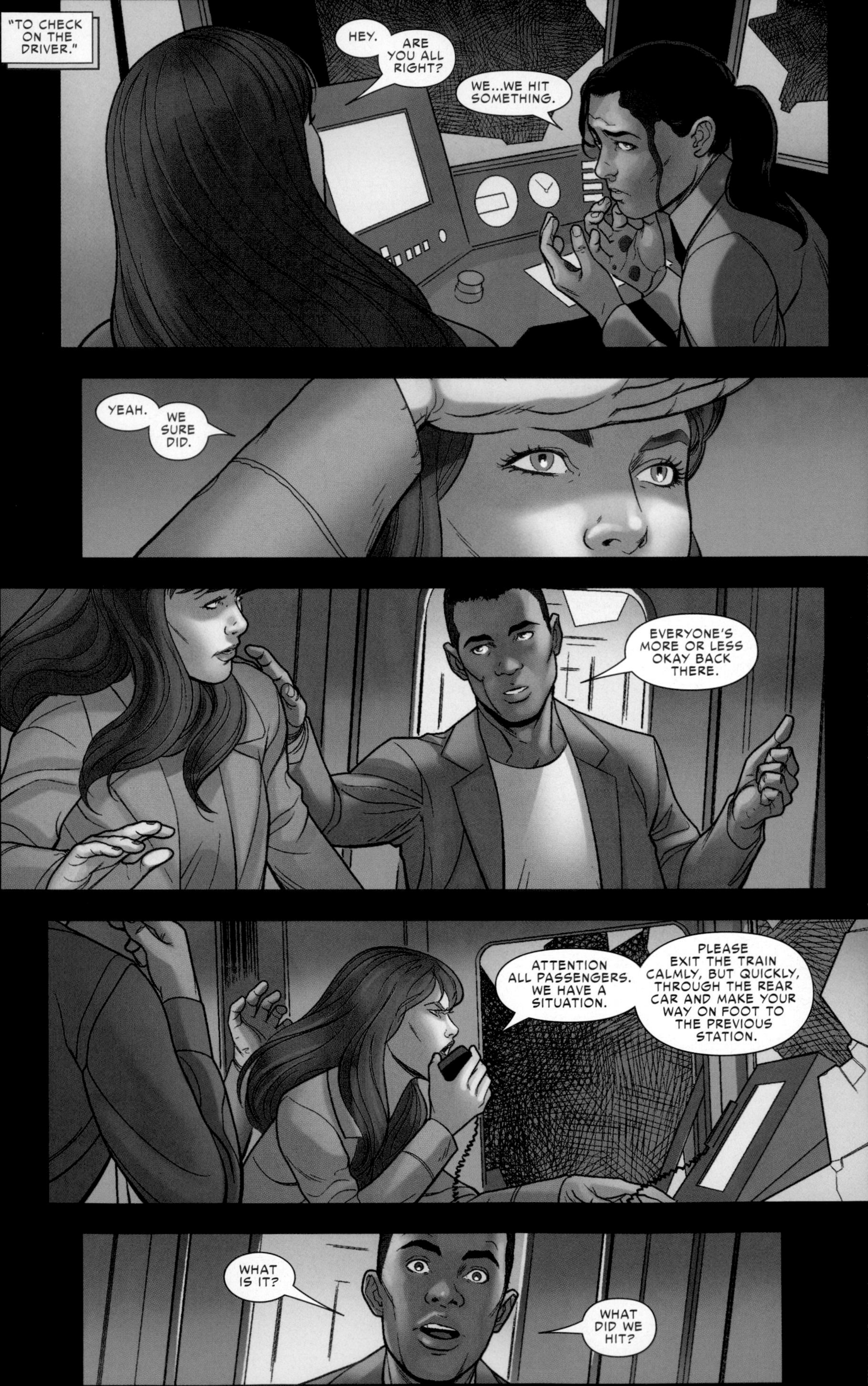
"TO CHECK ON THE DRIVER."
HEY.
ARE YOU ALL RIGHT?
WE...WE HIT SOMETHING.
YEAH.
WE SURE DID.
EVERYONE'S MORE OR LESS OKAY BACK THERE.
ATTENTION ALL PASSENGERS. WE HAVE A SITUATION.
PLEASE EXIT THE TRAIN CALMLY, BUT QUICKLY, THROUGH THE REAR CAR AND MAKE YOUR WAY ON FOOT TO THE PREVIOUS STATION.
WHAT IS IT?
WHAT DID WE HIT?

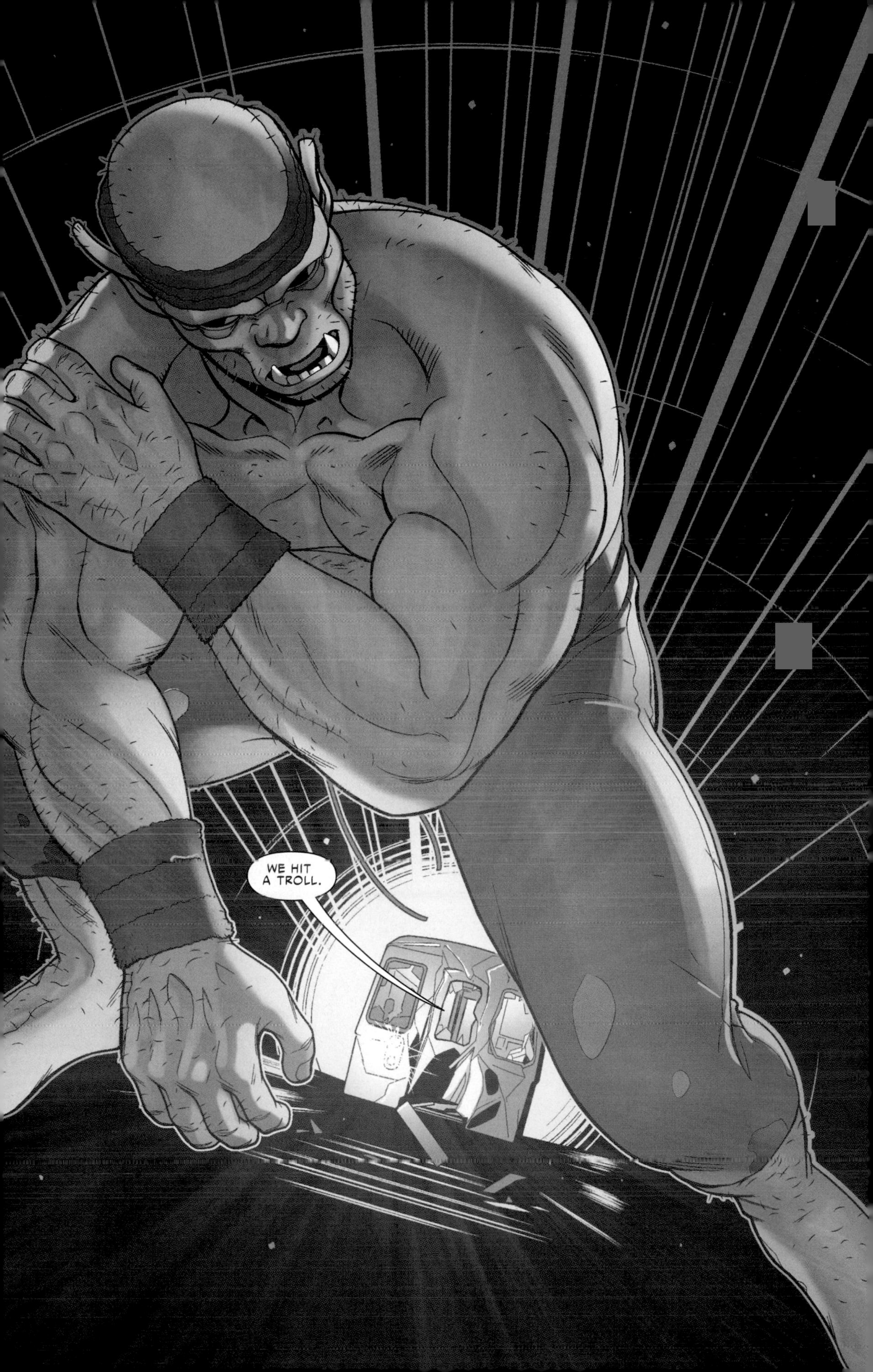
WE HIT A TROLL.

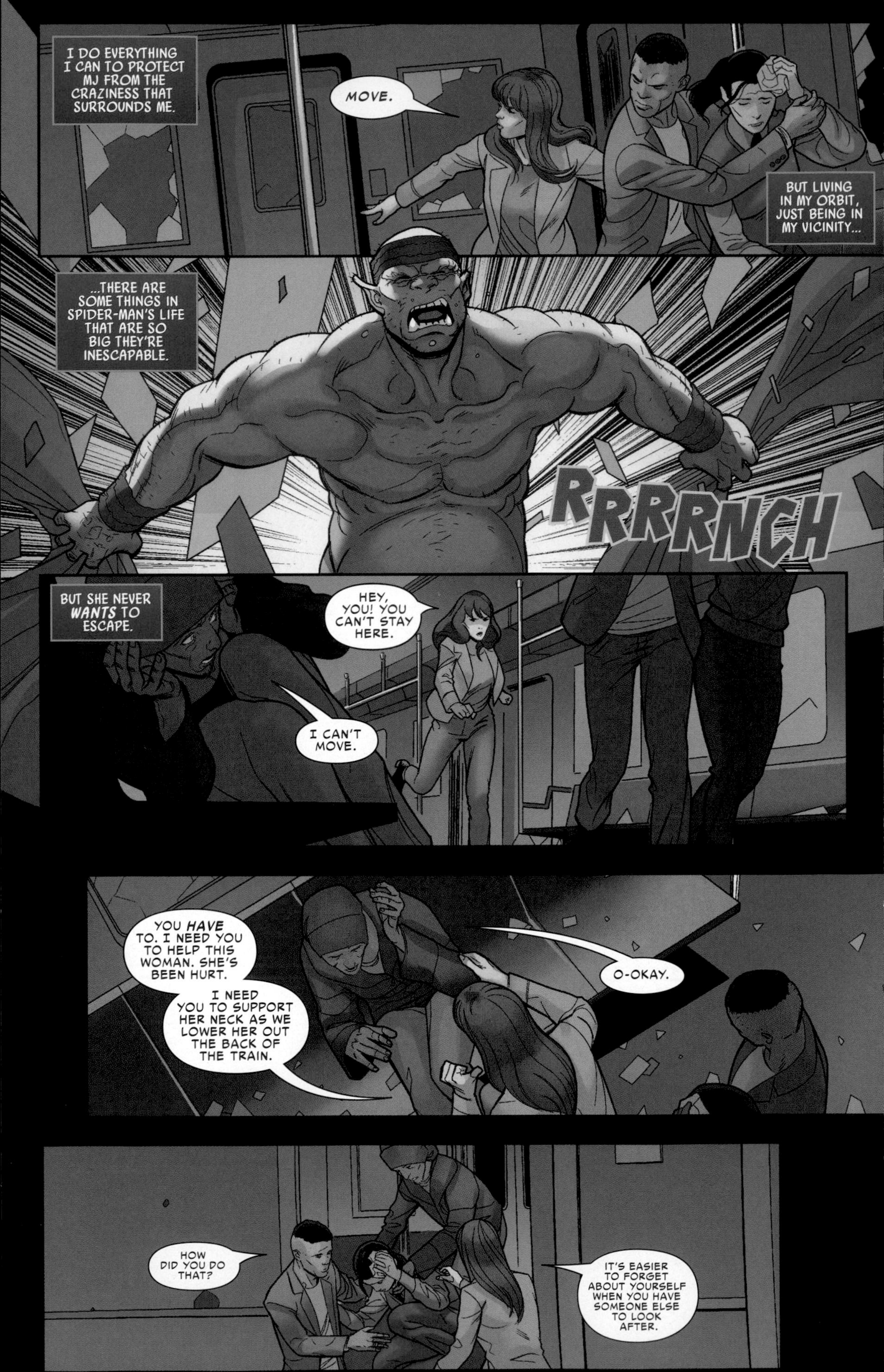
I DO EVERYTHING I CAN TO PROTECT MJ FROM THE CRAZINESS THAT SURROUNDS ME.
MOVE.
BUT LIVING IN MY ORBIT, JUST BEING IN MY VICINITY...
...THERE ARE SOME THINGS IN SPIDER-MAN'S LIFE THAT ARE SO BIG THEY'RE INESCAPABLE.
RRRRNCH
BUT SHE NEVER WANTS TO ESCAPE.
HEY, YOU! YOU CAN'T STAY HERE.
I CAN'T MOVE.
YOU HAVE TO. I NEED YOU TO HELP THIS WOMAN. SHE'S BEEN HURT.
I NEED YOU TO SUPPORT HER NECK AS WE LOWER HER OUT THE BACK OF THE TRAIN.
O-OKAY.
HOW DID YOU DO THAT?
IT'S EASIER TO FORGET ABOUT YOURSELF WHEN YOU HAVE SOMEONE ELSE TO LOOK AFTER.

ROOARGH

I'D UNDERSTAND IF SHE RAN AWAY TOMORROW.

AGHHHH!

BUT MJ DOESN'T RUN.

NO.

DON'T PANIC. DON'T SCREAM. THAT'S NO HELP TO ANYONE.

WORRY ABOUT THE PEOPLE AROUND YOU. DON'T LEAVE ANYONE BEHIND.

EVEN WHEN I WISH SHE WOULD.

EVEN WHEN I'VE BEGGED HER TO.

PANICKING AND SCREAMING FEELS PRETTY APPROPRIATE RIGHT NOW, SO WHY AREN'T YOU?

OH, MY DAMSEL DAYS ARE LONG BEHIND ME.

GET THE PASSENGERS AS FAR AWAY AS YOU CAN.

WHAT? WHAT ARE YOU GOING TO DO?

DON'T WORRY. I'M NOT AN IDIOT. I'M GOING TO DISTRACT IT A BIT AND THEN HIDE.

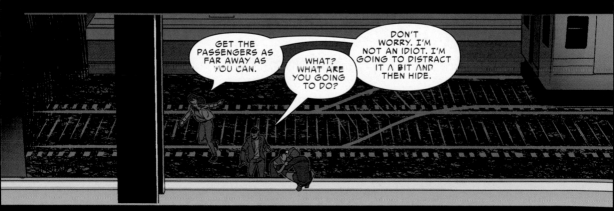

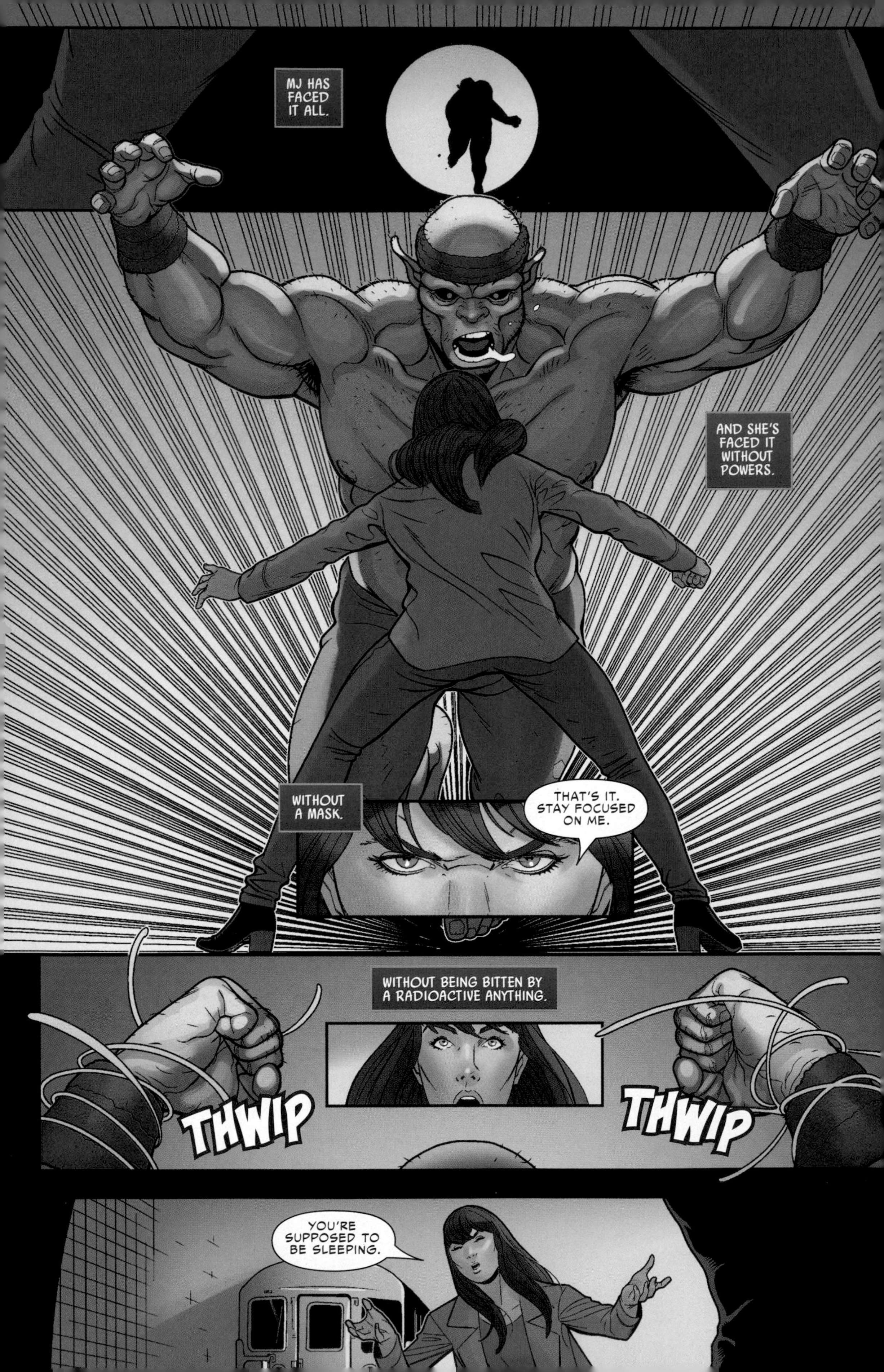
MJ HAS FACED IT ALL.
AND SHE'S FACED IT WITHOUT POWERS.
WITHOUT A MASK.
THAT'S IT. STAY FOCUSED ON ME.
WITHOUT BEING BITTEN BY A RADIOACTIVE ANYTHING.
THWIP
THWIP
YOU'RE SUPPOSED TO BE SLEEPING.

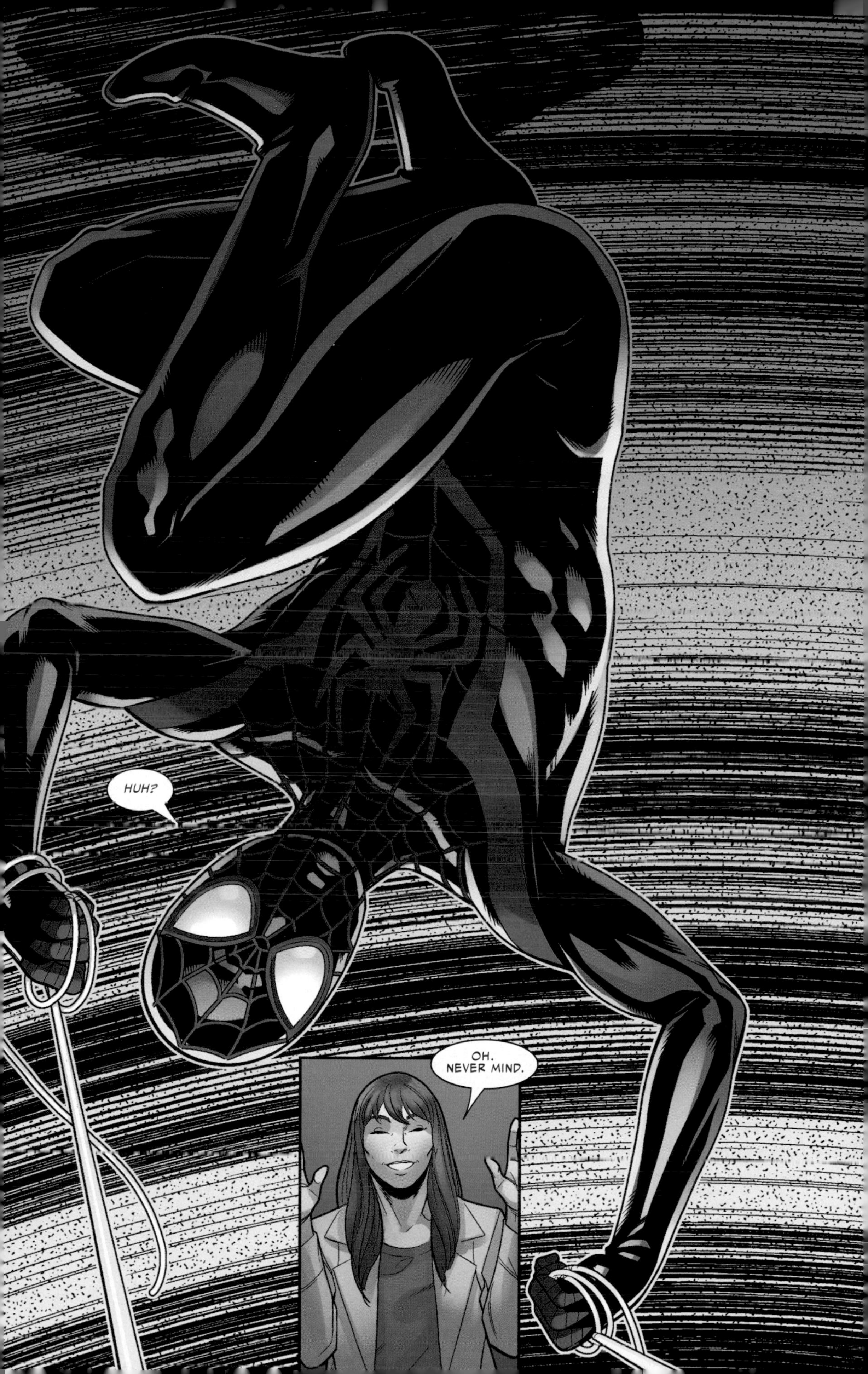
HUH?
OH. NEVER MIND.

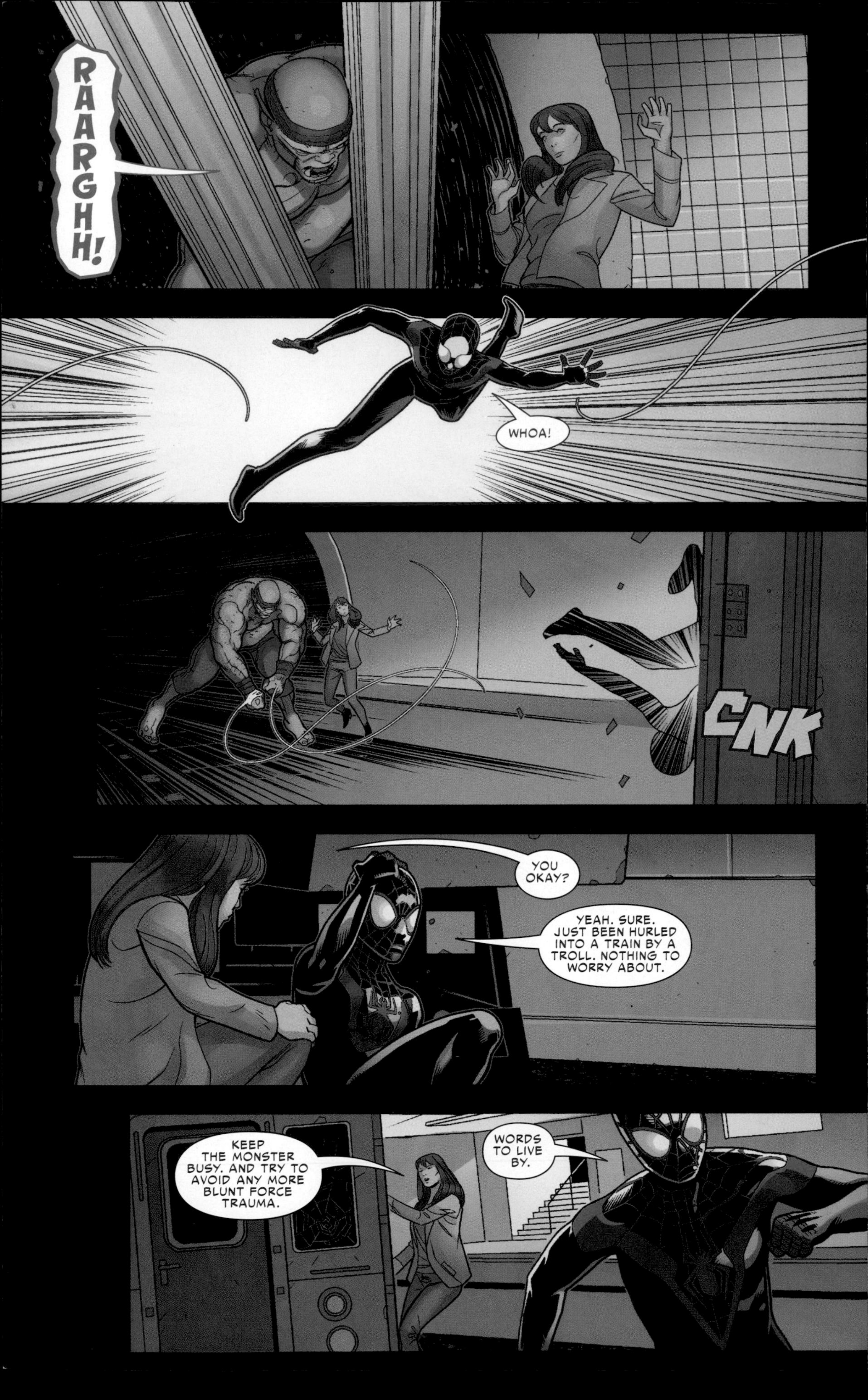
RAARGHH!
WHOA!
CNK
YOU OKAY?
YEAH. SURE. JUST BEEN HURLED INTO A TRAIN BY A TROLL. NOTHING TO WORRY ABOUT.
KEEP THE MONSTER BUSY. AND TRY TO AVOID ANY MORE BLUNT FORCE TRAUMA.
WORDS TO LIVE BY.

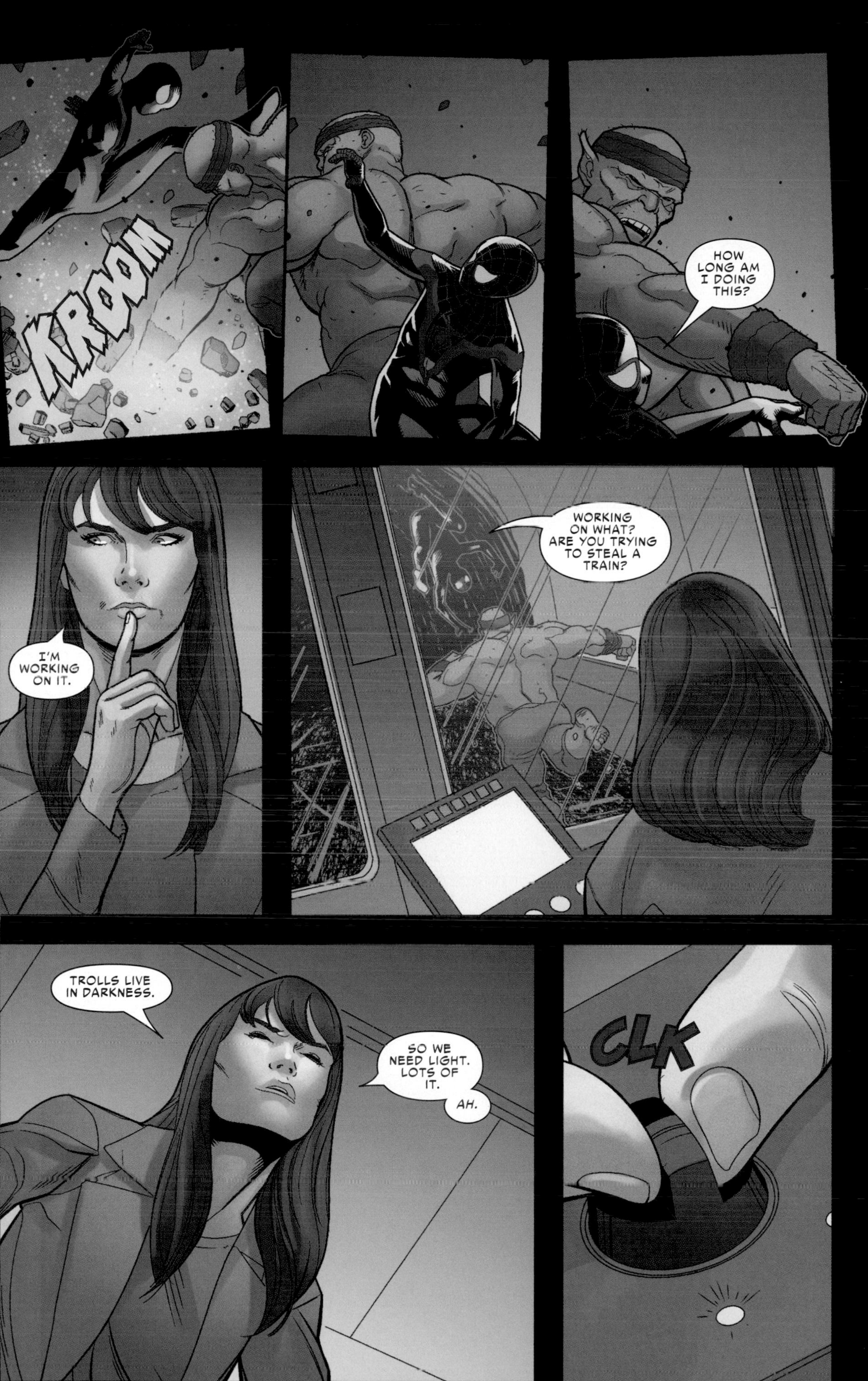
KROOM
HOW LONG AM I DOING THIS?
I'M WORKING ON IT.
WORKING ON WHAT? ARE YOU TRYING TO STEAL A TRAIN?
TROLLS LIVE IN DARKNESS.
SO WE NEED LIGHT. LOTS OF IT.
AH.
CLK

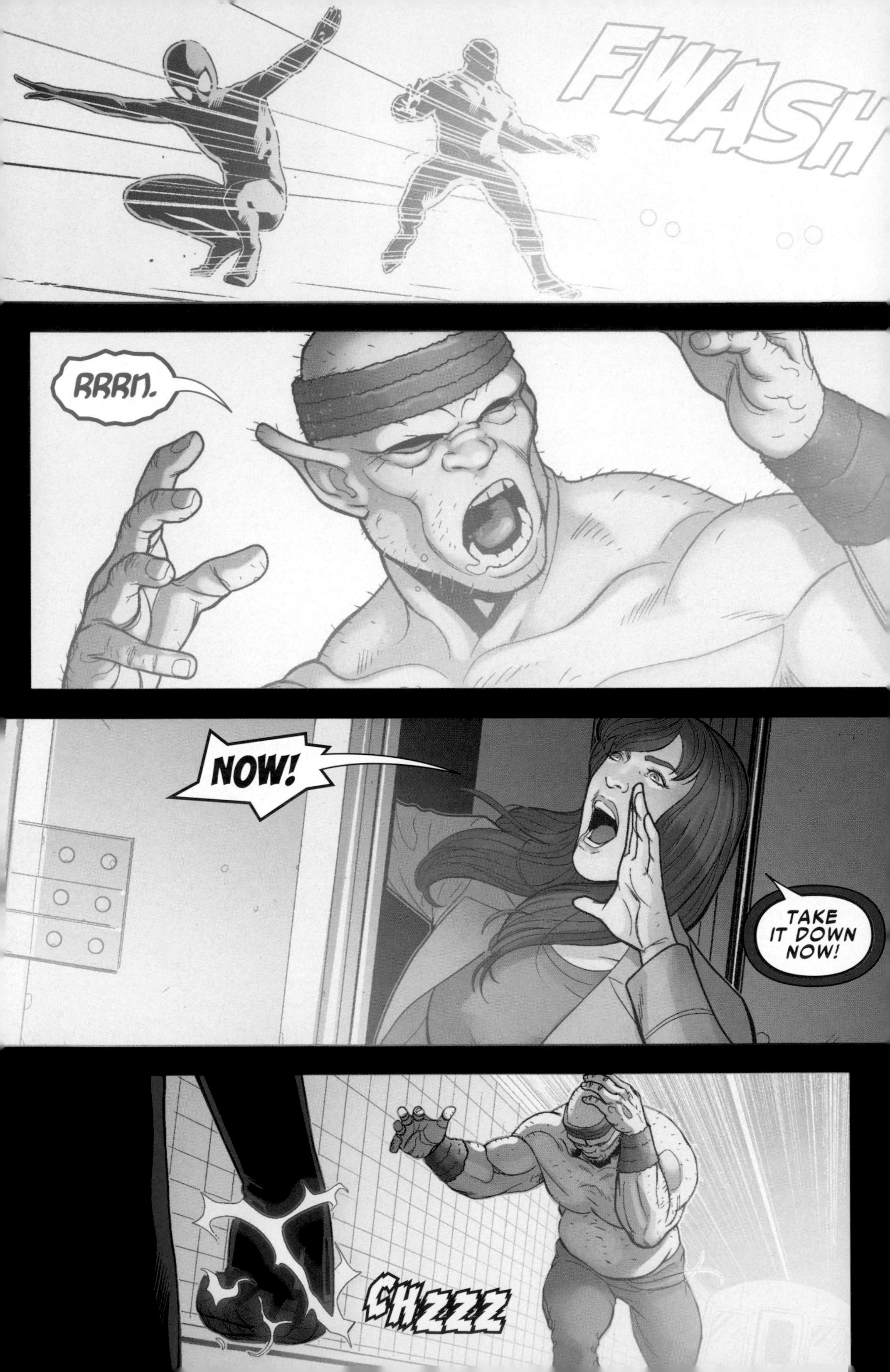

FWASH
RRRN.
NOW!
TAKE IT DOWN NOW!
CHZZZ

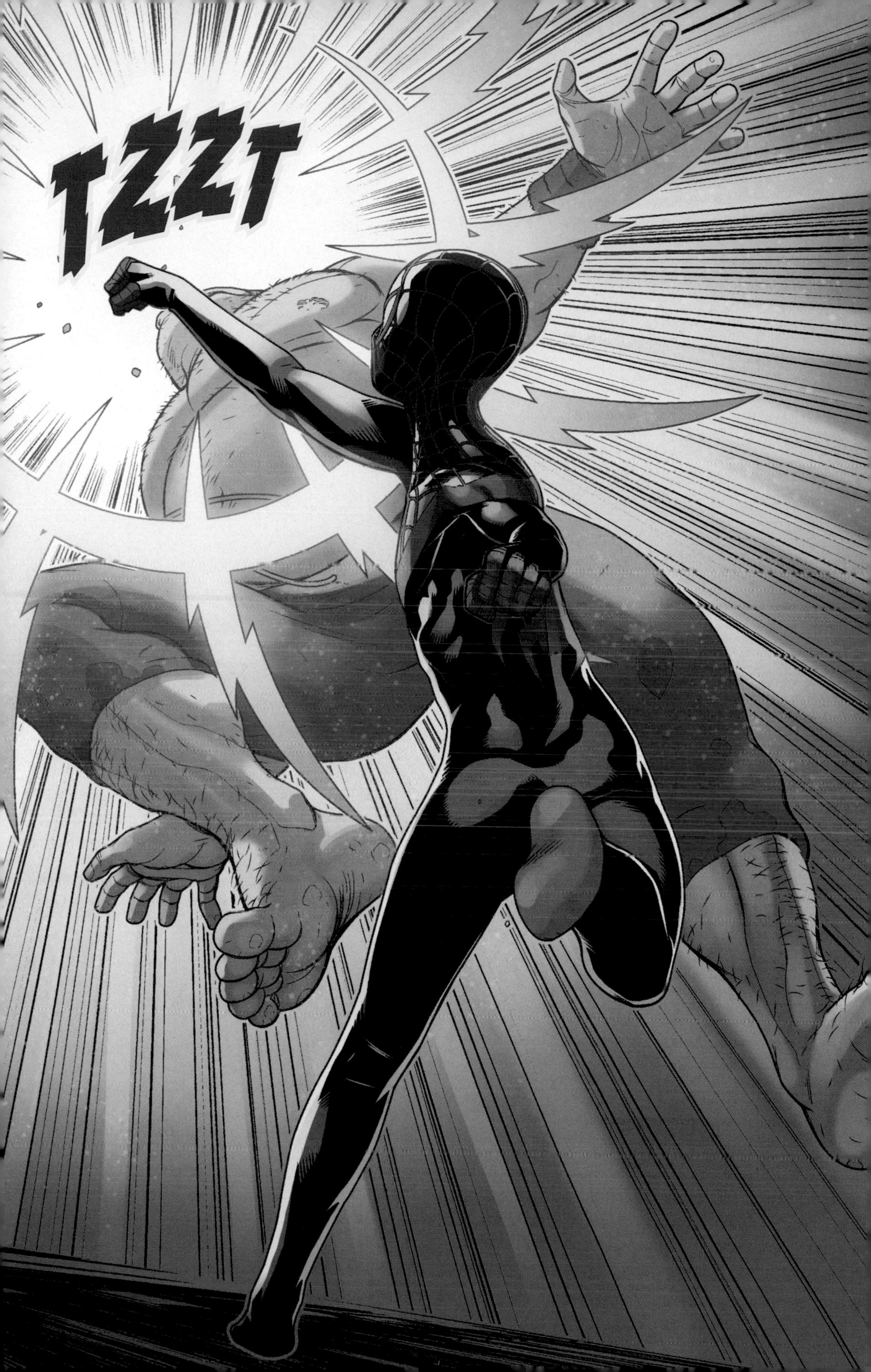
TZZT

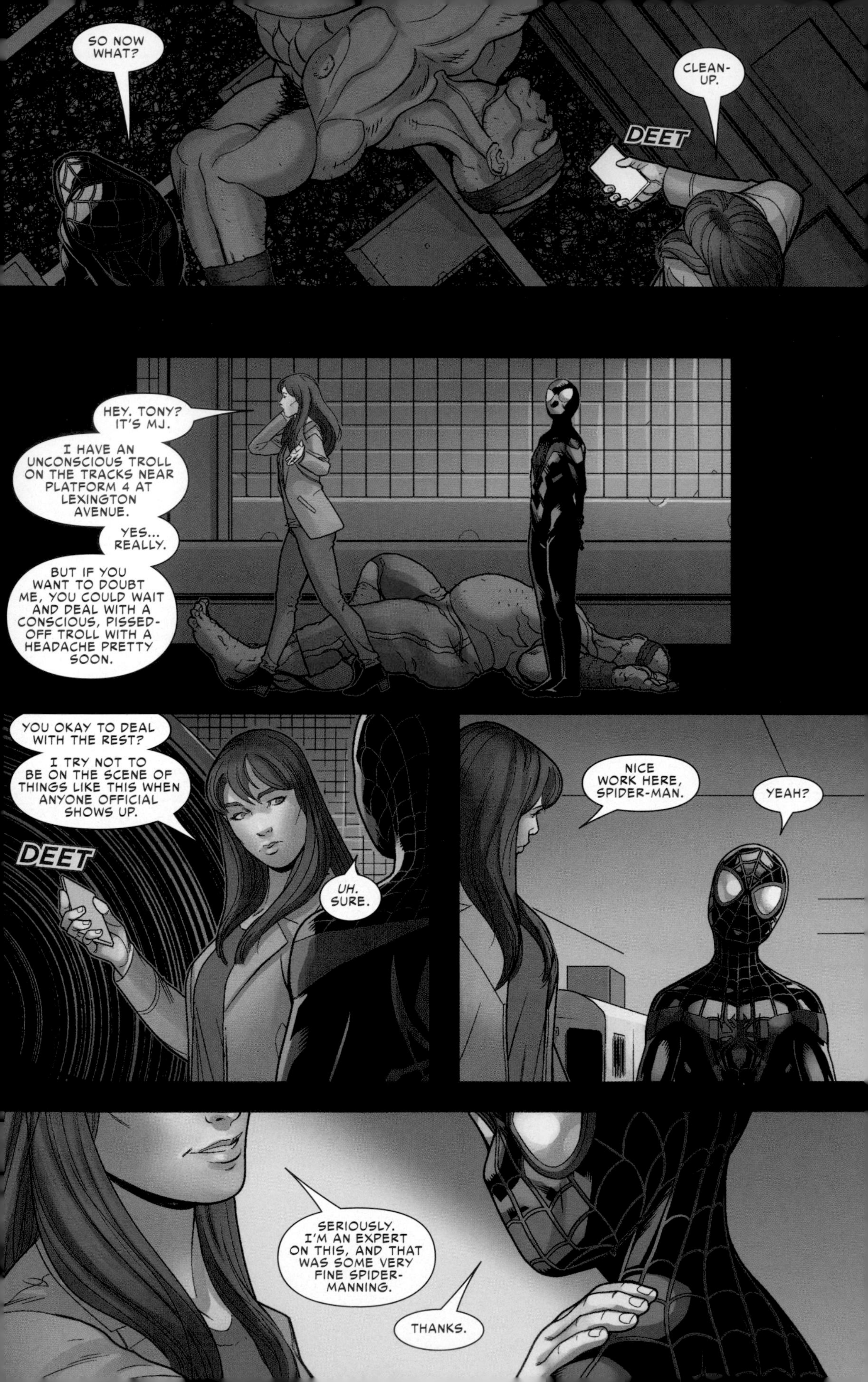
SO NOW WHAT?
CLEAN-UP.
DEET
HEY. TONY? IT'S MJ.
I HAVE AN UNCONSCIOUS TROLL ON THE TRACKS NEAR PLATFORM 4 AT LEXINGTON AVENUE.
YES... REALLY.
BUT IF YOU WANT TO DOUBT ME, YOU COULD WAIT AND DEAL WITH A CONSCIOUS, PISSED-OFF TROLL WITH A HEADACHE PRETTY SOON.
YOU OKAY TO DEAL WITH THE REST?
I TRY NOT TO BE ON THE SCENE OF THINGS LIKE THIS WHEN ANYONE OFFICIAL SHOWS UP.
DEET
UH. SURE.
NICE WORK HERE, SPIDER-MAN.
YEAH?
SERIOUSLY. I'M AN EXPERT ON THIS, AND THAT WAS SOME VERY FINE SPIDER-MANNING.
THANKS.

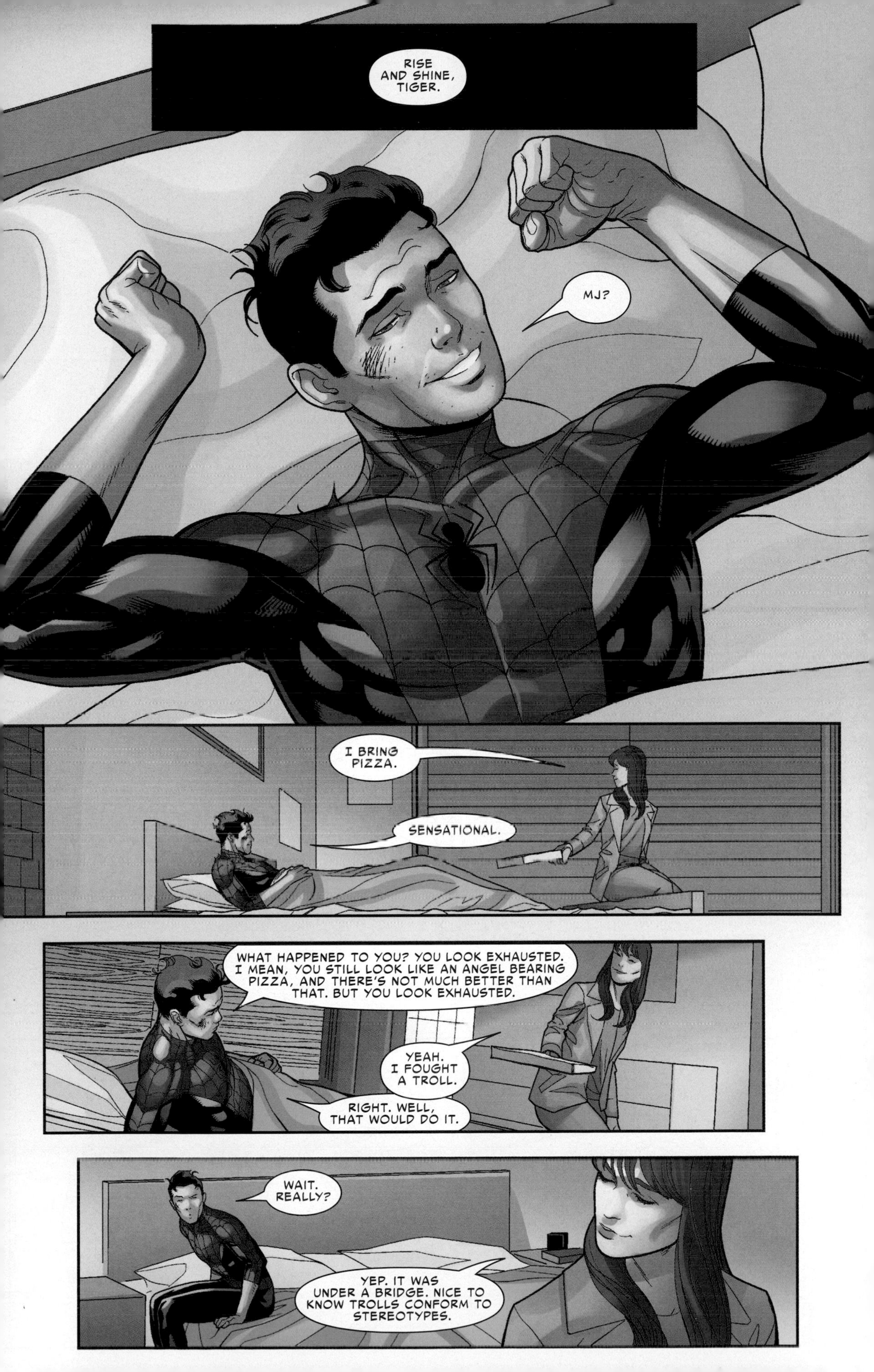
RISE AND SHINE, TIGER.
MJ?
I BRING PIZZA.
SENSATIONAL.
WHAT HAPPENED TO YOU? YOU LOOK EXHAUSTED. I MEAN, YOU STILL LOOK LIKE AN ANGEL BEARING PIZZA, AND THERE'S NOT MUCH BETTER THAN THAT. BUT YOU LOOK EXHAUSTED.
YEAH. I FOUGHT A TROLL.
RIGHT. WELL, THAT WOULD DO IT.
WAIT. REALLY?
YEP. IT WAS UNDER A BRIDGE. NICE TO KNOW TROLLS CONFORM TO STEREOTYPES.

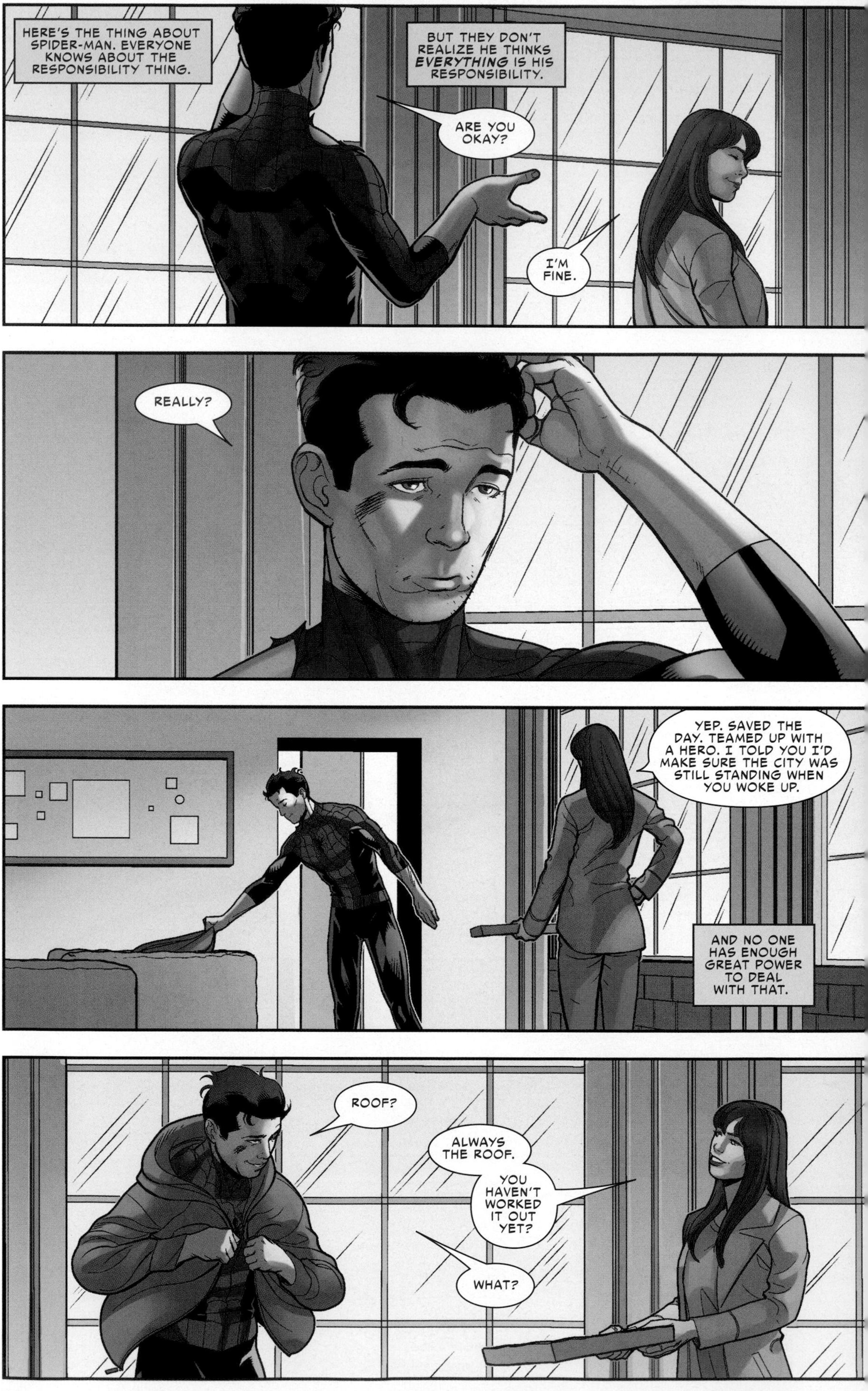
HERE'S THE THING ABOUT SPIDER-MAN. EVERYONE KNOWS ABOUT THE RESPONSIBILITY THING.
BUT THEY DON'T REALIZE HE THINKS *EVERYTHING* IS HIS RESPONSIBILITY.
ARE YOU OKAY?
I'M FINE.
REALLY?
YEP. SAVED THE DAY. TEAMED UP WITH A HERO. I TOLD YOU I'D MAKE SURE THE CITY WAS STILL STANDING WHEN YOU WOKE UP.
AND NO ONE HAS ENOUGH GREAT POWER TO DEAL WITH THAT.
ROOF?
ALWAYS THE ROOF.
YOU HAVEN'T WORKED IT OUT YET?
WHAT?

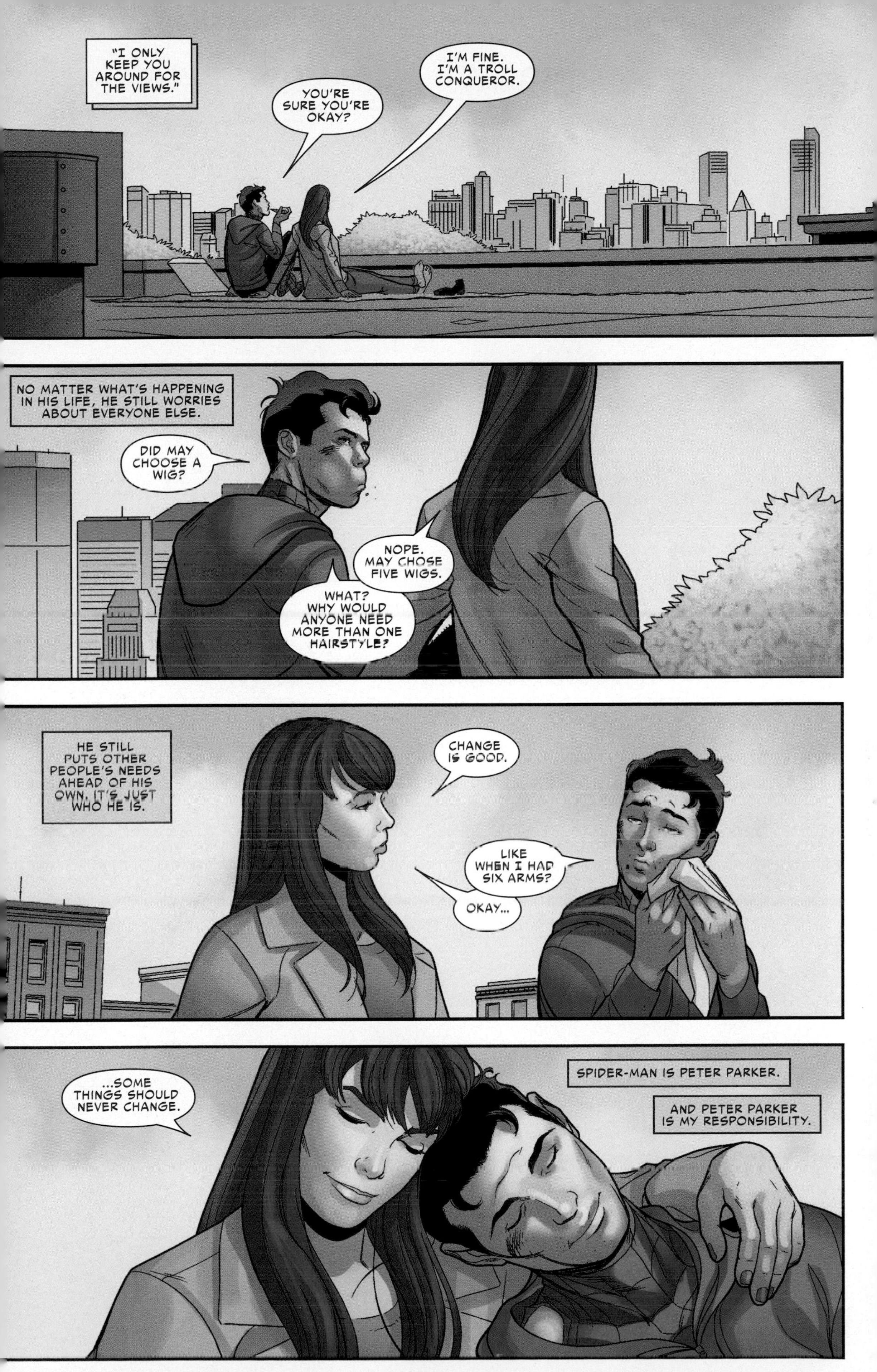
"I ONLY KEEP YOU AROUND FOR THE VIEWS."
YOU'RE SURE YOU'RE OKAY?
I'M FINE. I'M A TROLL CONQUEROR.
NO MATTER WHAT'S HAPPENING IN HIS LIFE, HE STILL WORRIES ABOUT EVERYONE ELSE.
DID MAY CHOOSE A WIG?
NOPE. MAY CHOSE FIVE WIGS.
WHAT? WHY WOULD ANYONE NEED MORE THAN ONE HAIRSTYLE?
HE STILL PUTS OTHER PEOPLE'S NEEDS AHEAD OF HIS OWN. IT'S JUST WHO HE IS.
CHANGE IS GOOD.
LIKE WHEN I HAD SIX ARMS?
OKAY...
...SOME THINGS SHOULD NEVER CHANGE.
SPIDER-MAN IS PETER PARKER.
AND PETER PARKER IS MY RESPONSIBILITY.

12

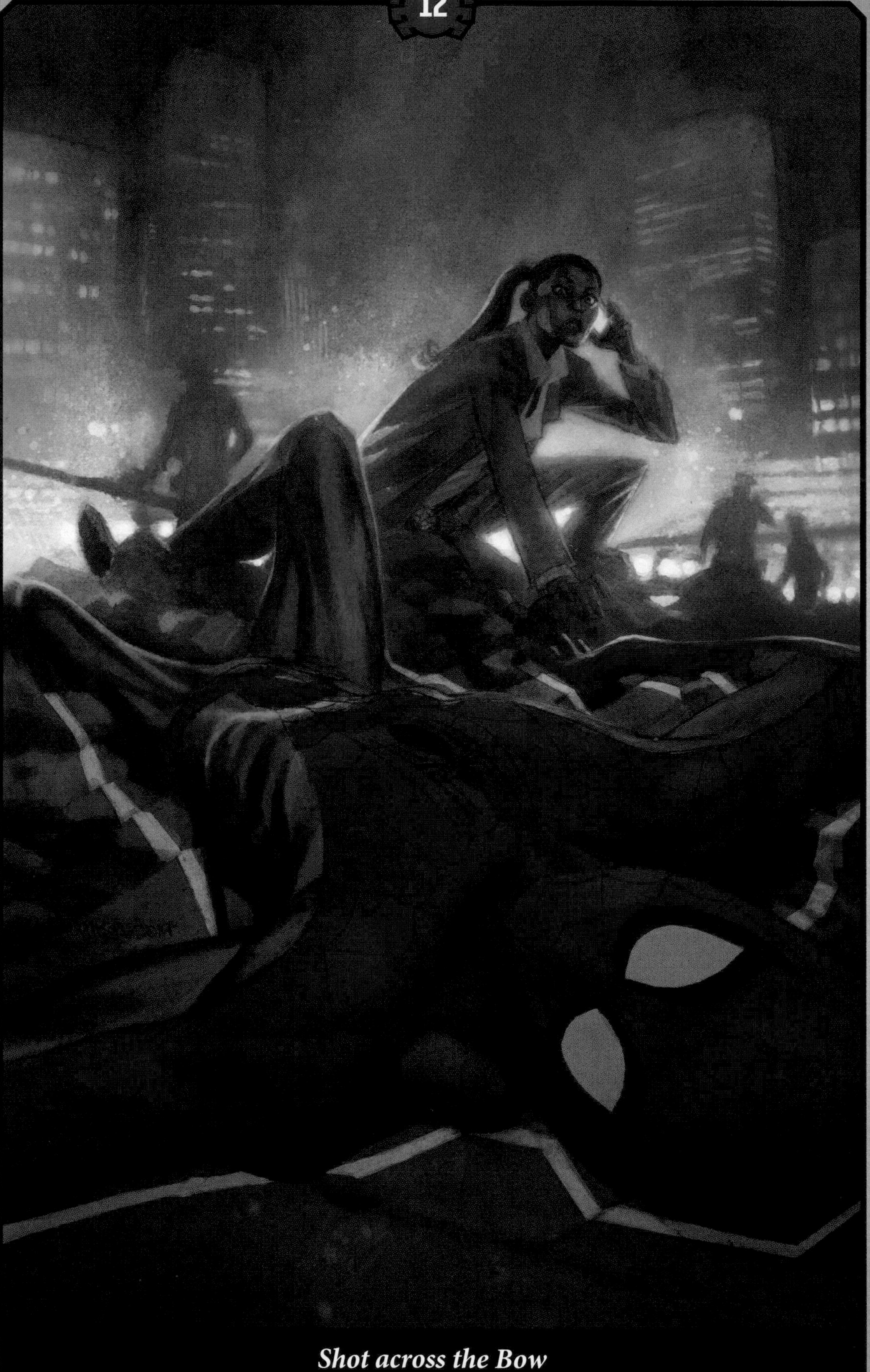

Shot across the Bow

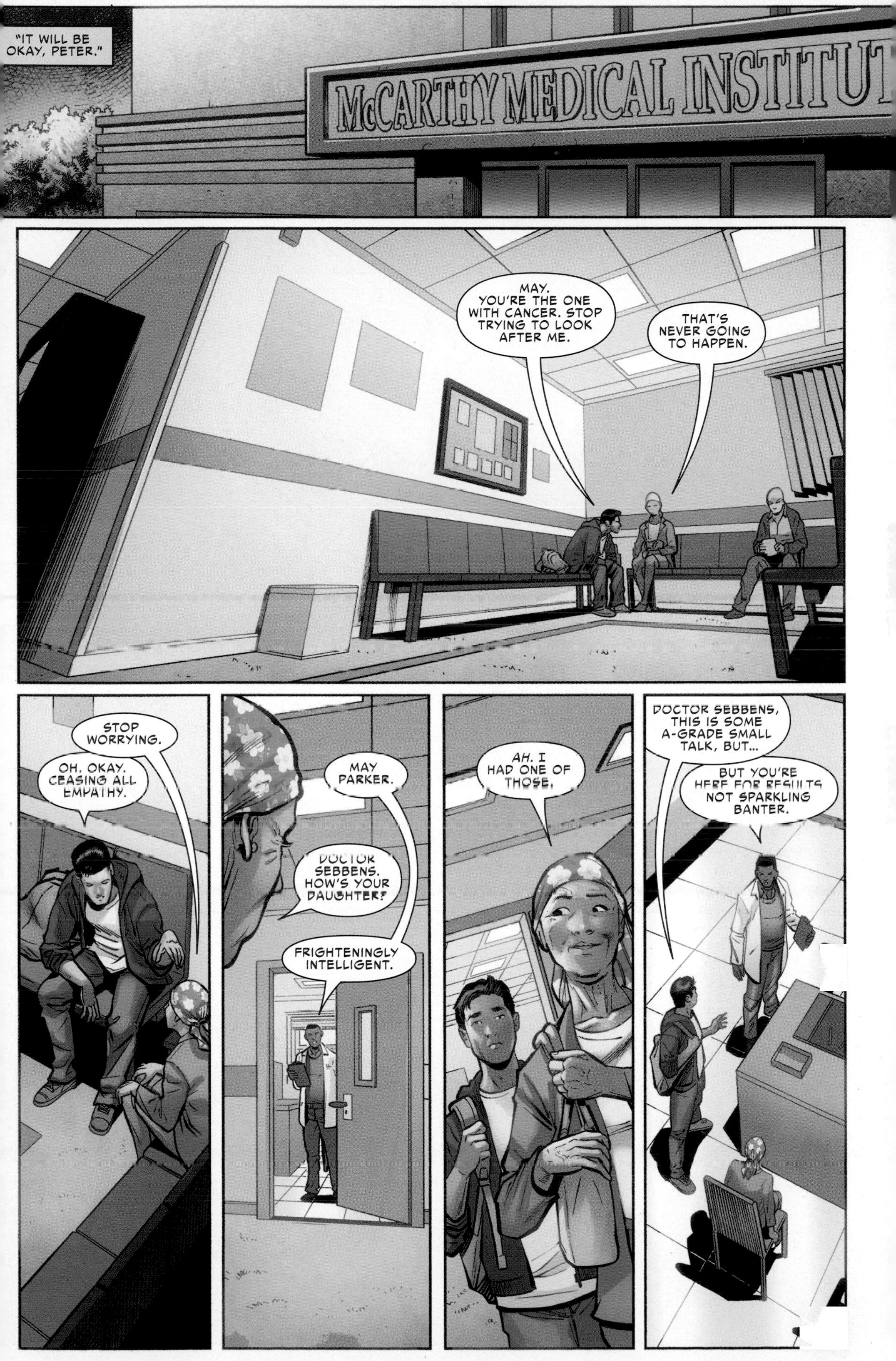
"IT WILL BE OKAY, PETER."
McCARTHY MEDICAL INSTITUT
MAY. YOU'RE THE ONE WITH CANCER. STOP TRYING TO LOOK AFTER ME.
THAT'S NEVER GOING TO HAPPEN.
STOP WORRYING.
OH. OKAY. CEASING ALL EMPATHY.
MAY PARKER.
DOCTOR SEBBENS. HOW'S YOUR DAUGHTER?
FRIGHTENINGLY INTELLIGENT.
AH. I HAD ONE OF THOSE.
DOCTOR SEBBENS, THIS IS SOME A-GRADE SMALL TALK, BUT...
BUT YOU'RE HERE FOR RESULTS NOT SPARKLING BANTER.

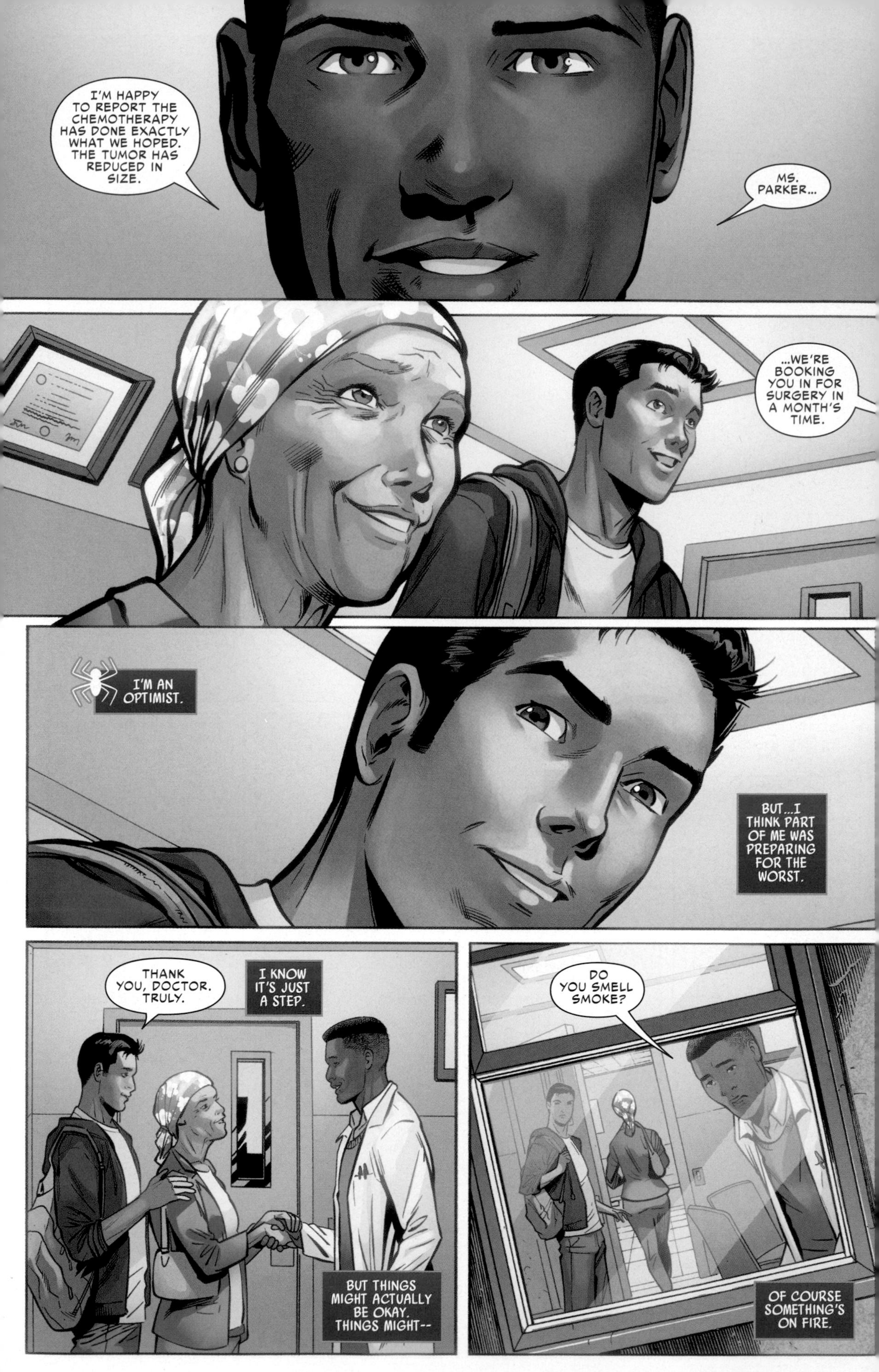
I'M HAPPY TO REPORT THE CHEMOTHERAPY HAS DONE EXACTLY WHAT WE HOPED. THE TUMOR HAS REDUCED IN SIZE.
MS. PARKER...
...WE'RE BOOKING YOU IN FOR SURGERY IN A MONTH'S TIME.
I'M AN OPTIMIST.
BUT...I THINK PART OF ME WAS PREPARING FOR THE WORST.
THANK YOU, DOCTOR. TRULY.
I KNOW IT'S JUST A STEP.
BUT THINGS MIGHT ACTUALLY BE OKAY. THINGS MIGHT--
DO YOU SMELL SMOKE?
OF COURSE SOMETHING'S ON FIRE.

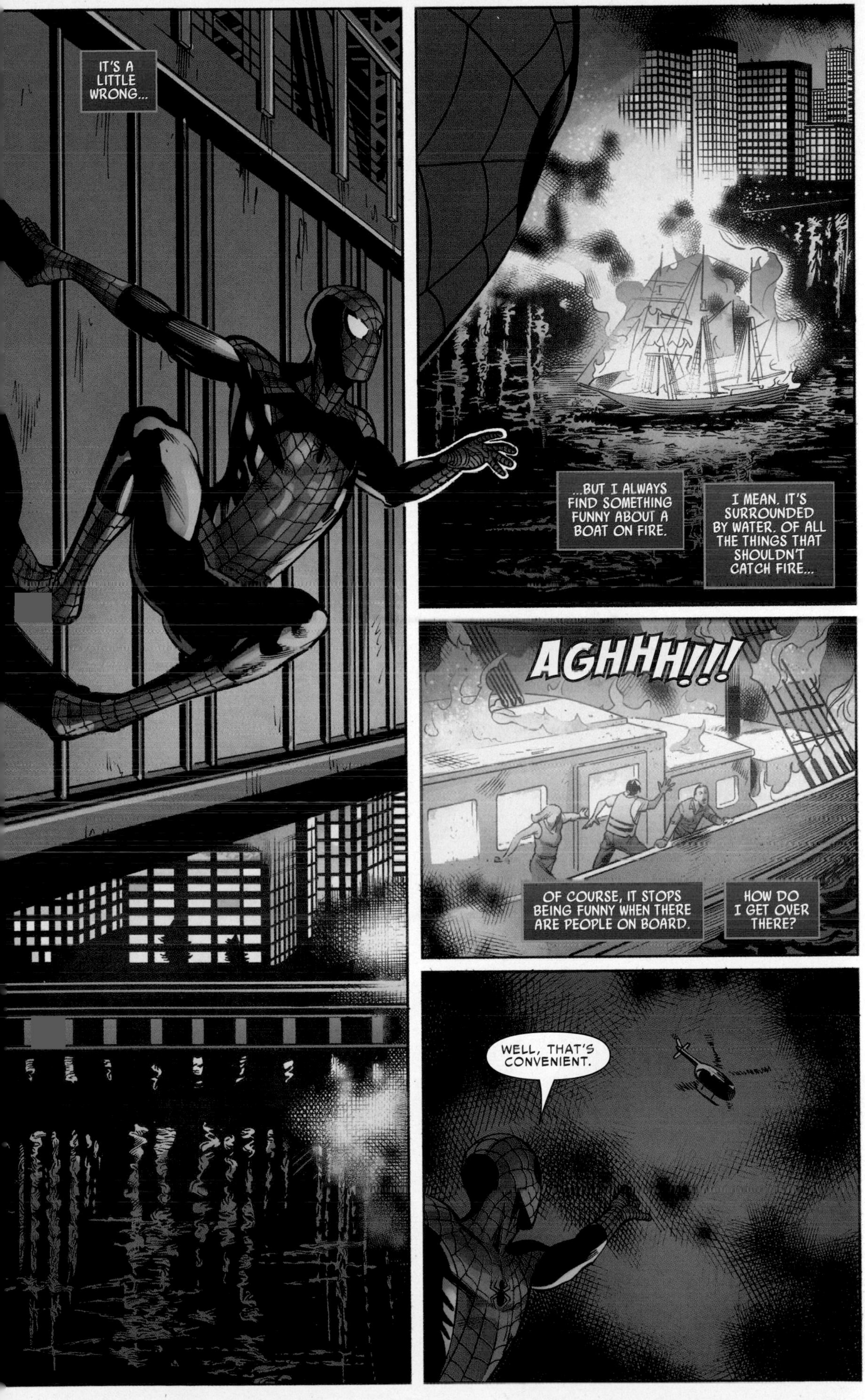
IT'S A LITTLE WRONG...
...BUT I ALWAYS FIND SOMETHING FUNNY ABOUT A BOAT ON FIRE.
I MEAN, IT'S SURROUNDED BY WATER. OF ALL THE THINGS THAT SHOULDN'T CATCH FIRE...
AGHHH!!!
OF COURSE, IT STOPS BEING FUNNY WHEN THERE ARE PEOPLE ON BOARD.
HOW DO I GET OVER THERE?
WELL, THAT'S CONVENIENT.

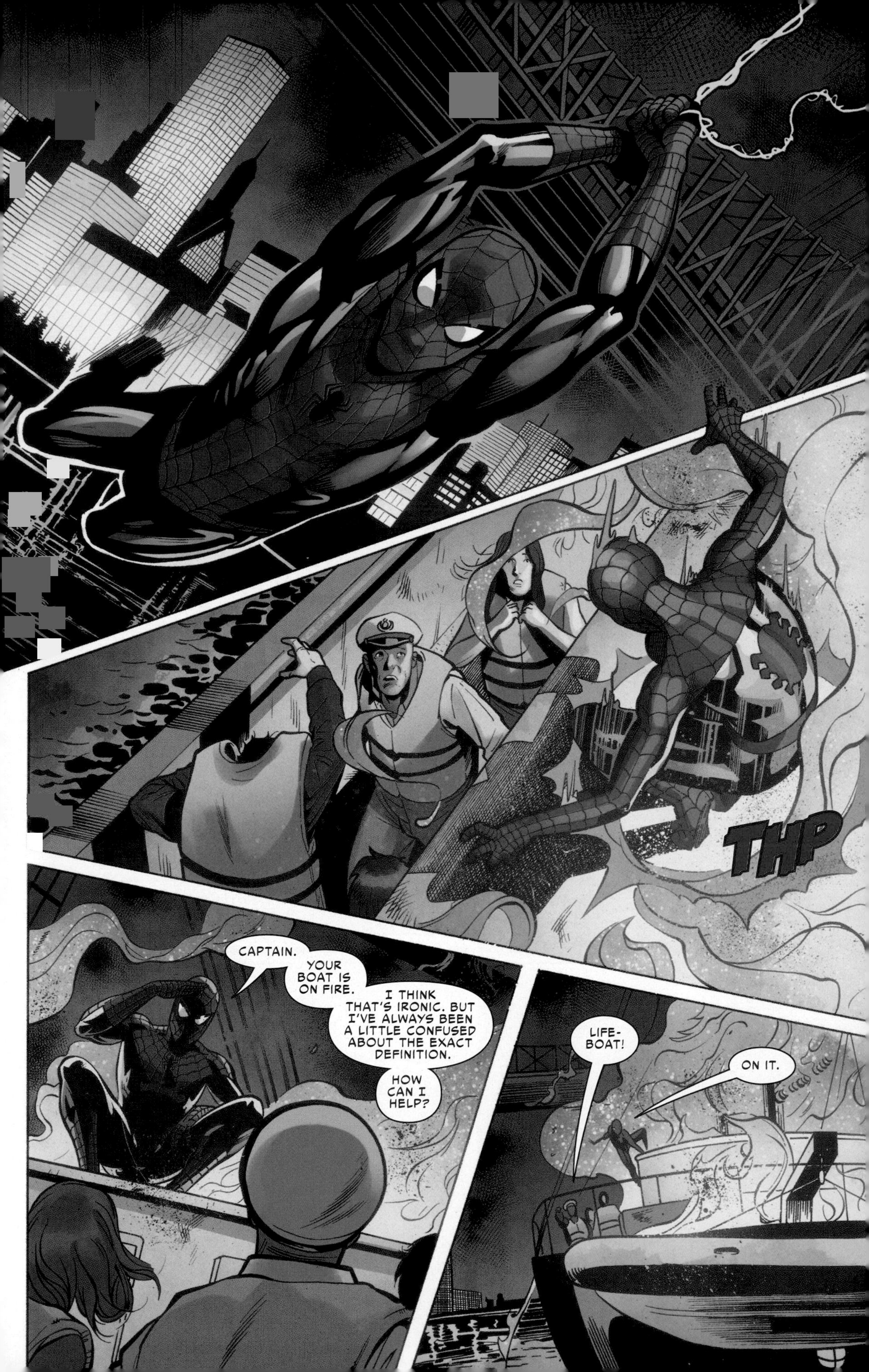
THP
CAPTAIN.
YOUR BOAT IS ON FIRE.
I THINK THAT'S IRONIC. BUT I'VE ALWAYS BEEN A LITTLE CONFUSED ABOUT THE EXACT DEFINITION.
HOW CAN I HELP?
LIFE-BOAT!
ON IT.

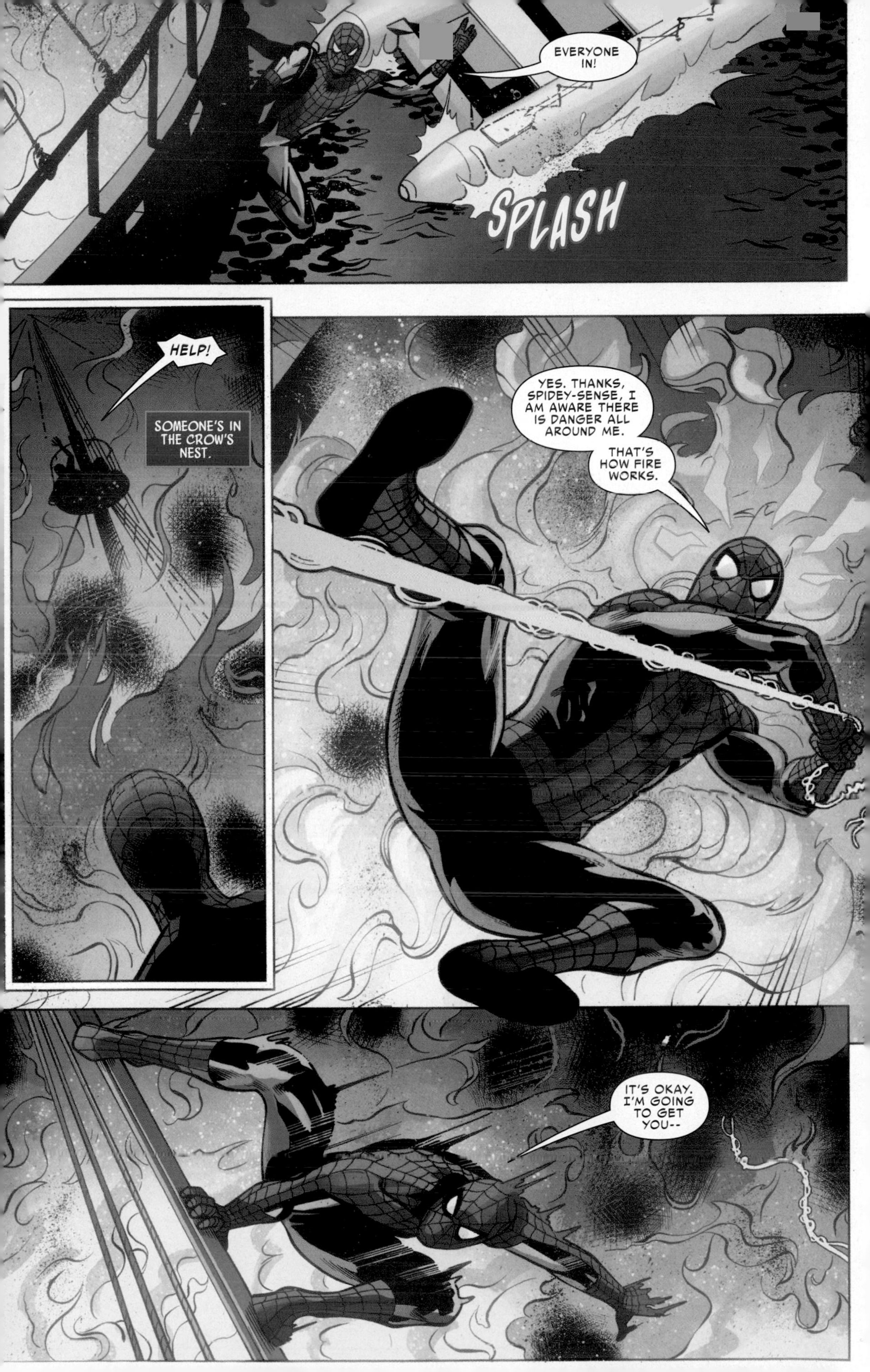

EVERYONE IN!
SPLASH
HELP!
SOMEONE'S IN THE CROW'S NEST.
YES. THANKS, SPIDEY-SENSE, I AM AWARE THERE IS DANGER ALL AROUND ME.
THAT'S HOW FIRE WORKS.
IT'S OKAY. I'M GOING TO GET YOU--

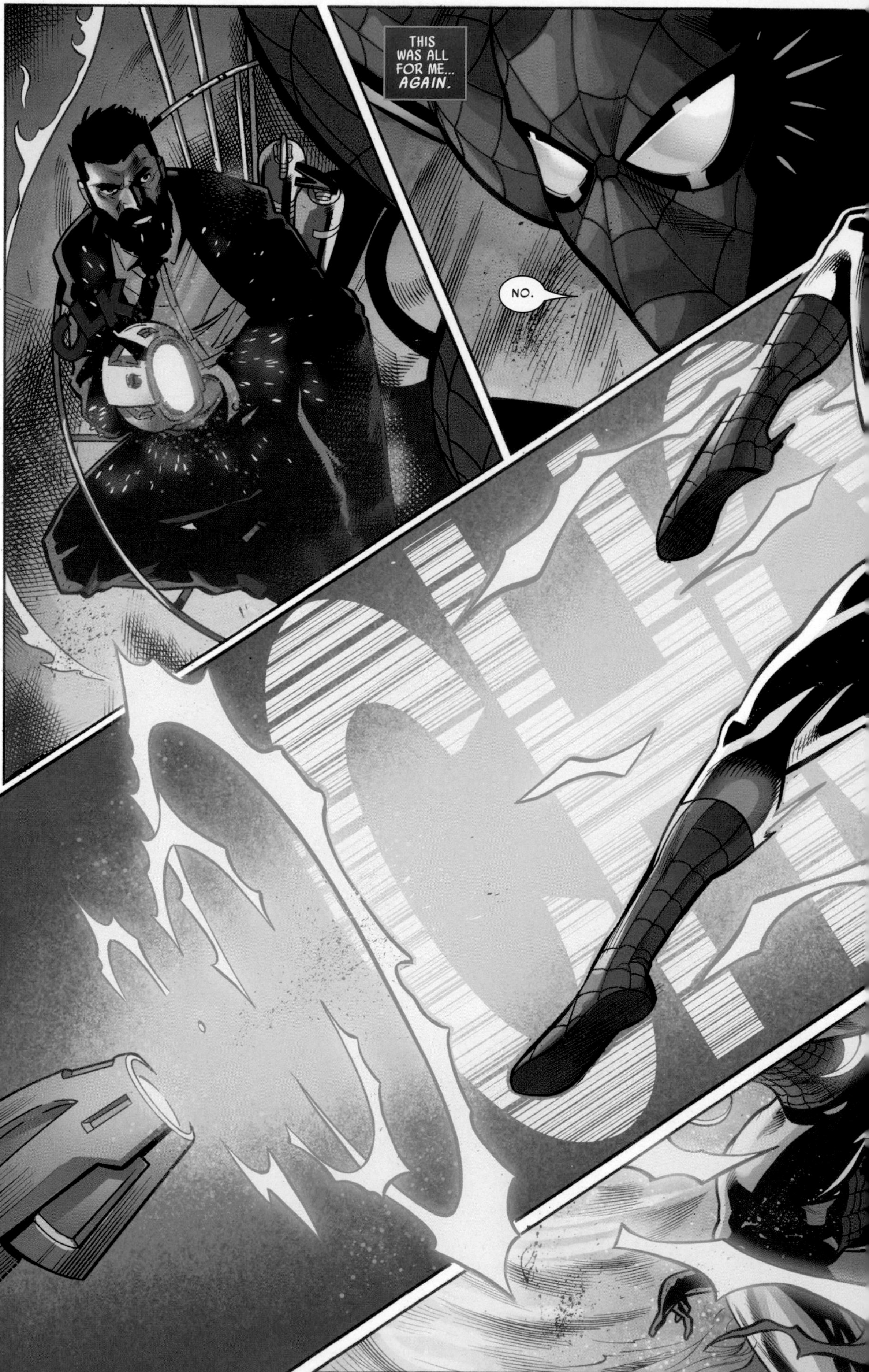
THIS WAS ALL FOR ME... AGAIN.
NO.

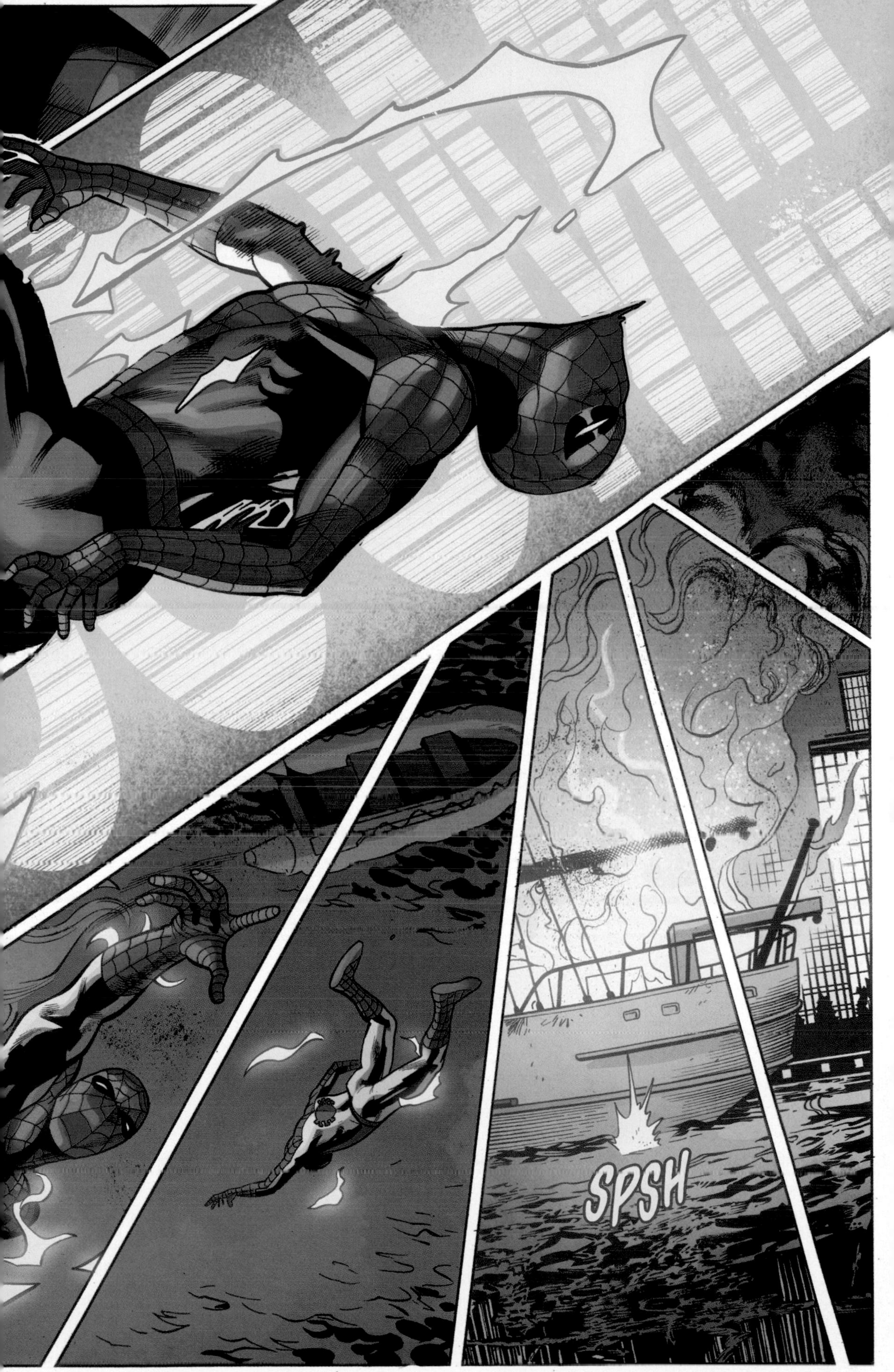
SPSH

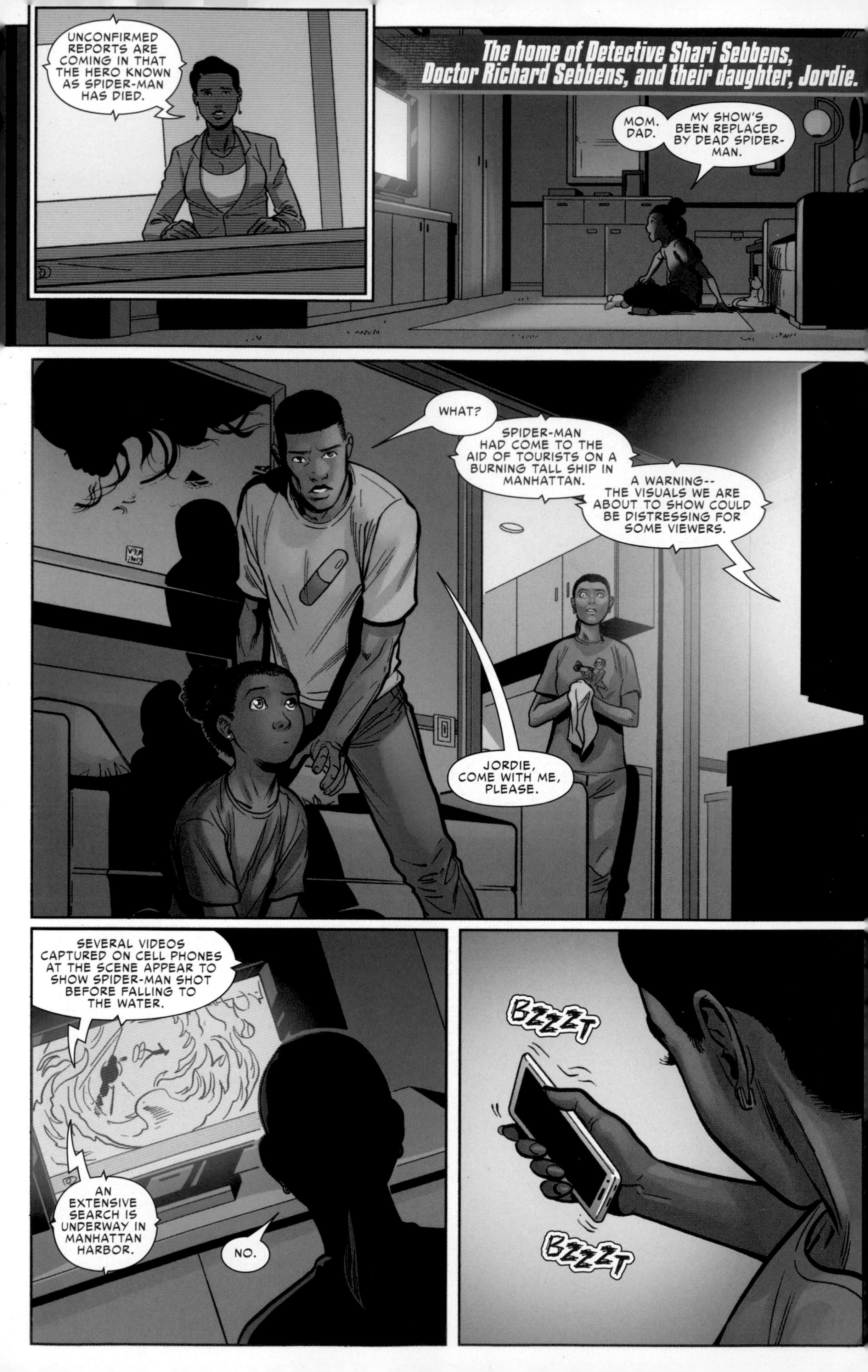
UNCONFIRMED REPORTS ARE COMING IN THAT THE HERO KNOWN AS SPIDER-MAN HAS DIED.
The home of Detective Shari Sebbens, Doctor Richard Sebbens, and their daughter, Jordie.
MOM. DAD.
MY SHOW'S BEEN REPLACED BY DEAD SPIDER-MAN.
WHAT?
SPIDER-MAN HAD COME TO THE AID OF TOURISTS ON A BURNING TALL SHIP IN MANHATTAN.
A WARNING-- THE VISUALS WE ARE ABOUT TO SHOW COULD BE DISTRESSING FOR SOME VIEWERS.
JORDIE, COME WITH ME, PLEASE.
SEVERAL VIDEOS CAPTURED ON CELL PHONES AT THE SCENE APPEAR TO SHOW SPIDER-MAN SHOT BEFORE FALLING TO THE WATER.
AN EXTENSIVE SEARCH IS UNDERWAY IN MANHATTAN HARBOR.
NO.
BZZZT
BZZZT

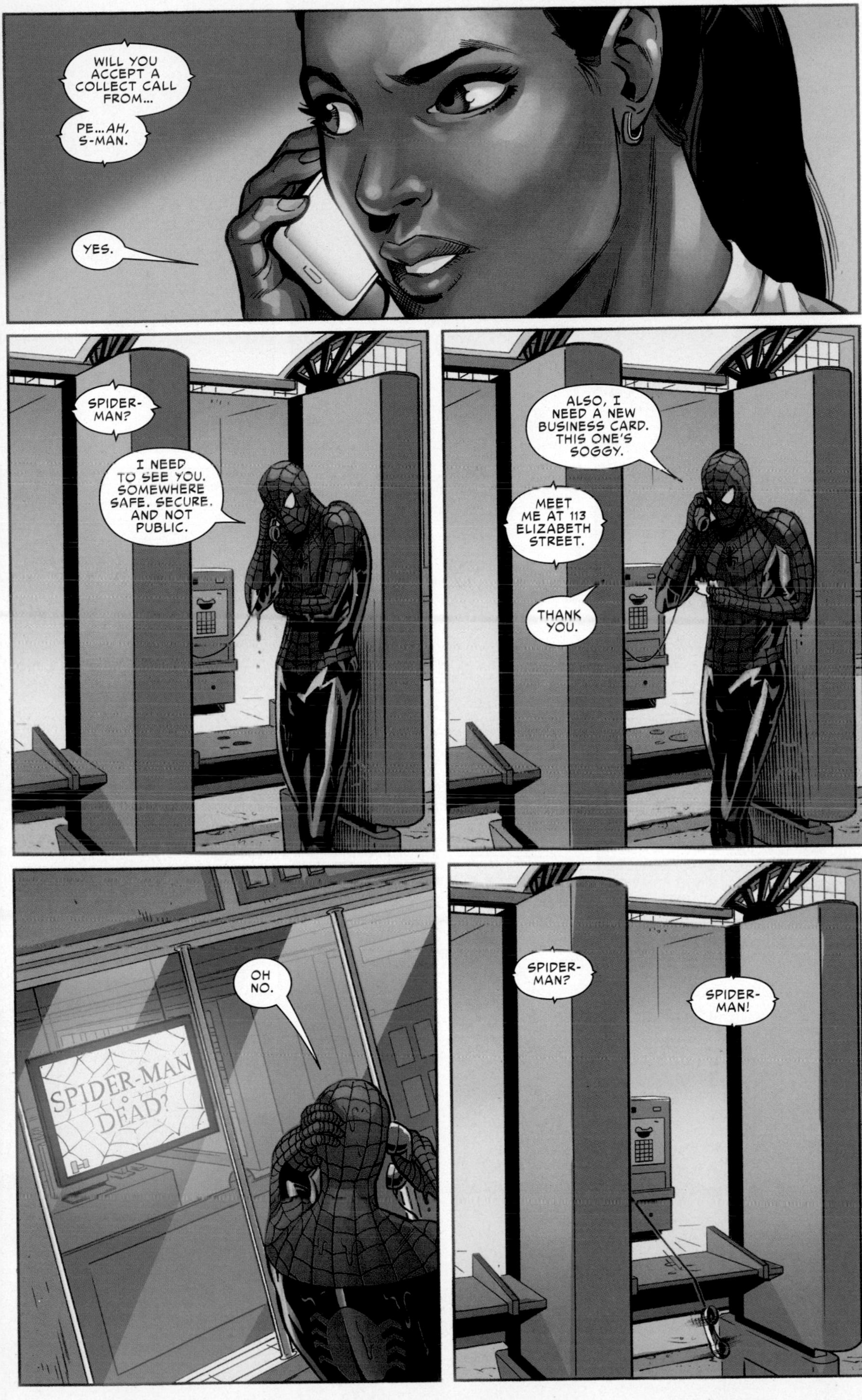
WILL YOU ACCEPT A COLLECT CALL FROM...
PE...AH, S-MAN.
YES.
SPIDER-MAN?
I NEED TO SEE YOU. SOMEWHERE SAFE. SECURE. AND NOT PUBLIC.
ALSO, I NEED A NEW BUSINESS CARD. THIS ONE'S SOGGY.
MEET ME AT 113 ELIZABETH STREET.
THANK YOU.
SPIDER-MAN DEAD?
OH NO.
SPIDER-MAN?
SPIDER-MAN!

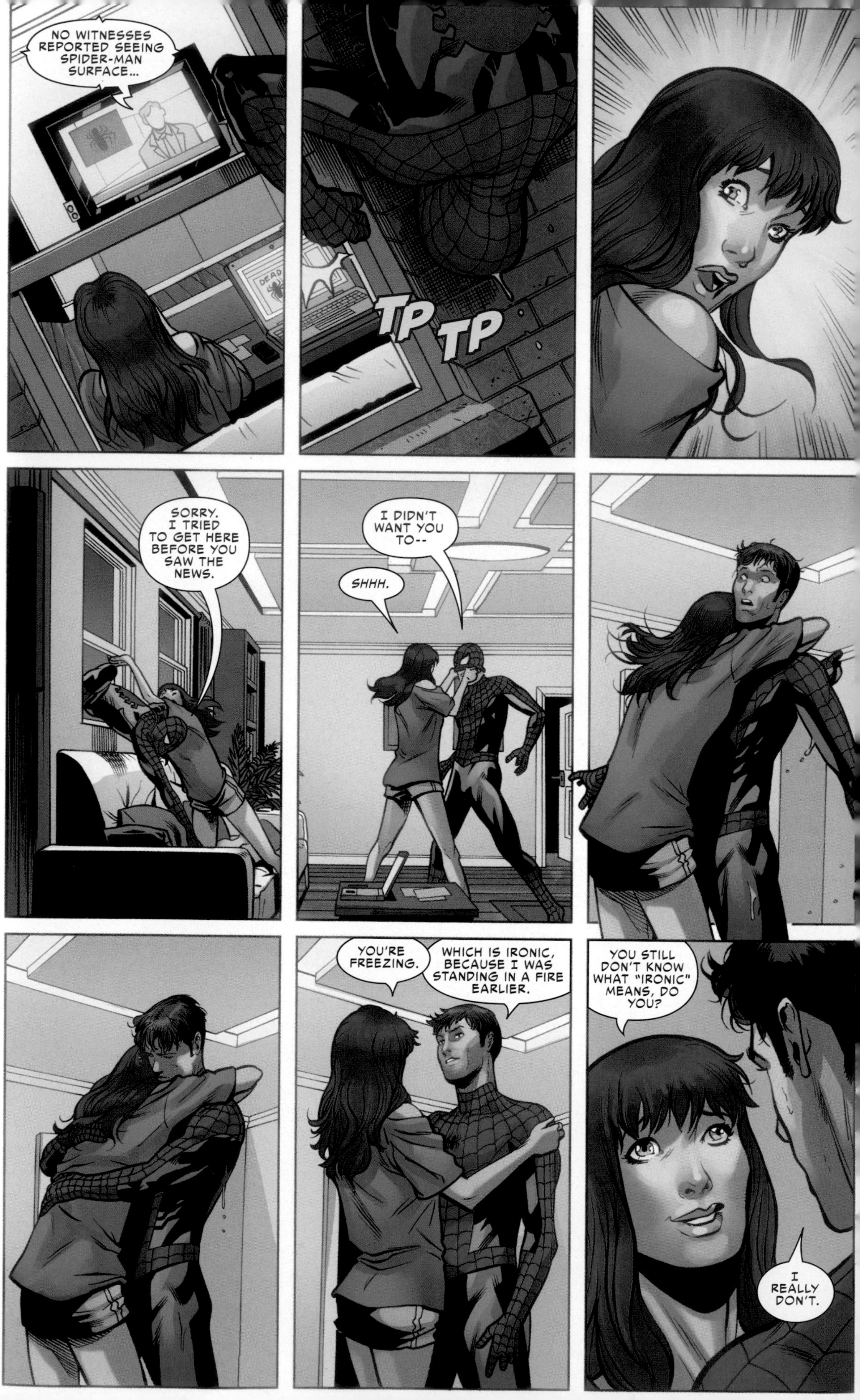
NO WITNESSES REPORTED SEEING SPIDER-MAN SURFACE...
DEAD
TP TP
SORRY. I TRIED TO GET HERE BEFORE YOU SAW THE NEWS.
I DIDN'T WANT YOU TO--
SHHH.
YOU'RE FREEZING.
WHICH IS IRONIC, BECAUSE I WAS STANDING IN A FIRE EARLIER.
YOU STILL DON'T KNOW WHAT "IRONIC" MEANS, DO YOU?
I REALLY DON'T.

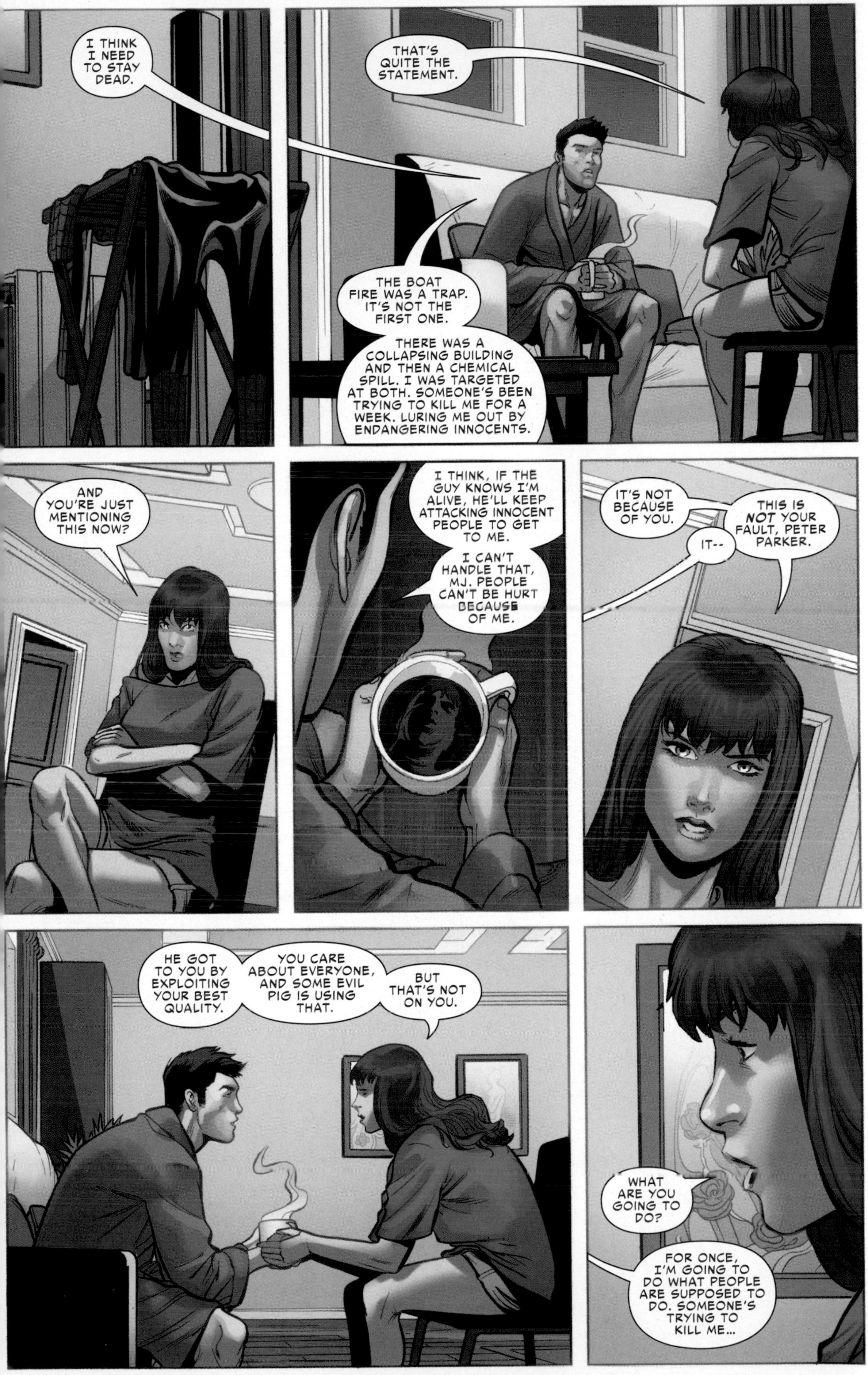
I THINK I NEED TO STAY DEAD.
THAT'S QUITE THE STATEMENT.
THE BOAT FIRE WAS A TRAP. IT'S NOT THE FIRST ONE.
THERE WAS A COLLAPSING BUILDING AND THEN A CHEMICAL SPILL. I WAS TARGETED AT BOTH. SOMEONE'S BEEN TRYING TO KILL ME FOR A WEEK. LURING ME OUT BY ENDANGERING INNOCENTS.
AND YOU'RE JUST MENTIONING THIS NOW?
I THINK, IF THE GUY KNOWS I'M ALIVE, HE'LL KEEP ATTACKING INNOCENT PEOPLE TO GET TO ME.
I CAN'T HANDLE THAT, MJ. PEOPLE CAN'T BE HURT BECAUSE OF ME.
IT'S NOT BECAUSE OF YOU.
IT--
THIS IS NOT YOUR FAULT, PETER PARKER.
HE GOT TO YOU BY EXPLOITING YOUR BEST QUALITY.
YOU CARE ABOUT EVERYONE, AND SOME EVIL PIG IS USING THAT.
BUT THAT'S NOT ON YOU.
WHAT ARE YOU GOING TO DO?
FOR ONCE, I'M GOING TO DO WHAT PEOPLE ARE SUPPOSED TO DO. SOMEONE'S TRYING TO KILL ME...

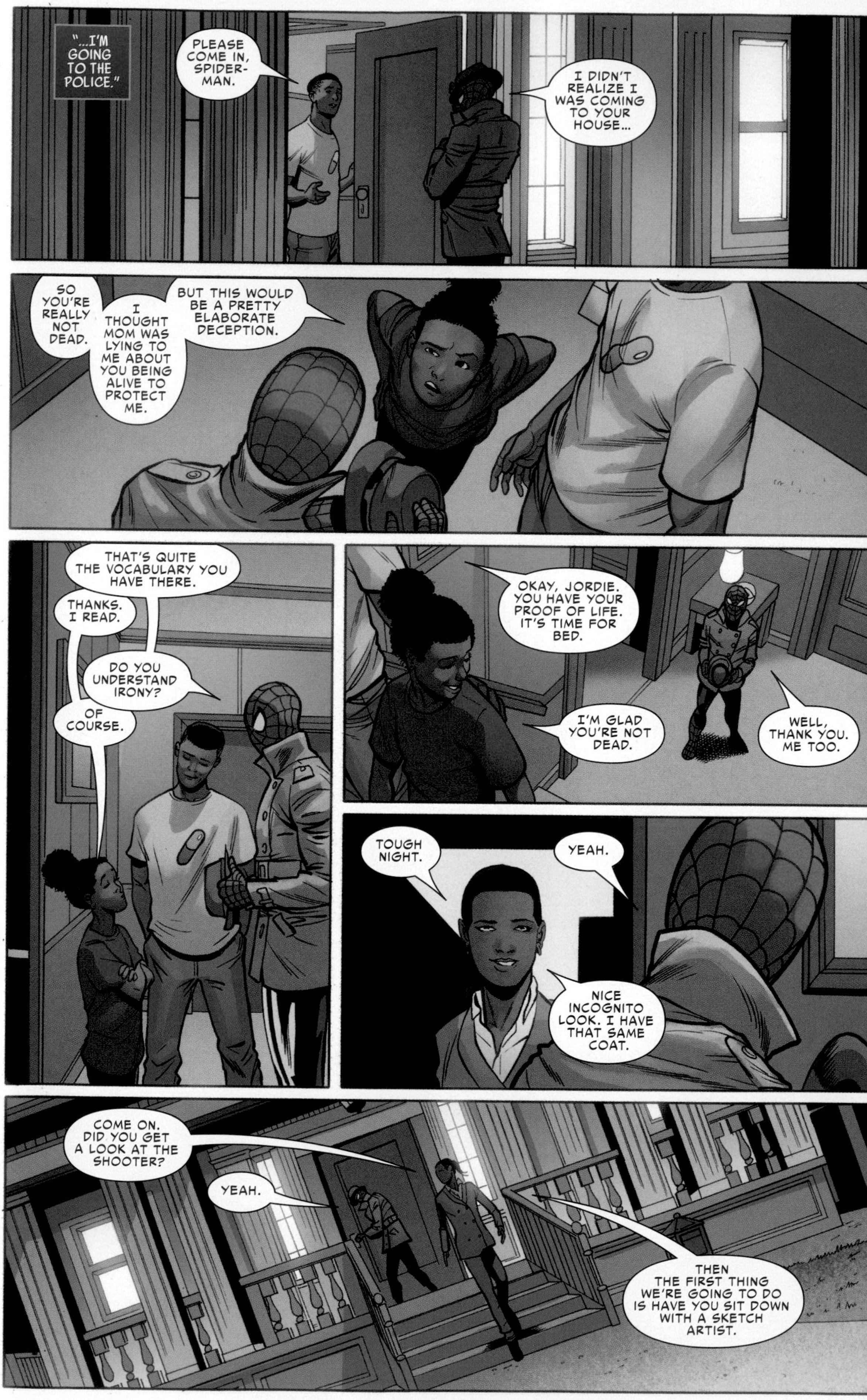
"...I'M GOING TO THE POLICE."
PLEASE COME IN, SPIDER-MAN.
I DIDN'T REALIZE I WAS COMING TO YOUR HOUSE...
SO YOU'RE REALLY NOT DEAD.
I THOUGHT MOM WAS LYING TO ME ABOUT YOU BEING ALIVE TO PROTECT ME.
BUT THIS WOULD BE A PRETTY ELABORATE DECEPTION.
THAT'S QUITE THE VOCABULARY YOU HAVE THERE.
THANKS. I READ.
DO YOU UNDERSTAND IRONY?
OF COURSE.
OKAY, JORDIE. YOU HAVE YOUR PROOF OF LIFE. IT'S TIME FOR BED.
I'M GLAD YOU'RE NOT DEAD.
WELL, THANK YOU. ME TOO.
TOUGH NIGHT.
YEAH.
NICE INCOGNITO LOOK. I HAVE THAT SAME COAT.
COME ON. DID YOU GET A LOOK AT THE SHOOTER?
YEAH.
THEN THE FIRST THING WE'RE GOING TO DO IS HAVE YOU SIT DOWN WITH A SKETCH ARTIST.

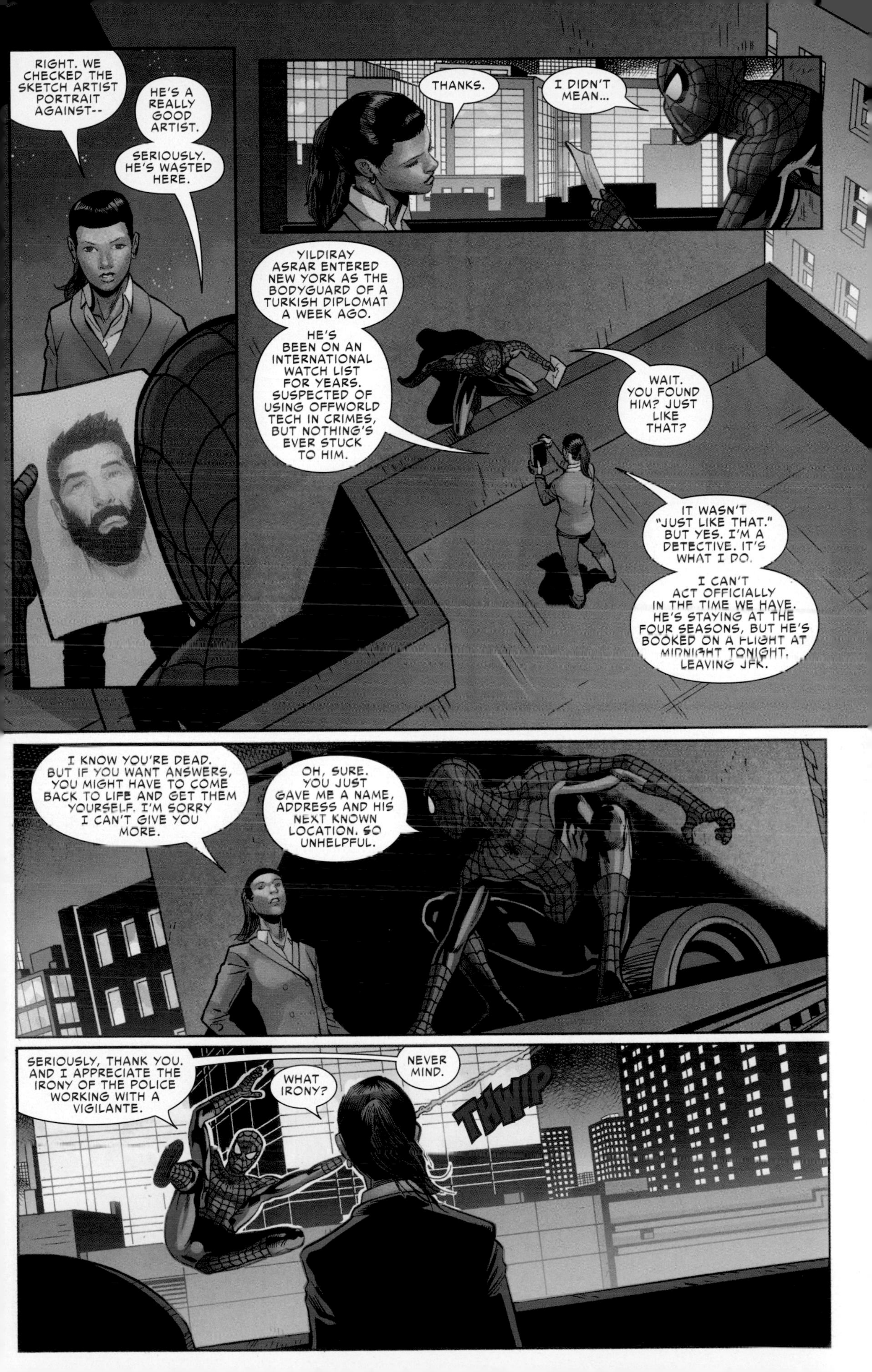
RIGHT. WE CHECKED THE SKETCH ARTIST PORTRAIT AGAINST--
HE'S A REALLY GOOD ARTIST.
SERIOUSLY. HE'S WASTED HERE.
THANKS.
I DIDN'T MEAN...
YILDIRAY ASRAR ENTERED NEW YORK AS THE BODYGUARD OF A TURKISH DIPLOMAT A WEEK AGO.
HE'S BEEN ON AN INTERNATIONAL WATCH LIST FOR YEARS. SUSPECTED OF USING OFFWORLD TECH IN CRIMES, BUT NOTHING'S EVER STUCK TO HIM.
WAIT. YOU FOUND HIM? JUST LIKE THAT?
IT WASN'T "JUST LIKE THAT." BUT YES. I'M A DETECTIVE. IT'S WHAT I DO.
I CAN'T ACT OFFICIALLY IN THE TIME WE HAVE. HE'S STAYING AT THE FOUR SEASONS, BUT HE'S BOOKED ON A FLIGHT AT MIDNIGHT TONIGHT, LEAVING JFK.
I KNOW YOU'RE DEAD. BUT IF YOU WANT ANSWERS, YOU MIGHT HAVE TO COME BACK TO LIFE AND GET THEM YOURSELF. I'M SORRY I CAN'T GIVE YOU MORE.
OH, SURE. YOU JUST GAVE ME A NAME, ADDRESS AND HIS NEXT KNOWN LOCATION. SO UNHELPFUL.
SERIOUSLY, THANK YOU. AND I APPRECIATE THE IRONY OF THE POLICE WORKING WITH A VIGILANTE.
WHAT IRONY?
NEVER MIND.
THWIP

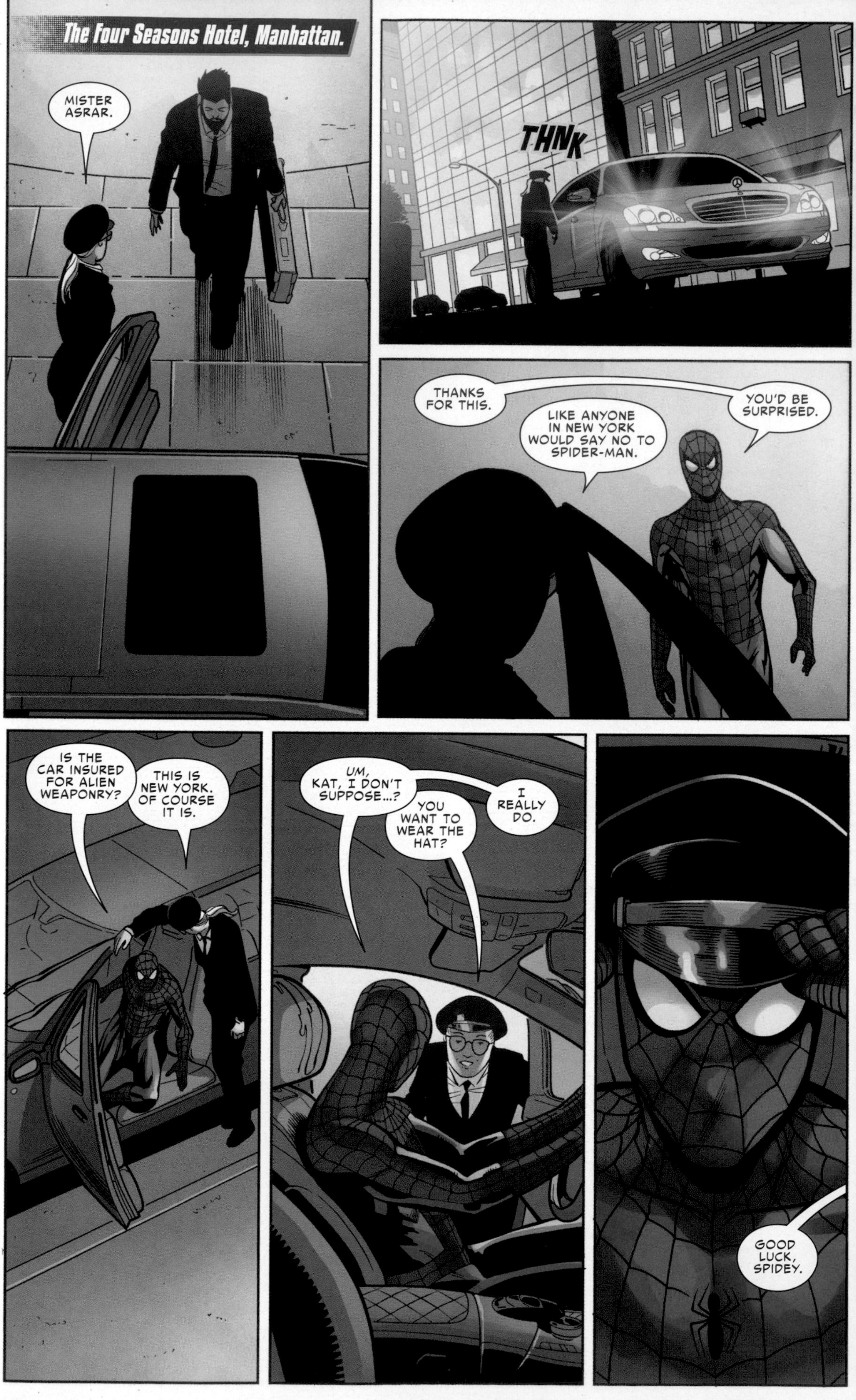
The Four Seasons Hotel, Manhattan.
MISTER ASRAR.
THNK
THANKS FOR THIS.
LIKE ANYONE IN NEW YORK WOULD SAY NO TO SPIDER-MAN.
YOU'D BE SURPRISED.
IS THE CAR INSURED FOR ALIEN WEAPONRY?
THIS IS NEW YORK. OF COURSE IT IS.
UM, KAT, I DON'T SUPPOSE...?
YOU WANT TO WEAR THE HAT?
I REALLY DO.
GOOD LUCK, SPIDEY.

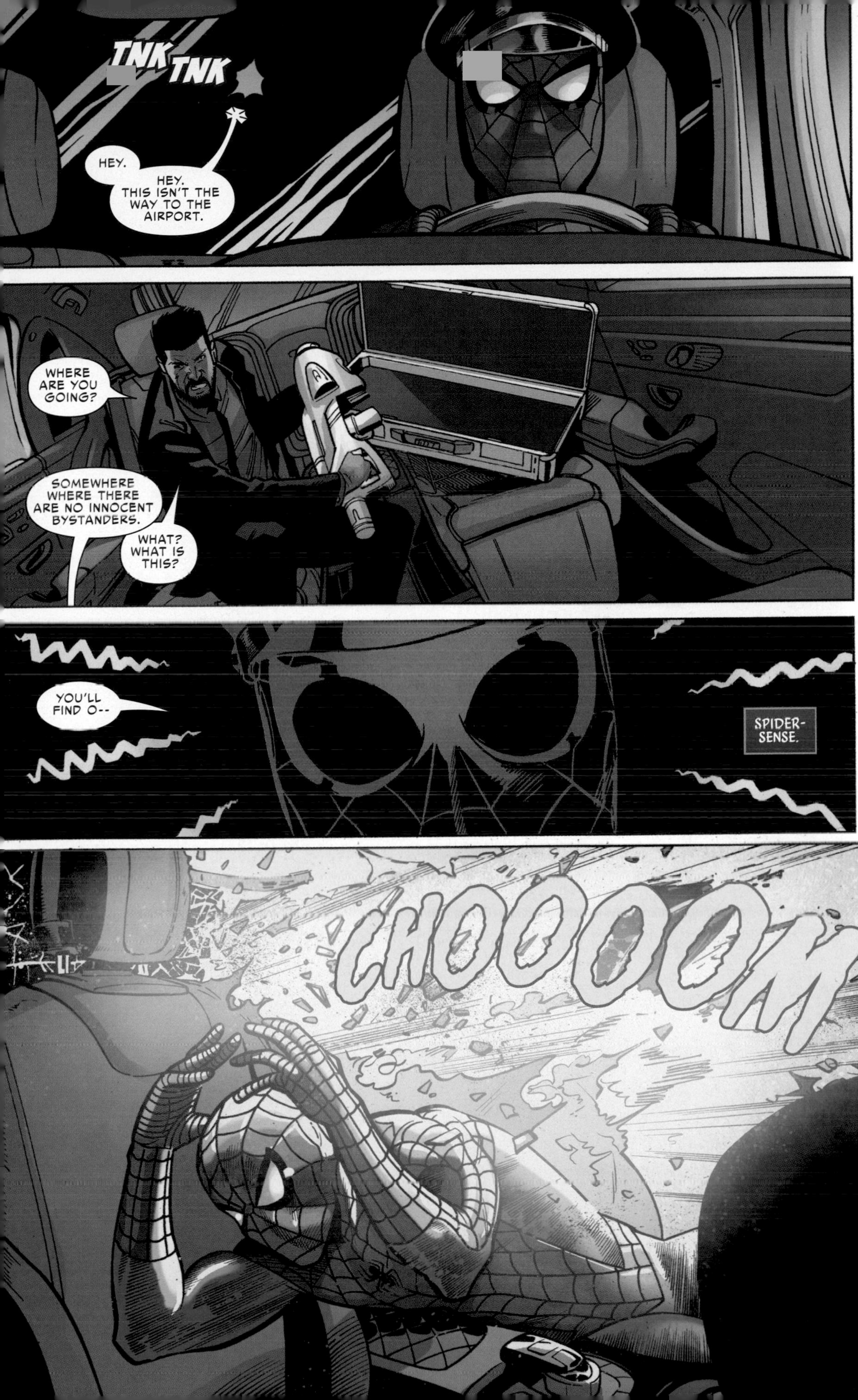
TNK TNK
HEY.
HEY. THIS ISN'T THE WAY TO THE AIRPORT.
WHERE ARE YOU GOING?
SOMEWHERE WHERE THERE ARE NO INNOCENT BYSTANDERS.
WHAT? WHAT IS THIS?
YOU'LL FIND O--
SPIDER-SENSE.
CHOOOOOM

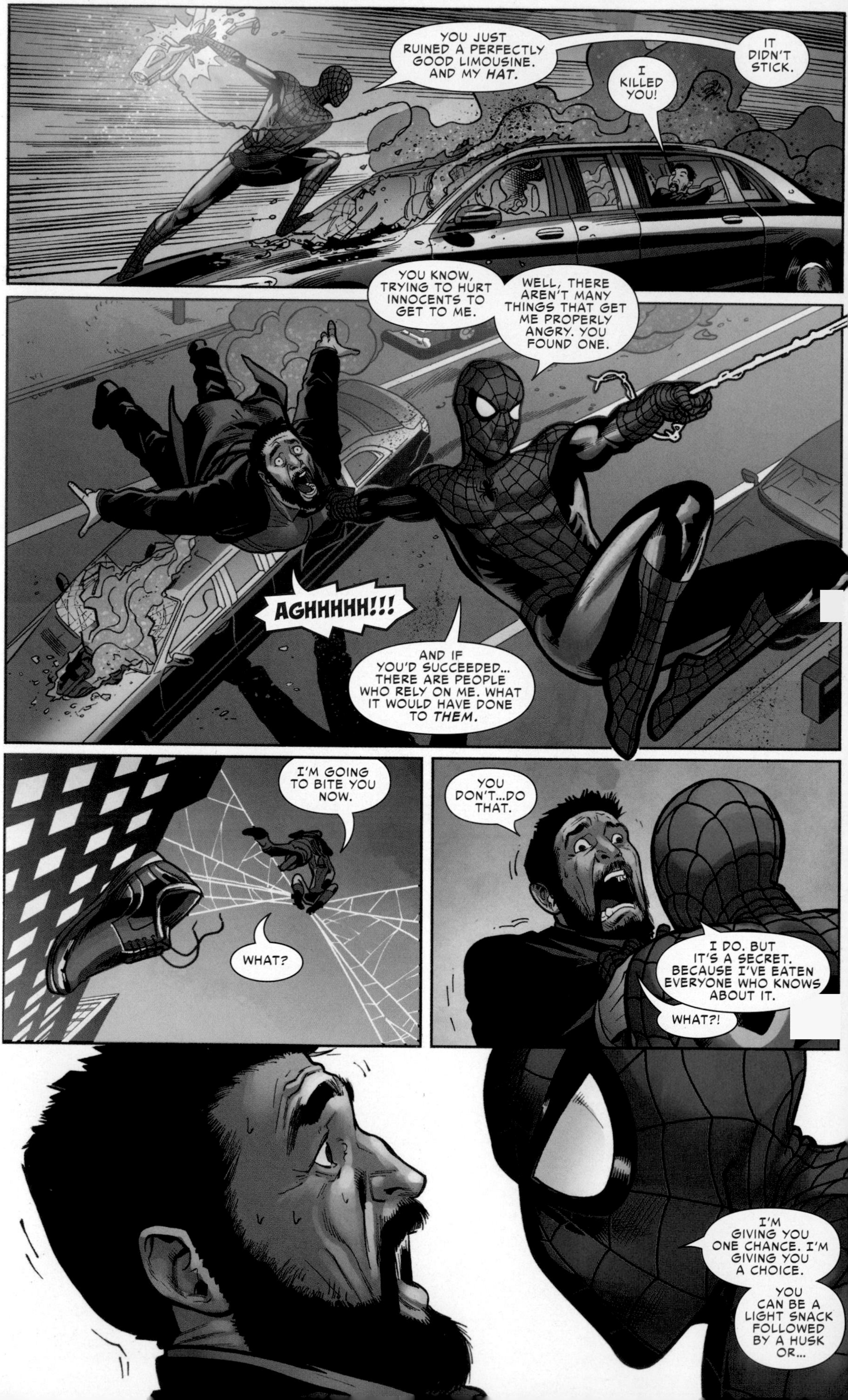

YOU JUST RUINED A PERFECTLY GOOD LIMOUSINE. AND MY HAT.
IT DIDN'T STICK.
I KILLED YOU!
YOU KNOW, TRYING TO HURT INNOCENTS TO GET TO ME.
WELL, THERE AREN'T MANY THINGS THAT GET ME PROPERLY ANGRY. YOU FOUND ONE.
AGHHHHH!!!
AND IF YOU'D SUCCEEDED... THERE ARE PEOPLE WHO RELY ON ME. WHAT IT WOULD HAVE DONE TO THEM.
I'M GOING TO BITE YOU NOW.
WHAT?
YOU DON'T...DO THAT.
I DO. BUT IT'S A SECRET. BECAUSE I'VE EATEN EVERYONE WHO KNOWS ABOUT IT.
WHAT?!
I'M GIVING YOU ONE CHANCE. I'M GIVING YOU A CHOICE.
YOU CAN BE A LIGHT SNACK FOLLOWED BY A HUSK OR...

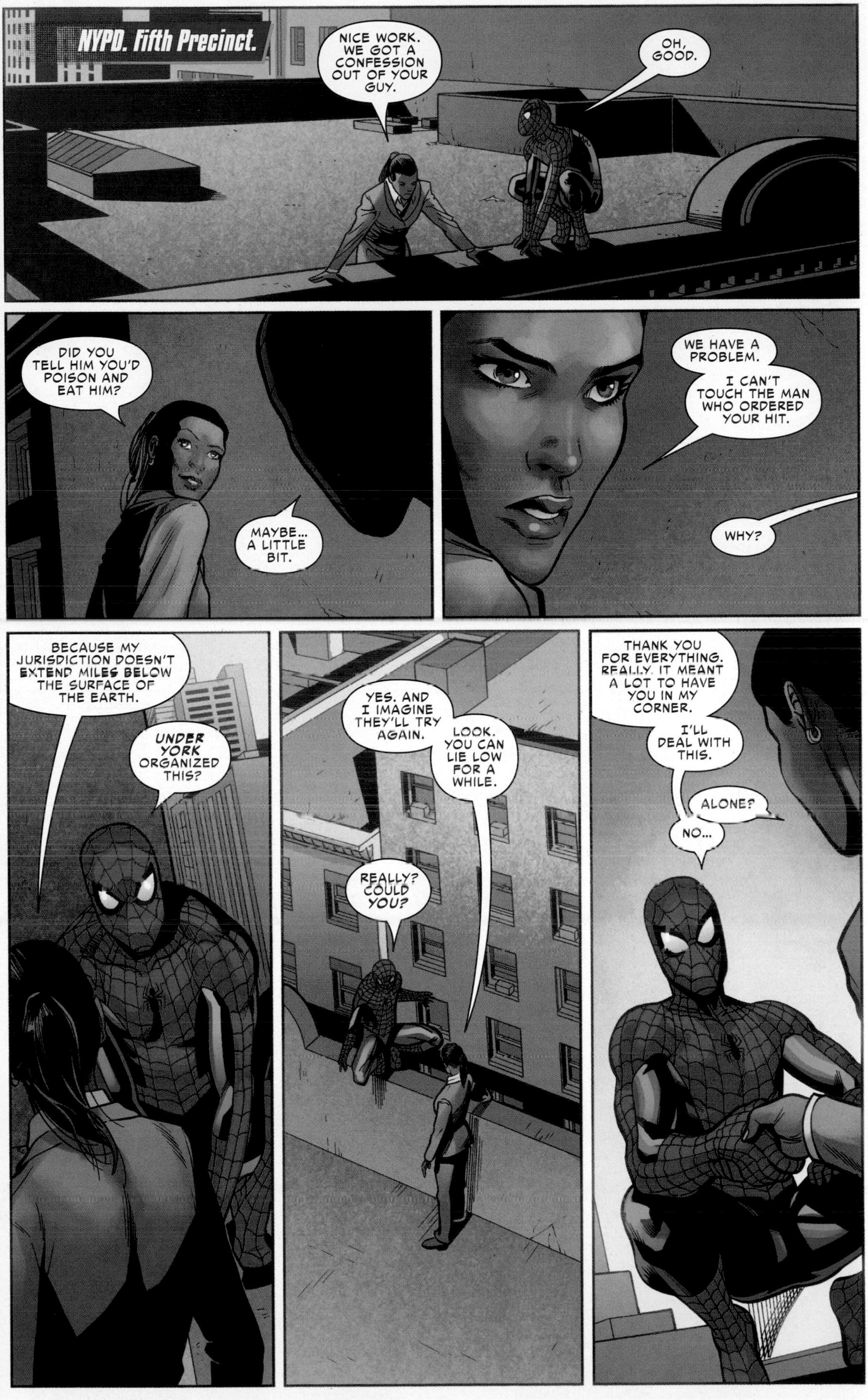
NYPD. Fifth Precinct.
NICE WORK. WE GOT A CONFESSION OUT OF YOUR GUY.
OH, GOOD.
DID YOU TELL HIM YOU'D POISON AND EAT HIM?
MAYBE... A LITTLE BIT.
WE HAVE A PROBLEM.
I CAN'T TOUCH THE MAN WHO ORDERED YOUR HIT.
WHY?
BECAUSE MY JURISDICTION DOESN'T EXTEND MILES BELOW THE SURFACE OF THE EARTH.
UNDER YORK ORGANIZED THIS?
YES. AND I IMAGINE THEY'LL TRY AGAIN.
LOOK. YOU CAN LIE LOW FOR A WHILE.
REALLY? COULD YOU?
THANK YOU FOR EVERYTHING. REALLY. IT MEANT A LOT TO HAVE YOU IN MY CORNER.
I'LL DEAL WITH THIS.
ALONE?
NO...

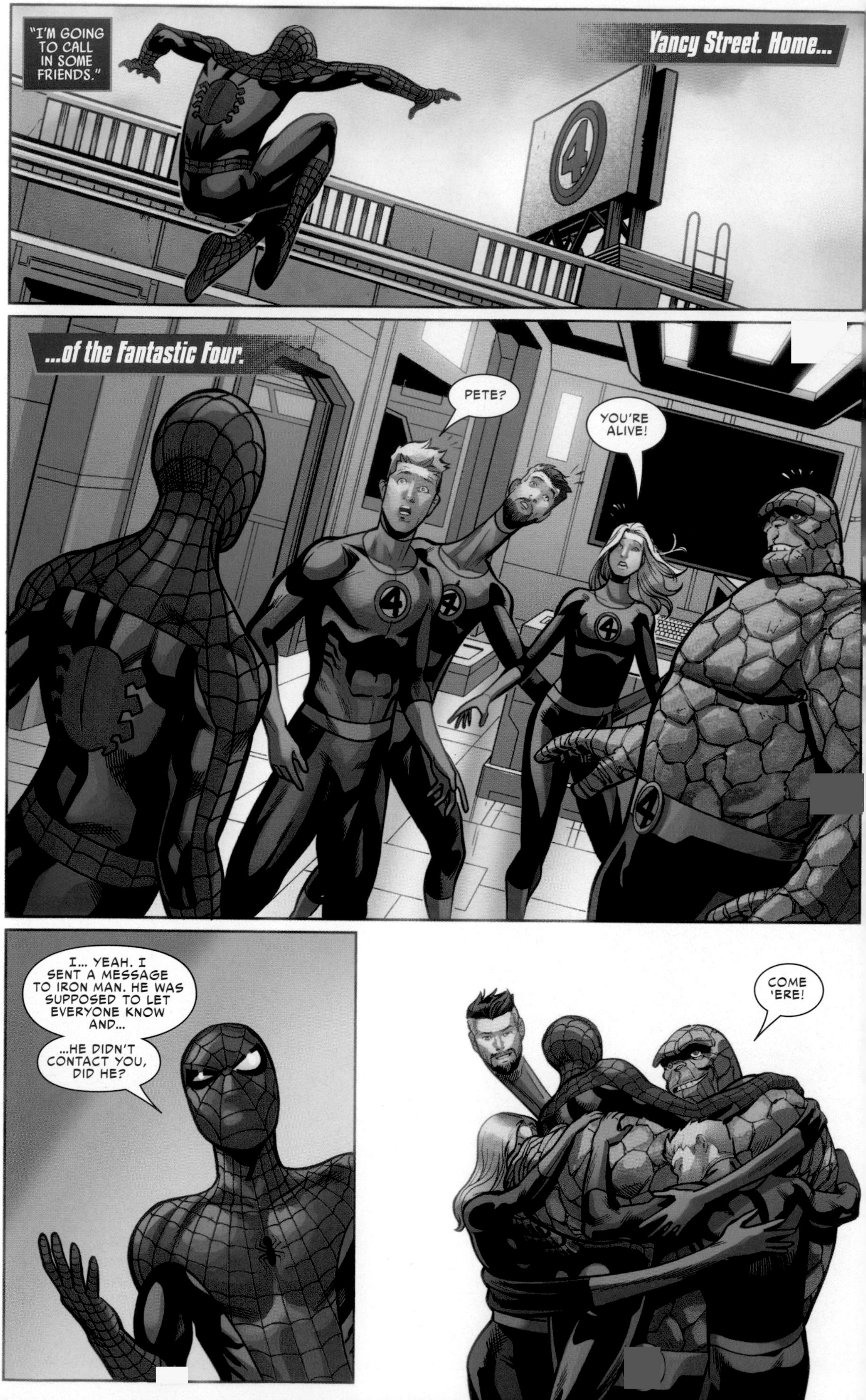
"I'M GOING TO CALL IN SOME FRIENDS."
Yancy Street. Home...
...of the Fantastic Four.
PETE?
YOU'RE ALIVE!
I... YEAH. I SENT A MESSAGE TO IRON MAN. HE WAS SUPPOSED TO LET EVERYONE KNOW AND...
...HE DIDN'T CONTACT YOU, DID HE?
COME 'ERE!

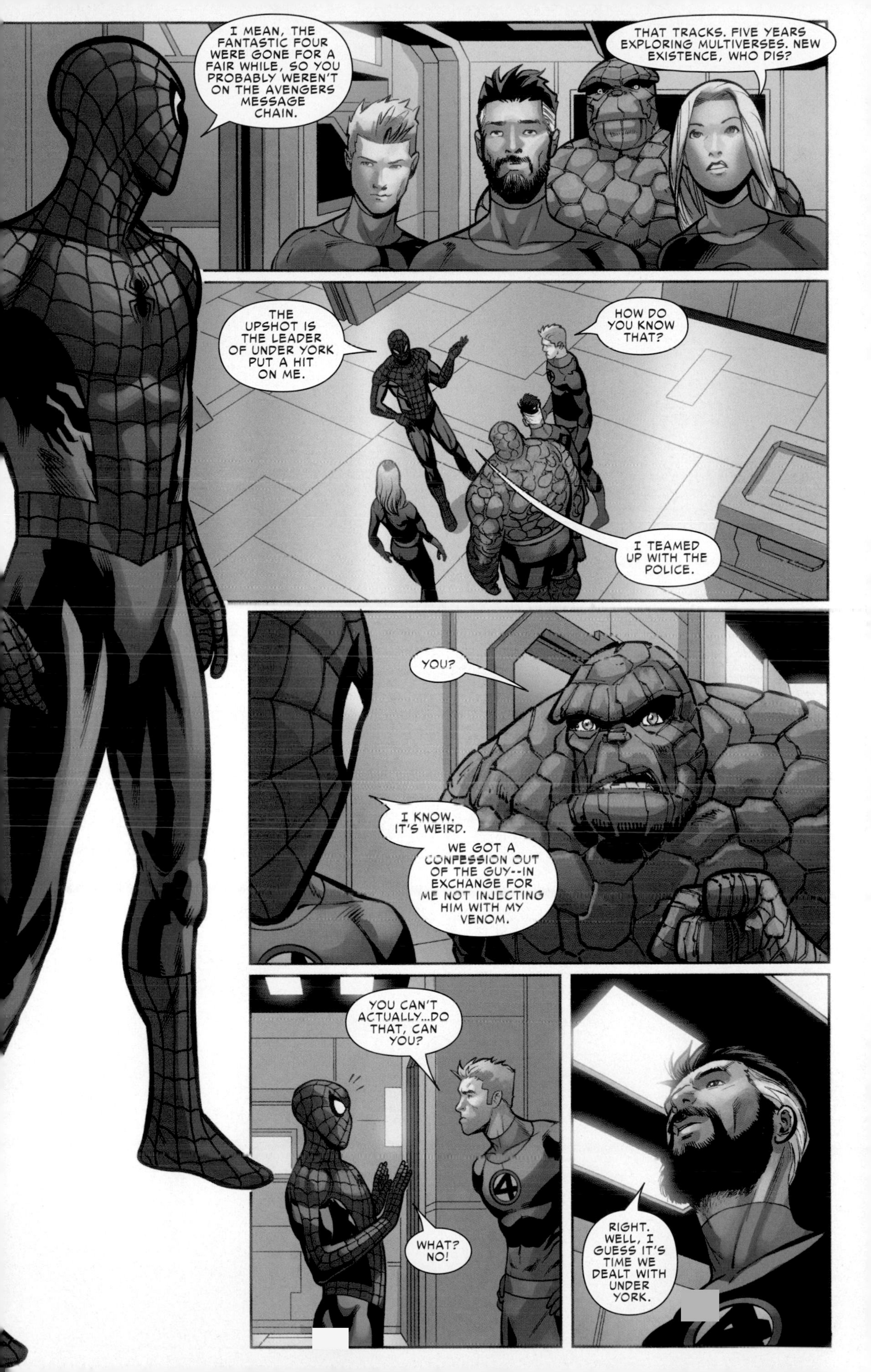
I MEAN, THE FANTASTIC FOUR WERE GONE FOR A FAIR WHILE, SO YOU PROBABLY WEREN'T ON THE AVENGERS MESSAGE CHAIN.
THAT TRACKS. FIVE YEARS EXPLORING MULTIVERSES. NEW EXISTENCE, WHO DIS?
THE UPSHOT IS THE LEADER OF UNDER YORK PUT A HIT ON ME.
HOW DO YOU KNOW THAT?
I TEAMED UP WITH THE POLICE.
YOU?
I KNOW. IT'S WEIRD.
WE GOT A CONFESSION OUT OF THE GUY--IN EXCHANGE FOR ME NOT INJECTING HIM WITH MY VENOM.
YOU CAN'T ACTUALLY...DO THAT, CAN YOU?
WHAT? NO!
RIGHT. WELL, I GUESS IT'S TIME WE DEALT WITH UNDER YORK.

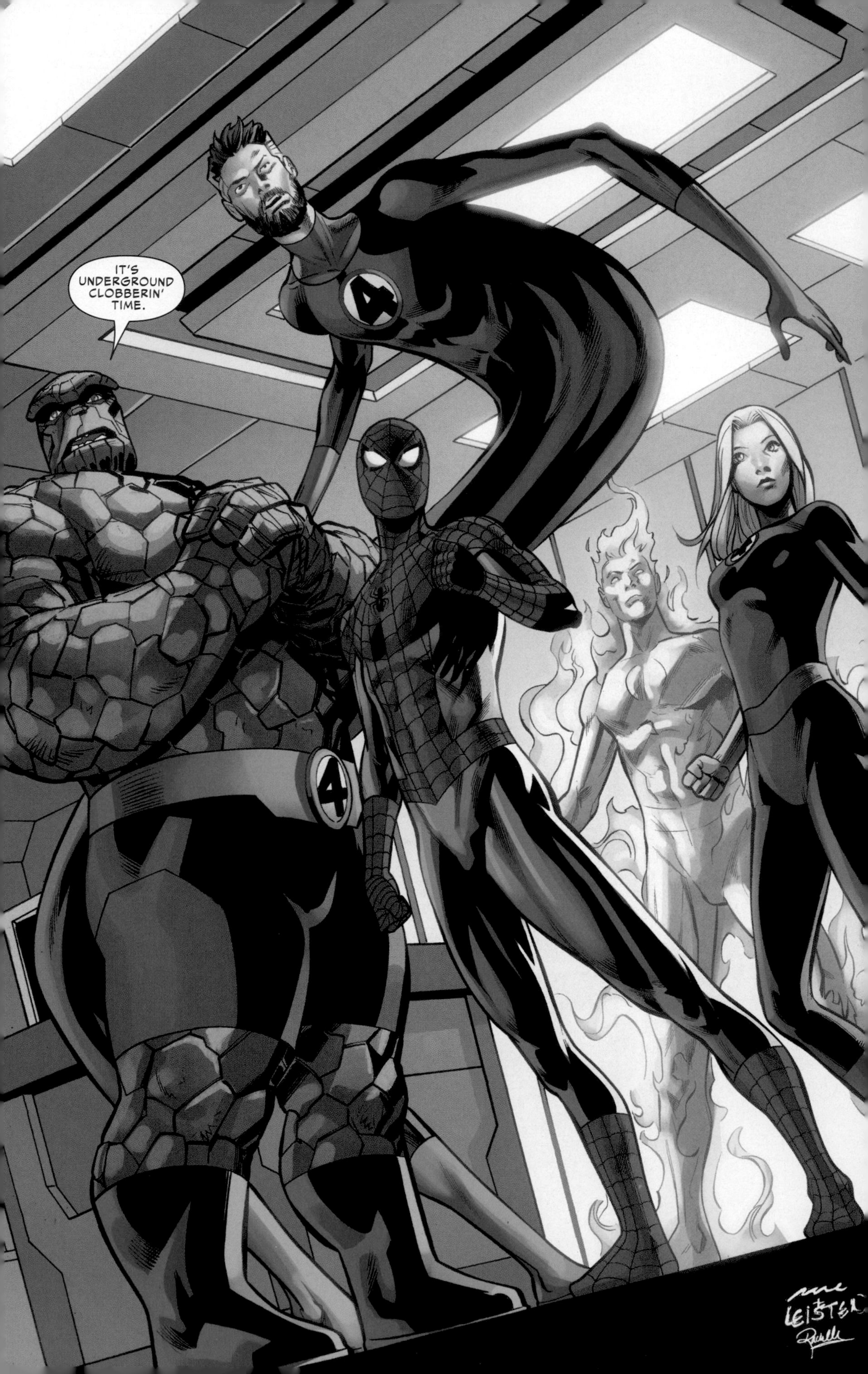
IT'S UNDERGROUND CLOBBERIN' TIME.

13

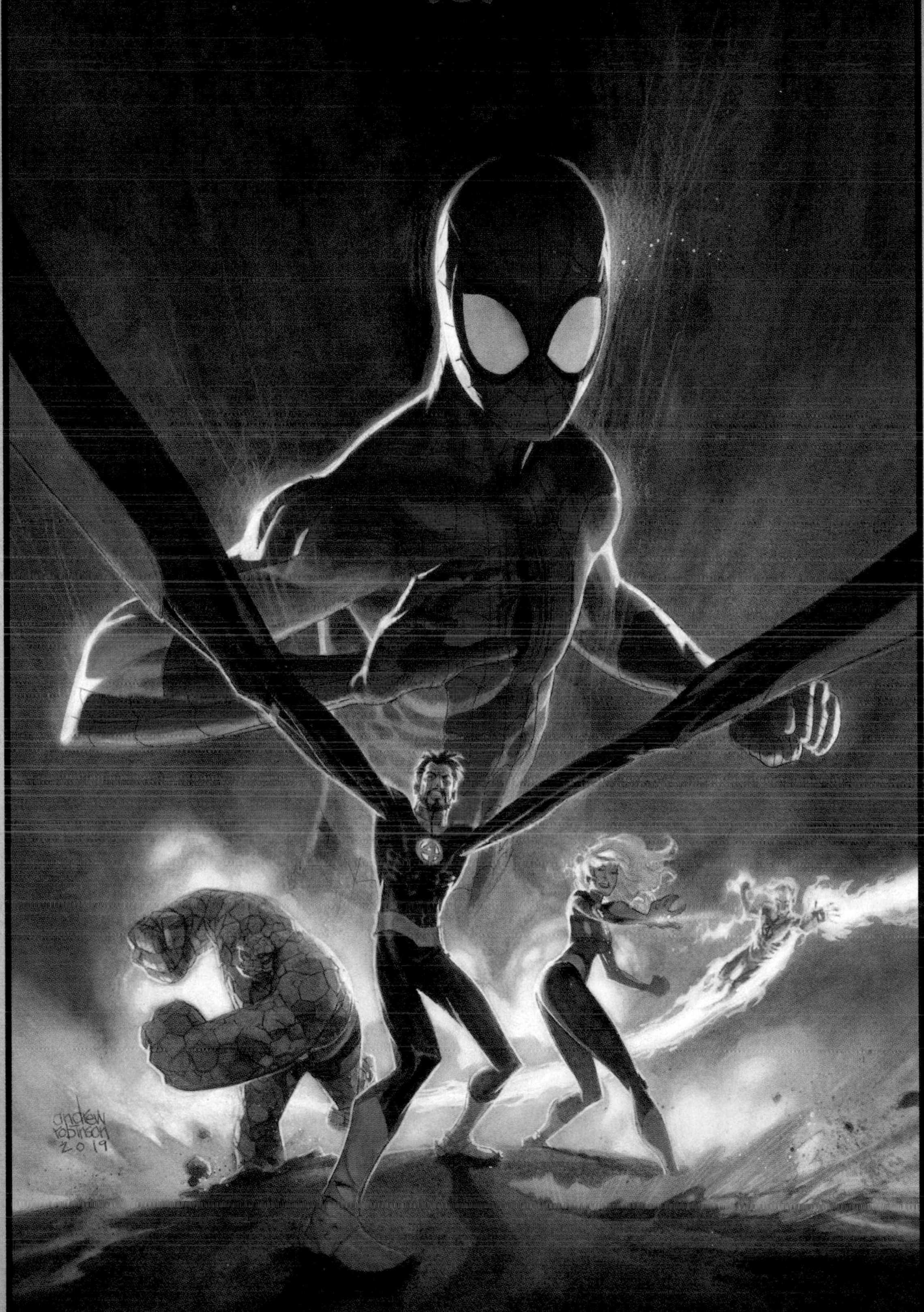
andrew robinson 2019

You Say You Want a Revolution

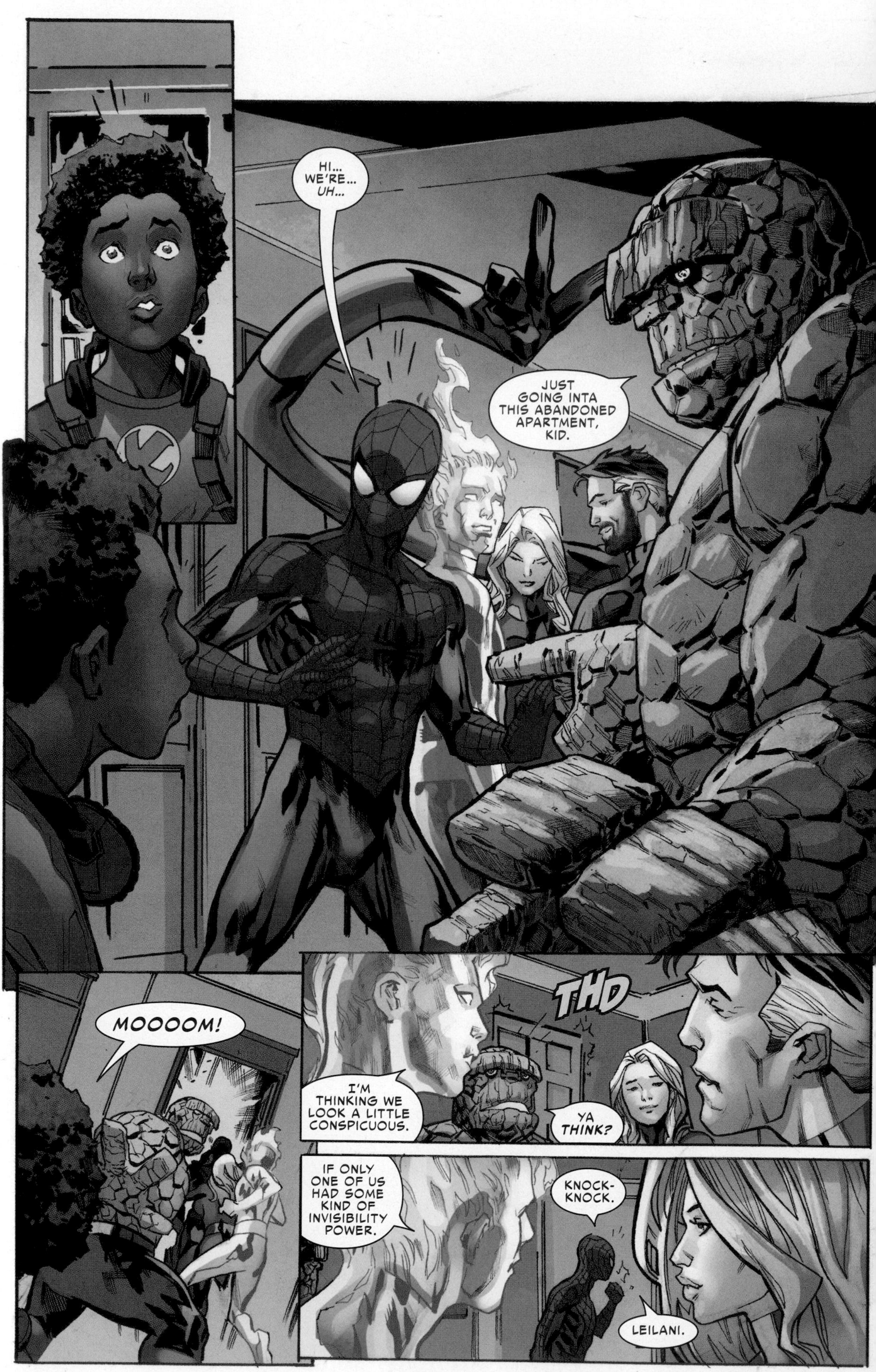
HI... WE'RE... UH...
JUST GOING INTA THIS ABANDONED APARTMENT, KID.
MOOOOM!
THD
I'M THINKING WE LOOK A LITTLE CONSPICUOUS.
YA THINK?
IF ONLY ONE OF US HAD SOME KIND OF INVISIBILITY POWER.
KNOCK-KNOCK.
LEILANI.

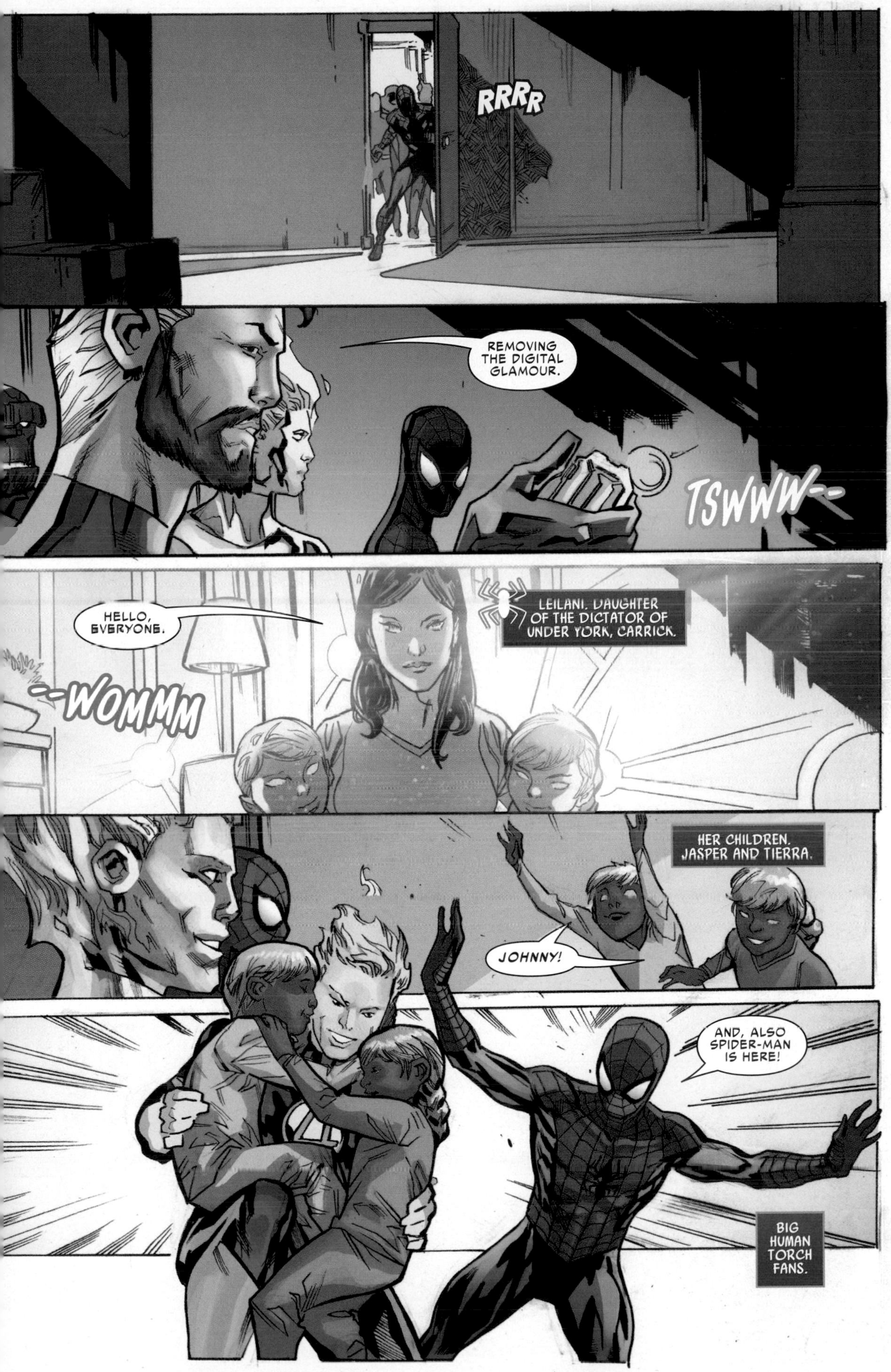
RRRR
REMOVING THE DIGITAL GLAMOUR.
TSWWW--
HELLO, EVERYONE.
LEILANI. DAUGHTER OF THE DICTATOR OF UNDER YORK, CARRICK.
--WOMMM
HER CHILDREN. JASPER AND TIERRA.
JOHNNY!
AND, ALSO SPIDER-MAN IS HERE!
BIG HUMAN TORCH FANS.

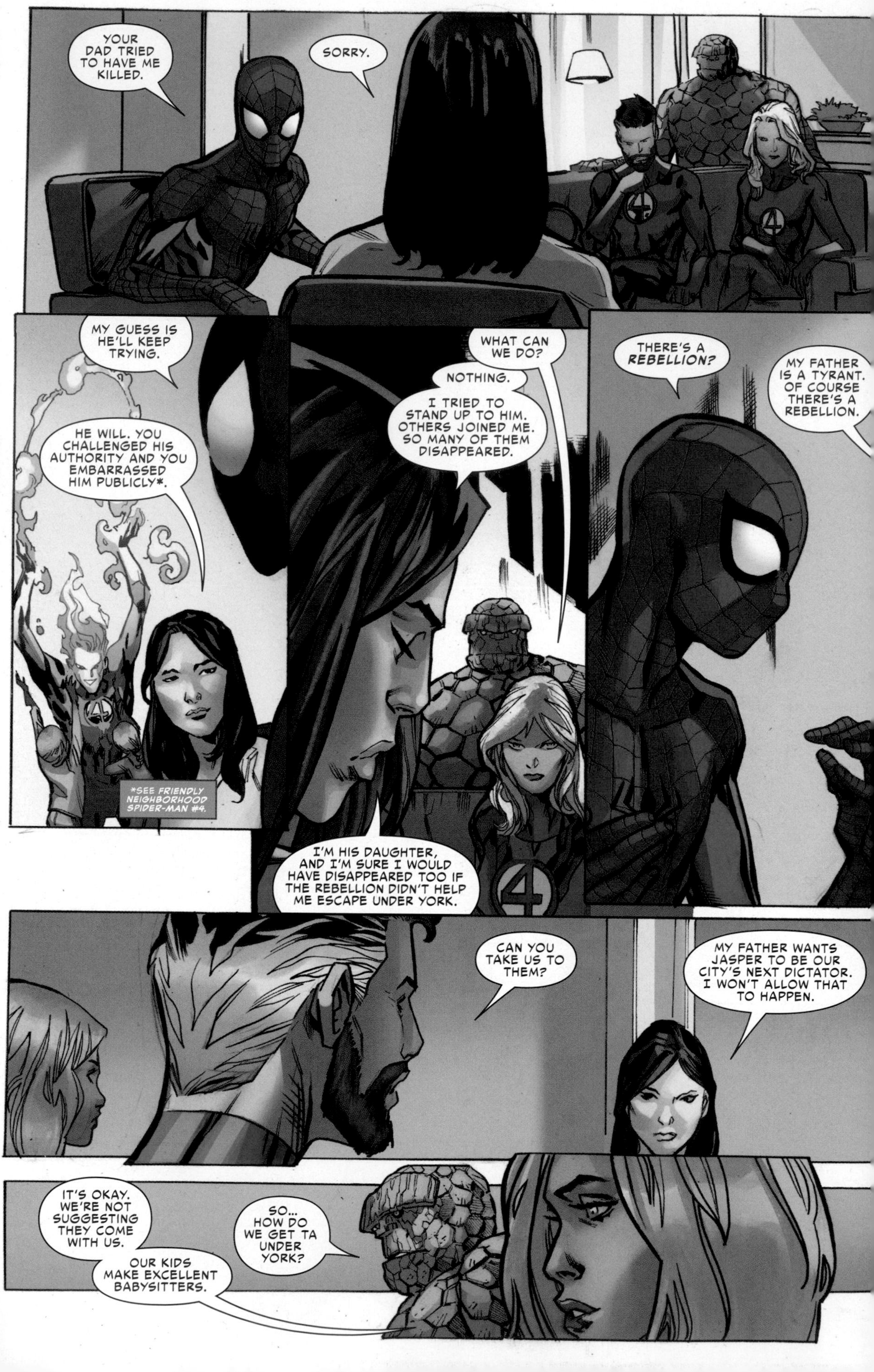
YOUR DAD TRIED TO HAVE ME KILLED.
SORRY.
MY GUESS IS HE'LL KEEP TRYING.
HE WILL. YOU CHALLENGED HIS AUTHORITY AND YOU EMBARRASSED HIM PUBLICLY*.
*SEE FRIENDLY NEIGHBORHOOD SPIDER-MAN #4.
WHAT CAN WE DO?
NOTHING.
I TRIED TO STAND UP TO HIM. OTHERS JOINED ME. SO MANY OF THEM DISAPPEARED.
I'M HIS DAUGHTER, AND I'M SURE I WOULD HAVE DISAPPEARED TOO IF THE REBELLION DIDN'T HELP ME ESCAPE UNDER YORK.
THERE'S A REBELLION?
MY FATHER IS A TYRANT. OF COURSE THERE'S A REBELLION.
CAN YOU TAKE US TO THEM?
MY FATHER WANTS JASPER TO BE OUR CITY'S NEXT DICTATOR. I WON'T ALLOW THAT TO HAPPEN.
IT'S OKAY. WE'RE NOT SUGGESTING THEY COME WITH US.
OUR KIDS MAKE EXCELLENT BABYSITTERS.
SO... HOW DO WE GET TA UNDER YORK?

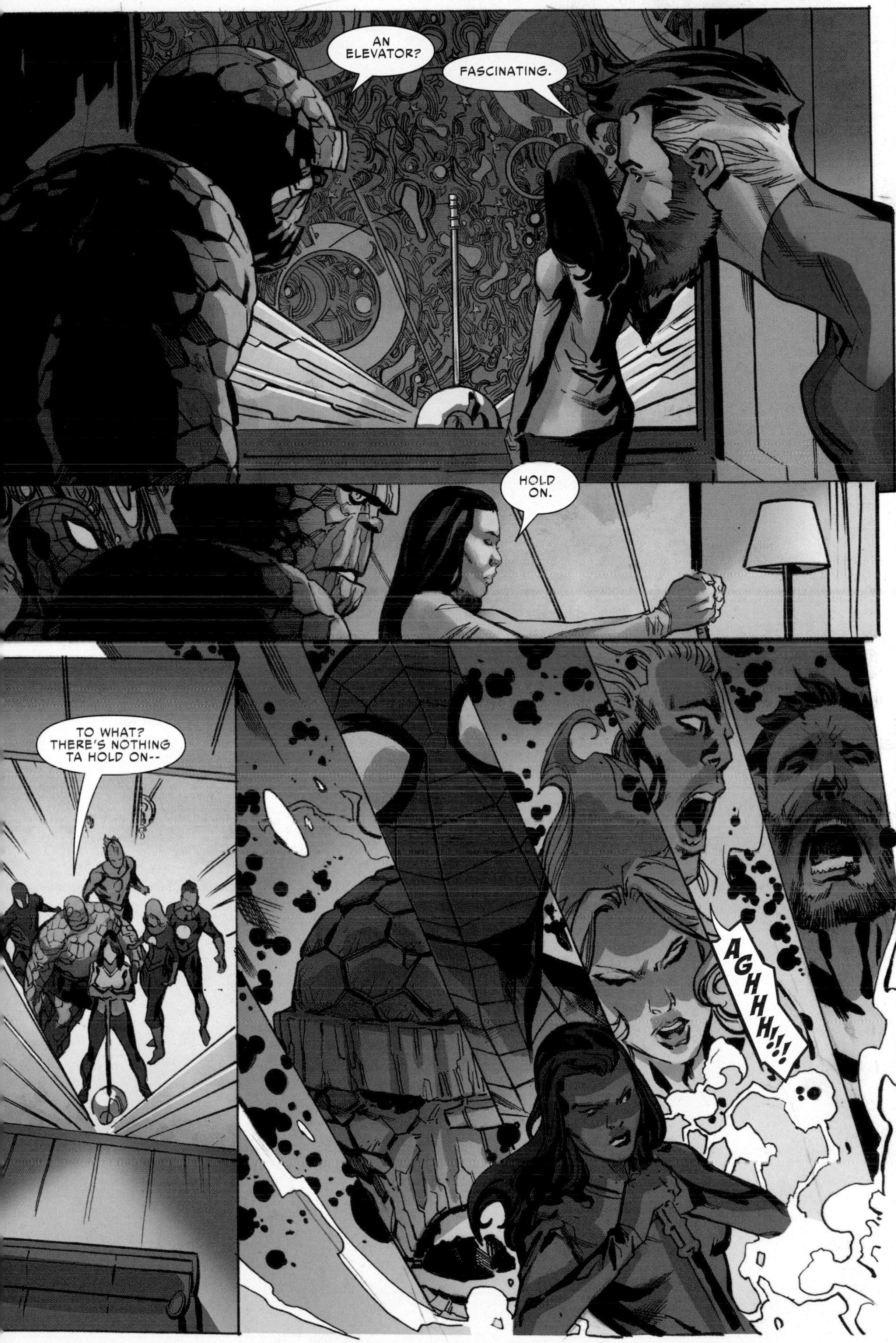
AN ELEVATOR?
FASCINATING.
HOLD ON.
TO WHAT? THERE'S NOTHING TA HOLD ON--
AGHHH!!!

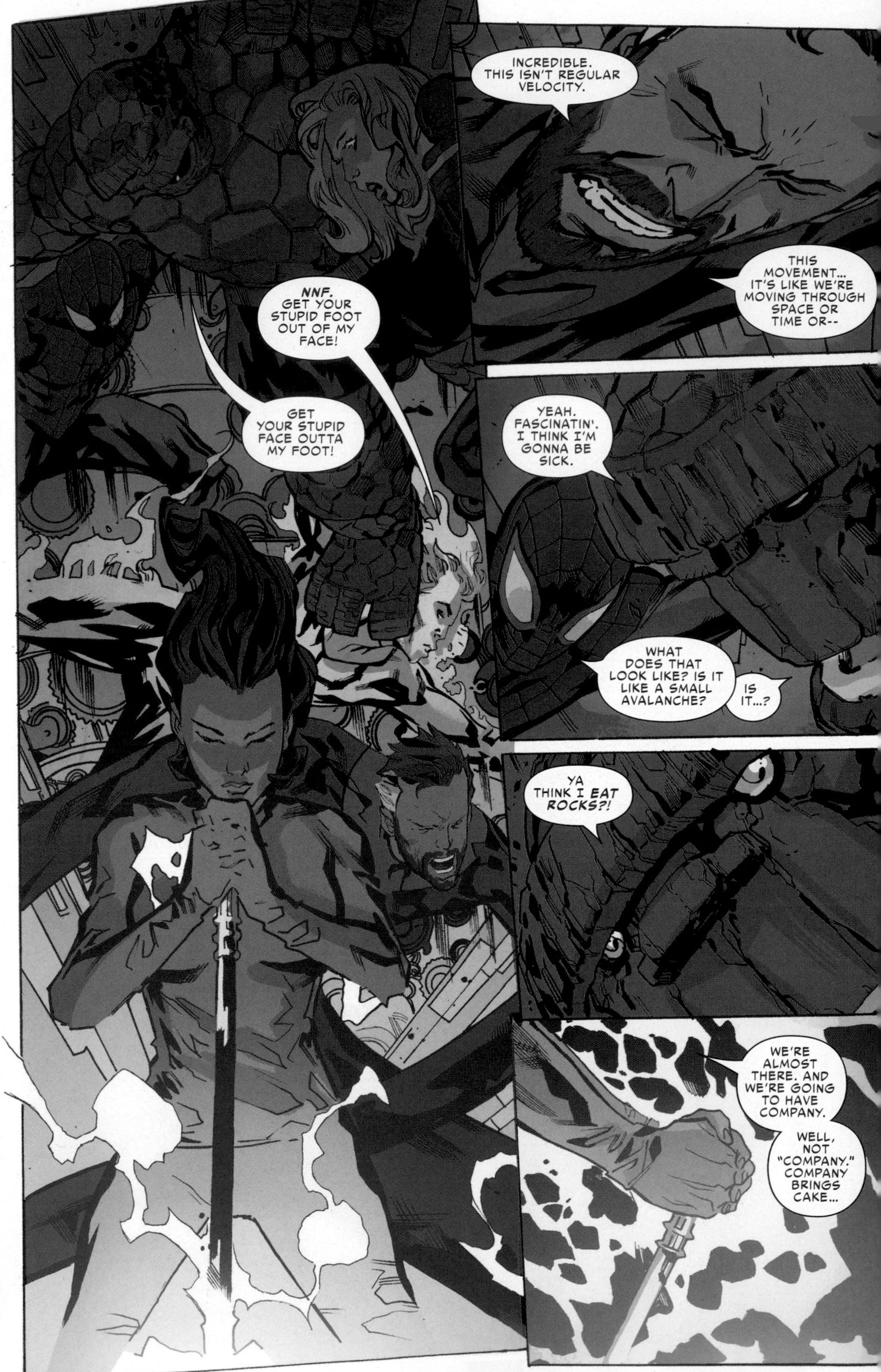
INCREDIBLE. THIS ISN'T REGULAR VELOCITY.
THIS MOVEMENT... IT'S LIKE WE'RE MOVING THROUGH SPACE OR TIME OR--
NNF. GET YOUR STUPID FOOT OUT OF MY FACE!
GET YOUR STUPID FACE OUTTA MY FOOT!
YEAH. FASCINATIN'. I THINK I'M GONNA BE SICK.
WHAT DOES THAT LOOK LIKE? IS IT LIKE A SMALL AVALANCHE?
IS IT...?
YA THINK I EAT ROCKS?!
WE'RE ALMOST THERE. AND WE'RE GOING TO HAVE COMPANY.
WELL, NOT "COMPANY." COMPANY BRINGS CAKE...

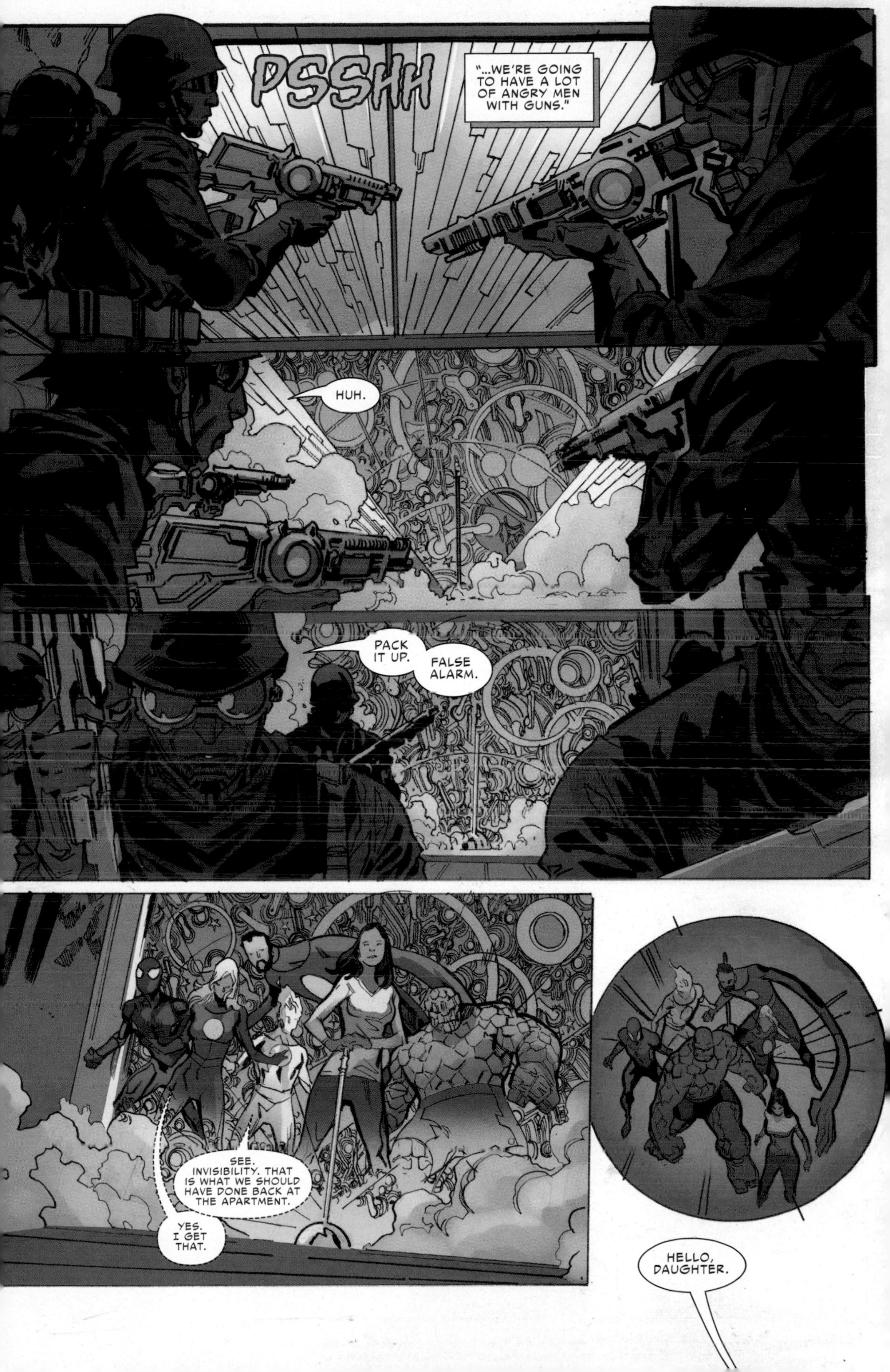
PSSHH
"...WE'RE GOING TO HAVE A LOT OF ANGRY MEN WITH GUNS."
HUH.
PACK IT UP.
FALSE ALARM.
SEE. INVISIBILITY. THAT IS WHAT WE SHOULD HAVE DONE BACK AT THE APARTMENT.
YES. I GET THAT.
HELLO, DAUGHTER.

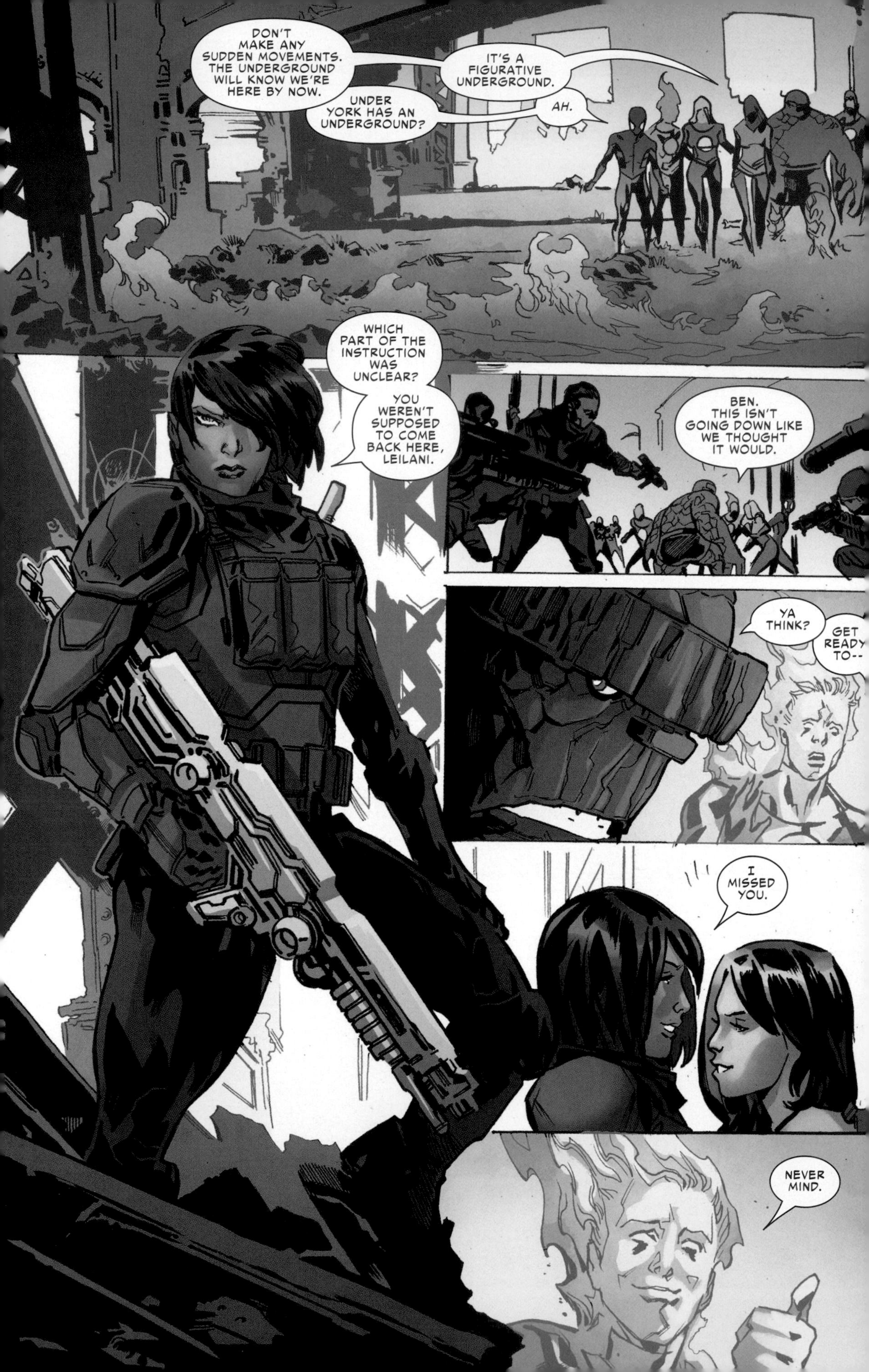
DON'T MAKE ANY SUDDEN MOVEMENTS. THE UNDERGROUND WILL KNOW WE'RE HERE BY NOW.
UNDER YORK HAS AN UNDERGROUND?
IT'S A FIGURATIVE UNDERGROUND.
AH.
WHICH PART OF THE INSTRUCTION WAS UNCLEAR?
YOU WEREN'T SUPPOSED TO COME BACK HERE, LEILANI.
BEN. THIS ISN'T GOING DOWN LIKE WE THOUGHT IT WOULD.
YA THINK?
GET READY TO--
I MISSED YOU.
NEVER MIND.

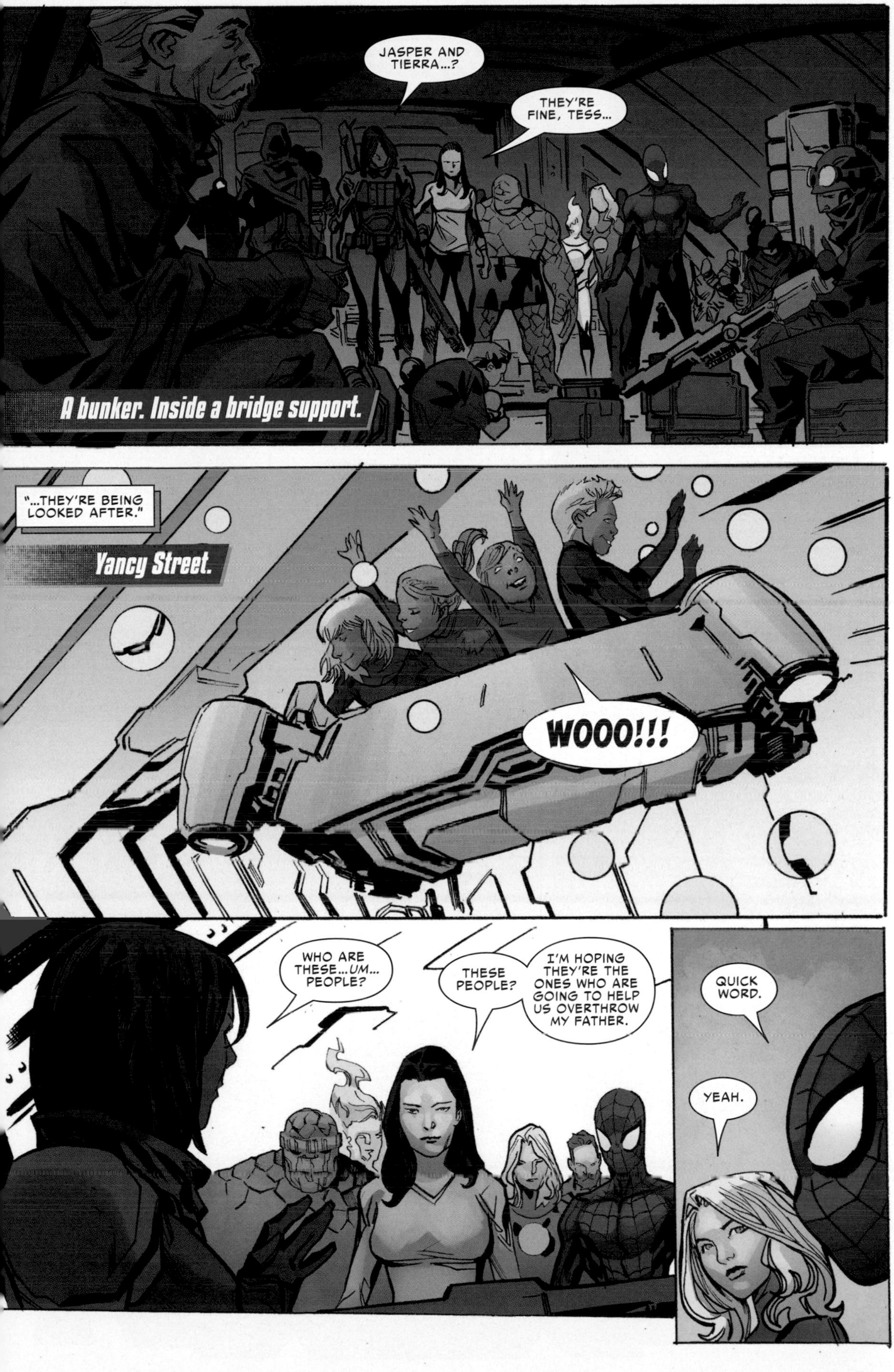
JASPER AND TIERRA...?
THEY'RE FINE, TESS...
A bunker. Inside a bridge support.
"...THEY'RE BEING LOOKED AFTER."
Yancy Street.
WOOO!!!
WHO ARE THESE...UM... PEOPLE?
THESE PEOPLE?
I'M HOPING THEY'RE THE ONES WHO ARE GOING TO HELP US OVERTHROW MY FATHER.
QUICK WORD.
YEAH.

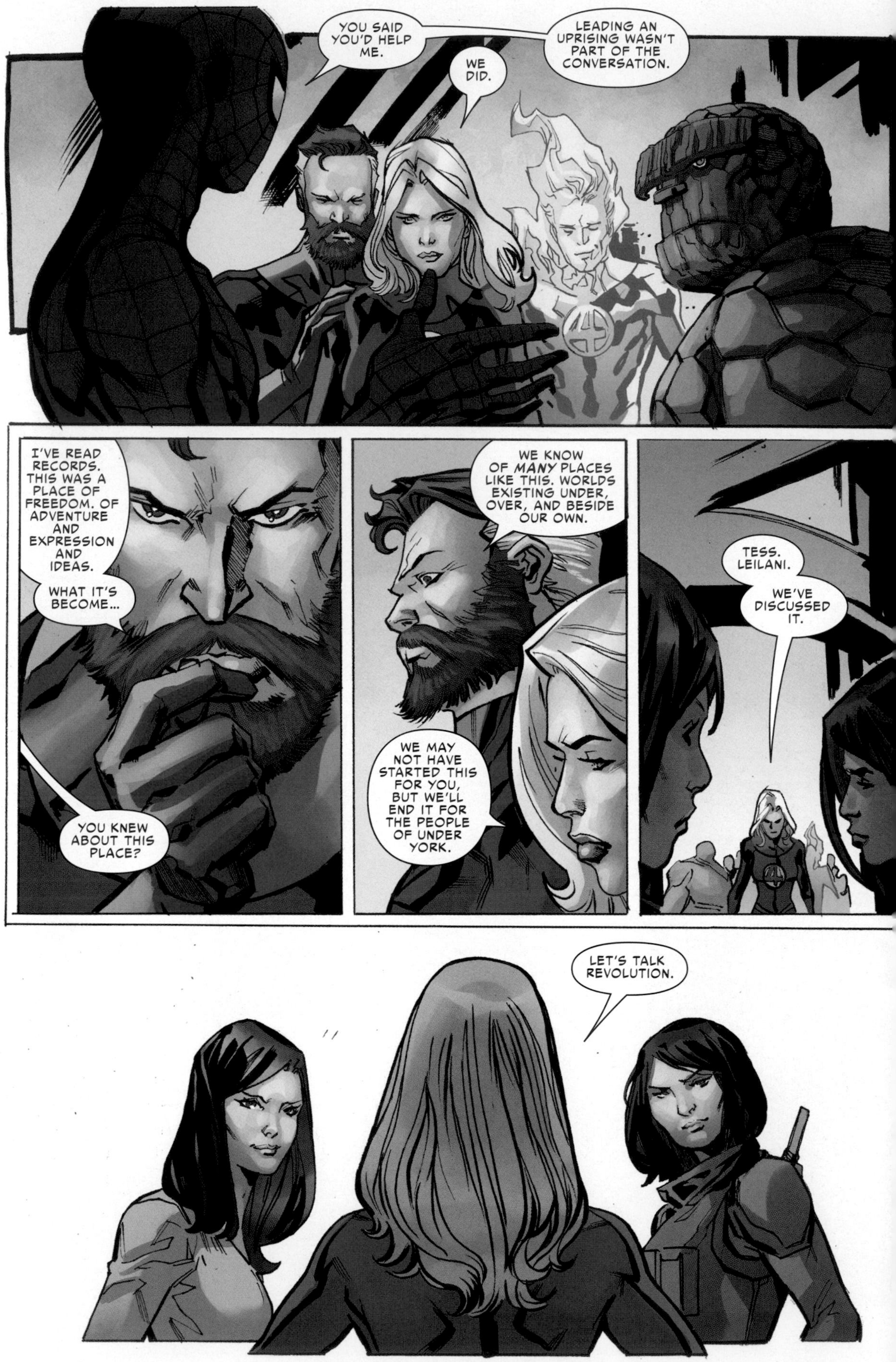
YOU SAID YOU'D HELP ME.
WE DID.
LEADING AN UPRISING WASN'T PART OF THE CONVERSATION.
I'VE READ RECORDS. THIS WAS A PLACE OF FREEDOM. OF ADVENTURE AND EXPRESSION AND IDEAS.
WHAT IT'S BECOME...
YOU KNEW ABOUT THIS PLACE?
WE KNOW OF MANY PLACES LIKE THIS. WORLDS EXISTING UNDER, OVER, AND BESIDE OUR OWN.
WE MAY NOT HAVE STARTED THIS FOR YOU, BUT WE'LL END IT FOR THE PEOPLE OF UNDER YORK.
TESS. LEILANI.
WE'VE DISCUSSED IT.
LET'S TALK REVOLUTION.

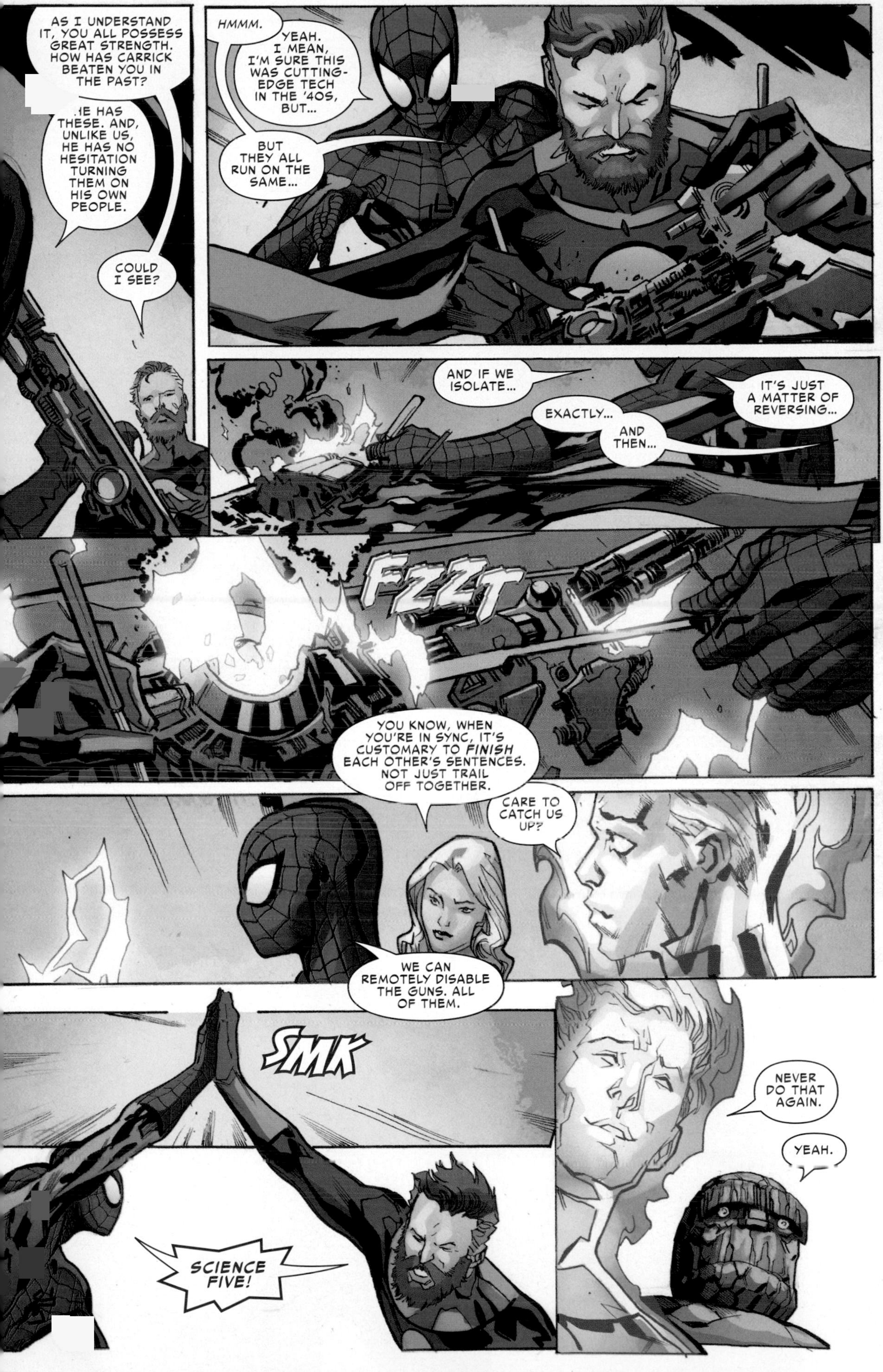
AS I UNDERSTAND IT, YOU ALL POSSESS GREAT STRENGTH. HOW HAS CARRICK BEATEN YOU IN THE PAST?
HE HAS THESE. AND, UNLIKE US, HE HAS NO HESITATION TURNING THEM ON HIS OWN PEOPLE.
COULD I SEE?
HMMM.
YEAH. I MEAN, I'M SURE THIS WAS CUTTING-EDGE TECH IN THE '40S, BUT...
BUT THEY ALL RUN ON THE SAME...
AND IF WE ISOLATE...
IT'S JUST A MATTER OF REVERSING...
EXACTLY...
AND THEN...
FZZT
YOU KNOW, WHEN YOU'RE IN SYNC, IT'S CUSTOMARY TO FINISH EACH OTHER'S SENTENCES. NOT JUST TRAIL OFF TOGETHER.
CARE TO CATCH US UP?
WE CAN REMOTELY DISABLE THE GUNS. ALL OF THEM.
SMK
SCIENCE FIVE!
NEVER DO THAT AGAIN.
YEAH.

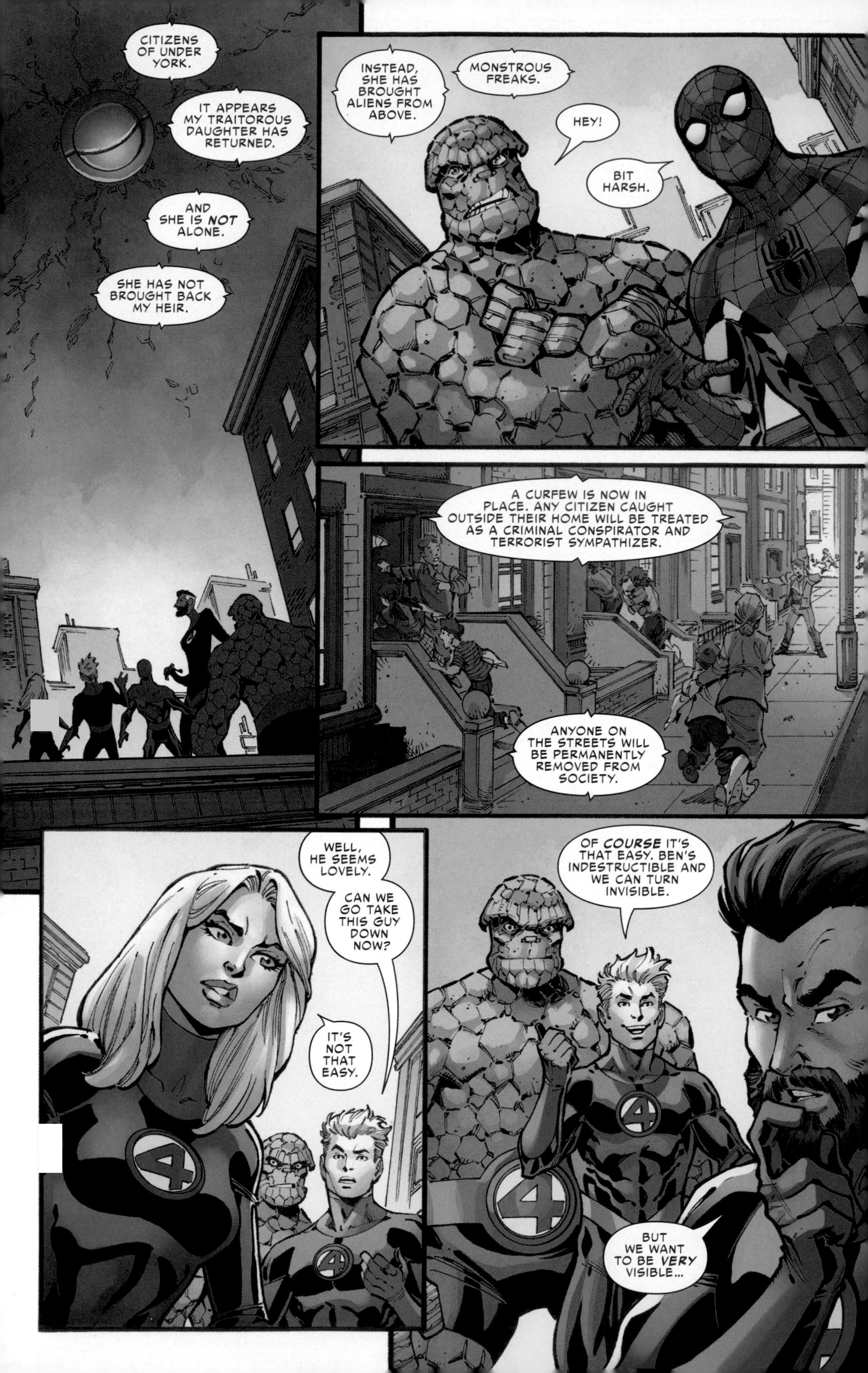

CITIZENS OF UNDER YORK.
IT APPEARS MY TRAITOROUS DAUGHTER HAS RETURNED.
AND SHE IS *NOT* ALONE.
SHE HAS NOT BROUGHT BACK MY HEIR.
INSTEAD, SHE HAS BROUGHT ALIENS FROM ABOVE.
MONSTROUS FREAKS.
HEY!
BIT HARSH.
A CURFEW IS NOW IN PLACE. ANY CITIZEN CAUGHT OUTSIDE THEIR HOME WILL BE TREATED AS A CRIMINAL CONSPIRATOR AND TERRORIST SYMPATHIZER.
ANYONE ON THE STREETS WILL BE PERMANENTLY REMOVED FROM SOCIETY.
WELL, HE SEEMS LOVELY.
CAN WE GO TAKE THIS GUY DOWN NOW?
IT'S NOT THAT EASY.
OF *COURSE* IT'S THAT EASY. BEN'S INDESTRUCTIBLE AND WE CAN TURN INVISIBLE.
BUT WE WANT TO BE *VERY* VISIBLE...

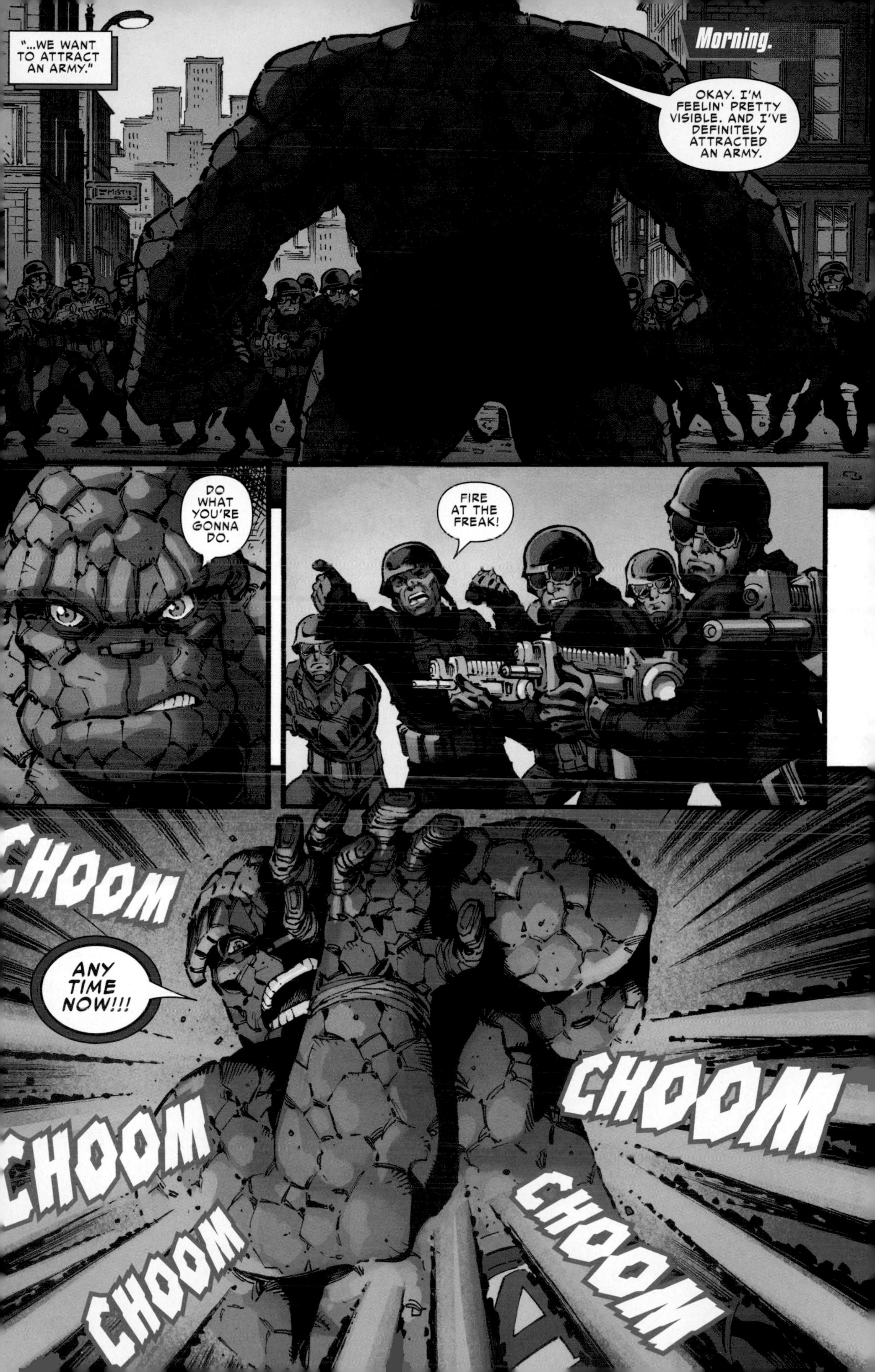
"...WE WANT TO ATTRACT AN ARMY."
Morning.
OKAY. I'M FEELIN' PRETTY VISIBLE. AND I'VE DEFINITELY ATTRACTED AN ARMY.
DO WHAT YOU'RE GONNA DO.
FIRE AT THE FREAK!
CHOOM
ANY TIME NOW!!!
CHOOM
CHOOM
CHOOM
CHOOM
CHOOM

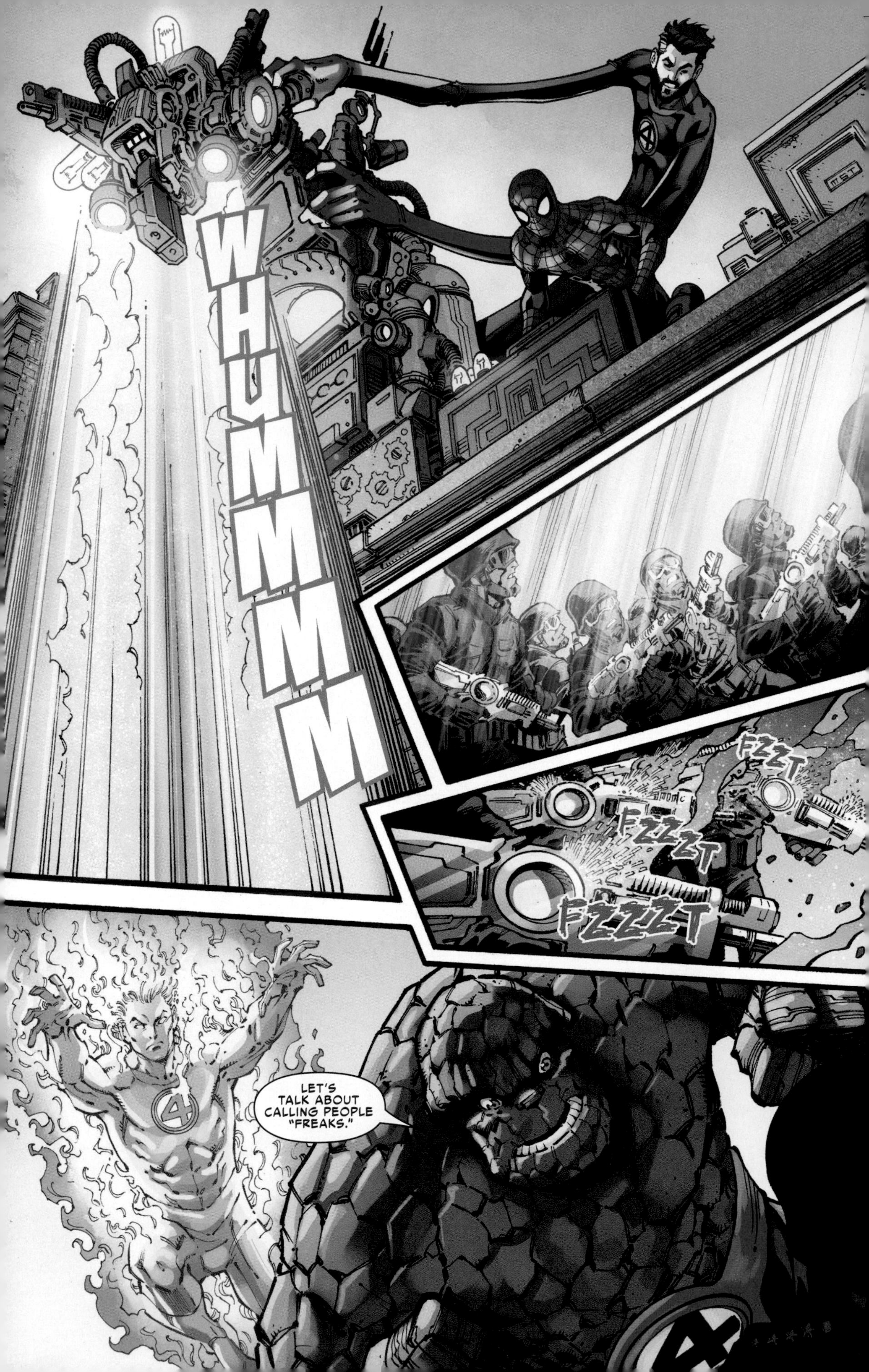
WHUMMMM
FZZZT
FZZZZT
FZZZZZT
LET'S TALK ABOUT CALLING PEOPLE "FREAKS."

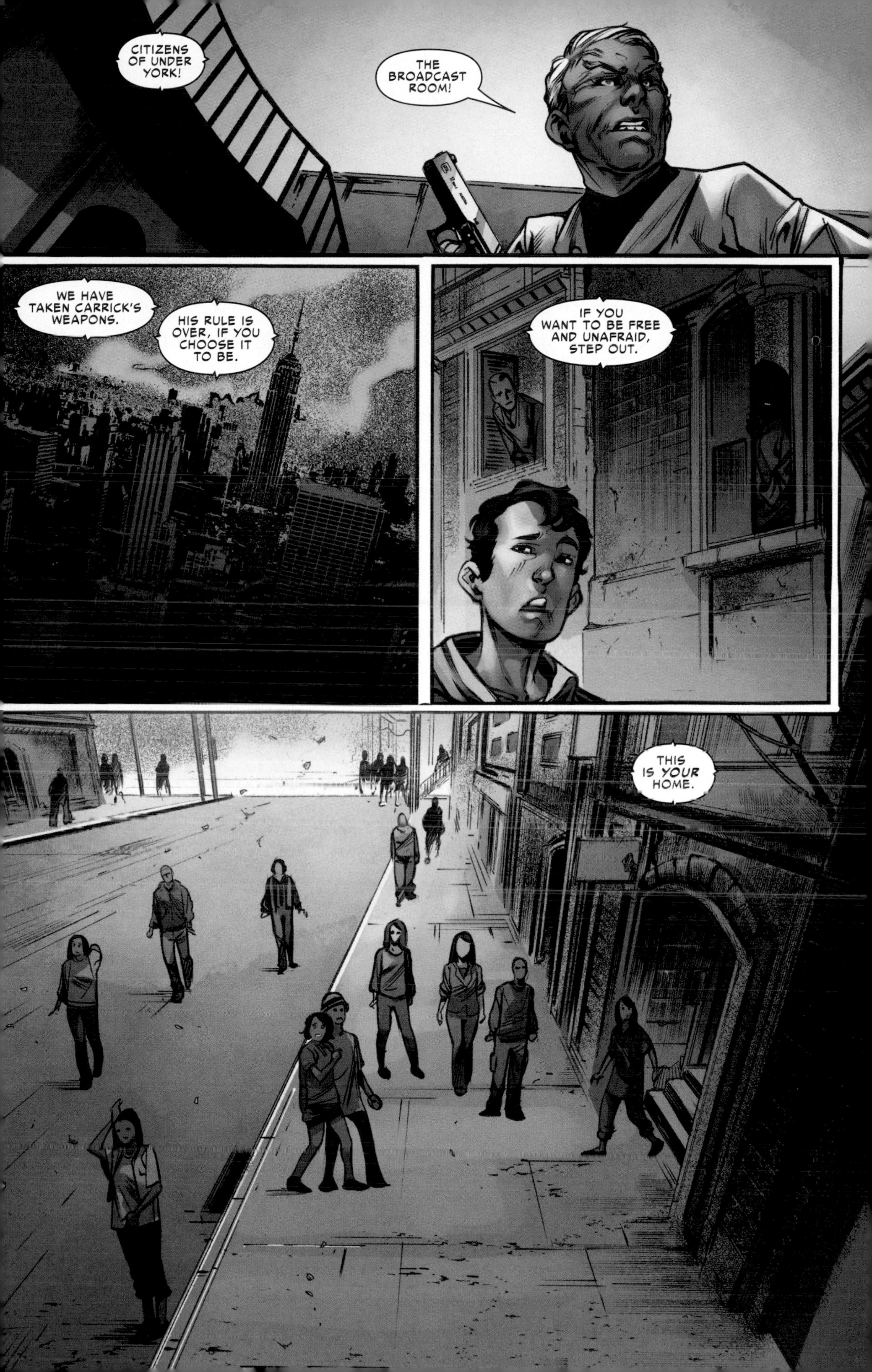
CITIZENS OF UNDER YORK!
THE BROADCAST ROOM!
WE HAVE TAKEN CARRICK'S WEAPONS.
HIS RULE IS OVER, IF YOU CHOOSE IT TO BE.
IF YOU WANT TO BE FREE AND UNAFRAID, STEP OUT.
THIS IS *YOUR* HOME.

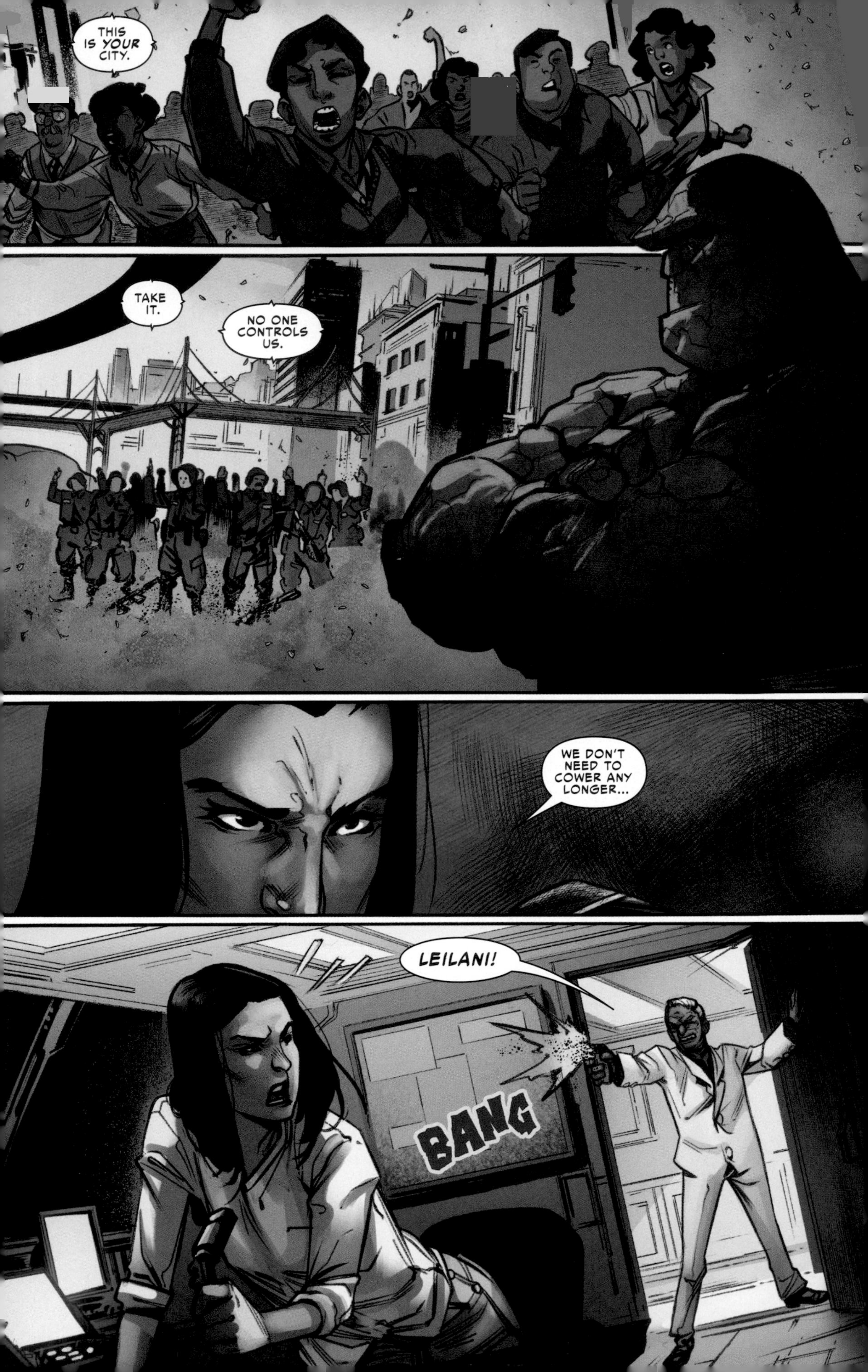
THIS IS YOUR CITY.
TAKE IT.
NO ONE CONTROLS US.
WE DON'T NEED TO COWER ANY LONGER...
LEILANI!
BANG

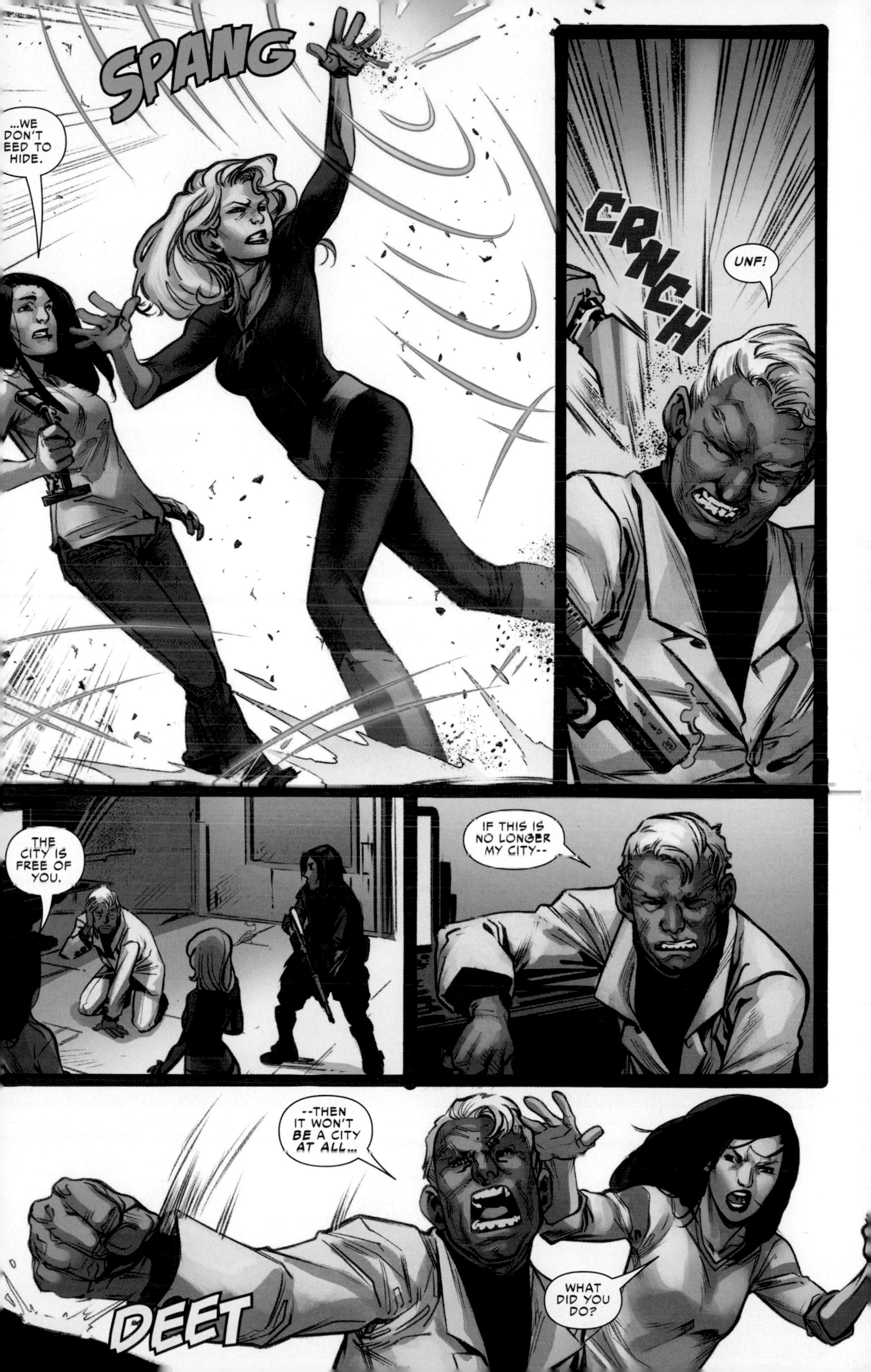
SPANG
...WE
DON'T
EED TO
HIDE.
CRNCH
UNF!
THE
CITY IS
FREE OF
YOU.
IF THIS IS
NO LONGER
MY CITY--
--THEN
IT WON'T
BE A CITY
AT ALL...
WHAT
DID YOU
DO?
DEET

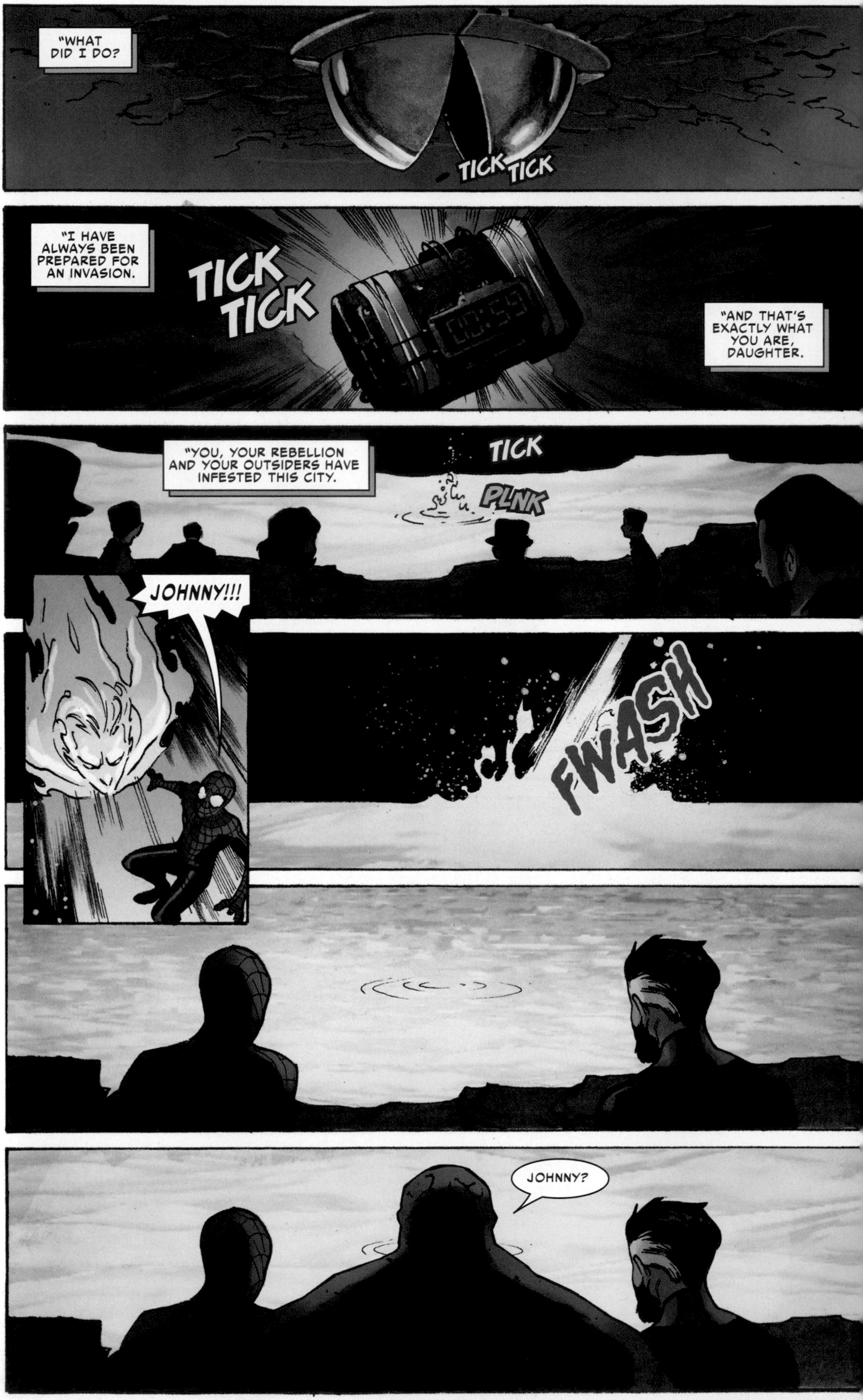
"WHAT DID I DO?
TICK TICK
"I HAVE ALWAYS BEEN PREPARED FOR AN INVASION.
TICK TICK
"AND THAT'S EXACTLY WHAT YOU ARE, DAUGHTER.
"YOU, YOUR REBELLION AND YOUR OUTSIDERS HAVE INFESTED THIS CITY.
TICK
PLNK
JOHNNY!!!
FWASH
JOHNNY?

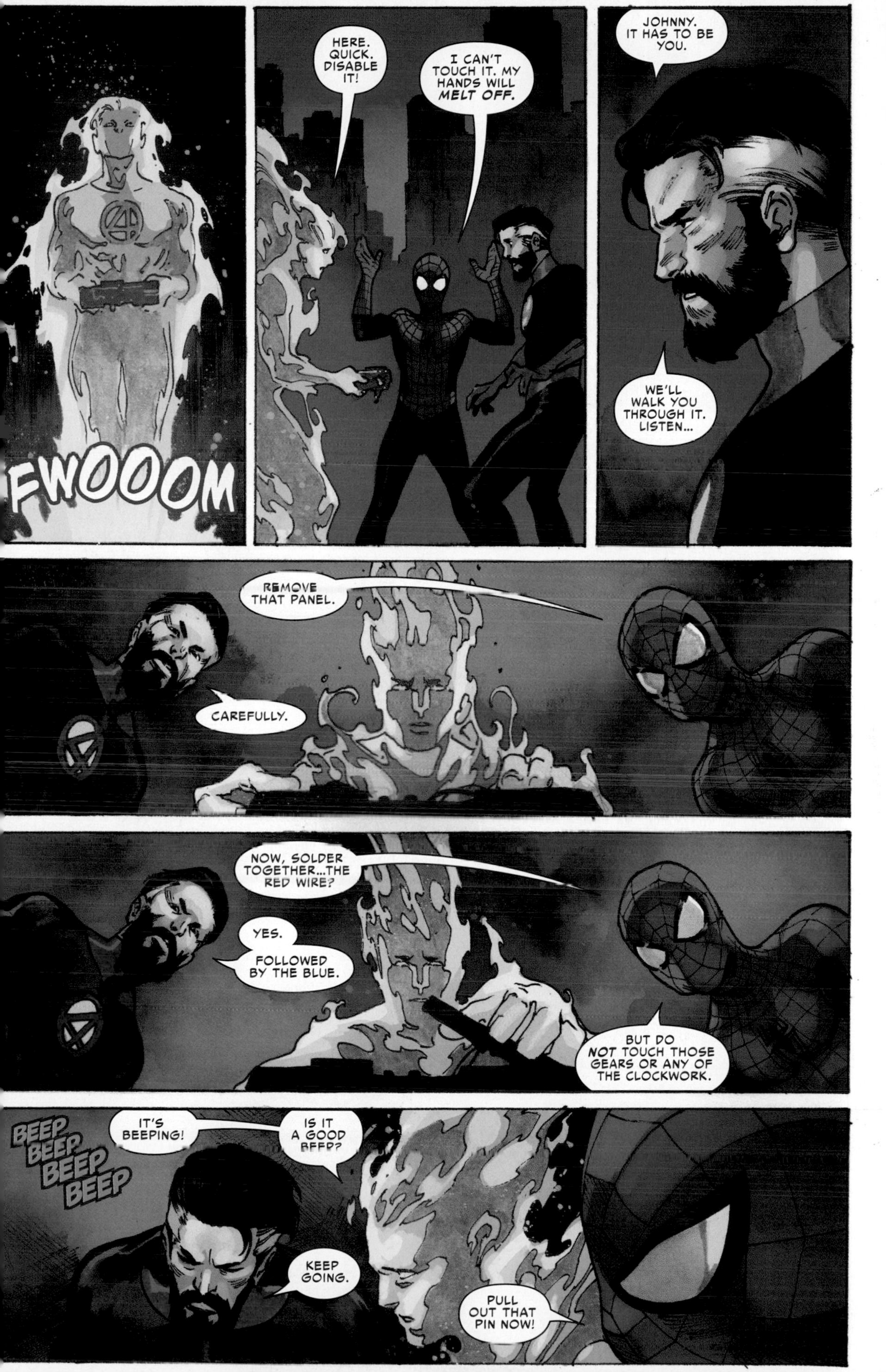
FWOOOM
HERE. QUICK. DISABLE IT!
I CAN'T TOUCH IT. MY HANDS WILL *MELT OFF*.
JOHNNY. IT HAS TO BE YOU.
WE'LL WALK YOU THROUGH IT. LISTEN...
REMOVE THAT PANEL.
CAREFULLY.
NOW, SOLDER TOGETHER...THE RED WIRE?
YES.
FOLLOWED BY THE BLUE.
BUT DO *NOT* TOUCH THOSE GEARS OR ANY OF THE CLOCKWORK.
BEEP BEEP BEEP BEEP
IT'S BEEPING!
IS IT A GOOD BEEP?
KEEP GOING.
PULL OUT THAT PIN NOW!

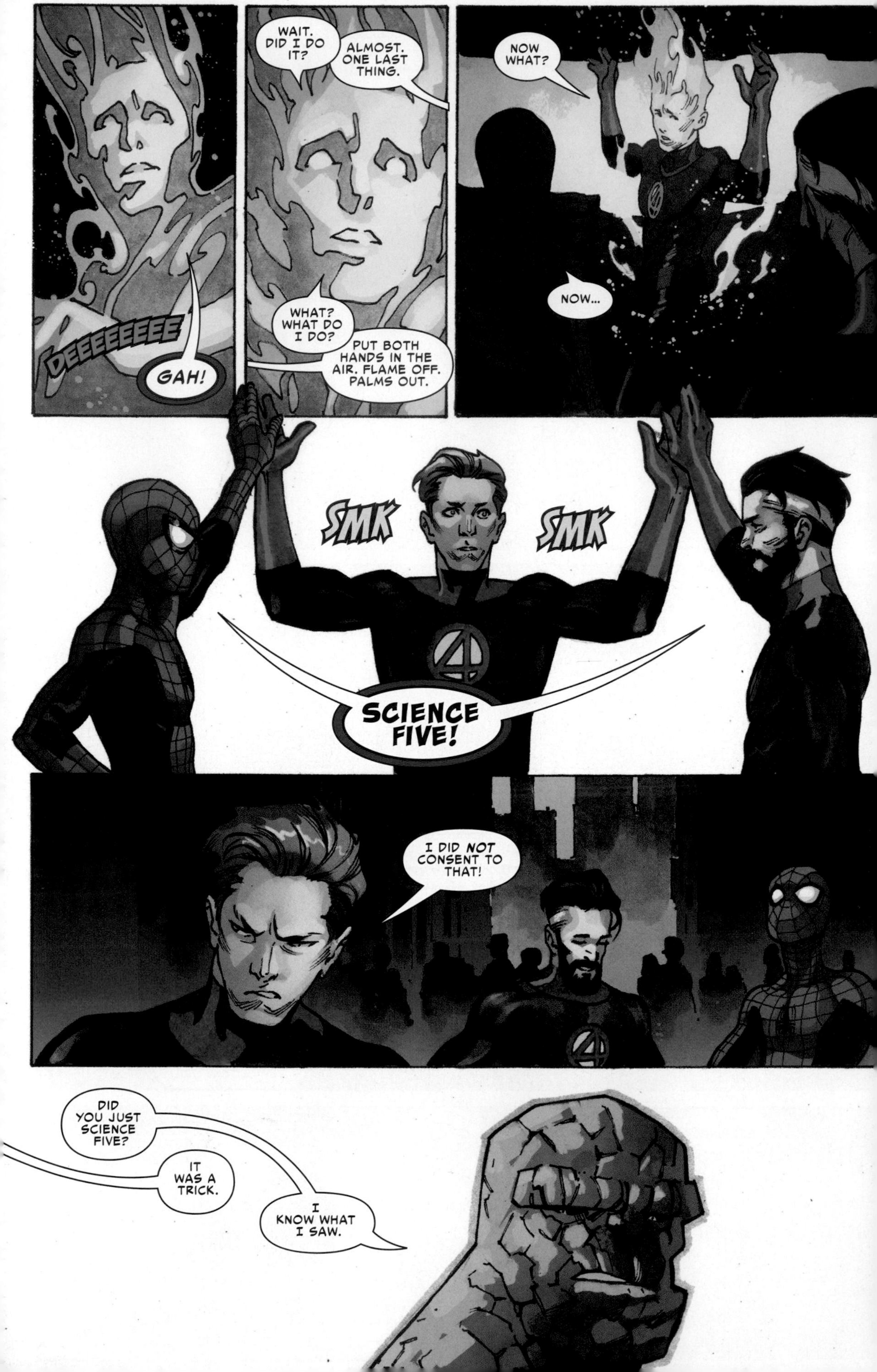

DEEEEEEEE
GAH!
WAIT. DID I DO IT?
ALMOST. ONE LAST THING.
WHAT? WHAT DO I DO?
PUT BOTH HANDS IN THE AIR. FLAME OFF. PALMS OUT.
NOW WHAT?
NOW...
SMK
SMK
SCIENCE FIVE!
I DID NOT CONSENT TO THAT!
DID YOU JUST SCIENCE FIVE?
IT WAS A TRICK.
I KNOW WHAT I SAW.

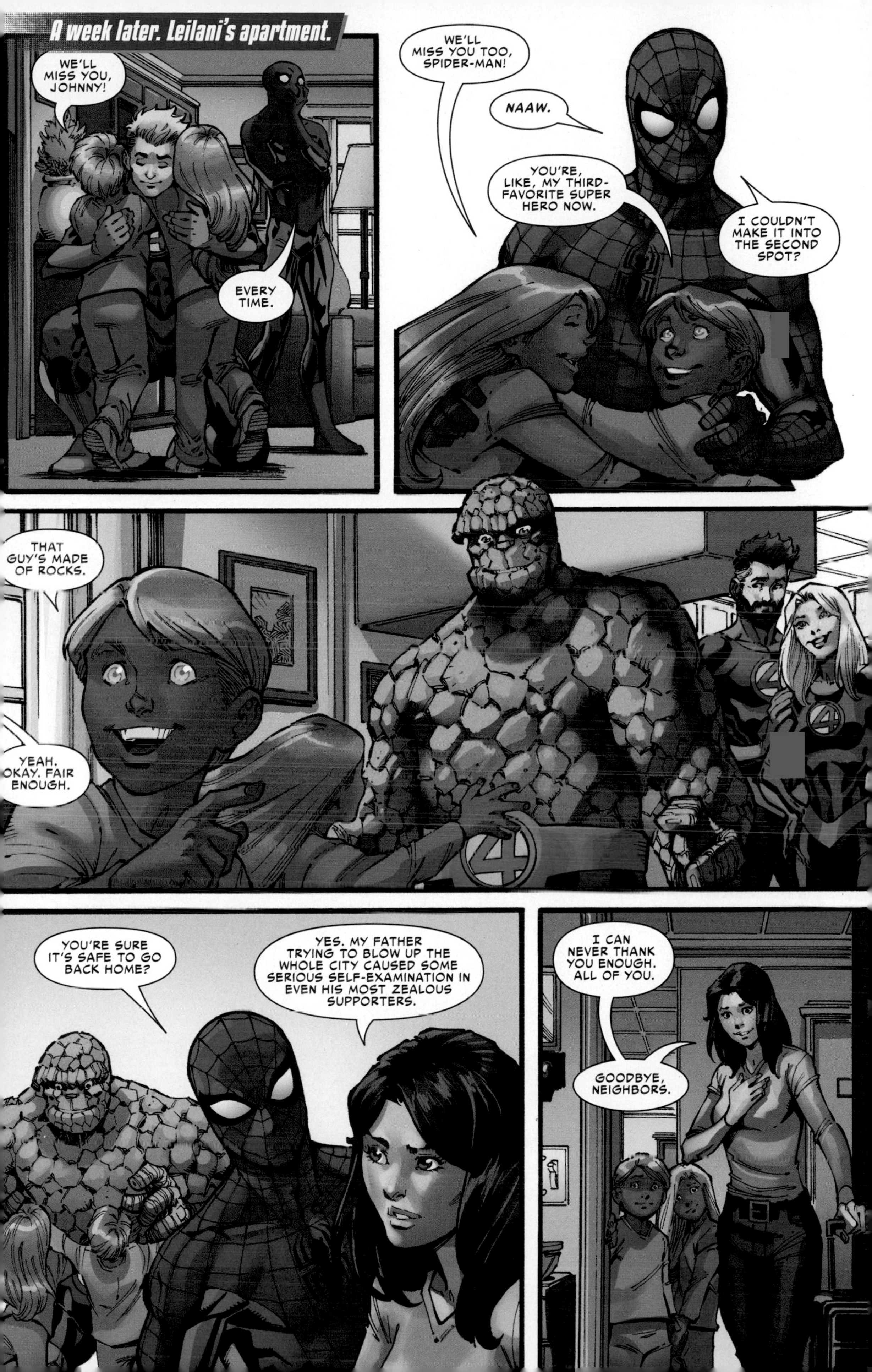
A week later. Leilani's apartment.
WE'LL MISS YOU, JOHNNY!
EVERY TIME.
WE'LL MISS YOU TOO, SPIDER-MAN!
NAAW.
YOU'RE, LIKE, MY THIRD-FAVORITE SUPER HERO NOW.
I COULDN'T MAKE IT INTO THE SECOND SPOT?
THAT GUY'S MADE OF ROCKS.
YEAH. OKAY. FAIR ENOUGH.
YOU'RE SURE IT'S SAFE TO GO BACK HOME?
YES. MY FATHER TRYING TO BLOW UP THE WHOLE CITY CAUSED SOME SERIOUS SELF-EXAMINATION IN EVEN HIS MOST ZEALOUS SUPPORTERS.
I CAN NEVER THANK YOU ENOUGH. ALL OF YOU.
GOODBYE, NEIGHBORS.

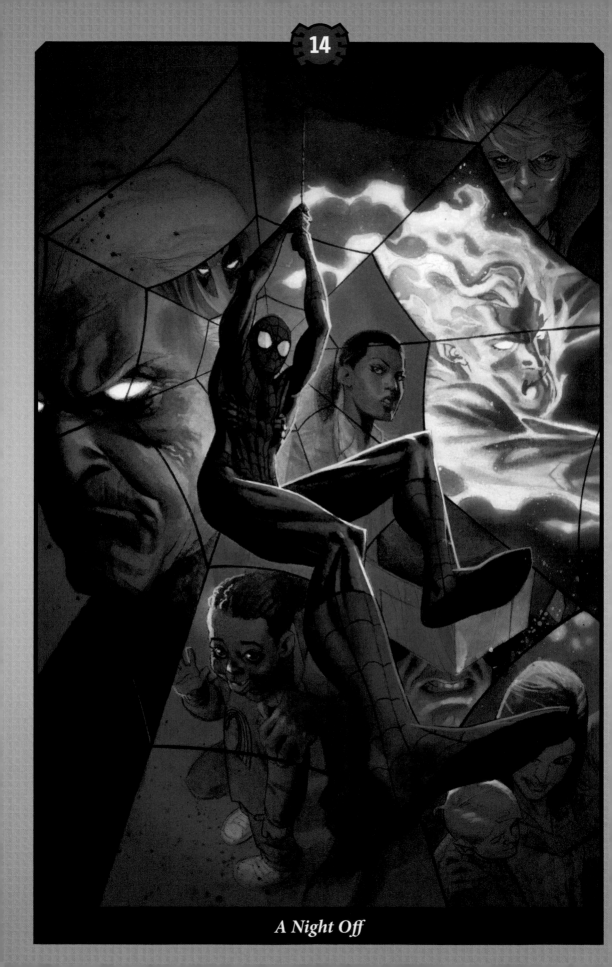

A Night Off

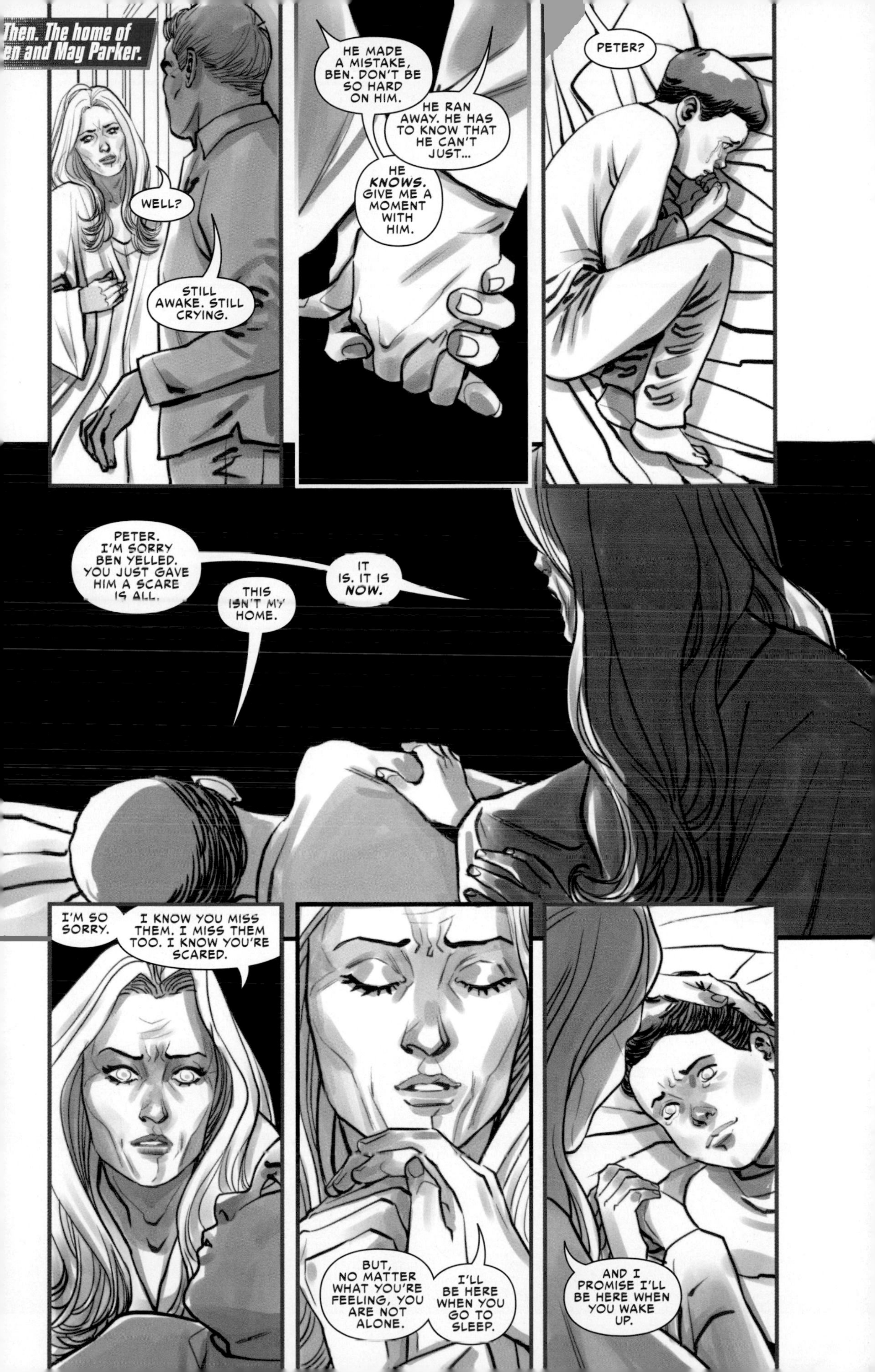
Then. The home of
en and May Parker.
WELL?
STILL AWAKE. STILL CRYING.
HE MADE A MISTAKE, BEN. DON'T BE SO HARD ON HIM.
HE RAN AWAY. HE HAS TO KNOW THAT HE CAN'T JUST...
HE KNOWS. GIVE ME A MOMENT WITH HIM.
PETER?
PETER. I'M SORRY BEN YELLED. YOU JUST GAVE HIM A SCARE IS ALL.
THIS ISN'T MY HOME.
IT IS. IT IS NOW.
I'M SO SORRY.
I KNOW YOU MISS THEM. I MISS THEM TOO. I KNOW YOU'RE SCARED.
BUT, NO MATTER WHAT YOU'RE FEELING, YOU ARE NOT ALONE.
I'LL BE HERE WHEN YOU GO TO SLEEP.
AND I PROMISE I'LL BE HERE WHEN YOU WAKE UP.

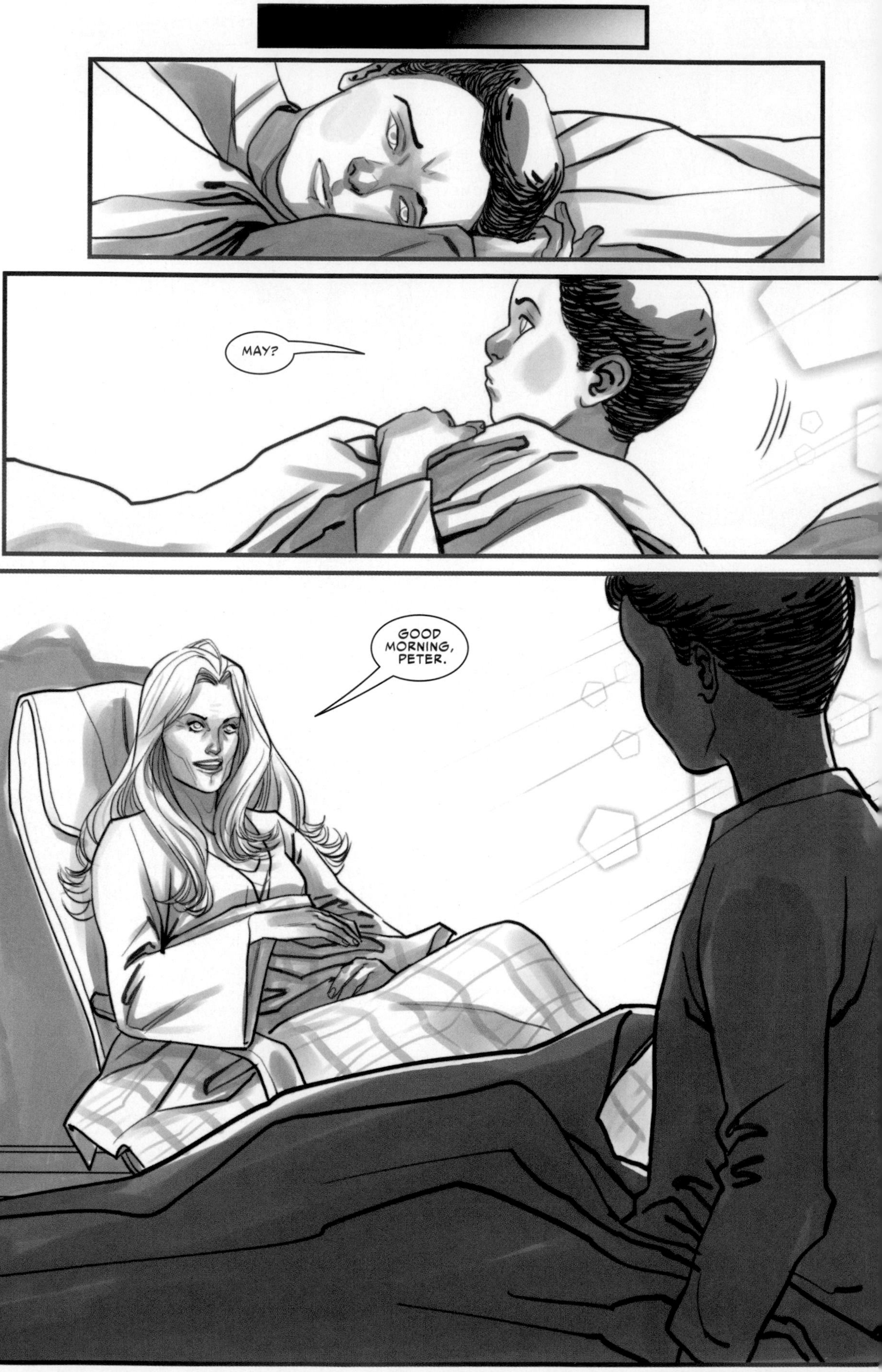
MAY?
GOOD MORNING, PETER.

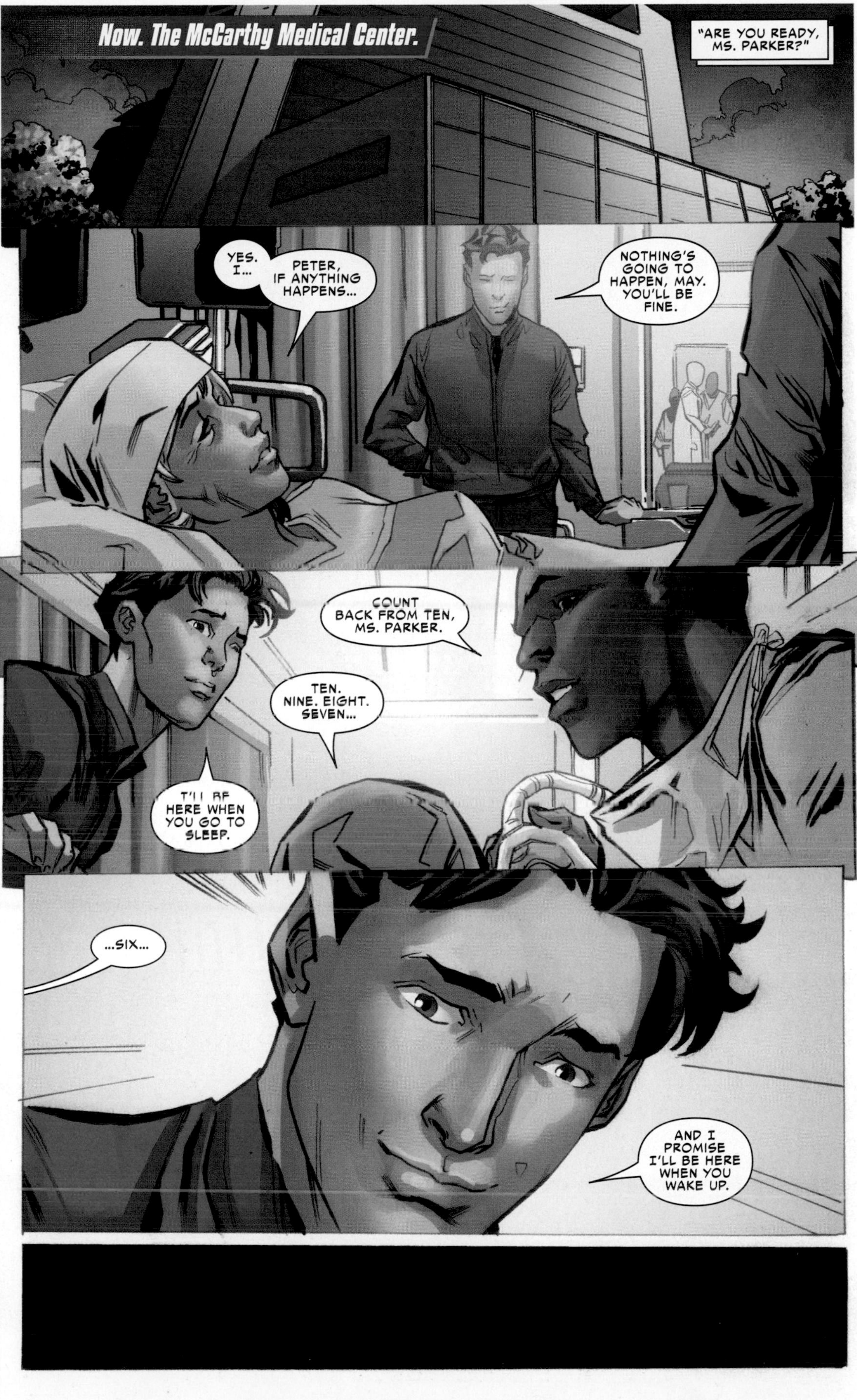
Now. The McCarthy Medical Center.
"ARE YOU READY, MS. PARKER?"
YES. I...
PETER, IF ANYTHING HAPPENS...
NOTHING'S GOING TO HAPPEN, MAY. YOU'LL BE FINE.
COUNT BACK FROM TEN, MS. PARKER.
TEN. NINE. EIGHT. SEVEN...
I'LL BE HERE WHEN YOU GO TO SLEEP.
...SIX...
AND I PROMISE I'LL BE HERE WHEN YOU WAKE UP.

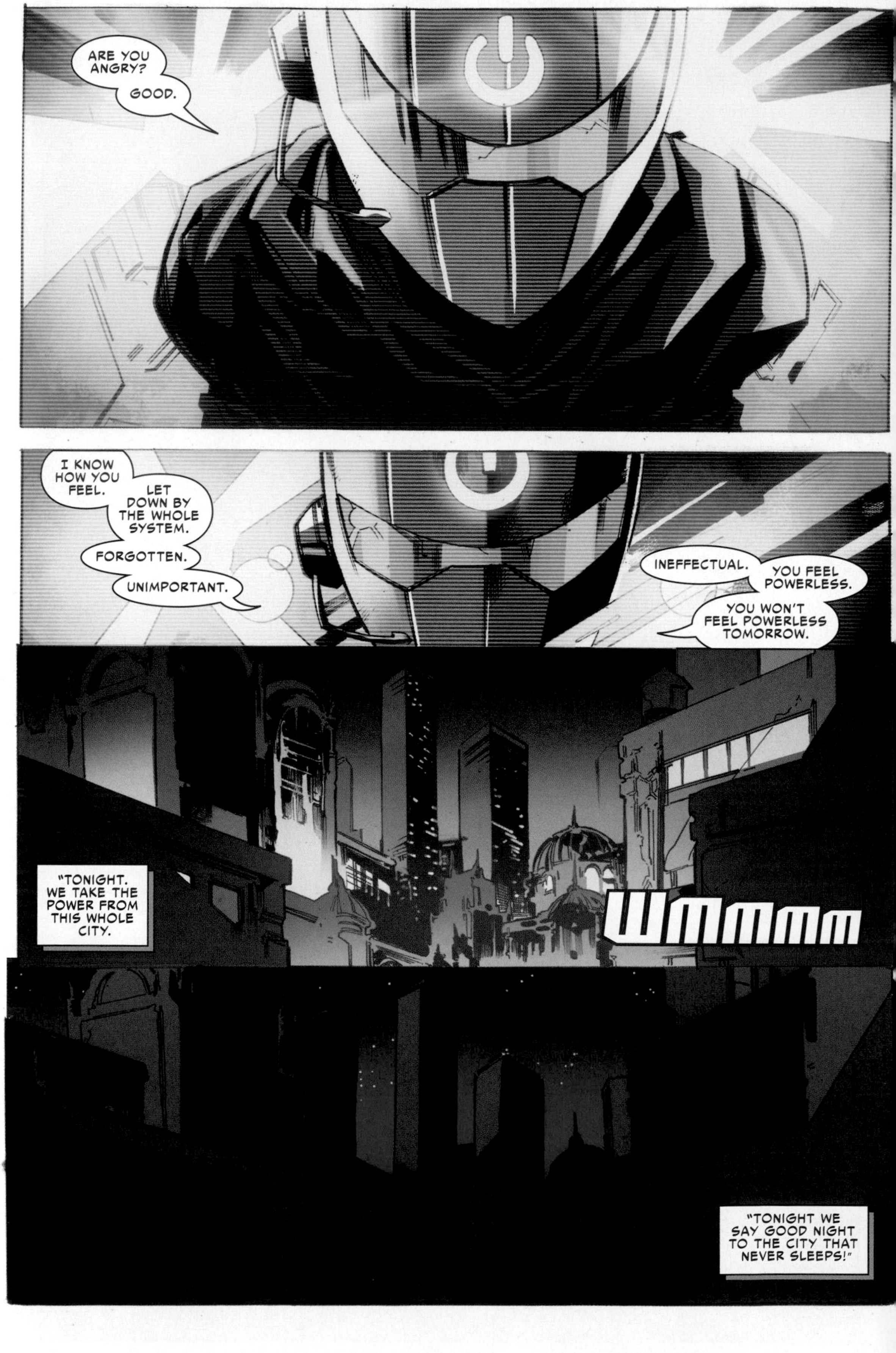
ARE YOU ANGRY?
GOOD.
I KNOW HOW YOU FEEL.
LET DOWN BY THE WHOLE SYSTEM.
FORGOTTEN.
UNIMPORTANT.
INEFFECTUAL.
YOU FEEL POWERLESS.
YOU WON'T FEEL POWERLESS TOMORROW.
"TONIGHT. WE TAKE THE POWER FROM THIS WHOLE CITY.
WMMMMM
"TONIGHT WE SAY GOOD NIGHT TO THE CITY THAT NEVER SLEEPS!"

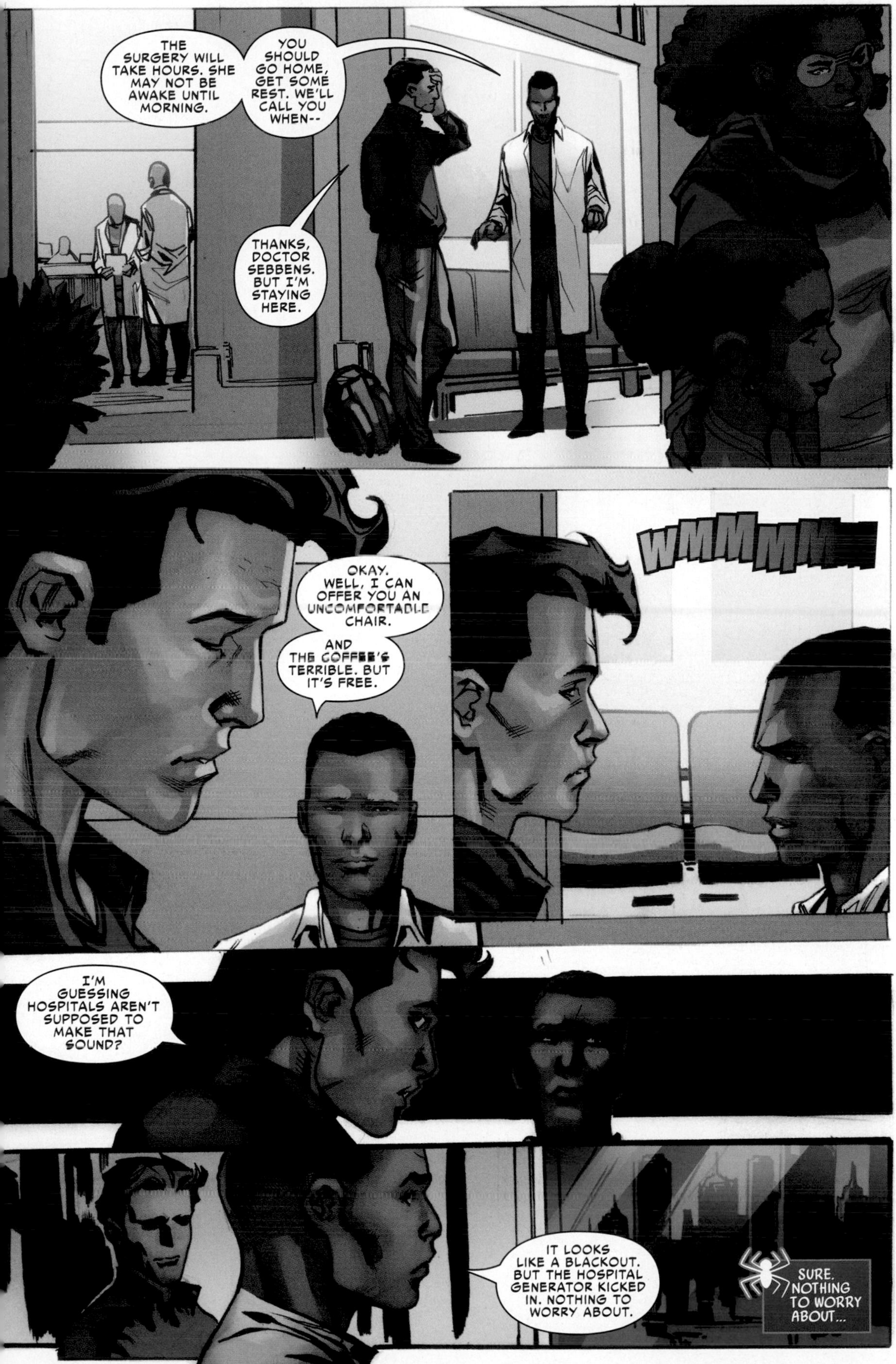

THE SURGERY WILL TAKE HOURS. SHE MAY NOT BE AWAKE UNTIL MORNING.
YOU SHOULD GO HOME, GET SOME REST. WE'LL CALL YOU WHEN--
THANKS, DOCTOR SEBBENS. BUT I'M STAYING HERE.
OKAY. WELL, I CAN OFFER YOU AN UNCOMFORTABLE CHAIR.
AND THE COFFEE'S TERRIBLE. BUT IT'S FREE.
WMMMMM
I'M GUESSING HOSPITALS AREN'T SUPPOSED TO MAKE THAT SOUND?
IT LOOKS LIKE A BLACKOUT. BUT THE HOSPITAL GENERATOR KICKED IN. NOTHING TO WORRY ABOUT.
SURE. NOTHING TO WORRY ABOUT...

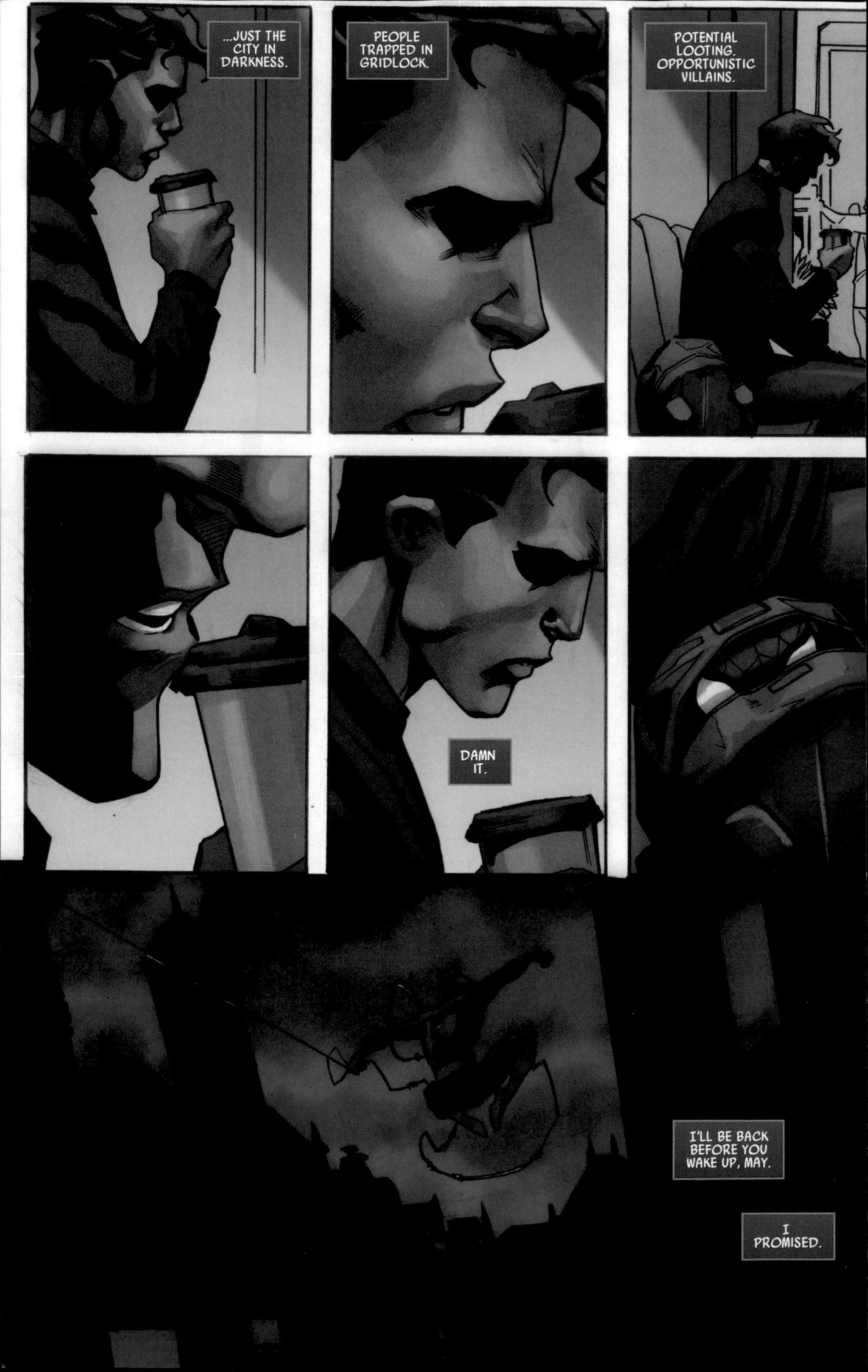
...JUST THE CITY IN DARKNESS.
PEOPLE TRAPPED IN GRIDLOCK.
POTENTIAL LOOTING. OPPORTUNISTIC VILLAINS.
DAMN IT.
I'LL BE BACK BEFORE YOU WAKE UP, MAY.
I PROMISED.

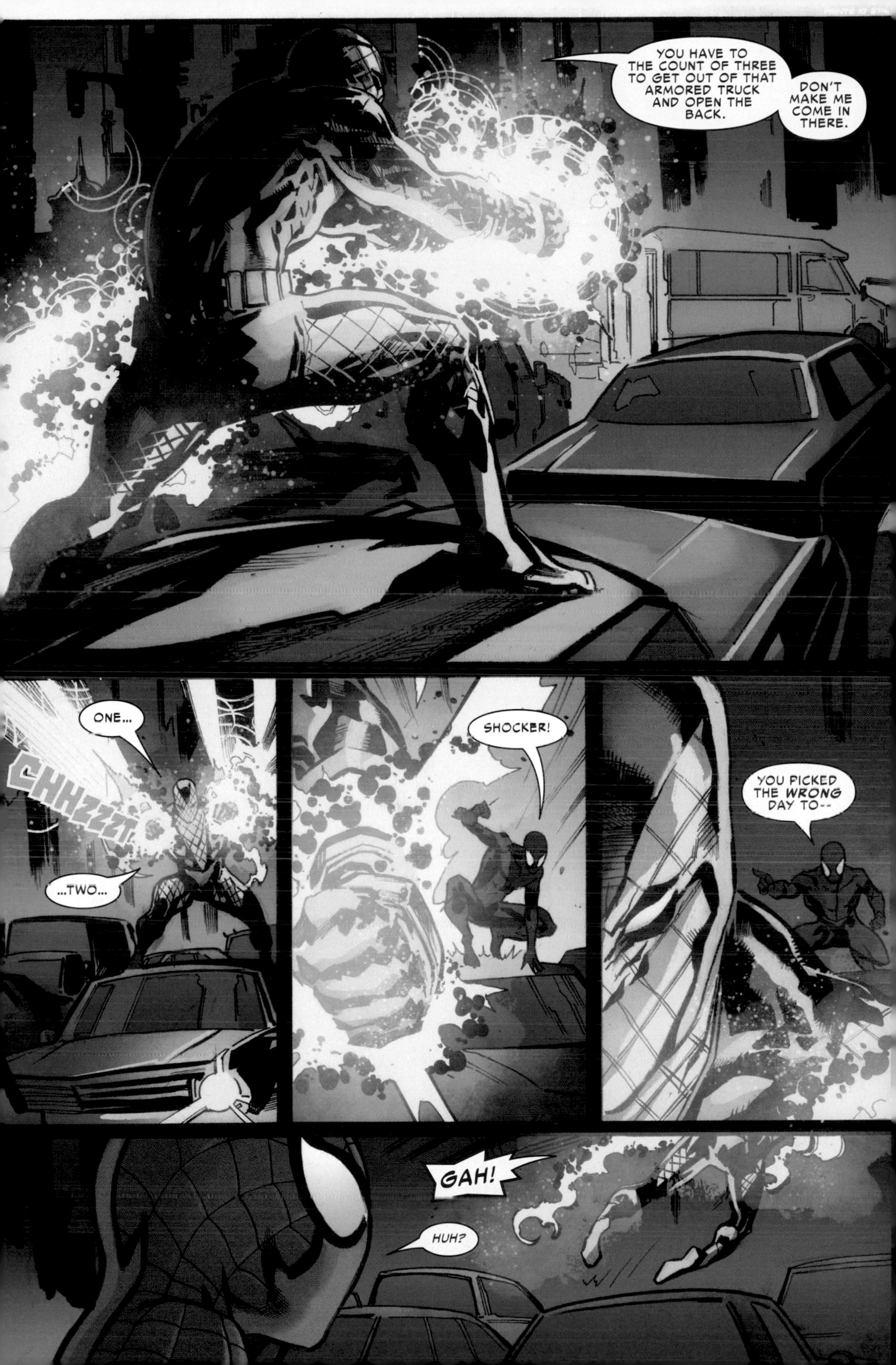
YOU HAVE TO THE COUNT OF THREE TO GET OUT OF THAT ARMORED TRUCK AND OPEN THE BACK.
DON'T MAKE ME COME IN THERE.
ONE...
CHHZZZT
...TWO...
SHOCKER!
YOU PICKED THE *WRONG* DAY TO--
GAH!
HUH?

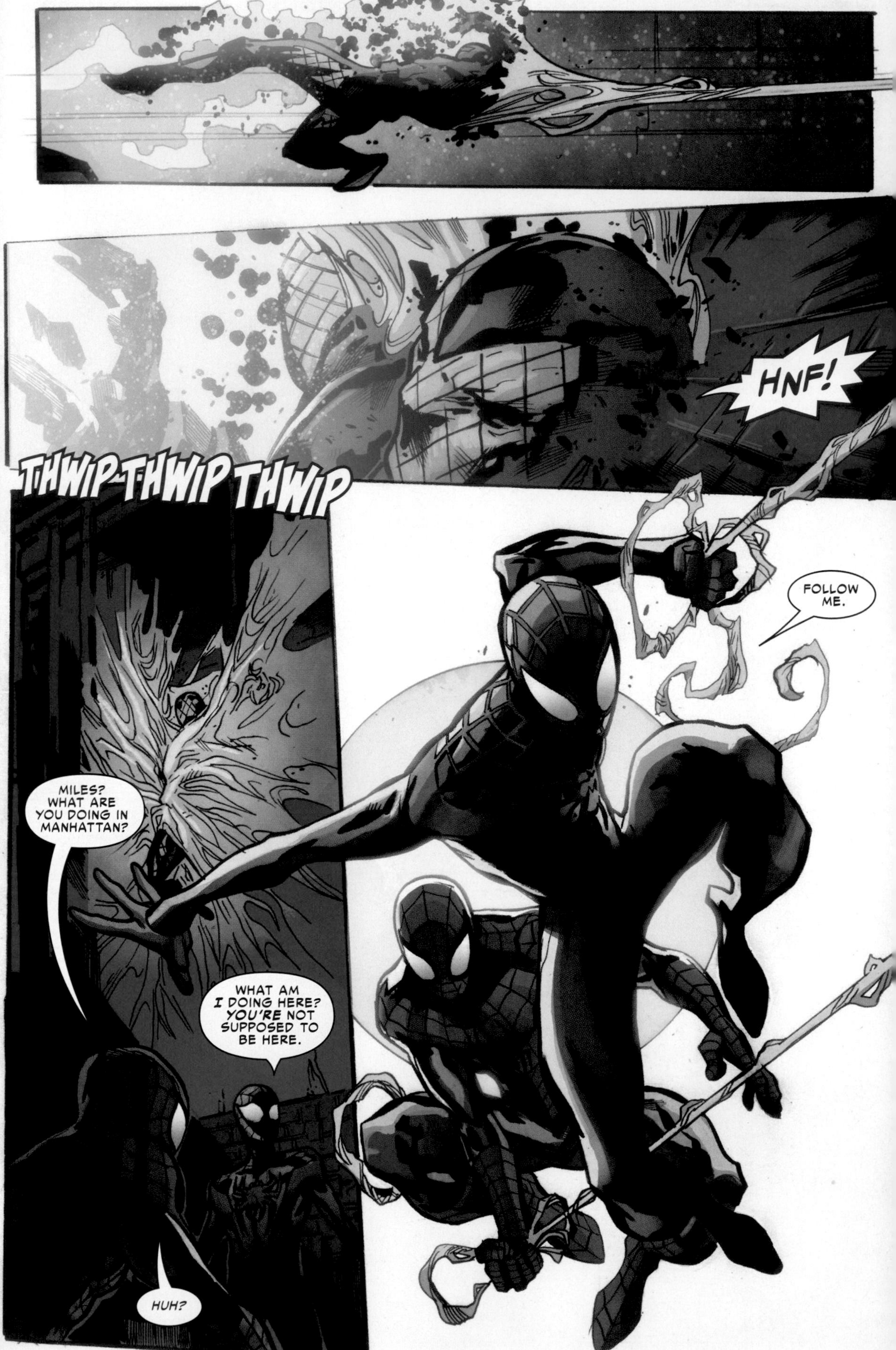
HNF!
THWIP THWIP THWIP
FOLLOW ME.
MILES? WHAT ARE YOU DOING IN MANHATTAN?
WHAT AM I DOING HERE? YOU'RE NOT SUPPOSED TO BE HERE.
HUH?

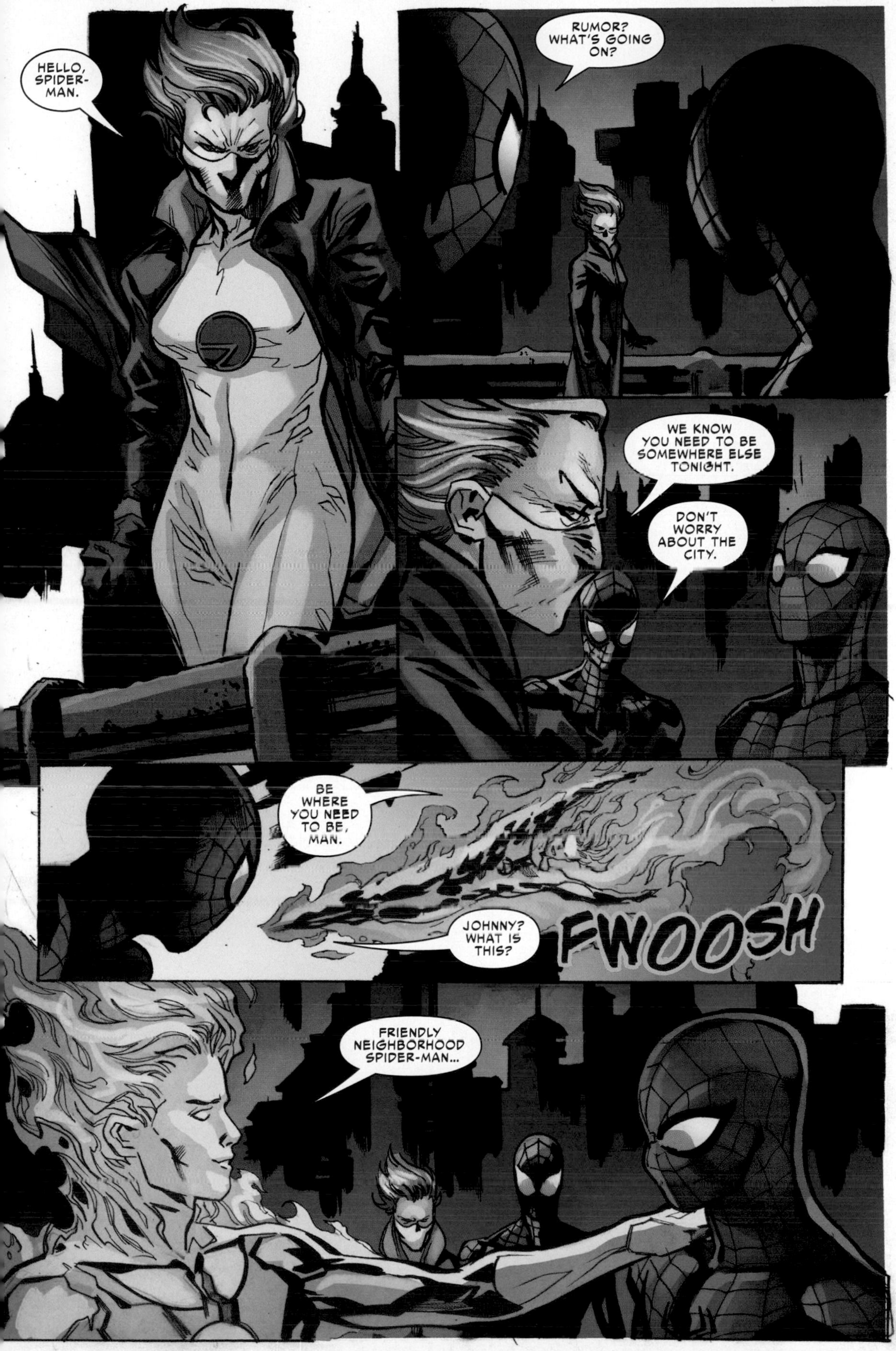
HELLO, SPIDER-MAN.
RUMOR? WHAT'S GOING ON?
WE KNOW YOU NEED TO BE SOMEWHERE ELSE TONIGHT.
DON'T WORRY ABOUT THE CITY.
BE WHERE YOU NEED TO BE, MAN.
JOHNNY? WHAT IS THIS?
FWOOSH
FRIENDLY NEIGHBORHOOD SPIDER-MAN...

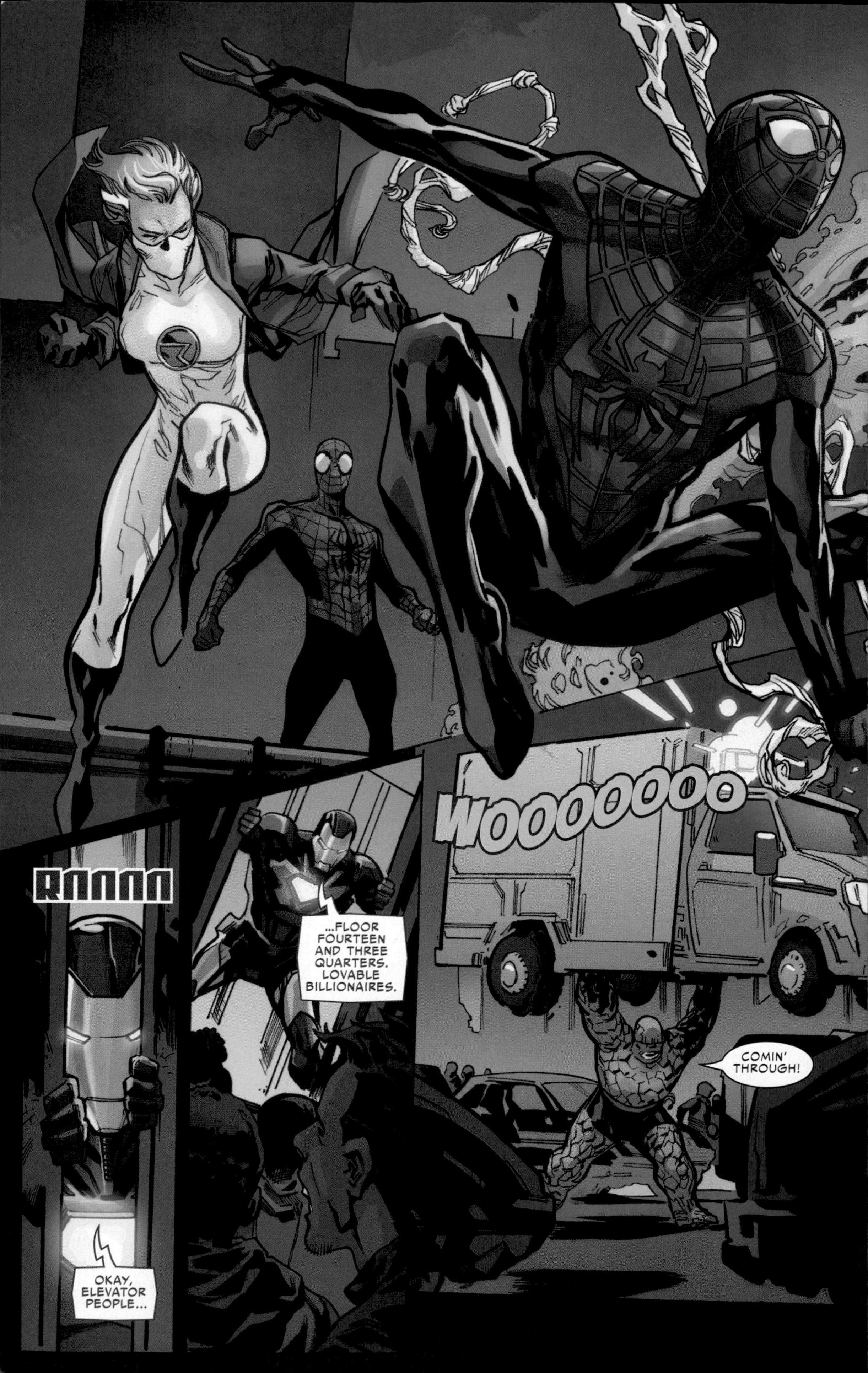
WOOOOOOO
RNNNN
...FLOOR FOURTEEN AND THREE QUARTERS. LOVABLE BILLIONAIRES.
COMIN' THROUGH!
OKAY, ELEVATOR PEOPLE...

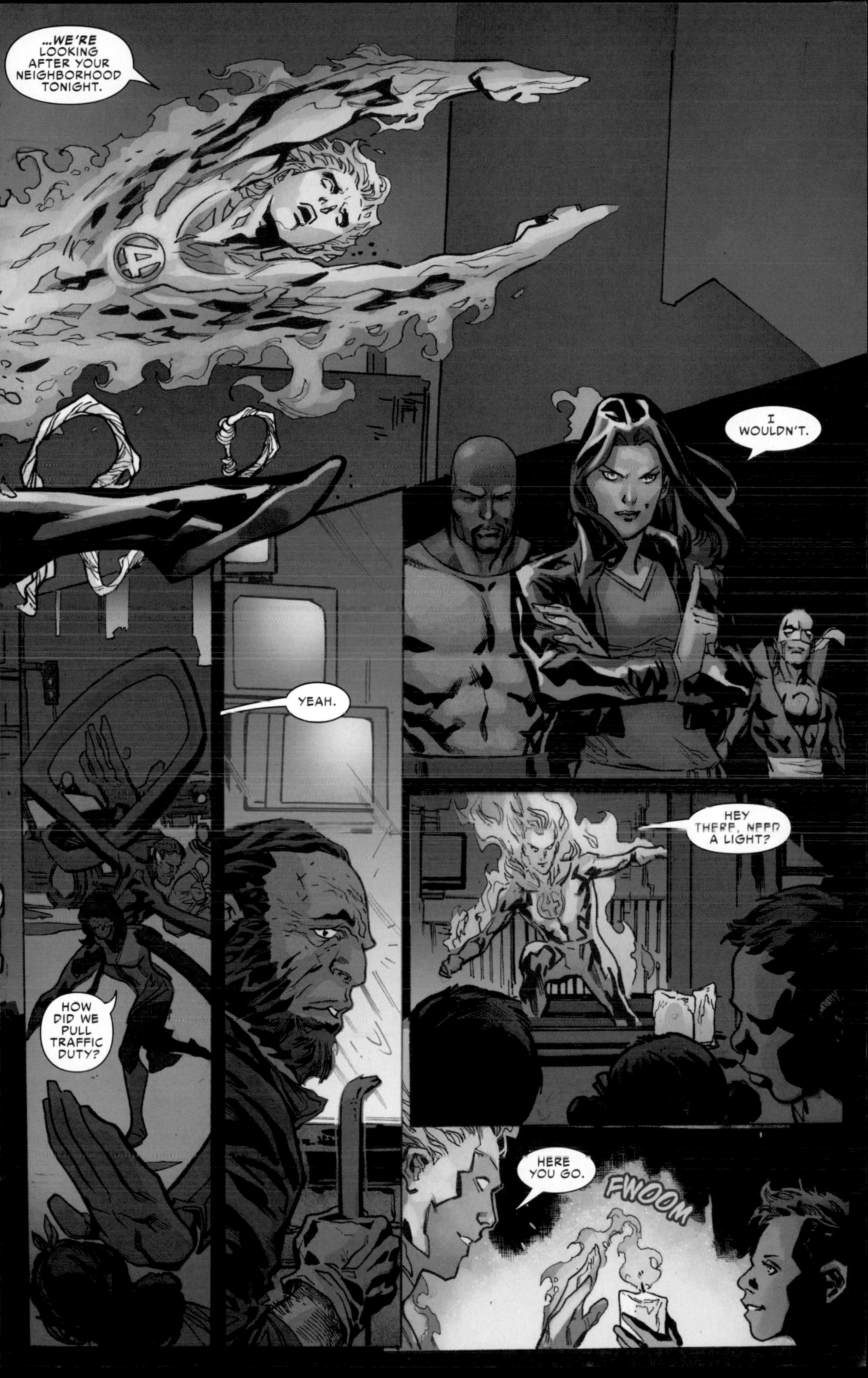
...WE'RE LOOKING AFTER YOUR NEIGHBORHOOD TONIGHT.
I WOULDN'T.
YEAH.
HOW DID WE PULL TRAFFIC DUTY?
HEY THERE, NEED A LIGHT?
HERE YOU GO.
FWOOM

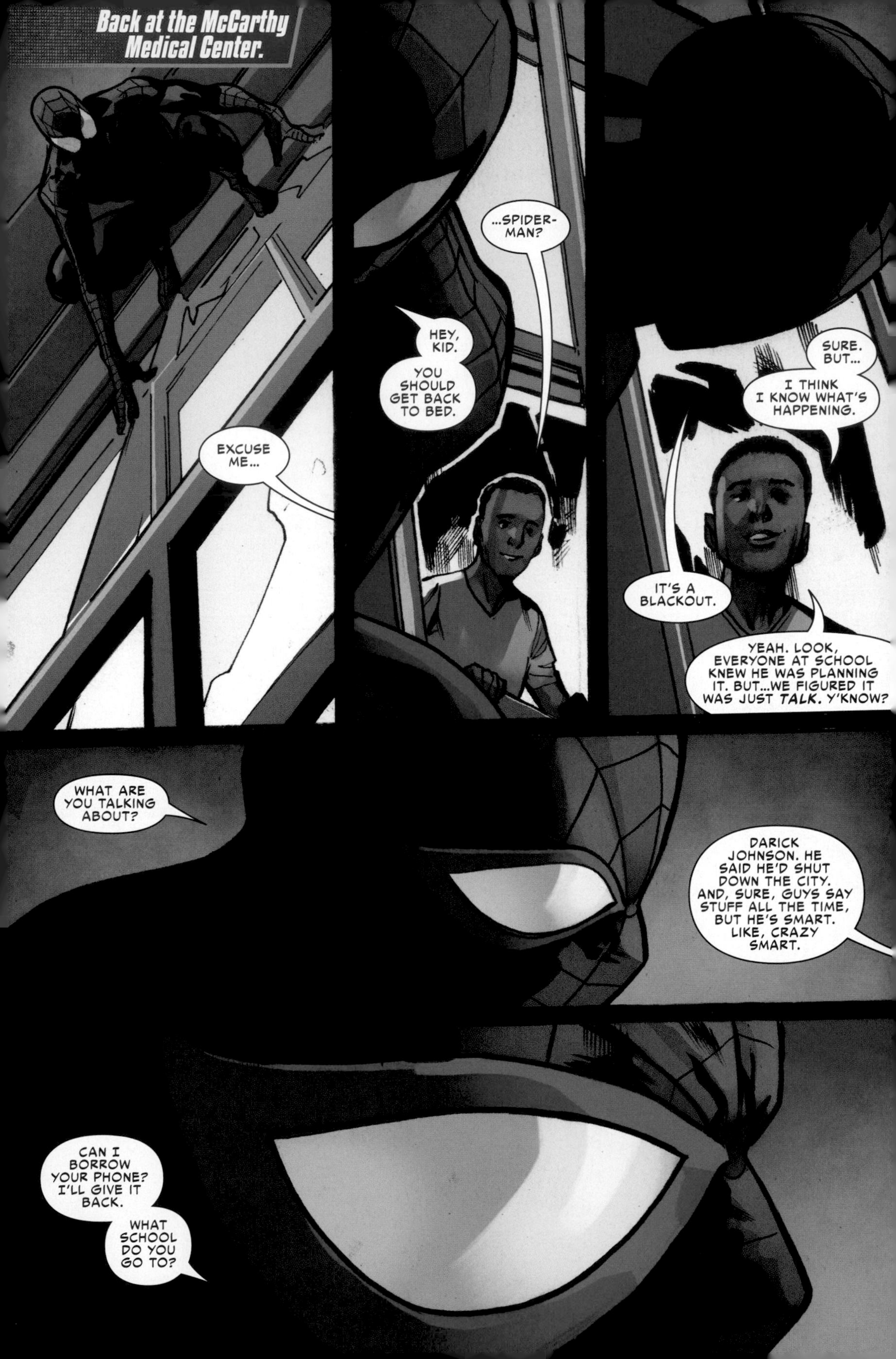
Back at the McCarthy Medical Center.
EXCUSE ME...
...SPIDER-MAN?
HEY, KID.
YOU SHOULD GET BACK TO BED.
SURE. BUT...
I THINK I KNOW WHAT'S HAPPENING.
IT'S A BLACKOUT.
YEAH. LOOK, EVERYONE AT SCHOOL KNEW HE WAS PLANNING IT. BUT...WE FIGURED IT WAS JUST TALK. Y'KNOW?
WHAT ARE YOU TALKING ABOUT?
DARICK JOHNSON. HE SAID HE'D SHUT DOWN THE CITY. AND, SURE, GUYS SAY STUFF ALL THE TIME, BUT HE'S SMART. LIKE, CRAZY SMART.
CAN I BORROW YOUR PHONE? I'LL GIVE IT BACK.
WHAT SCHOOL DO YOU GO TO?

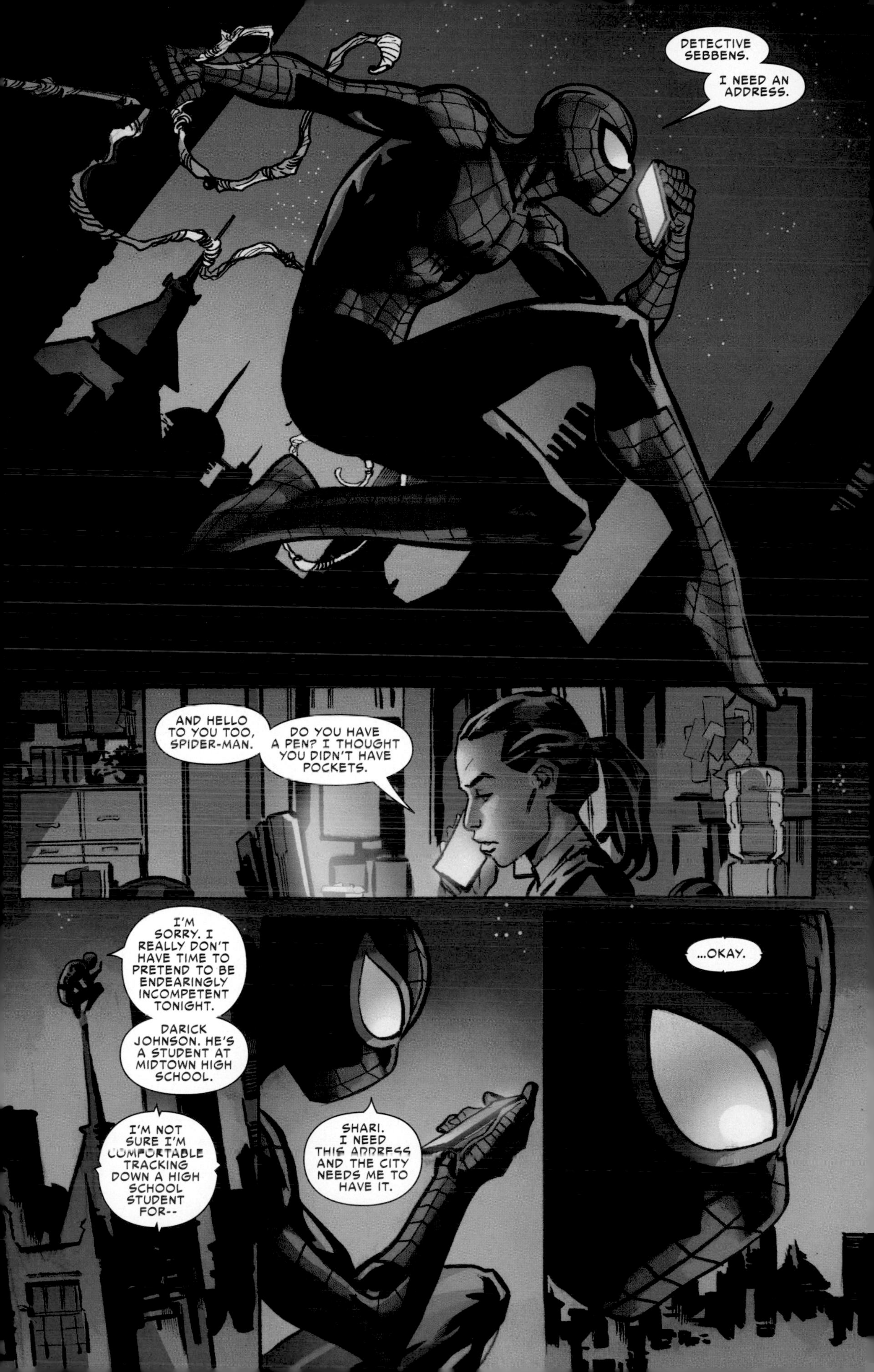
DETECTIVE SEBBENS.
I NEED AN ADDRESS.
AND HELLO TO YOU TOO, SPIDER-MAN.
DO YOU HAVE A PEN? I THOUGHT YOU DIDN'T HAVE POCKETS.
I'M SORRY. I REALLY DON'T HAVE TIME TO PRETEND TO BE ENDEARINGLY INCOMPETENT TONIGHT.
DARICK JOHNSON. HE'S A STUDENT AT MIDTOWN HIGH SCHOOL.
I'M NOT SURE I'M COMFORTABLE TRACKING DOWN A HIGH SCHOOL STUDENT FOR--
SHARI. I NEED THIS ADDRESS AND THE CITY NEEDS ME TO HAVE IT.
...OKAY.

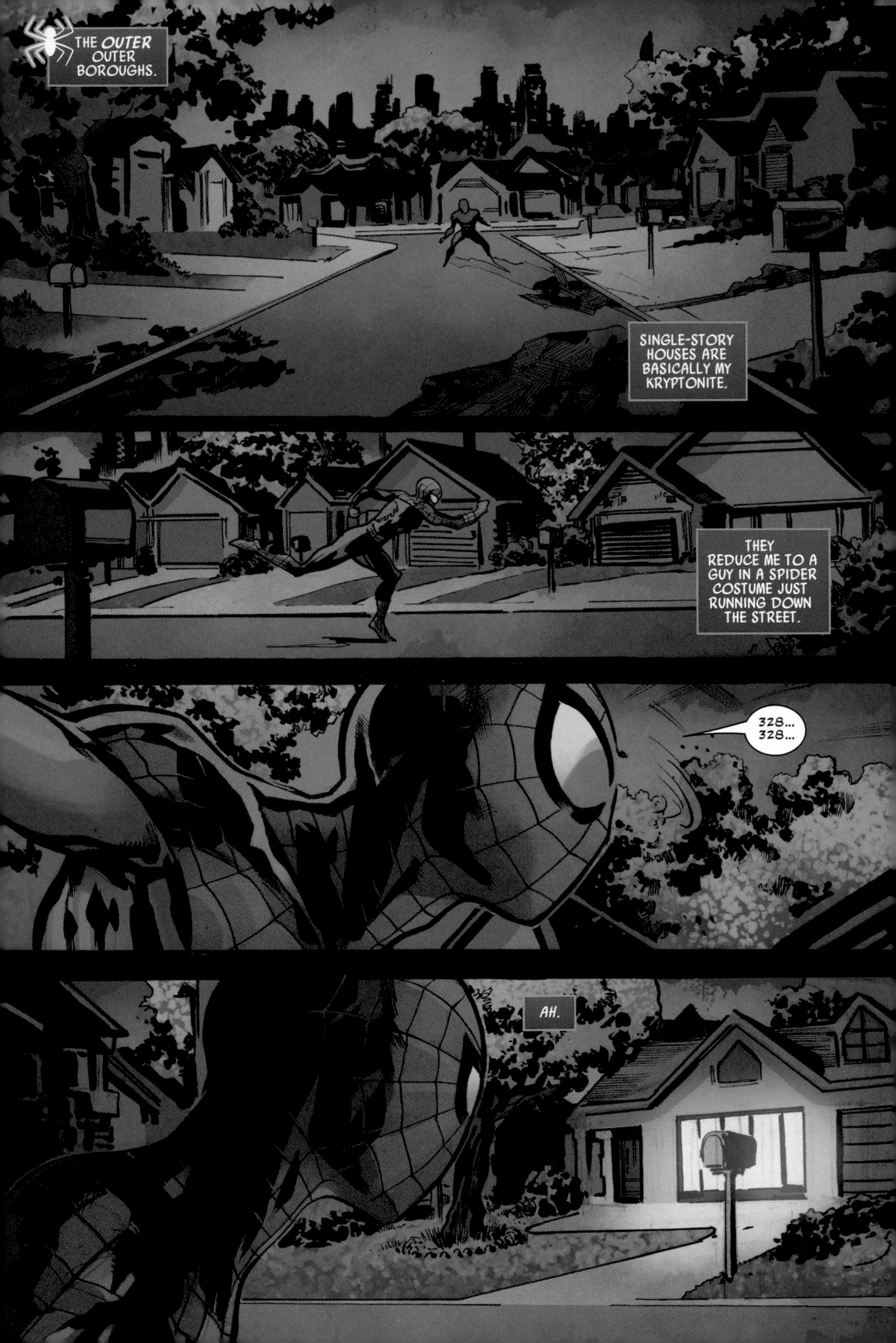
THE OUTER OUTER BOROUGHS.
SINGLE-STORY HOUSES ARE BASICALLY MY KRYPTONITE.
THEY REDUCE ME TO A GUY IN A SPIDER COSTUME JUST RUNNING DOWN THE STREET.
328... 328...
AH.

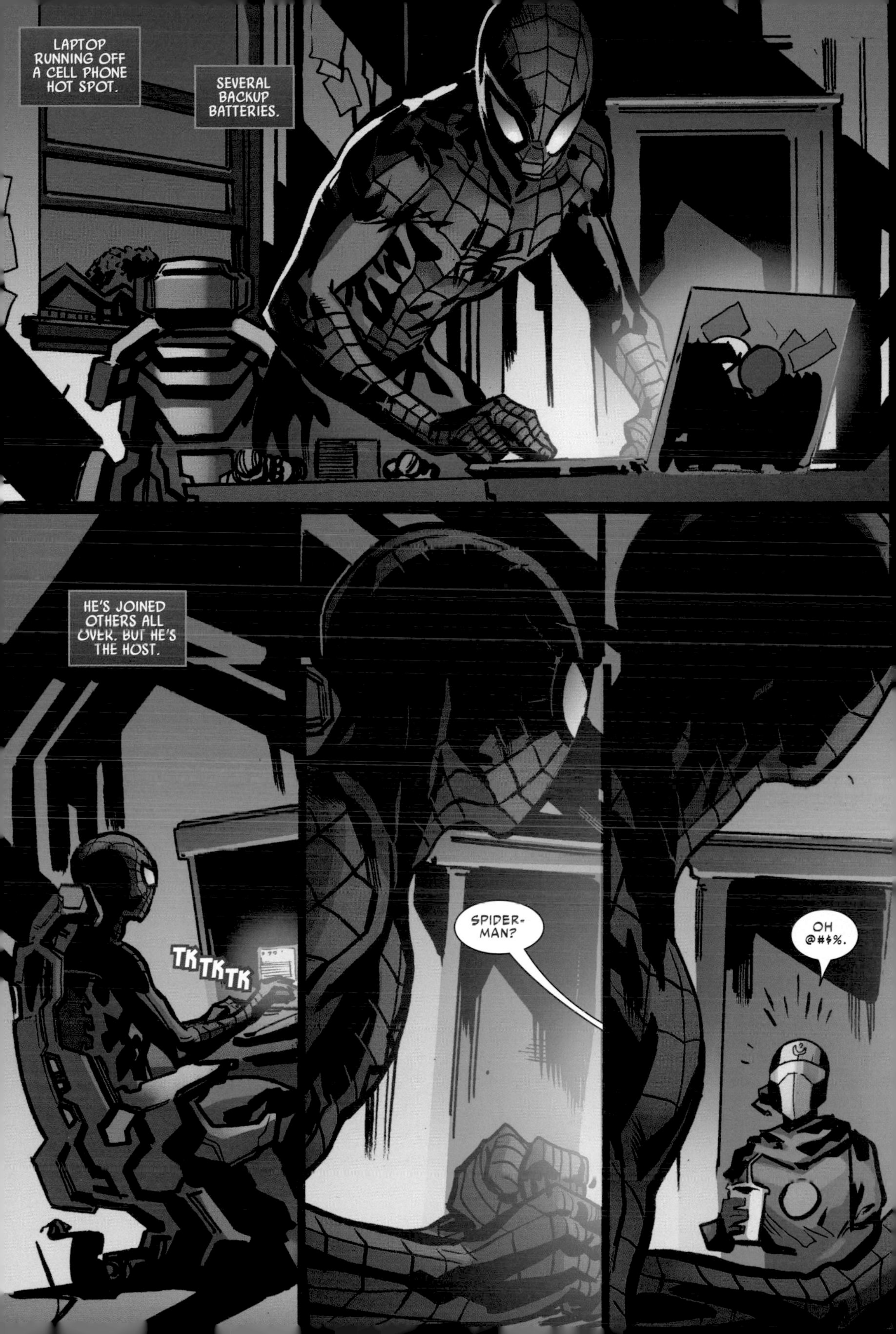
LAPTOP RUNNING OFF A CELL PHONE HOT SPOT.
SEVERAL BACKUP BATTERIES.
HE'S JOINED OTHERS ALL OVER. BUT HE'S THE HOST.
TKTKTK
SPIDER-MAN?
OH @#$%.

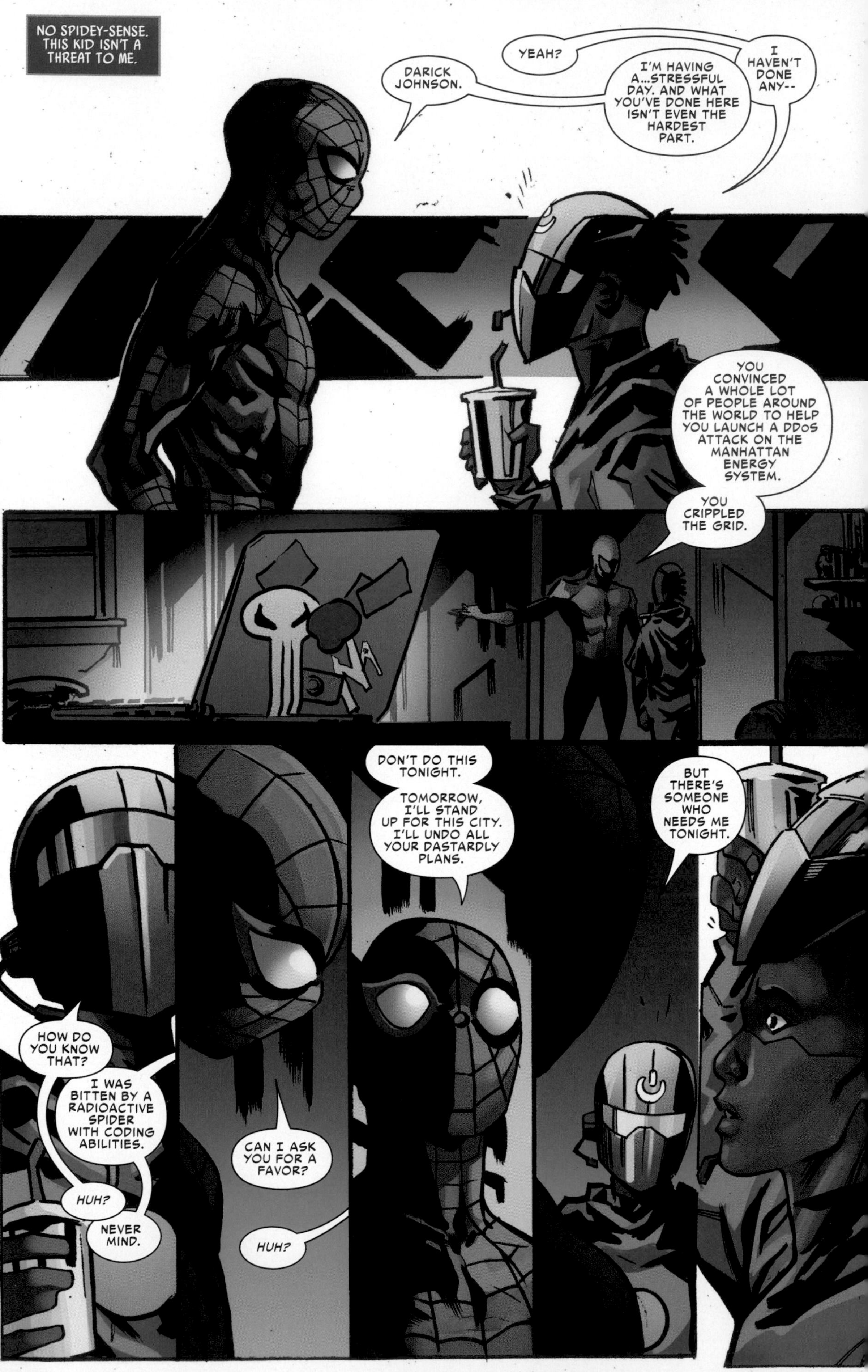
NO SPIDEY-SENSE. THIS KID ISN'T A THREAT TO ME.
DARICK JOHNSON.
YEAH?
I'M HAVING A...STRESSFUL DAY. AND WHAT YOU'VE DONE HERE ISN'T EVEN THE HARDEST PART.
I HAVEN'T DONE ANY--
YOU CONVINCED A WHOLE LOT OF PEOPLE AROUND THE WORLD TO HELP YOU LAUNCH A DDoS ATTACK ON THE MANHATTAN ENERGY SYSTEM.
YOU CRIPPLED THE GRID.
HOW DO YOU KNOW THAT?
I WAS BITTEN BY A RADIOACTIVE SPIDER WITH CODING ABILITIES.
HUH?
NEVER MIND.
CAN I ASK YOU FOR A FAVOR?
HUH?
DON'T DO THIS TONIGHT.
TOMORROW, I'LL STAND UP FOR THIS CITY. I'LL UNDO ALL YOUR DASTARDLY PLANS.
BUT THERE'S SOMEONE WHO NEEDS ME TONIGHT.

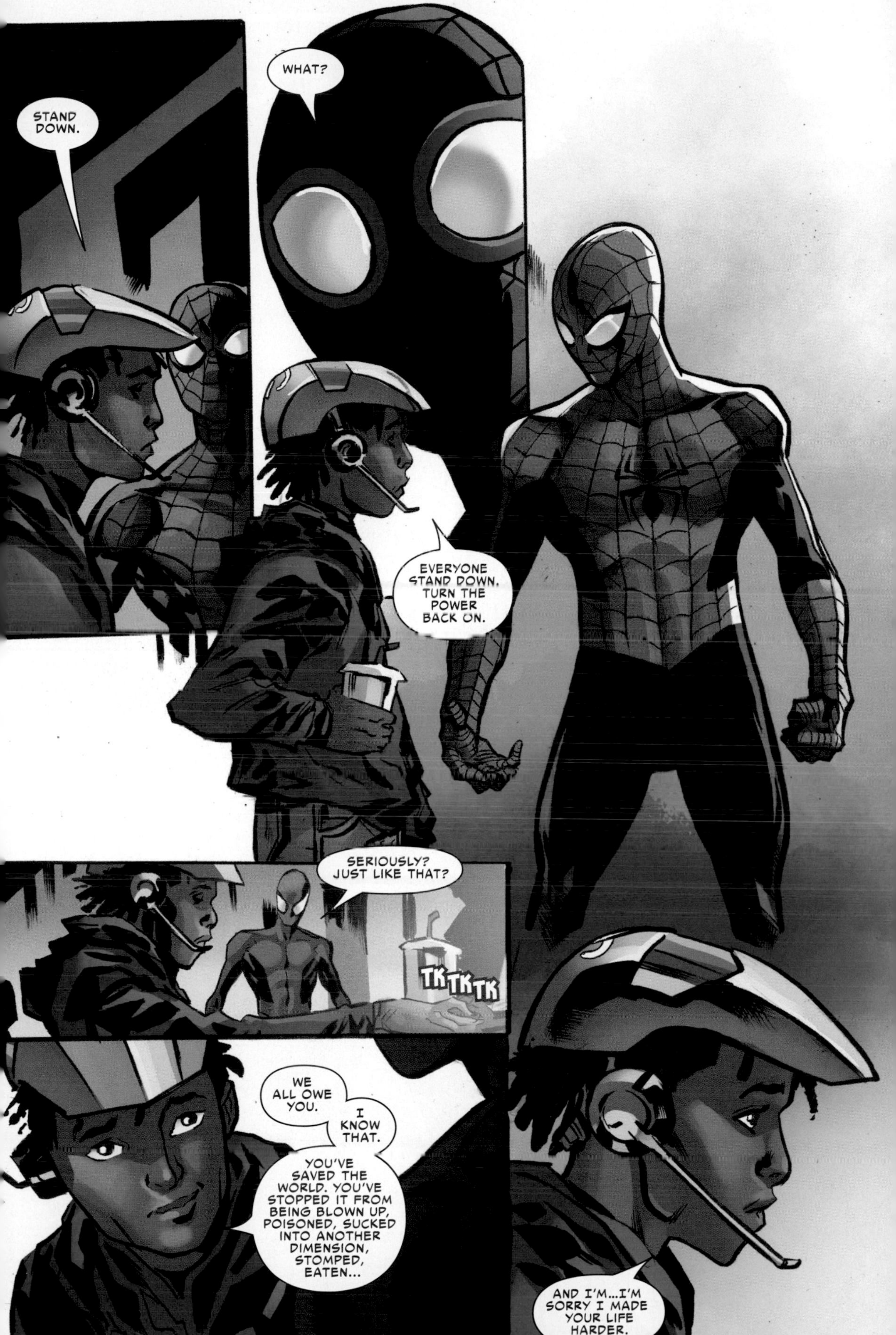
STAND DOWN.
WHAT?
EVERYONE STAND DOWN. TURN THE POWER BACK ON.
SERIOUSLY? JUST LIKE THAT?
TKTKTK
WE ALL OWE YOU.
I KNOW THAT.
YOU'VE SAVED THE WORLD. YOU'VE STOPPED IT FROM BEING BLOWN UP, POISONED, SUCKED INTO ANOTHER DIMENSION, STOMPED, EATEN...
AND I'M...I'M SORRY I MADE YOUR LIFE HARDER.

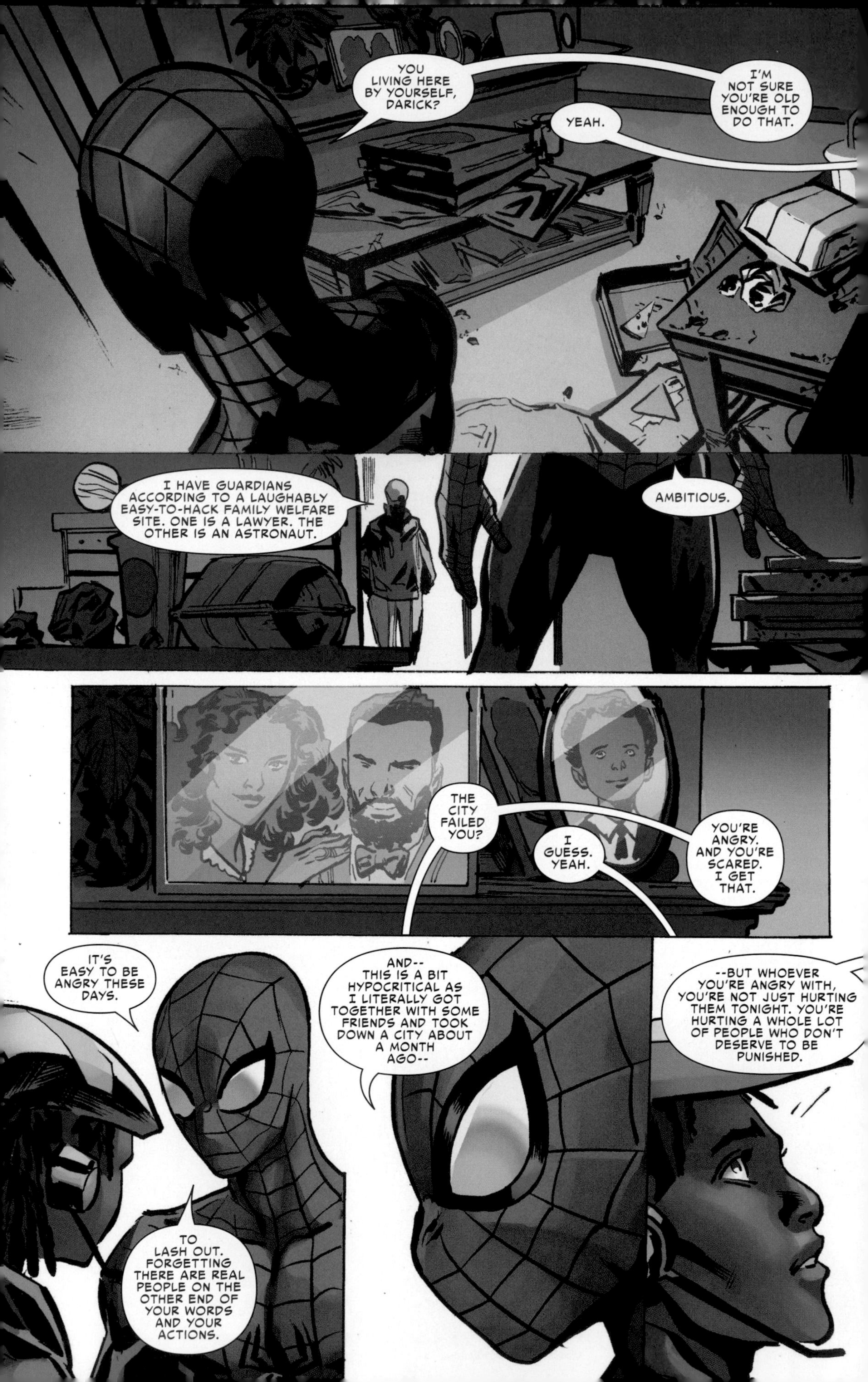
YOU LIVING HERE BY YOURSELF, DARICK?
YEAH.
I'M NOT SURE YOU'RE OLD ENOUGH TO DO THAT.
I HAVE GUARDIANS ACCORDING TO A LAUGHABLY EASY-TO-HACK FAMILY WELFARE SITE. ONE IS A LAWYER. THE OTHER IS AN ASTRONAUT.
AMBITIOUS.
THE CITY FAILED YOU?
I GUESS. YEAH.
YOU'RE ANGRY. AND YOU'RE SCARED. I GET THAT.
IT'S EASY TO BE ANGRY THESE DAYS.
TO LASH OUT. FORGETTING THERE ARE REAL PEOPLE ON THE OTHER END OF YOUR WORDS AND YOUR ACTIONS.
AND-- THIS IS A BIT HYPOCRITICAL AS I LITERALLY GOT TOGETHER WITH SOME FRIENDS AND TOOK DOWN A CITY ABOUT A MONTH AGO--
--BUT WHOEVER YOU'RE ANGRY WITH, YOU'RE NOT JUST HURTING THEM TONIGHT. YOU'RE HURTING A WHOLE LOT OF PEOPLE WHO DON'T DESERVE TO BE PUNISHED.

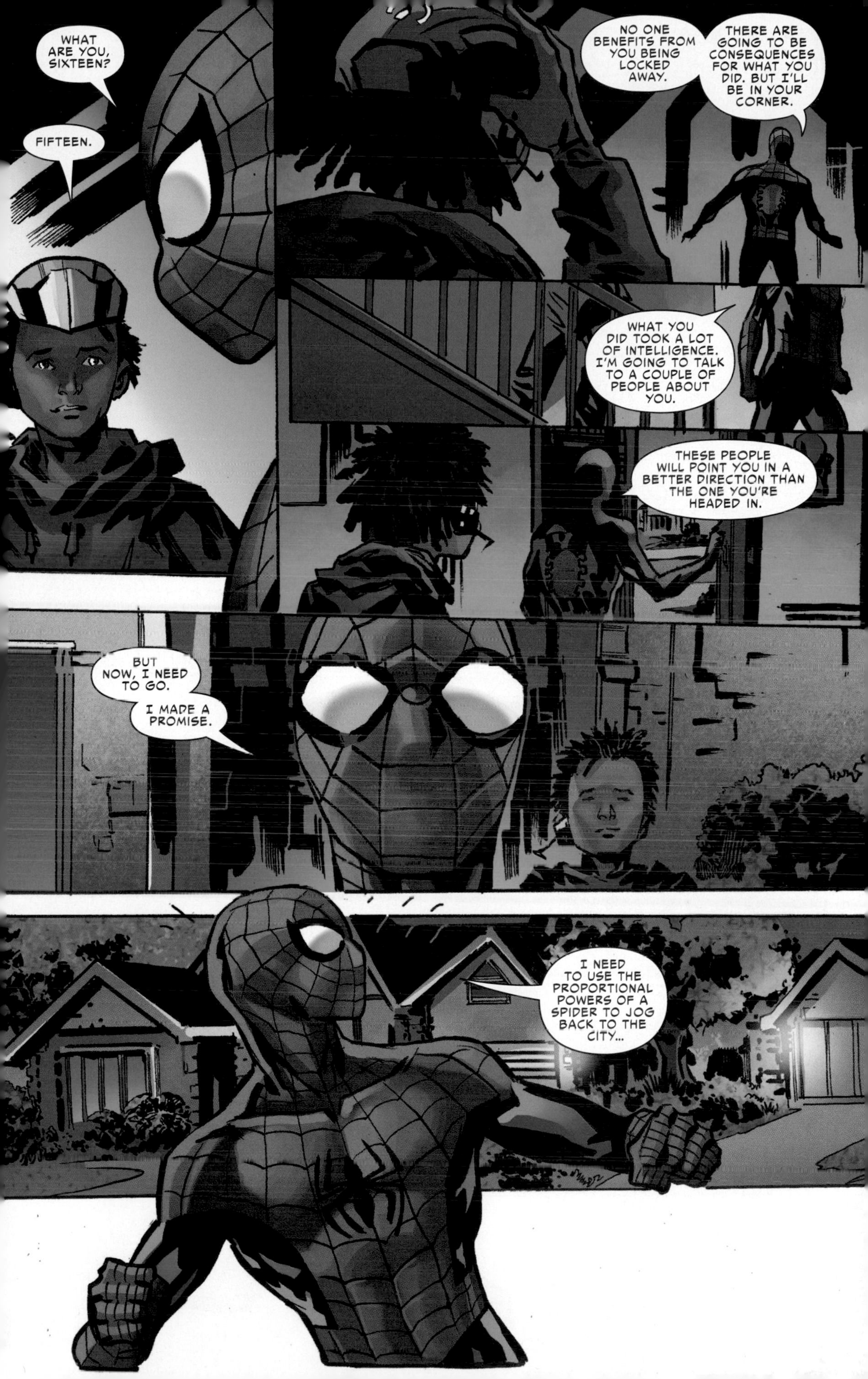
WHAT ARE YOU, SIXTEEN?
FIFTEEN.
NO ONE BENEFITS FROM YOU BEING LOCKED AWAY.
THERE ARE GOING TO BE CONSEQUENCES FOR WHAT YOU DID. BUT I'LL BE IN YOUR CORNER.
WHAT YOU DID TOOK A LOT OF INTELLIGENCE. I'M GOING TO TALK TO A COUPLE OF PEOPLE ABOUT YOU.
THESE PEOPLE WILL POINT YOU IN A BETTER DIRECTION THAN THE ONE YOU'RE HEADED IN.
BUT NOW, I NEED TO GO.
I MADE A PROMISE.
I NEED TO USE THE PROPORTIONAL POWERS OF A SPIDER TO JOG BACK TO THE CITY...

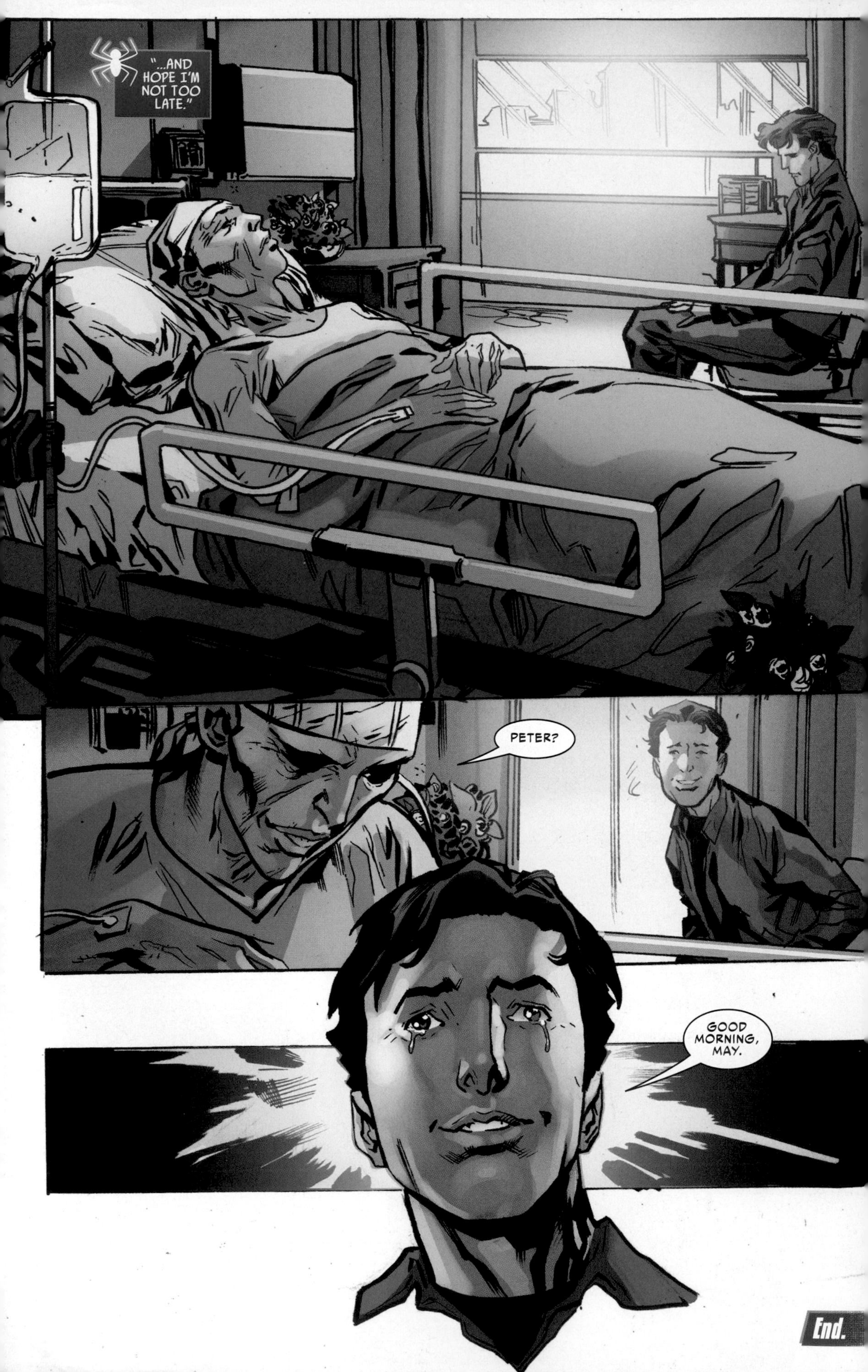
"...AND HOPE I'M NOT TOO LATE."
PETER?
GOOD MORNING, MAY.
End.

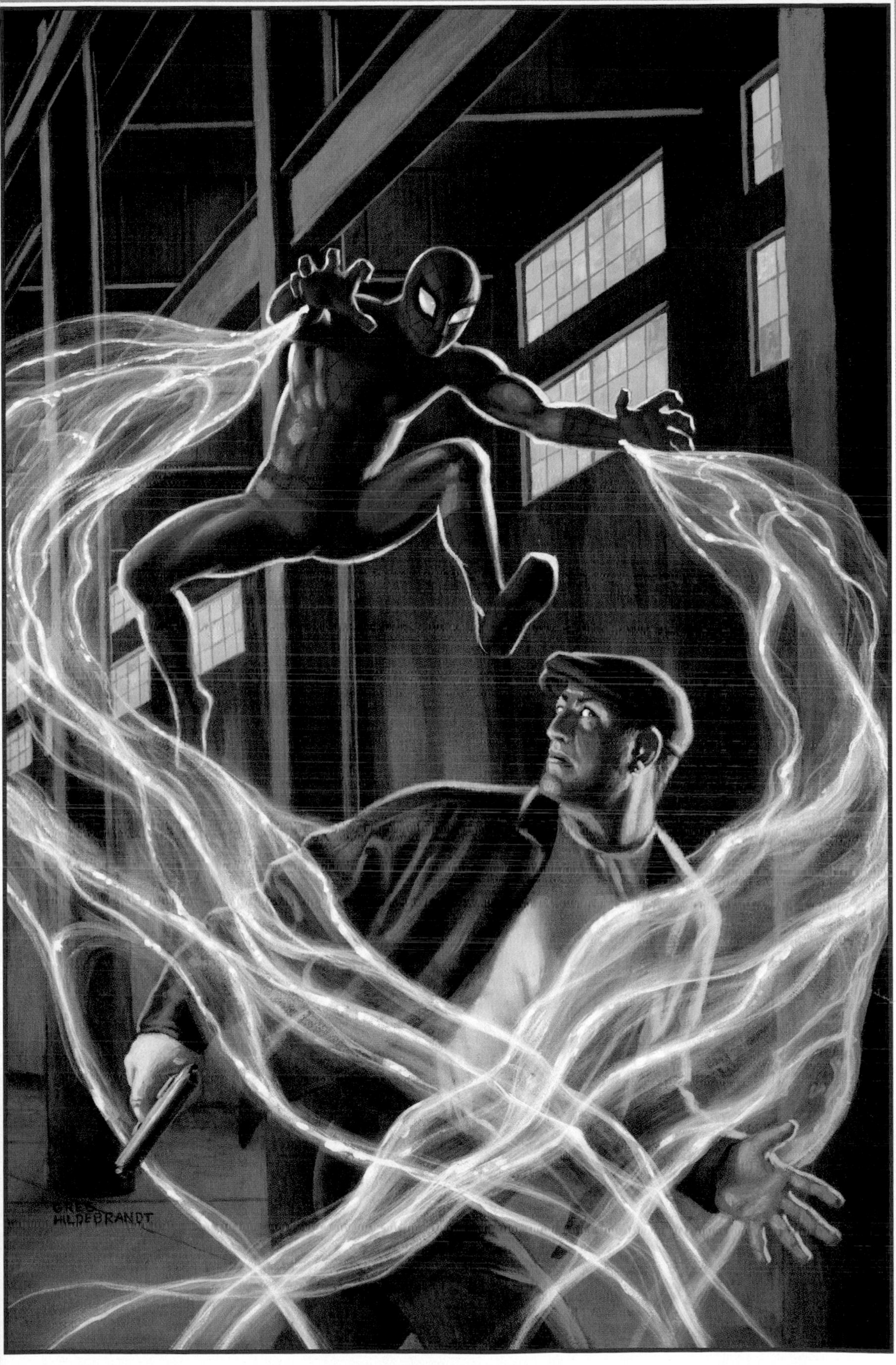
GREG
HILDEBRANDT

Greg Hildebrandt
#11 Bring on the Bad Guys Variant

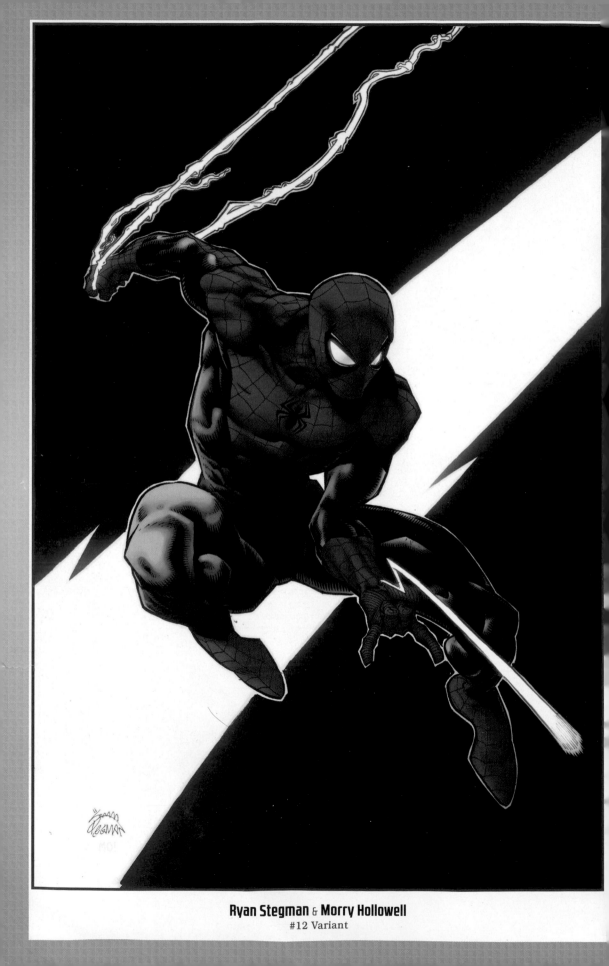

Ryan Stegman & **Morry Hollowell**
#12 Variant